THE ISRAEL–PALESTINE CONFLICT

WITHDRAWN

The conflict between the Israelis and the Palestinians is considered intractable by many, and is frequently characterized by the violence between the two sides. In attempts at peace, the starting point for negotiations is a cessation of violence; beneath this, however, lies a plethora of other issues to be addressed.

This unique text brings together Israeli and Palestinian viewpoints on a number of key issues and topics, making clear the points of agreement as well as the views that divide. The chapters deal first with three issues that require compromise and resolution for a peace treaty to be realized – water, refugees, and borders, territory and settlements – and then with three important concepts that can either impede or promote peace: democracy, human rights, and peace culture and education. Thus, the book provides an invaluable opportunity to understand, at least in part, the divergent and even convergent interests and understandings of Israelis and Palestinians on issues and concepts important to the peace process. As such, it will be a valuable resource for courses on conflict resolution, the Middle East peace process, and political science.

Elizabeth G. Matthews is Assistant Professor in the Department of Political Science at California State University San Marcos, USA. She has written a number of books and articles on world politics and US foreign policy, and is co-editor of the Routledge *UCLA Center for Middle East Development (CMED)* series.

David Newman is Dean of the Faculty of Humanities and Social Sciences and Professor of Political Geography at Ben-Gurion University. Since 1999, he has been the chief editor of the international journal *Geopolitics*, and he is currently co-editing *The Routledge Handbook of the Israeli–Palestinian Conflict* with Joel Peters. He has published widely on issues related to territory and borders and the changing role of borders in a globalized world.

Mohammed S. Dajani Daoudi holds two doctorate degrees from the University of South Carolina at Columbia and the University of Texas at Austin. He is the founding director of the American Studies Center at al-Quds University, the Wasatia Movement – Palestine, and the Jerusalem Studies and Research Institute, and is the author of numerous books and academic articles in English and Arabic.

UCLA Center for Middle East Development (CMED)
Series Editors
Steven L. Spiegel, UCLA
Elizabeth G. Matthews, California State University San Marcos

The UCLA Center for Middle East Development (CMED) series on Middle East security and cooperation is designed to present a variety of perspectives on a specific topic, such as democracy in the Middle East, dynamics of Israeli–Palestinian relations, Gulf security, and the gender factor in the Middle East. The uniqueness of the series is that the authors write from the viewpoints of a variety of countries so that no matter what the issue, articles appear from many different states, both within and beyond the region. No existing series provides a comparable, multi-national collection of authors in each volume. Thus, the series presents a combination of writers from countries who, for political reasons, do not always publish in the same volume. The series features a number of sub-themes under a single heading, covering security, social, political, and economic factors affecting the Middle East.

1. The Struggle over Democracy in the Middle East
Regional politics and external policies
Edited by Nathan J. Brown and Emad El-Din Shahin

2. Women in the Middle East and North Africa
Agents of change
Edited by Fatima Sadiqi and Moha Ennaji

3. The Israel–Palestine Conflict
Parallel discourses
Edited by Elizabeth G. Matthews with David Newman and Mohammed S. Dajani Daoudi

THE ISRAEL–PALESTINE CONFLICT

Parallel discourses

Edited by Elizabeth G. Matthews

WITH

DAVID NEWMAN AND
MOHAMMED S. DAJANI DAOUDI

LONDON AND NEW YORK

First published 2011 by Routledge
2 Park Square, Milton Park, Abingdon, Oxon OX14 4RN

Simultaneously published in the USA and Canada
by Routledge
270 Madison Ave, New York, NY 10016

Routledge is an imprint of the Taylor & Francis Group, an informa business

© 2011 UCLA

Typeset in Bembo
by Keystroke, Station Road, Codsall, Wolverhampton
Printed and bound in Great Britain
by CPI Antony Rowe, Chippenham, Wiltshire

British Library Cataloguing in Publication Data
A catalogue record for this book is available from the British Library

Library of Congress Cataloging in Publication Data
The Israel–Palestine conflict : parallel discourses / edited by Elizabeth G.
Matthews.
    p. cm. – (UCLA Center for Middle East development (CMED); 3)
Includes biographical references and index
1. Arab–Israeli conflict–1993– 2. Arab–Israeli conflict–1993–Peace.
I. Matthews, Elizabeth G.
DS119.76.I8197 2010
956.9405'4–dc22
2010019495

ISBN 978–0–415–43478–2 (hbk)
ISBN 978–0–415–43479–9 (pbk)
ISBN 978–0–203–83939–3 (ebk)

CONTENTS

ILLUSTRATIONS

Figures

Tables

CONTRIBUTORS

Amjad Aliewi is the Director General of House of Water and Environment, Palestine and a Senior Researcher at Newcastle University, UK.

Karen Assaf is the Head of the Water Environment Section, and Co-Director, of ASIR – Arab Scientific Institute for Research and Transfer of Technology, Palestine.

Salem Aweiss teaches at Stanford University. His fields of specialization are foreign language education and peace education in the Israeli–Palestinian context.

Daniel Bar-Tal is Branco Weiss Professor of Research in Child Development and Education at the School of Education, Tel Aviv University. His research interests are in political and social psychology, studying socio-psychological foundations of intractable conflicts and peacemaking, as well as development of political under-standing among children and peace education. He has published over fifteen books and over 250 articles and chapters in major social and political psychological journals and books. He has served as a President of the International Society of Political Psychology and received various awards for his work.

Mohammed S. Dajani Daoudi holds two doctorate degrees from the University of South Carolina at Columbia and the University of Texas at Austin. He is the founding director of the American Studies Center at al-Quds University, the Wasatia Movement – Palestine, and the Jerusalem Studies and Research Institute, and is the author of numerous books and academic articles in English and Arabic.

Bassem Eid is the Executive Director of the Palestinian Human Rights Monitoring Group (PHRMG). PHRMG is a Palestinian, independent, non-governmental organization working to end human rights violations committed against Palestinians in the West Bank, Gaza Strip, and East Jerusalem, regardless of who is responsible.

Galia Golan is Professor Emerita at the Hebrew University, Jerusalem, where she was head of the Political Science Department and founder and chair of the Lafer

Center for Women's Studies. She is the founder and chair of the Program on Diplomacy and Conflict Studies at the Interdisciplinary Center, Herzliya; a peace and feminist activist, she is author of nine books. Her most recent works include *Israel and Palestine: Peace Plans and Proposals from Oslo to Disengagement* and "Globalization, Non-state Actors, and the Transformation of Conflict," in Bruce Dayton and Louis Kreisberg, *Conflict Transformation and Peace-building* (Taylor & Francis, 2009).

Jad Isaac is general director of the Applied Research Institute Jerusalem.

Edward (Edy) Kaufman is a Senior Research Associate and former Director at International Development and Conflict Management at the University of Maryland and Visiting Professor at the Interdisciplinary Center in Hertzlyia and Haifa University, Israel. He has also been a Senior Researcher and the Executive Director of the Harry S. Truman Research Institute for the Advancement of Peace at the Hebrew University of Jerusalem from 1983 to 2004. He has authored and co-authored twelve books including *Bridging Across the Divide – Peacebuilding in the Israeli/Palestinian Conflict* (Lynne Rienner, 2006).

Elizabeth G. Matthews is Assistant Professor in the Department of Political Science at California State University San Marcos, USA. She has written a number of books and articles on world politics and US foreign policy, and is co-editor of the Routledge *UCLA Center for Middle East Development (CMED)* series.

David Newman is Dean of the Faculty of Humanities and Social Sciences and Professor of Political Geography at Ben-Gurion University. Since 1999, he has been the chief editor of the international journal *Geopolitics*, and he is currently co-editing *The Routledge Handbook of the Israeli–Palestinian Conflict* with Joel Peters. He has published widely on issues related to territory and borders and the changing role of borders in a globalized world.

Enda O'Connell is Professor of Water Resources Engineering and Climate Change at Newcastle University, UK.

Geoff Parkin is a Senior Lecturer in Hydrology at Newcastle University, UK.

Joel Peters is Associate Professor in Government and International Affairs at the School of Public and International Affairs, Virginia Tech. Prior to joining Virginia Tech, Peters was the founding Director of the Centre for the Study of European Politics and Society (CSEPS) and was a senior lecturer in the Department of Politics and Government at Ben Gurion University, Israel.

Walid Salem was born in East Jerusalem in 1957. He is the author of thirty books and manuals and tens of research papers on democracy, civil society, citizenship, refugees, Jerusalem, and peace building issues. He has also been a trainer for thirty thousand people on democracy issues since 1993 and he is the Director of the Center for Democracy and Community Development, East Jerusalem.

Hillel Shuval is Head of the Department of Environmental Health Sciences, Hadassah Academic College, Jerusalem and Kunen-Lunenfeld Emeritus Professor of Environmental Sciences, The Hebrew University of Jerusalem.

PREFACE

The Center for Middle East Development of the International Institute at UCLA (CMED) is pleased to present the third installment in our book series on Middle East security and cooperation. The series is designed to offer discussions on the current problems in the Middle East with volumes that are unique because the participating authors are from a variety of countries and provide a range of perspectives on a specific topic. We envision that this diversity will contribute directly to the global discourse on the ongoing developments in the region.

The editors wish to extend our deepest gratitude to James Whiting, Acquisitions Editor for Middle Eastern and Islamic Studies, of Routledge, Taylor and Francis Group, who has served as such a critical asset to us in the complex preparation of these exciting, but complicated to prepare, volumes. We greatly appreciate the patience and dedication of Suzanne Richardson, Senior Editorial Assistant, Middle East and Islamic Studies, for Routledge, Taylor & Francis Group, who assisted us so admirably in preparing this manuscript. We also want to extend our thanks to Professor David Newman, who first conceived of the exercise and placed us in contact with Routledge. And we deeply appreciate the work and gargantuan efforts that are being pursued by the editors and authors responsible for each volume, and of course our International Advisory Board. We also wish to recognize the support to this project provided by CMED's Faculty Advisory Committee and the Institute on Global Conflict and Cooperation (IGCC) of the University of California based at UC San Diego.

CMED conducts research and provides educational programs on political, economic, and diplomatic development in the Middle East. CMED programs approach these issues through a multi-tiered regional security program. Through reports and monographs, CMED explores key subjects on the region, including but by no means limited to democratic culture, regional business and economics, gender issues, media, technological cooperation across borders, and a full range of security and political issues, including strategic challenges in cooperative and conflictual contexts, Mediterranean and Gulf security, threats of weapons of mass destruction, and specific dynamics of regional problems such as the Arab–Israeli dispute, Iraq, and Iran. This series is a product of these studies and the promotion of intellectual interchange to which CMED is committed.

We are proud of the first two books in the series, *The Struggle over Democracy in the Middle East: Regional Politics and External Policies* (2009) and *Women in the Middle East and North Africa: Agents of Change* (2010). This third book, *The Israel–Palestine Conflict: Parallel Discourses*, continues our goal of offering the highest possible quality to our readers and providing unique and stimulating discussions as the series expands.

This book is slightly different than our first two offerings. As mentioned above, one of the goals and unique features of this series is that the authors are from a variety of countries and provide a range of perspectives on a specific topic. In this volume, however, we seek only two perspectives, those of the Israelis and the Palestinians, on a broad range of topics: refugees, borders, territory and settlements, water, democratization, human rights, and peace culture and education. The beauty of this volume is that it offers, side by side, the approaches and ideas of one Israeli and one Palestinian speaking on the same subject. All are subjects that relate to the current peace process between the parties and readers will see the areas of agreement and disagreement.

Although many view the conflict between the Palestinians and Israelis as intractable, this volume highlights the possibility of compromise. As stated in the Introduction, "What you should learn from the arguments of the authors is that there are areas of agreement – and, yes, of disagreement, too – but it might be possible to move in a positive direction if we build from the areas of agreement." We are very pleased to present in this volume a unique view of one of the most analyzed conflicts in the world. We hope it will enlighten and enrich both those well acquainted with the conflict and those who are confronting its major issues for the first time.

Steven L. Spiegel, UCLA
Elizabeth G. Matthews, CSUSM

INTRODUCTION

Elizabeth G. Matthews

When we contemplate the possibility of peace between the Israelis and the Palestinians we cannot help but conjure up images of numerous wars, suicide bombings, and the loss of innocent civilians on both sides. When we witness, and many experience, the effects of events such as the al–Aqsa Intifada, the building of the West Bank security barrier, the battle between Hamas and Fatah fighters that resulted in Hamas control of Gaza in 2007, and the Israeli incursion into Gaza in 2008/2009, it may become difficult to imagine a peace settlement between these two peoples. In fact, in every attempt at peace throughout the Oslo process and the Roadmap, the opening requirement has always been, and will continue to be in any future peace proposal, the cessation of violence. As a consequence of this very real concern, it becomes difficult to look past the violence toward the other issues that need resolution for a lasting peace. When we are in the midst of a violent confrontation, like the one in late 2008 into 2009, it is easy to believe that this is simply a never-ending conflict; that the Israelis and Palestinians can never arrive at an acceptable compromise to allow their people to live in peace, security, and prosperity.

Despite its understandable prominence in peace discussions, violence, *per se*, is not the subject of this book. Violence has been and will continue to be a source and/or consequence related to the focus of this book, but it is not in and of itself the purpose of our discussion. The work presented in this book is a reminder that even when the violence stops, there is still a plethora of issues to be addressed, and this is where our attention rests. In Part I, we deal with three of the glut of issues that require compromise and resolution for a peace treaty to be realized: water, refugees, and borders, territory and settlements. In Part II, three important concepts that can either impede or promote peace are addressed: democracy, human rights, and peace culture and education. The unique contribution of this text is that for each one of these issues and concepts, one point of view presented is Israeli and the other is Palestinian. Thus, this provides an invaluable opportunity to understand, at least in part, the divergent and even convergent interests and understandings of Israelis and Palestinians on issues and concepts important to the peace process.

Obviously, only one perspective from each camp (Israelis, for example, can have divergent interests and understandings among themselves) is provided here, but the authors in this volume are experts in their fields and provide a significant contribution to the evaluation of Israeli–Palestinian relations. In addition, there are many other topics of importance that are not discussed in this book, most notably Jerusalem, reconciliation, and the roles of the media, third-party intervention, public opinion, and religion. These issues are clearly important components of the Israel–Palestinian conflict and their resolution will be required for a comprehensive peace. Although we cannot address them here, the reader is encouraged to investigate these issues elsewhere. While there are numerous topics that could be covered in this book, the chosen issues and concepts provide an enlightening overview of attitudes and opinions that punctuate the Israeli–Palestinian relationship. The reader will discover two facets of the conflict. First, the obvious, is that the Israelis and the Palestinians have fundamental differences about important aspects of the peace process. Second, the conflicting parties also share commonalities in approach and perspective that could be used to promote progress in negotiations. For example, Chapters 5 and 6 demonstrate that there is room for compromise over the issue of water sharing. Further, Chapters 11 and 12 show agreement over the importance of peace education as a tool for improving the relationship between the Israelis and the Palestinians.

The reader should keep in mind that these chapters are not meant to be unbiased views of the conflict. The point here is to discover the arguments and understanding of the authors on these important topics, and recognizing bias is part of that investigation. There are obviously differences at play among the parties in this conflict and allowing the authors to express their viewpoints highlights these divergent approaches. Part I of this volume, as mentioned above, deals with three of the very serious issues dividing the parties. Due to the nature of these issues, bias is much more prevalent in their discussion than is obvious in Part II. Interested readers should undertake a thorough investigation of approaches on each issue before criticizing and evaluating the Israeli and Palestinian sides in this conflict.

This introduction will provide a brief overview of each issue and concept to be discussed in the following chapters. The purpose is to put the proceeding discussion into context, fitting each author's approach and perspective into the larger picture of each topic. This chapter will provide some historical background and contextual facts to put the authors' arguments in perspective.

Refugees

According to the United Nations Relief and Works Agency for Palestine Refugees (UNRWA, n.d), "Palestinian refugees are persons whose normal place of residence was Palestine between June 1946 and May 1948, who lost both their homes and means of livelihood as a result of the 1948 Arab–Israeli conflict." This definition also covers the descendants of persons who meet the definition of a refugee. The UNRWA places the number of refugees in 1950 at 914,000, and at more than 4 million in 2010. (It is important to keep in mind that these figures are open to debate and controversy. Some claim they are too high and some claim they are too low. These figures are provided here only to give the reader an idea of the numbers of people who claim to be, or are believed to be, refugees.) About one-third of the registered refugees live in UNRWA-operated refugee camps in Jordan, Lebanon, Syria, the West Bank, and Gaza (the other two-thirds live near the cities in the host countries and the West Bank and Gaza). While most of the fifty-eight UNRWA camps were opened after the 1948 conflict, ten opened after the 1967 war to accommodate the newly displaced persons. Despite the UNRWA's provision of schools and health and distribution centers, conditions in the camps are poor. The population in the camps has grown remarkably over the years, leading to crowded living conditions and inadequate infrastructure (UNRWA, n.d.).

The Palestinian refugees were the true losers of the 1948 war (known as the "catastrophe" by the Palestinians) and the fate of these displaced persons continues to be a highly divisive issue today. Although there are differing estimates, according to the United Nations roughly 726,000 persons fled during the 1948 conflict (estimates range from 472,000 to 1 million). There is a continuing controversy over why they left and this helps to fuel the ongoing disagreement concerning what should happen to the refugees in any peace agreement between the Israelis and the Palestinians. On one hand, the Israelis argue that the Palestinian refugees left willingly to avoid the dangers of war. Some claim that Arab leaders actually requested that the Palestinians leave to avoid getting in the way of advancing Arab armies or being caught in the cross-fire of the conflict. The argument continues that the refugees were told that they would be able to return after the Arab states had defeated Israel. On the other hand, the Palestinians claim that they were driven from their homes by threats and violence. An Irgun and Lehi attack on the village of Deir Yassin that killed between 110 and 250 Arabs (estimates vary) shortly before Israeli independence is often cited as an example of the tactics used by the Israelis to compel the Arabs to flee. As word of Deir Yassin spread, many Palestinians fled their homes out of fear that they would suffer a similar fate. Regardless of the reason why they left, the outcome was the same. After the cease-fire, they were not allowed to return, their property was declared abandoned, and resentment and hatred have grown among those who were displaced and their descendants.

The Palestinians argue that the refugees have a "right of return" to their land and homes. They have a moral and legal right to reclaim what is rightfully theirs, even in what is now Israel. In fact, there are some refugees who still possess the keys to homes that are now occupied by Israelis or no longer exist. The Palestinians cite United Nations General Assembly Resolution 194, passed in 1948, as the basis for their claim. Resolution 194 states, "Refugees wishing to return to their homes and live at peace with their neighbors should be permitted to do so at the earliest practical date." Hence, Palestinians believe they have the right to return as a matter of international law. For the Israelis, on the other hand, there can be no absolute right of return. Allowing that to occur would be the opening salvo in the death of the Jewish state. With a population of roughly 7 million, approximately 76 percent of whom are Jewish, allowing potentially 4.5 million returnees would undermine the demographic balance in Israel and deny Jewish self-determination. The Israelis will not and cannot surrender the identity of their state. Many argue that General Assembly resolutions are not binding and that the resolution leaves vague whether returning is actually a "right," especially in light of the possibility that returnees could be hostile to Israel. Israel asserts that it is not responsible for the creation of the refugees and has no obligation to repatriate hostile belligerents. It passed laws preventing the return of the refugees (in particular, the Prevention of Infiltration Law, 1954) and expropriating their property, but also unblocked refugees' bank accounts and reunited some Arab families.

The Palestinian refugees are labeled a "final status" issue. Israel would like to see them absorbed by their host countries and the future Palestinian state, but at Camp David in 2000, Ehud Barak did offer the return of a number of refugees for "family reunifications" and was willing to consider compensation for the refugees. Arab states have no interest in keeping the refugees (Jordan has granted them citizenship), the territory of the future independent state of Palestine is too small to accept vast numbers of refugees adequately, and Camp David collapsed with no agreement, even in principle, about any of the issues. Israeli leaders, including Barak at Camp David, are unwilling to accept any moral or legal responsibility for the refugee problem or the concept of "right of return" while the Palestinians continue to insist that they must. In late 2000, US President Bill Clinton proposed a compromise: a right of return, but only to the refugees' homeland, meaning the future Palestinian state. At the Taba summit in January 2001, however, the Palestinians presented their hard-line position: Israel must accept moral and legal responsibility for the refugee problem as well as for preventing the implementation of Resolution 194; allow the right of return and pay compensation for lost property and suffering; and compensate the Arab states which have hosted the refugees. In response, the Israelis offered the return of tens of thousands of refugees over a number of years for family reunifications and agreed that Israel would be a leading contributor to a new international body established to regulate compensation to refugees and the Arab states (Tovy, 2003). Taba concluded without an agreement, but the summit does at least demonstrate that there may be some room for maneuver on this issue.

The controversies and differing interpretations of the causes and consequences of the refugee issue are addressed in Chapters 1 and 2 of this book. As demonstrated above, these differences dramatically impact negotiations and whether a compromise between the parties is possible. In Chapter 1, Joel Peters explains that the refugee issue continues to be somewhat taboo in Israel, in part because, much as Israel would like to avoid the topic (it is seen as the most threatening of all the final status issues), there is a realization that it could prevent a comprehensive peace with the Palestinians. Peters provides a closer look at the attitudes and opinions inside Israel about who is responsible for the refugee problem and thus what should be done about it. He provides a narrative of the Israeli approach to the refugee problem in peace negotiations from 1991 to 2000 and the backlash in Israel following public knowledge of Israeli concessions offered on the issue. In Chapter 2, Mohammed S. Dajani Daoudi discusses the interesting dynamics surrounding the perceptions of the Israeli–Palestinian conflict and how these perceptions frame the understanding of the 1948 conflict and the plight of the refugees. He addresses the question of why the Palestinians left in 1948 and discusses some possible solutions to the dilemma of where the refugees should go. Taken together, these chapters illuminate the issues relating to finding a mutually acceptable, negotiated solution to the problem of the Palestinian refugees.

Borders, territory, and settlements

Saeb Erakat, the Palestinian chief negotiator, once said that the settlements are to the Palestinians as bombs in Tel Aviv are to the Israelis. Thus, as mentioned above, all attempts at peace begin with two imperatives: the cessation of violence and the cessation of settlement construction. These are not "final status" issues but "starting line" issues. The controversial nature of Israeli settlements derives from the fact that, at its heart, the Israeli–Palestinian conflict is over land. Two peoples lay claim to the same piece of territory. Wars have been fought, negotiations tried, but sixty years later there are still no permanent borders for Israel or a Palestinian state. Peace agreements with Jordan and Egypt meant Israel established certain borders (1949 cease-fire lines became borders), but a lack of agreement with Syria, Lebanon, and the Palestinians means the conflict still rests on who gets what territory.

In 1947, the United Nations Partition Plan allotted Israel 55 percent of the territory of Palestine, but when British rule ended in 1948 and Israel declared its independence in the territory, Arab armies invaded and Israel came out of the war with 78 percent of the former Palestine. The remaining percentage of the former Mandate came under the control of Arab states: the West Bank under Jordan and the Gaza Strip under Egypt. This lasted until 1967, when Israel gained control of the West Bank and Gaza Strip, as well as the Golan Heights, captured from Syria, and the Sinai Peninsula, captured from Egypt. Israel exchanged land for peace with Egypt in the Camp David Accords (1979) by returning the Sinai Peninsula (thus recognizing the border between Egypt and Israel) and agreed to borders with Jordan in 1994 (river borders in the north and desert borders south of the Dead Sea). The West Bank, Gaza, and the Golan Heights remain contested territories occupied by Israel.

Israeli settlers, many at the request of the Israeli government, have moved into the Occupied Palestinian Territories (OPT). In 2005, Israel unilaterally disengaged from Gaza, ending thirty-eight years of military rule (Ariel Sharon proposed the plan in December 2003, Israel's cabinet approved it in June 2004, and the Knesset approved it in October 2004). In doing so, settlements were abandoned, although many of the settlers had to be removed by force. The Israeli government argued that, although it has "security needs and other vital interests," it was not "Israel's intention to rule over a large Palestinian population" and there was "optimism that the Disengagement Plan will succeed to advance peace efforts where previous attempts have failed" (Israel Ministry of Foreign Affairs, 2005). The disengagement from Gaza has not resulted in further steps toward peace – in fact, ultimately peace took some significant steps backwards. A poll found that 84 percent of Palestinians believed that armed violence was the reason for the Israeli withdrawal from Gaza, and 40 percent credited Hamas directly for the pullout (Associated Press, 2009). These results were harbingers of what was to come. Partially related to the Gaza disengagement, Hamas won the Palestinian parliamentary elections in 2006 (securing 76 of the 132 parliamentary seats), prompting Israel (and others, notably the United States) to declare that there would be no negotiations with a Hamas-led government. The situation deteriorated when fighting erupted between Hamas and Fatah fighters in Gaza, ultimately leading to the Hamas takeover of Gaza in 2007. Gaza was sealed off, a humanitarian crisis ensued, and in December 2008, in an effort to stop Hamas from firing rockets into southern Israel, the Israeli Defense Forces (IDF) launched an assault on Gaza that killed hundreds of Palestinians and scores of Israeli soldiers.

The West Bank has also been a difficult issue for the Israelis and the Palestinians. It is strategically significant to Israel, but also historically and religiously significant, partially due to the fact that Jerusalem lies within the territory. Jewish religious nationalism was a strong impetus for the settlement movement, and merely suggesting pulling back from the settlements is risky for Israeli politicians. Despite this, ending settlement construction has been a provision in several agreements signed by Israeli governments, in addition to the Road Map proposed in 2003 by the Quartet (the United States, the United Nations, the European Union, and Russia). Further settlement construction is viewed by many as an impediment to the peace process. Palestinian Authority President Mahmoud Abbas has said, "We consider settlements to be the greatest obstacle to the road of peace" (CNN, 2008). In December 2008, Gordon Brown, the Prime Minister of Great Britain, argued that while "everyone now sees the contours of what a two-state solution would look like . . . One of the blockages to that is clearly the settlement issue . . . [and] we've consistently seen that as a barrier to reaching the agreement that everybody thinks is possible" (Sparrow, 2008). Even Israel's firmest ally, the United States, has questioned the purpose and wisdom of settlement construction. For example, in 2008, in response to an Israeli plan to build 1,300 additional homes in East Jerusalem, Secretary of State Condoleezza Rice said, "I'm very concerned that at a time when we need to build confidence between the parties, the continued building and the settlement activity has the potential to harm the negotiations going forward . . . This is simply not helpful to building confidence" (CNN, 2008).

The situation in the West Bank is complicated by Israel's building of a barrier known by many names, including the "security [or anti-terrorism] fence" by Israelis and the "apartheid [or colonization] wall" by Palestinians. Work began on the structure in June 2002 and Israel claims that its intended purpose is to prevent would-be suicide bombers from entering and blowing themselves up in Israel. Prime Minister Ehud Olmert declared in December 2008 that the barrier is a model of "how to defend against terrorism." He stated, "Wherever there is a fence, terrorism against Israel is prevented. Countries that wish to fight the kind of terrorism that we have absorbed in Jerusalem and other cities throughout Israel will yet study the model of the security fence" (Yahoo News, 2008). The Palestinians view the wall quite differently. Primarily it is viewed as a land grab. The structure cuts deep into the West Bank, surrounding Israeli settlements in the territory, creating a non-negotiated border. It also separates Palestinian traders and farmers from their livelihoods, and restricts Palestinian freedom of movement (Human Rights Watch, 2004). Palestinians also argue that the building of the wall impedes attempts to negotiate a comprehensive peace between the parties. In support of the Palestinian claims, in 2004 the International Court of Justice ruled that the barrier was illegal, declared it violates the human rights of the Palestinians, and called for it to be dismantled. In response, Olmert declared, "It's certainly unpleasant to have the ruling, but it's more unpleasant to have suicide attacks from territories not defended by the fence . . . The fence is removable and reversible, and death is not" (Richburg, 2004). The Israeli Supreme Court, while recognizing Israel's need for security, has declared that there are limits to the construction of the barrier in response to several Palestinian petitioners and human rights groups. In September 2007, for example, the Court ruled that the barrier could not impose undue hardship on Palestinians, and ordered that the portion that divided the village of Bilin from much of its farmland should be rerouted. In December 2008, the Court ruled again that the revised path was also unacceptable and not based solely on security needs (the plan appeared to be an attempt to protect new Jewish housing activity). The Court therefore recognized that Israel's security concerns needed to be balanced against the needs and suffering of the Palestinians. However, despite the opposition, the barrier exists and new Jewish housing continues to be constructed in the West Bank.

In Chapter 3, David Newman addresses the question of how two peoples divide the same piece of territory through an analysis of territorial discourses in Israel and Palestine: the partition, the homeland, the securitization, the binational, and the border discourses. He traces the territorial and border discourses from the Oslo Accords to the Gaza disengagement, demonstrating that the attempts to solve the conflict have been transformed from bilateral and negotiated to unilateral and superimposed. Most today accept that the solution to the puzzle of what happens with two peoples who lay claim to the same piece of territory is one of two states: Israel and Palestine living side by side in peace and security. Extremists on both sides still argue that each is entitled to the entirety of the territory, but a negotiated solution will undoubtedly be for two states.

In Chapter 4, Jad Isaac provides a detailed description of the building of Israeli settlements and outposts (communities that extend further into Palestinian lands) in the Occupied Territories as well as a discussion of the evolution of negotiations over the settlements from Oslo to Camp David, and ends with a discussion of the segregation and disengagement plans. Isaac, arguing strongly from the Palestinian point of view, concludes with a list of failures of the peace process and calls for strong third-party intervention to improve conditions for the Palestinians.

Chapters 3 and 4 both present some of the issues that have featured in attempts to solve the conflict that is at the heart of the Israeli–Palestinian dispute.

Water

Drinkable water is a scarce resource in the Middle East. While our focus here is on Israeli–Palestinian issues, it is important to remember that they do not have a monopoly on the problems associated with water scarcity. Most Middle Eastern countries have a shortage, and water is used as a political lever by many. Yemen, for example, has undertaken a significant domestic campaign to convince its population that conservation is necessary and urgent. It has even been argued that future wars in the region will be fought over water. As has been mentioned, the Arab–Israeli conflict revolves primarily over land, but with that land is the water that flows through it, and that water is potentially as crucial as the territory itself.

The land that is shared by the Israelis and the Palestinians is desert, and one of the most arid environments on earth. It experiences extreme variations in climate: cold with potential snowfall in the winter, and blisteringly hot in the summer. Droughts are common, and much of the yearly rainfall is lost through evaporation and transpiration. In years of relatively low annual rainfall, there is an added pressure to manage the water resources properly. The scarce water supply has to serve not only the indigenous population but the vast number of Jewish immigrants who have been flocking to the area for well over a hundred years. Even though demand already outstrips supply, water use is increasing as the population and economic activity continue to grow.

There are two main sources of water for Israel and the future independent state of Palestine. The first of these, and arguably the more important, are aquifers, openings in permeable rocks that contain or conduct groundwater. Second, rivers, in particular the Jordan and the Banyas, flowing through the West Bank and the Golan Heights, respectively, provide water for the Israelis and Palestinians as well as the Syrians. In 1967, Israel gained control of the West Bank's mountain aquifer and the Sea of Galilee. Intense arguments abound over the mountain aquifer, with Israelis consuming about 80 percent of its output. Israel argues that the rain that feeds this aquifer may fall in the West Bank, but the water flows into pre-1967 Israel. The Palestinians, on the other hand, argue that a stronger military power is preventing them from using their own water resource, allocating several times more water to Israeli citizens, and severely undermining the Palestinian agricultural economy.

In addition to its scarcity, groundwater can be contaminated in ways that make it unusable for human consumption. A common problem is the encroachment of saline water from the Mediterranean and Red seas, the migration of brines, and salt emanating from rocks throughout the area. Groundwater can also be contaminated via human-produced pollutants. Agricultural and industrial activity, combined with human waste and improper waste management techniques, can significantly contaminate otherwise usable water supplies. The situation in Gaza, for example, is "catastrophic." Significant financial difficulties, compounded by the sanctions placed on the territory in response to the election of Hamas, drought, and mismanagement have left it with polluted water, most of which is undrinkable. As a result, the head of the Palestinian Water Authority, Shaddad Attili, declared in summer 2008 that all he could do was engage in "crisis management" (UN Office for the Coordination of Humanitarian Affairs, 2008).

A solution must be found to allow for the careful management of the limited availability of water resources, and negotiations on this issue are as contentious as any. Negotiations on water resources occur on two fronts. First, Syria and Israel have made attempts since the 1990s to negotiate a peace settlement revolving around the Golan Heights. Israel occupied the Golan Heights in 1967, annexed it in 1980, and controls the water from the Jordan and Yarmouk rivers. Syria wants a return to the pre-1967 borders, with which would come access to the water from these two rivers; the Israelis want a return to 1923 borders, allowing them to maintain control of the water. Second, the Israelis and the Palestinians have numerous issues to confront concerning water in their attempts to negotiate a peace agreement. The Oslo process has involved attempts to address water issues. The Oslo Accords promoted the process of "equitable utilization" and the 1995 Taba Agreement (Oslo II) included Israel's recognition of Palestinian water rights. Like many of the most contentious issues (including Jerusalem, the right of return, and borders), water rights were included as a final status issue (Asser, 2007). Like the other final status issues, little progress has been made because the two parties simply cannot reach the point of final status. As mentioned above, all agreements demand a cessation of violence and the cessation of Israeli settlement-building, neither of which has occurred for a prolonged period of time. As a result, insufficient attention has been given to final status issues.

Israel has proposed solving the water problem with "regional desalination." This will certainly increase the amount of water available, but concerns have been raised that it will not result in a more equal distribution. Israel has long considered water access a security issue, while the Palestinians feel that control over their own resources is a vital component of independence and sovereignty. Complicating the situation, the West Bank security barrier encroaches into occupied territory and allows Israel to control areas of high water yield. Palestinians suffer from severe water deprivation, the worst in the Jordan River Basin, and finding an equitable solution that protects the interests of both sides will be difficult.

In Chapter 5, Hillel Shuval proposes that the parties must give priority to meeting the vital human needs of the Palestinians. To achieve this, Israel could relinquish a portion of the water from the Mountain Aquifer, while Lebanon and Syria relinquish a portion of the Jordan River to the Palestinians. Shuval concludes that Israel could easily afford to make this concession as it could replace the lost aquifer water with an unlimited supply of desalinated seawater, which it could purchase at a reasonable price. (Of course, the Palestinians cannot so readily afford the cost of such water.)

In Chapter 6, Amjad Aliewi, Enda O'Connell, and Geoff Parkin, and Karen Assaf provide a comprehensive look at the water situation experienced by the Palestinians.

Their chapter addresses the availability of water and the challenges of managing the Palestinian water sector, and concludes with ways in which the situation might be improved.

Taken together, these two chapters provide a comprehensive overview of the problems of water distribution and suggest some possible solutions.

Democratization and the domestic political environment

The concept of democracy creation and development is the subject of significant debate in the Israeli–Palestinian relationship, but the nature of that debate is very different for the two groups. Chapters 7 and 8 explore two stages in the evolution of democracy. For both Palestinians and Israelis, this is a matter of development, but the Palestinians are starting their democracy in a non-state while Israel is an established democratic state. Thus, the issues facing the two differ significantly.

In contrast to the Palestinians' nascent democracy, the Israelis live in a well-established democratic system. In fact, on Israel's sixtieth anniversary of statehood (2008), George W. Bush called it "one of the world's great democracies." This does not mean, however, that all issues relating to democracy in Israel have been resolved. Even in the most highly touted democracies, inequalities, discrimination, and electoral irregularities occur. Further progress in these areas is needed in all the world's "great" democracies.

In Chapter 7, Galia Golan deals with one such area where progress still needs to be made: the role of women in Israel. Israel has legally protected women's rights ever since the passing of the Women's Equal Rights Law, 1951, which prohibits discrimination on the basis of gender. However, despite the apparent progress of women in Israel, where they are employed in all professions and have had prominent roles in government, they remain a historically underrepresented group. Traditional cultural pressures to marry and start a family are still strong, patriarchy still dominates the social structure, and a 2007 study showed that women are paid on average one-third less than men for the same job (Sandler, 2007). In an effort to enhance the role of women in government, Israel has built upon UN Security Council Resolution 1325 (2000), which called for women's involvement in all efforts to promote peace and security. This resolution expresses "concern that civilians, especially women and children, account for the vast majority of those adversely affected by armed conflict." With the recognition that women play an important role in preventing and resolving conflict, and in peace-building, the resolution "urges Member States to ensure increased representation of women at all decision-making levels in national, regional, and international institutions and mechanisms for the prevention, management, and resolution of conflict" (UN Security Council, 2000). Golan discusses how Israel has built on the resolution, with particular emphasis on the area of military service. Women now play roles in all units of the IDF, but Golan details the continuing inequality, and she concludes with a discussion about whether the inclusion of more women in the decision-making arena would make any significant difference.

In attempts to promote peace between the Israelis and the Palestinians, third parties (in particular the United States) have stressed the importance of democratic development for the Palestinians. One of the highlights of the Oslo Accords was the general election to create the governing body known as the Palestinian Authority. Similarly, Phase One of the Roadmap proposed by the Quartet included new Palestinian elections. Despite espousing the importance of democracy, however, third parties have criticized Palestinian democracy and the use of elections as political tools. For example, in 2002, George W. Bush called on the Palestinian people to elect new leaders – in other words, oust the democratically elected Yasser Arafat. The United States and Israel had come to the conclusion that Arafat could not be reasoned with and that he was an impediment to peace. (Bush's predecessor, Bill Clinton, had come to a similar conclusion after the failure of Camp David in 2000.) Bush called on "the Palestinian people to elect new leaders, leaders not compromised by terror" and "to build a practicing democracy, based on tolerance and liberty." He then went on to promise, "When the Palestinian people have new leaders, new institutions and new security arrangements with their neighbors, the United States of America will support the creation of a Palestinian state whose borders and certain aspects of sovereignty will be provisional until resolved as part of a final settlement in the Middle East" (Bush, 2002).

Dissatisfaction with the outcome of the Palestinian political process intensified in 2006 when Hamas won the majority of seats in the Palestinian parliamentary elections. This was a democratic nightmare for the Unites States, Israel, and their allies. A fair and free election brought to power an entity that denies Israel's right to exist and utilizes violence against civilians as a means of political persuasion. Immediately after the Hamas victory, Israeli Prime Minister Olmert declared, "Israel will not conduct any negotiations with a Palestinian government if it includes any [members of] an armed terrorist organization that calls for Israel's destruction" (BBC, 2006). The United States also declared that it would not have dealings with a Hamas-led government, unless the latter renounced its call to destroy Israel. Along with the European Union, the United States and Israel have taken steps to isolate the Hamas wing of the Palestinian Authority.

While it is difficult for many to contemplate working with Hamas, others are critical of the tactic of isolating the Palestinian regime. Former US President Jimmy Carter, while certainly not condoning terrorism, has claimed that the United States' stance on the 2006 election smacks of hypocrisy. In an interview in March 2006, he said, "Since the Hamas victory [came] as a result of an election that the United States encouraged – even forced on the reluctant Israelis – this punishment undermines the credibility of our commitment to democracy, unless we control the outcome of an election" (Council on Foreign Relations, 2006). While Western governments rhetorically promote democracy, there seems to be little hesitation in undermining any unfriendly administrations that emerge as the victors in elections. (The Palestinians are not alone in having their electoral choice questioned, and the United States has on occasion overthrown democratically elected governments that do not conform to its interests: for example, Prime Minister Mossadegh in Iran in 1953 and the Arbenz government in Guatemala in 1954.)

In Chapter 8, Walid Salem looks at Palestinian "transitional democracy" (pre-state democracy in transition to statehood) and discusses the nascent stages of democracy, explaining how it has developed as well as its advantages and problems.

Human rights

While there is no universally agreed definition of human rights, the Universal Declaration of Human Rights does at least provide a frame of reference for debates on the issue in relation to the Israelis and Palestinians. It was adopted by the General Assembly of the United Nations in December 1948 and includes the following in its list of basic human rights:

- life, liberty, and security of the person;
- freedom from slavery or servitude;
- freedom from torture or cruel, inhuman or degrading treatment or punishment;
- equal protection under the law;
- freedom from arbitrary arrest, detention, or exile;
- freedom of movement and residence within the borders of a state;
- right to own property and not be deprived of that property;
- freedom of thought, conscience, and religion;
- freedom of opinion and expression;
- freedom of peaceful assembly and association;
- the right to work, rest and leisure;
- a standard of living adequate for the health and well-being of a person and his or her family; and
- the right to education.

The human rights situation in Israel and the Occupied Territories is complicated for two main reasons. First, Israel has a legitimate need for security. It faces a significant and real security threat emanating from the Occupied Territories. As mentioned above, Hamas has habitually fired rockets from Gaza into southern Israel. This, coupled with the use of suicide attacks, has led to a sense of insecurity in Israel and a consequent response. The belief of most Israelis (and their allies) is that it is unreasonable to expect them to sit by idly and allow themselves to be attacked, kidnapped, or killed. Hence, the response to each Palestinian action is an equal (or harsher) reaction. And indeed, Israeli actions to impede the movement of suicide bombers and other terrorists (such as the separation barrier, checkpoints, and segregated roads) may be having the desired effect. There was a nine-month period from April 2006 to January 2007 without a single suicide bombing in Israel, and a cease-fire between Israel and Hamas that began in mid-2008 led to a period of calm that lasted roughly five months. (Unfortunately, when the cease-fire broke, the Israelis promptly launched an attack on Gaza.) As discussed above, Israelis firmly believe that the West Bank barrier is preventing the movement of would-be suicide bombers from the Occupied Territories into Israel. However, while these are positive outcomes for the Israelis, they are having negative effects in the Occupied

Territories, especially when considered alongside Palestinian infighting and the Israeli military action in Gaza (Callaway and Matthews, 2008).

If there is to be progress in the peace process between the Israelis and the Palestinians, what approach should be taken with respect to human rights? In Chapter 9, Edward Kaufman discusses whether adherence to human rights principles will help push forward the peace process. He addresses two schools of thought: those who believe that human rights should be guiding principles in negotiations and codified in peace agreements; and those who believe that the issue can be resolved once the main negotiations have been concluded. After examining the arguments and counter-arguments, Kaufman concludes that the former approach would be more productive. Understanding that concern for security often overrides concern for human rights, it is argued that respect for human rights in the negotiation process will assist in moving the process forward, something that is greatly desired by the Israelis. Thus, pursuing improvements in human rights for the Palestinians will benefit the Israelis, too.

The second issue that complicates the human rights situation in Israel and the Occupied Territories is that conditions are very different for Israeli citizens, on the one hand, and for Palestinians in the Occupied Territories, on the other. As mentioned above, Israel is a democracy that holds free elections and guarantees enumerated fundamental rights for its citizens. Admittedly, its Arab citizens continue to face discrimination, violence persists against women, and even trafficking in women is a problem, but Israeli citizens generally enjoy a high level of human rights. One cannot, however, remove the Occupied Territories from the reality of the human rights situation, and thus conditions in Israel overall are considered very poor (as indicated by annual reports from Amnesty International and Human Rights Watch). While Israeli citizens rarely suffer atrocities, the situation for the Palestinians is quite different. For example, in its 2007 report on the Occupied Territories, Amnesty International concluded,

> Military blockades and increased restrictions imposed by Israel on the movement of Palestinians and the confiscation by Israel of Palestinian customs duties caused a significant deterioration in living conditions for Palestinian inhabitants in the Occupied Territories, with poverty, food aid dependency, health problems and unemployment reaching crisis levels. Israeli soldiers and settlers committed serious human rights abuses, including unlawful killings, against Palestinians, mostly with impunity. Thousands of Palestinians were arrested by Israeli forces throughout the Occupied Territories on suspicion of security offences and hundreds were held in administrative detention.
>
> *(Amnesty International, 2007a)*

Thus, Palestinians in the Occupied Territories face an unsafe security environment and are living through a humanitarian disaster.

The situation in Gaza, in particular, has reached catastrophic levels. The victory of Hamas in the 2006 parliamentary elections resulted in a deterioration on two fronts. First, the Israelis cracked down even harder on border crossings as Qassam rockets continued to fly into southern Israel. Few goods were reaching Gaza, partly because of the blockade that has been enforced along the Egyptian–Gazan border. Although parts of the barrier separating Egypt from Gaza were torn down by Hamas in 2008 and Egypt periodically allows Gazans across the border to obtain food and medical supplies and treatment (and materials and supplies enter Gaza through tunnels from Egypt), the people of Gaza now find themselves in an untenable situation. The quality of life for them diminished further with the eruption of hostilities in late 2008. As mentioned above, this conflict left hundreds of Palestinians dead and the infrastructure decimated.

Second, following the election triumph for Hamas, Palestinian factions turned on each other. After months of factional street-fighting and a failed attempt to form a unity government, the conflict between Fatah and Hamas culminated in the bloody takeover of Gaza by the latter in 2007. (Consequently, Hamas controlled Gaza while Fatah remained in power on the West Bank.) There were reports of terrible atrocities committed by both sides, and claims (denied by Hamas) that Fatah fighters remaining in Gaza were executed in the streets.

In Chapter 10, Bassem Eid details the violations of Palestinian rights from April 2006 through December 2007. Eid has a clear focus and point of view as he outlines abuses by Hamas and Fatah against each other. The chapter provides a detailed and disturbing look at how the two factions have treated one another's members.

Peace culture and education

While education is not a panacea, it is an important element in reducing misunderstandings, prejudice, and hatred. Chapters 11 and 12 deal with the concept of peace education and how it might be utilized as an effective tool in changing the underlying hostility that permeates relations between the Israelis and the Palestinians. Peace education is aimed primarily at children and youth and is designed to help them understand the origins and consequences of violence, recognize injustice and prejudice, and enhance self-awareness. The United Nations, in particular UNICEF and UNESCO, has put considerable effort into this area. It defines peace education as being "directed to the full development of the human personality and to the strengthening of respect for human rights and fundamental freedoms." It is designed to promote "understanding, tolerance and friendship among nations, racial or religious groups" and to assist the UN in furthering peace. It was originally developed to reduce the possibility of nuclear war, but it now seeks to create a culture of peace (UN Peace Education, n.d.). Further, UNICEF defines peace education as "the process of promoting the knowledge, skills, attitudes and values needed to bring about behavior change that will enable children, youth and adults to prevent conflict and violence, both overt and structural; to resolve conflict peacefully; and to create the conditions conducive to peace, whether at an interpersonal, intergroup, national or international level." UNICEF promotes the idea that peace education is of value in all societies, not just those in conflict, and that this is "a long-term process, not a short-term intervention" (UNICEF, n.d.). Lastly, UNESCO spends a significant portion of its resources promoting "Education for peace, human rights, and democracy." The Yamoussoukro Declaration of 1989 called on UNESCO "to construct a new vision of peace, liberty, justice, solidarity, tolerance, human rights and equality between women and men," and peace education is an important part of that vision (UN Peace Education, n.d.).

So how is the principle of peace education being applied by the Israelis and Palestinians? While the latter have been building their education system from the ground up, the former already had a fully functioning education system in place at the time of Israeli independence. One of the biggest challenges faced by Israel has been integrating large numbers of immigrants from different cultural backgrounds into its educational system. Children from over seventy countries have come to Israel and special programs have been designed to assist their transition. While the educational system has been criticized for its bias, in Chapter 11 Daniel Bar-Tal suggests how peace culture and education might be developed in Israel. He discusses the development of beliefs and attitudes that are formed in the midst of seemingly intractable conflicts and how peace education can assist in reconciliation. The Israelis and the Palestinians are in a period of transition – from intractable conflict to tractable conflict – and they need to make the transition from conflict culture to peace culture. Peace education is critical if this transition is to succeed.

Criticism leveled at the education system of the Palestinians has been widespread – the common belief is that Palestinian textbooks and curricula are anti-Semitic and preach the destruction of Israel. Nathan Brown (2001) concluded that such criticism was unfounded and was being used simply to attack the Palestinian National Authority. However, although the Palestinian curriculum does not incite hatred of the Jews, one could criticize it for failing to support peace. Brown concluded, "The Palestinian educational system is designed to serve other goals, most prominently the inculcation of identity and legitimation of authority – largely ignoring the sensitive issues connected with peace" (Brown, 2001). Attempts to institute concepts of peace education are further complicated by the living conditions of the Palestinians, especially in Gaza. The challenges faced by the Palestinian Ministry of Education are daunting. It was established in 1994, the point at which education services were handed over to the Palestinians for the first time. UNESCO, among others, has assisted in the development of both the ministry and the whole education system, but efforts to improve education for the Palestinians are consistently hampered by violence, poor conditions, and a lack of funding.

In Chapter 12, Salem Aweiss addresses the development of the Palestinian curriculum through the lens of peace education. He discusses the role of peace education in facilitating reconciliation and peace, and explains the development of the Palestinian curriculum. While there is no formal peace education included in the curriculum, Aweiss describes social and education initiatives designed to overcome stereotyping, intolerance, and prejudice. He ends with an important discussion of the obstacles to developing peace education in the Palestinian context and makes recommendations as to how these might be overcome.

Conclusion

On reading the chapters of this book, a number of questions might be considered. In what ways do the attitudes and suggestions of the authors diverge – where do they disagree? In what ways do their arguments converge – where do they agree? Are the areas of disagreement over the various issues (water, refugees, and borders, settlements and territory) intractable? Can the areas of agreement be used as building blocks toward a solution? What role can the concepts of democracy, human rights, and peace education play in promoting peace between the Israelis and the Palestinians? What do the arguments and evidence presented here tell us about the future of the Israeli–Palestinian conflict?

While this book will not give you definitive answers to all of these questions, the authors provide an illuminating view of a conflict that many believe cannot be resolved. What you should learn from the arguments of the authors is that there are areas of agreement – and, yes, of disagreement, too – but it might be possible to move in a positive direction if we build from the areas of agreement.

PART I
Issues

PART I.

Issues

Refugees

1

ISRAEL AND THE PALESTINIAN REFUGEE ISSUE

Joel Peters[1]

Introduction

Since the beginning of the Oslo process in 1993 the relative weight and attention given by Israeli policy-makers to each of the final status issues has significantly evolved. Initially, the greatest political and conceptual challenge centered on the question of Palestinian statehood, and the territorial configuration of a future Palestinian state. The refugee issue was largely ignored by Israel and was postponed to the latter stages of the negotiations. Indeed, it was not until early summer 2000, just prior to the Camp David summit, that Israeli policy-makers undertook any significant preparatory work on this issue.

The convergence of various political, economic, and cultural forces has reshaped Israeli perceptions and expectations, however. Palestinian statehood is now generally accepted as a given by most Israelis. Questions of a territorial withdrawal from the West Bank and the division of Jerusalem, even the idea of shared sovereignty of the holy sites, have become central parts of the Israeli discourse on the peace process. The refugee issue, however, still receives scant attention in Israel. It remains highly sensitive and potential solutions are rarely discussed within the general public domain. Israeli academia and media have been largely silent on this question, and the little coverage there has been has uncritically repeated the dominant Israeli discourse as to the causes, and the possible outcomes, of the refugee problem.

Israel's approach to the refugee question is deeply conflicted. Israel has consistently tried to deflect international discussion of the issue, arguing that such discussions are inimical to Israel's interests, and has sought to frame any such discussions in purely humanitarian rather than political terms. At the same time, there is a quiet realization within decision-making circles that a failure to address the issue could ultimately prevent a final peace settlement with the Palestinians, thus closing the window of opportunity on what is still held as Israel's leading strategic objective – a negotiated, comprehensive permanent status agreement. Yet the limited expertise, inside and outside government, on the complexities involved in resolving the refugee question has resulted in a failure of Israel to articulate its interests clearly on the various components of the issue and to develop a critical assessment of the various policy choices it faces in resolving it.

Israeli discourse on the refugee issue

Of all the final status issues, the refugee question is seen by Israel as the most threatening. It touches on a number of socio-political elements that embody deep-seated Israeli fears that are both past and future oriented. While the basic framework for the peace process draws on concluding the historical conflict between Jews and Palestinians, the question of the refugees is the only core issue that relates directly to the events of 1948 rather than to those of 1967. In that regard, the outbreak of the 1948 war and its consequences touch on what both sides see as constituting events in their national identities – the establishment of the state of Israel for the Jews and the Naqba and the creation of the refugee problem for the Palestinians.[2]

Palestinian demands for the right of return and calls for compensation are seen by Israel as challenges to its legitimacy and to the moral foundation of the Jewish state. Confronting these issues forces an uncomfortable reexamination of historical narratives, collective identity, and constituting myths, and touches on questions of Israeli culpability and responsibility for the refugee problem. Whereas all other aspects of the conflict with the Palestinians have generated contending and contested positions in Israel, a common narrative, with little open dissent, has emerged on the refugee issue. Israel's approach to the refugee problem has centered on three guiding principles forged shortly after the war in 1948. Those principles have held true, and have directed much of Israeli thinking on this issue, ever since.

First, Israel has consistently maintained that the responsibility for the creation of the refugee problem lies solely with the Arab states, which never accepted the creation of the state of Israel in 1948, and declared war on the nascent Jewish state. The Arab states that attacked Israel in 1948 created the refugee problem by calling on the Palestinians to leave their homes during the war, and to return later with the victorious Arab armies.[3] Second, Israel has sought to prevent the mass return of the refugees, and has denied that the Palestinians possess any legal, or moral, right to return to their homes and reclaim their property. Finally, Israel has argued that the solution to the plight of the refugees lies in their absorption and rehabilitation in their current places of residence, namely the Arab host countries.

The Arab states, along with the Palestinian leadership, are also accused by Israel of perpetuating the refugee problem, and of manipulating the refugees' plight for political advantage. Instead of offering the refugees the opportunity to assimilate into their host societies, the Arab states have confined them to camps, and to a life of misery. In this they have been abetted by the international community through the setting up in 1949 of the UNRWA (United Nations Relief and Works Agency) –

the international agency responsible for providing services to the refugees – and its continuous and extensive financial underwriting of the work of the UNRWA. By contrast, Israel points to the experience of some 600,000 Jewish refugees who were expelled from their homes by Arab governments following the war in 1948, but who were successfully absorbed into Israeli society.

Central to the Israeli discourse and its positioning on the refugee issue has been the prevention of the right of return. This issue has elicited a wall-to-wall consensus across Israeli civil society and the political establishment. Israel has consistently denied that the Palestinian refugees possess a legal or moral right to return to their homes. It has refuted Palestinian claims that UN General Assembly Resolution (UNGAR) 194 of December 1948 affords them any such legal right (Benvenisti 2002; Lapidoth 2002). Any Palestinian return, if at all, would be granted on a limited, case-by-case basis, using humanitarian criteria that allow solely for family reunification. Shlomo Gazit best presents the political argument:

> Israel denies the legality of the Palestinian claim. If it recognizes the right of return it would be admitting responsibility, and perhaps even culpability for creating the problem. But Israel categorically denies any responsibility for the War of 1948. On the contrary, the guilt and responsibility are all Arab-Palestinian, and it is completely irrelevant whether the Arab leaders encouraged the local population to leave their homes, or whether they departed to escape the fighting. Israel would deny any responsibility even if there were no practical demands for a "return" of refugees; even more so when recognition of such a right would deny Israel the right to control and veto the number of returnees.
>
> *(Gazit 1995: 7–8)*

Any discussion of the "right of return" is regarded as unacceptable for the vast majority of Israelis, and is a subject not open for any negotiation. The idea of acknowledging any Palestinian right, even symbolically, is viewed as a step that would only entrench this issue as a source of future tension between Israel and the Palestinians rather than help to bring closure on their conflict.

The rejection of a Palestinian "right of return" is not, however, just tied to the denial of any past culpability or responsibility. The Israeli discourse has securitized the question of repatriation of the Palestinian refugees. In recent years, the demographic issue has been viewed as a significant challenge to the Jewish-democratic nature of Israel and has become a major driver behind arguments for the need for an Israeli withdrawal from the West Bank. The advocacy for the Palestinian right of return to Israel is regarded within Israel as an ongoing challenge from the Palestinian leadership to the very foundation of the Jewish state, and therefore, in practice, as a rejection of the two-state solution. For Israel, accepting an unlimited number of Palestinian refugees is seen as nothing short of national suicide. Allowing a return of Palestinian refugees into Israel, however limited, is viewed as a threat to the demographic, social, and, above all, Jewish character of the state. Shlomo Ben

Ami, Israel's foreign minister at the Camp David summit, gave a forthright expression of his country's framing of the right of return as posing an existential threat to Israel. In a speech shortly after the collapse of those talks, he stated bluntly: "We want peace but we are not lunatics."

For Israel, any repatriation of Palestinian refugees, and thereby fulfillment of the right of return, would occur only in the context of a return to a future Palestinian state. In the past, even a return of the refugees to a Palestinian state in the West Bank and Gaza was questioned, especially by those on the right wing of the Israeli political spectrum. This was reflected in the 1996 Israeli government guidelines, presented by Benjamin Netanyahu, in which it was stated that Israel would "oppose 'the right of return' of Arab populations to any part of the Land of Israel west of the Jordan River" (Government of Israel 1996). Even for analysts who accept that imposing such conditions on the Palestinian leadership is politically unsustainable, there is a deep concern that the mass and uncontrolled return of refugees to the West Bank or Gaza would not be economically or socially viable. And that it would result in future destabilization, thereby presenting Israel with a potential new geostrategic threat.

The question of any past culpability or responsibility for the refugee problem has also influenced Israel's approach toward the question of compensation for the Palestinian refugees. Israel has rejected the Palestinian position that it bears the sole responsibility for the payment of financial compensation to the refugees both for their material loss and for their personal suffering. Israel has refused to talk in terms of personal compensation paid out to the refugees. Instead Israel has preferred to speak in terms of a rehabilitation fund, to which it too would be prepared to contribute, so as to assist in the resettlement of the refugees in their current places of residence. In that respect, Israel has traditionally argued that any form of reparation should be distributed on a collective basis, rather than through individual or family claims. Moreover, whenever the issue of compensation for Palestinian refugees has been raised, Israel has sought to broaden the discussion to include reparations to Jews expelled from Arab countries after 1948 for their loss, arguing that these two phenomena are connected, and thus they need to be treated in a similar fashion (Fischbach 2008: 6–24).

The refugee question and the peace process

These principles influenced the strategy and the approach Israel adopted throughout the peace process from 1991 to 2000. With the start of the Madrid peace conference and the signing of the Oslo Accords in 1993, Israel could no longer deflect discussion of the refugee problem and keep it off the political agenda. And with the onset of final status talks at Camp David in the summer of 2000, it was forced to address the issue directly, and modify many of its long-standing positions.

The Refugee Working Group

The Madrid peace conference of November 1991 led not only to the start of bilateral negotiations between Israel and Jordan, Israel and Syria, and Israel and the Palestinians but to the establishment of a set of multilateral talks aimed at dealing with problems of a regional nature, such as water, the environment, regional economic development, arms control and regional security, and refugees (Peters 1996). The decision to include a working group on refugees was made at the behest of the Palestinians, over the reservations of Israel. The Palestinians saw the establishment of the Refugee Working Group (RWG) as an opportunity to address the substantive concerns and the political rights of the refugees, and to send a signal to the refugee community that they had not been excluded from the peace process.

Israel's strategy towards the RWG was consistent with its approach to the refugee question during the previous forty years. It was prepared to discuss any initiatives that might lead to international efforts aimed at improving the welfare and living conditions of the Palestinian refugees, but it would resist the introduction of any political issues into the deliberations of the RWG. This position hardened after the signing of the Oslo Accords, with Israel insisting that all political issues should be excluded from the RWG since they would be addressed as part of the proposed final status negotiations.

Given the divergent starting points of Israel and the Palestinians, the functioning of the working group was fraught with difficulties from the outset. The first two meetings of the RWG were dominated by procedural problems centering on the composition of the Palestinian team, with Israel boycotting the first plenary meeting in Ottawa in May 1992 in protest at the inclusion of Palestinians from outside the West Bank and Gaza within the Palestinian delegation. At the first meeting, the RWG drew up its agenda. It identified six themes and allocated countries (or "shepherds," to use the official terminology of the multilateral talks) to be responsible for work in those areas: databases (Norway); human resources, job creation and training (USA); public health (Italy); child welfare (Sweden); economic and social infrastructure (EU); and family reunification (France).

Israel regarded the inclusion of family reunification among these six themes with deep suspicion, seeing it as a potential back door for a discussion of the right of return. Consequently, it was determined to limit the scope of discussion on this issue, and many of the deliberations in this sub-group revolved around developing criteria for defining the terms of family reunification. In April 1993, Israel agreed that it would increase the annual quota of applications for the reunification of families displaced from the West Bank and Gaza in 1967 to 2000 per year, a fourfold increase on the previous figure. It also agreed to reduce the time taken to process those applications from an average of one year to a maximum of three months. But in practice neither of these concessions was ever implemented.

The multilateral talks were short-lived and ceased to take place after the election of Benjamin Netanyahu as Israeli Prime Minister in May 1996. The substantive achievements of the RWG were limited. From the outset Israel was determined to limit the scope of the activities of the working group. It showed little enthusiasm and was deeply suspicious of the RWG, never viewing it as a valuable arena for addressing the various regional elements that any resolution of the refugee question would comprise, many of which cannot be settled directly between Israel and the Palestinians. In part, Israel viewed itself as outnumbered by the Arab states in the RWG and was untrusting of the intentions of other states in the working group. But, in reality, Israel had yet to start thinking systematically about solutions to the refugee issue, let alone the broader international and regional implications of this question.

The Oslo Accords

On September 13, 1993, Israel and the PLO signed the Declaration of Principles (DOP) on the White House lawn. This outlined a framework for the establishment of a self-governing Palestinian Authority in parts of the West Bank and Gaza and a timetable for the initiation and completion of final status talks on the outstanding contested issues. Article V of the Declaration of Principles explicitly stated that the refugee issue would be included as one of the five final status issues. For the first time ever, Israel and the Palestinians agreed to negotiate a resolution to the refugee issue. They also agreed to establish a mechanism for resolving the issue of those Palestinian refugees displaced from the West Bank and Gaza in the Six-Day War of 1967. Article XII stipulated that a Quadripartite Committee consisting of joint Palestinian–Jordanian–Egyptian–Israeli delegations would "decide by agreement on the modalities of admission of persons displaced form the West Bank and Gaza strip in 1967, together with the necessary measures to prevent disruption and disorder."

The Quadripartite Committee first met in Amman in March 1995. It soon became apparent, however, that progress would be slow, and that Israel was not willing to accept the return of significant numbers of Palestinians displaced in 1967 to the West Bank and Gaza. Discussion within the Quadripartite Committee quickly became bogged down over definitions of what comprised a displaced person and the various modalities for return. Israel held out for a minimalist definition of a "displaced person" (namely, those actually displaced by the fighting in 1967), totaling around 200,000 people. This definition was unacceptable to the Arab parties, who were pushing for a much larger figure of 1.1 million. The Committee failed to resolve the differences on numbers and could not produce any agreement over modalities. The talks broke down in 1997 and, despite a ministerial-level meeting in February 2000, never resumed.

The Stockholm Track

It was not until April 2000, nearly seven years after the signing of the Oslo Accords, that Israel and the Palestinians first addressed the refugee issue in any substantive form. Those discussions took place from April to June 2000 within the context of a secret back-channel aimed at formulating a draft for a Framework Agreement on Permanent

Status (FAPS). They culminated in a series of meetings held in Stockholm under the auspices of the Swedish government. The Israeli team consisted of Israel's foreign minister, Shlomo Ben Ami, and Gilead Sher, the head of Israel's negotiating team with the Palestinians, who arrived in Stockholm with a detailed set of ideas on the refugee issue.

In the discussions there was no meeting of minds, either on the origins of the refugee problem or on the question of right of return. Ben Ami and Sher refused to accept any language through which Israel would be held responsible for the creation of the refugee problem. Nor were they prepared to include any specific reference to UN Resolution 194 or acknowledge the Palestinian right of return, as demanded by Abu Ala, who led the Palestinian team. Israel did, however, express a willingness to accept up to 15,000 refugees, spread over a period of several years, who would be allowed to return on humanitarian grounds.

Agreement, in principle, was reached over various questions of compensation. The two sides agreed on the need for two new international mechanisms to deal with the technical aspects of this issue. The first would be an international commission that would address questions concerning the rehabilitation and resettlement of the refugees; the second, an international fund, would deal with the distribution of compensation to the refugees. It was also accepted that each Palestinian household that had fled in 1948 would be entitled to submit a claim for compensation, and that the registration of refugees for the work of the commission and the fund would be based upon data provided by the UNRWA (Sher 2001; Ben Ami 2001; Enderlin 2003).

The Camp David summit

None of the understandings reached in Stockholm fed into the discussions held at the Camp David summit. The Israeli team at the refugee sub-committee at Camp David now comprised Elyakim Rubinstein and Dan Meridor, both of whom had been included by Ehud Barak only at the last minute in order to add some right-wing balance to the composition of the Israeli delegation. The Palestinians interpreted handing the refugee portfolio to Rubinstein, who was briefed on developments in the refugee file only on the plane to Camp David, as proof that Barak had no intention of addressing the issue seriously (Drucker 2001; Swisher 2004).

In the initial exchanges at Camp David both sides presented well-rehearsed arguments. Israel refused to accept any of the Palestinian opening positions. It was unwilling to admit responsibility for the creation of the refugee problem in 1948, refused to recognize the principle of right of return, and refused to include any reference to UN Resolution 194. Furthermore, it rejected the Palestinian demand that it alone would be accountable for compensating the refugees for their suffering and for the material loss of their property. Israel countered by raising the claims of Jews who had been expelled from Arab lands and demanded that they should be equally compensated. It also proposed that the UNRWA should be dismantled within a ten-year period and be replaced by a new international body that would be responsible for the resettlement and rehabilitation of the refugees (Sher 2001; Swisher 2004; Enderlin 2003).[4]

However, it was not the refugee issue but Jerusalem that was the central focus, and the main point of contention, at the Camp David summit. In fact, Israel and the Palestinians did not engage in any serious negotiations about the refugees at Camp David. The refugee sub-committee met only briefly and carried on in the same vein as it had at the opening session, simply exchanging mutually counter-productive arguments.

The Taba talks

It was only during the negotiations in Taba at the end of January 2001, during the death throes of the peace process, that Israel and the Palestinians negotiated seriously on the refugee question. Yossi Beilin, who had not been present at Camp David, now headed the Israeli team on refugees. He brought with him his own set of ideas on the issue, many of which had been developed in the previous months by the Economic Cooperation Foundation (ECF), one of the few Israeli institutions that had been thinking seriously about potential solutions to the problem.

The negotiations at Taba were ultimately unsuccessful and failed to reach any signed agreement, and they have been a source of controversy ever since. Beilin has said the parties were very close to reaching a comprehensive agreement on the refugee issue. Others, though, including Ehud Barak, have dismissed the relevance of Taba, arguing that the achievements were limited and that any supposed meeting of minds has been greatly overstated.

Israel's thinking on the refugee issue at Taba can be gleaned from the "Private Response on Palestinian Refugees," submitted on January 23, 2001 in reply to Palestinian proposals presented the previous day.[5] In addition, a summary of the discussions at Taba was prepared by the EU's special envoy to the peace process, Miguel Moratinos (Eldar 2002; Moratinos 2001). The Israeli response (as well as the Moratinos report) has no official legal standing, and the ideas presented are not binding on the Israeli government in any future negotiations with the Palestinians. But the ideas contained within it are significant. They broke new ground and represent the most far-reaching and systematic Israeli thinking on the refugee issue: addressing the need to develop a common narrative on the origins of the refugee problem; presenting a number of options in respect of the repatriation and resettle-ment of the refugees; trying to grapple with the right of return and UN Resolution 194; and offering a set of practical measures in the area of compensation.

In his inaugural address to the Knesset as Prime Minister, Ehud Barak acknow-ledged the suffering caused to the Palestinians resulting from the conflict:

> To our neighbors the Palestinians, I wish to say: the bitter conflict between us has brought great suffering to both our peoples. We cannot change the past; we can only make the future better. I am not only cognizant of the sufferings of my people, but I also recognize the sufferings of the Palestinian people.
>
> *(Barak 1999)*

Barak's statement was unprecedented for an Israeli prime minister. It reflected a growing awareness that any peace agreement with the Palestinians could not just deal with the present reality and future relations, but would have to address, in some form, questions arising from the past.

At Taba, Israel acknowledged that the refugee issue was central and that its "comprehensive and just resolution" was essential. The Israeli response attempted to deal with the past suffering of the refugees. While falling far short of an apology, the second clause at least affirmed that "The State of Israel solemnly expresses its sorrow for the tragedy of the Palestinian refugees, their suffering and losses and will be an active partner in ending this terrible chapter that was opened 53 years ago, contributing its part to the attainment of a comprehensive and fair solution to the Palestinian refugee problem."

Israel again rejected the Palestinian demand that it should bear the sole moral and legal responsibility for the displacement of the Palestinians in 1948 and refused to accept that it alone was responsible for the resolution of the refugee problem. Instead, the Israeli text suggested that "For all those parties directly or indirectly responsible for the creation of the status of Palestinian refugeeism, as well as those for whom a just and stable peace in the region is an imperative, it is incumbent to take upon themselves responsibility to assist in resolving the Palestinian refugee problem of 1948." It also proposed that the two sides should work together to produce a shared historical narrative on the origins of the refugee problem, and this joint narrative should be included in any signed agreement.

The Palestinians reiterated their demand that the refugees should be afforded the right of return in accordance with UN Resolution 194. In response, Israel adopted the formula proposed by President Clinton one month earlier whereby the refugees would be given a choice of five options: the state of Palestine; areas in Israel that would be transferred to Palestine in the framework of a territorial exchange (the land swap); rehabilitation in their current host country; resettlement in a third country; admission to Israel. Although all options would be given equal status, the decisions made by the refugees would be linked with the compensation package, and financial incentives would be offered to encourage them to waive their right to return to Israel. In addition, Israel discussed potential numbers and a timetable by which some refugees might be allowed to return. No numbers were officially agreed upon, but informally Israel proposed a three-track program spread over fifteen years whereby 25,000 people would be admitted in the first three years and 40,000 after five years. In all events, Israel would retain its sovereign right to determine who would be allowed to return and whom it would bar (Clinton 2000).

Clinton had also tried to address the question of UN Resolution 194 by suggesting that the parties would in effect regard any agreement reached between them as implementing that resolution. Israel adopted Clinton's approach, and in its response proposed that the five resettlement options offered to the refugees should be regarded as fulfilling the relevant clause of Resolution 194. The agreement signed would serve as "a complete and final implementation of Article 11 of UNGAR 194."

When it came to the question of compensation, the two sides returned to the understandings reached in Stockholm. Two new international bodies, an international commission and an international fund, in which Israel would serve as a full member, would be created to implement the agreement. The Taba talks established a two-track procedure for submitting claims for compensation. According to Moratinos (2001), "Both sides agreed that 'small-sum' compensation shall be paid to the refugees in the 'fast-track' procedure, claims of compensation for property losses below a certain amount shall be subject to 'fast-track' procedures." Israel rejected the Palestinian proposal that the future state of Palestine would have sole responsibility for the distribution of funds. Instead it proposed that all funds would remain under the control of the international commission and that the commission "would have full and exclusive" responsibility. Israel agreed to contribute to the international fund, though the total sum of its contribution and how this amount would be assessed were never determined. A significant element of Israel's contribution would, however, comprise assets and property that it would leave behind following a withdrawal from any part of the West Bank, Gaza, and East Jerusalem.

Israel has historically insisted that any agreement on the refugee question would constitute an end to all claims by Palestinians on this issue and that it would signify a complete and final resolution of this problem. At Taba, it repeated this demand. The Israelis also called for UNRWA to be dismantled within a period of five years, with the refugee camps incorporated into the national and municipal structures of the host countries, so that the term "Palestinian refugee" would be consigned to the history books.

The Geneva Accord

By the time the details of the Taba negotiations were revealed in February 2002, the Al-Aqsa Intifada was at its height. Israelis no longer saw the Palestinians as a partner to be trusted and had begun to lose faith in the peace process. In addition, the concessions offered at Taba were associated with Yossi Beilin, who was becoming increasingly discredited in the public's eyes. Beilin was seen as acting independently at Taba, representing his own views in the negotiations, not those of the Israeli government.

Following the Taba talks, Beilin had continued to meet privately with his Palestinian counterparts in order to explore additional areas of potential agreement. Working with Yasser Abed Rabbo, the two succeeded in producing a detailed blueprint for an Israeli–Palestinian permanent status agreement, popularly known as the "Geneva Accord," following its public launch in Geneva on December 1, 2003. Dubbed by Beilin as the "eight days of Taba," the Geneva Accord builds on much of the previous understandings reached on the refugee issue, though notably the attempt to craft a shared narrative was dropped (Beilin 2004; Geneva Initiative 2003). Not surprisingly, the question of the right of return drew the most attention. When details of the Geneva Accord were first released, members of the Israeli team were quick to note that they had resolved this question and that the Palestinians had forgone the right of return, marking this as one of their main achievements.

In general, the Geneva Accord outlines the same five choices that were included in the Clinton Parameters and the Taba negotiations. It differs, however, in the way the number of possible returnees to Israel are to be determined. At Taba the parties tried, but failed, to arrive at a fixed number that would be allowed back. The Israeli side suggested 25,000 persons over a three-year period, or 40,000 over five, with all refugee return to be completed within a fifteen-year time-frame. The Palestinians had no fixed number in mind but were looking at "six figures" (at least 100,000) in the negotiations. By contrast, the Geneva Accord allows Israel to set its own number at its "sovereign discretion." But that figure would take into consideration and be in line with the average total numbers absorbed by various third countries.[6]

At first the Geneva Accord garnered considerable public support in Israel, but interest soon tapered off. It never truly caught the imagination of the Israeli people. In part, Israelis had become too untrusting of Beilin, and then the Accord was knocked off center stage by the announcement of Ariel Sharon's disengagement plan in December 2003. Israelis were also skeptical of the extent to which the Palestinians involved in the Geneva meetings were truly representative of Palestinian viewpoints, and whether they enjoyed the support of the Palestinian leadership. The ambiguous statements of Yasser Arafat on the Geneva initiative and the widespread criticism the Accord drew in the West Bank and Gaza only added to these doubts. In addition, the strenuous denials by various Palestinian participants that they had sold out the right of return only heightened Israeli suspicions. Given the contradictory comments by Palestinians, it is not surprising that in polls on the Geneva Accord the refugee section of the agreement had less support than almost any other component, with only 35 percent of Israelis expressing support for this aspect of the agreement (Brynen 2003).

Back to the right of return

The discussions at Taba were the last good-faith negotiations between Israel and the Palestinians on the refugee issue. Since then, the collapse of the peace process, the rise of the Intifada and the breakdown of trust between Israel and the Palestinians have resulted in a hardening of attitudes in Israel on this issue. The Israeli public is now more resistant to entertaining thoughts of compromise and concession in this area.

It was Jerusalem, not refugees, that plagued the negotiations at Camp David in July 2000. However, it was Palestinian intransigence over the right of return, not differences over Jerusalem, that was publicly flagged as the primary reason for the breakdown of those talks. For Israel, Arafat's refusal to compromise on this issue was highlighted as revealing his true intentions. The advocacy of the right of return was seen as simply a "demographic-political weapon for subverting the Jewish state" (Barak 2002). Israelis, of all political persuasions, saw the raising of the right of return as evidence that the Palestinians had yet to reconcile themselves to the idea of

coexistence. On January 2, 2001, thirty-three Israeli intellectuals published a state-
ment addressed to the Palestinian leadership. "We want to clarify," it stated, "that
we shall never be able to agree to the return of the refugees within the borders of
Israel, for the meaning of such a return would be the elimination of the State of
Israel." The signatories included known Israeli liberals such as the novelists Amos
Oz and David Grossman (Oz 2002).

The outbreak of the Intifada in September 2001, combined with the protests by
Israel's Arab population in its early months, substantially undercut the already weak
support for the return of any refugees to Israel. The widespread suspicion of
Palestinian motives had been expressed the previous year in *Ha'aretz*, Israel's leading
liberal newspaper, by Ze'ev Schiff (2000):

> it is doubtful whether those responsible for the riots among Israeli Arabs took
> into account how this behavior would influence negotiations on the sensitive
> issue of the Palestinian refugees. So far, Israel has shown a willingness to absorb
> into its territory, in stages, tens of thousands of refugees. Now it is clear that
> it would be madness, from a security as well as a demographic point of view,
> to add to the Arab minority – many of whose members raised the banner of
> revolt against Israel – tens of thousands of Palestinians who feel cheated and
> oppressed.

The backlash on the refugee question after the failure of the Camp David summit
was not just confined to rhetorical statements. On January 1, 2001, the Knesset
enacted legislation which stated that any agreement including the repatriation of
refugees to Israel would require parliamentary approval. The resolution had 61
co-sponsors, out of the 120 members, and won a majority of 90, attesting to its overwhelming cross-party support.

In 2002 the Israeli Ministry of the Interior began to limit the possibility of family
reunification by freezing permits allowing Palestinians from the West Bank and Gaza
married to Israeli citizens from residing with their spouses in Israel. The Israeli
cabinet gave a green light to this policy "in light of the security situation and because
of the implication of the immigration and the establishment in Israel of foreigners
of Palestinian descent including through family reunification." On July 31, 2003,
the Knesset enacted the Nationality and Entry into Israel Law (Temporary Order).
This law was then extended on several occasions, with 2005's extension adding
amendments that allow for family unification in only very limited circumstances.
The law includes age- and gender-related stipulations, which impose a sweeping
ban on applications from all Palestinian men under thirty-five years of age, and all
Palestinian women under twenty-five (Adalah 2003).

The Israeli government has also intensively lobbied the United States government
to back its position on the right of return publicly, and has achieved a significant
degree of success. Israel conditioned its acceptance of the Roadmap in May 2003
with fourteen reservations, including a demand that "references must be made to
Israel's right to exist as a Jewish state and to the waiver of any right of return for

Palestinian refugees to the State of Israel" (Government of Israel 2003). In the lead-up to Israel's withdrawal from Gaza and the dismantling of Jewish settlements in August 2005, Ariel Sharon succeeded in eliciting a statement from the American government reflecting Israel's stance on the right of return. In an exchange of letters aimed at bolstering domestic support for Sharon's disengagement plan, President George Bush wrote on April 14, 2004: "It seems clear that an agreed, just, fair and realistic framework for a solution to the Palestinian refugee issue as part of any final status agreement will need to be found through the establishment of a Palestinian state, and the settling of Palestinian refugees there, rather than in Israel" (Bush 2004).

Conclusion

After a hiatus of almost eight years, Israel and the Palestinians returned to the negotiating table following the Annapolis summit at the end of November 2007. In his speech to the Annapolis meeting Israeli Prime Minister Ehud Olmert (2007) acknowledged the importance and centrality of the refugee issue:

> Many Palestinians have been living for decades in camps, disconnected from the environment in which they grew up, wallowing in poverty, in neglect, alienation, bitterness, and a deep, unrelenting sense of humiliation . . . I know that this pain and this humiliation are the deepest foundations which fomented the ethos of hatred toward us. We are not indifferent to this suffering. We are not oblivious to the tragedies that you have experienced.

Olmert continued by committing Israel to play its part in any international mechanisms aimed at finding a solution to the refugee issue. His acknowledgment of the tragedy experienced by the Palestinian refugees was an important step. Yet in an interview several months earlier, in response to the issuing of the Arab Peace Initiative in March 2007, Olmert had been categorical in rejecting the possibility of any return of Palestinian refugees to Israel: "I'll never accept a solution that is based on their return to Israel, any number . . . I will not agree to accept any kind of Israeli responsibility for the refugees" (*Jerusalem Post* 2007).

The post-Annapolis talks failed to address the refugee issue in any great depth. Instead, Israel has been willing only to postpone any discussion of the operational components to a later stage, and has been interested only in a general declaration outlining the principles involved in finding a solution to the refugee issue. In the summer of 2009, the Palestinians and the Israelis offered differing accounts of the degree of understanding that had been reached on the refugee issue. In an interview with the *Washington Post*, Palestinian President Mahmoud Abbas claimed that Ehud Olmert had "accepted the principle" of the right of return of Palestinian refugees – something no previous Israeli prime minister had done – and that he had offered to resettle thousands in Israel (*Washington Post* 2009). Olmert categorically refuted Abbas's claim. In an interview with *Newsweek*, he stressed that he had rejected the Palestinian right of return but had offered instead to allow a small number of returnees into Israel as a "humanitarian gesture." This number was "smaller than the Palestinians wanted – a very, very limited number" (*Newsweek* 2009).

Since the collapse of the peace process in 2000, many Israelis have lost hope in the possibility of a negotiated settlement with the Palestinians. Ideas of unilateralism and separation have replaced strategies of conflict resolution. The debate on the refugee issue has hardened and become further securitized. Over the past decade Israeli academia, civil society, and policy-making circles have devoted little time to thinking systematically through potential solutions to this issue.[7] Little effort has been made to deepen understanding of the complexities involved in resolving the problem, and in encouraging an informed public debate. Post-Annapolis, Israel has been as reluctant to address the refugee issue as it was prior to the Camp David summit. Any resumption of negotiations brokered by George Mitchell is likely to falter over the lack of creative thinking and detailed proposals on the issue.

To ensure a successful and sustainable outcome to any future Israeli–Palestinian negotiations, more systematic work and strategic thinking, taking into account the socio-economic context facing the Palestinian refugee population and incorporating recent research on the issue, need to be undertaken within Israel. Such work would offer Israeli decision-makers a set of alternative operational frameworks and policy options and would allow them to assess the potential trade-offs emerging from alternative ideas. It would also enable Israel to think in more creative terms, and adopt a more flexible and imaginative approach towards negotiations with the Palestinians on this question.

To a large degree, the refugee issue remains the unresolved piece of the peace process puzzle. Israel has a strong strategic interest in addressing it, and in seeking a viable and durable solution to it. Any strategy that seeks to treat the refugee issue as a solely humanitarian concern, and to skirt round its political dimension, will not provide a long-lasting resolution. Ignoring the needs, interests, and political concerns of the refugees within the peace process, and in any final settlement reached between Israel and the Palestinians, will merely provide a focus for future resentment and potential destabilization. There is little chance of achieving a true reconciliation and an end to the conflict between Israel and the Palestinians if the refugee question is not addressed in *all* of its aspects, and in good faith.

Notes

1   The author would like to thank Michal Eskenazi for her research assistance in the preparation of this chapter.
2   I am grateful to Orit Gal for sharing these ideas with me. See Orit Gal, *Israeli Perspectives on the Palestinian Issue*, Middle East Programme Briefing Paper (London: Chatham House, 2008).
3   Recent scholarship on the 1948 war and the origins of the refugee problem has challenged this position. But such scholarship has been widely rejected in Israel as being biased and politically motivated, and it has had little impact on Israeli perceptions. See Benny Morris, *The Birth of the Palestinian Refugee Problem Revisited* (Cambridge: Cambridge University Press, 2003), and Ilan Pappe, *The Making of the Arab–Israeli Conflict* (London: I.B. Tauris, 1994). For an attack on this scholarship for its political bias, see Ephraim Karsh, *Fabricating Israeli History; The "New Historians"* (London: Frank Cass, 2000).

4 Dennis Ross, in his book on the peace process, *The Missing Peace* (New York: Farrar, Straus and Giroux, 2004), makes little mention of the refugee issue in his account of the Camp David summit.

5 Published by *Le Monde Diplomatique* and to be found at <http://www.monde-diplomatique.fr/cahier/proche-orient/israelrefugees-en> and <http://www.monde-diplomatique.fr/cahier/proche-orient/refugeespal-en>.

6 See Rex Brynen, "The Geneva Accord and the Palestinian Refugee Issue," mimeo, at: <http://www.arts.mcgill.ca/mepp/new_prrn/research/papers/geneva_refugees_2.pdf>. The text of the Geneva Accord reads: "Section 7 article 4.5.c. Option iv . . . [Israel as a permanent place of residence] shall be at the sovereign discretion of Israel and will be in accordance with a number that Israel will submit to the International Commission. This number shall represent the total number of Palestinian refugees that Israel shall accept. As a basis, Israel will consider the average of the total numbers submitted by the different third countries to the International Commission."

7 One notable exception is the work on the economic aspect of the refugee issue carried out by the Aix Group, available at <http://www.aixgroup.org/economic_dimensions_english_website.pdf>.

2

PALESTINIAN REFUGEES

Mohammed S. Dajani Daoudi

Introduction

The Palestinian refugee problem is one of the most intractable and controversial issues of the Arab–Israeli conflict, with the Palestinian refugees being one of the largest and longest-standing displaced populations in the world today. In fact, a majority of the Palestinian people remain displaced.[1] Throughout the history of the conflict, the Zionist movement and the state of Israel, according to Nur Masalha, pushed strongly in three directions: trying to wipe the refugee issue off the peace agenda, attempting to resettle the refugees away from Palestine, and uprooting the Palestinians who had not yet become refugees (Masalha 2003).[2] This relentless effort at dispossession has failed to undermine Palestinian emotional feeling on this issue. Even for the younger generation of Palestinians who never experienced life in refugee camps, the "right of return" remains a vital national and moral demand which Palestinian political leaders cannot ignore (Masalha 2001).

This chapter explores and analyzes the controversial central issues related to the refugee problem and addresses several questions. How and why does the Palestinian narrative conflict and contrast sharply with the Israeli narrative on the refugee question? What is the pervasive influence of "mythology" on finding an acceptable solution for the refugees' predicament? What lessons may we learn from the 1948 episode? Is the Palestinian refugee problem soluble? Does international law provide a practical framework for resolving the refugee problem?

Background

The majority of Palestinian refugees were displaced during the armed conflict of the 1948 Israeli–Arab war. According to Palestinian sources as well as others, between 750,000 and 900,000 Palestinians were displaced or expelled between late 1947 and the first half of 1949 (Sayigh 1952; Schechtman 1952). Israel has officially maintained that the number of refugees in 1948 was 520,000, while UNRWA's lists registered 726,000 refugees (Ju'beh 2002).[3] Of the roughly 150,000 Palestinians who remained in the part of Palestine that became the state of Israel on May 15, 1948, approximately 32,000 were internally displaced (Nazzal 1978). Between 350,000 and 400,000 Palestinians were displaced during the 1967 Israeli–Arab war (Dodd and Barakat 1969). Approximately 95,000 of the 1948 refugees became refugees for a second time as a result of the later war.[4]

UN General Assembly Resolution 194 (III), passed on December 11, 1948, reaffirms the right of Palestinian refugees to housing and property restitution. The resolution specifically gave the refugees the option of returning to their homes, or of resettlement elsewhere and compensation for loss of or damage to movable and immovable property. Persons choosing to return and those choosing to resettle elsewhere are both entitled to compensation. A broader set of claims under the resolution may include compensation for human capital losses and psychological suffering. International proposals for the solutions to the refugee problem include return for some, repatriation, host-country integration and third-country resettlement. Palestinian rights are affirmed in international law. UN Security Council Resolution 237 reaffirmed these rights (United Nations 1978; Buehrig 1971). A statistical report shows that more than 80 percent of the Palestinian people who are still living at a distance of 100 kilometers from their original birth place, "Palestine," inside the so-called "Green Line" that was created in 1948, are refugees.[5]

On March 14, 1950, Israel passed the Absentee Property Law, which considered the custodian as the "owner" until an "absentee" could prove that he was not absent or not considered legally absent. This law also prevented the custodian from transferring ownership to any party other than the "development authority." An Israeli government decision issued on September 29, 1953 made the custodian transfer land under his control to the "development authority," which in turn handed over large tracts of land to the Israeli Land Administration (ILA; Wakim 2002). Under this law, Israel offered financial compensation to the "absentees" whose property was transferred to the custodian but only a very small percentage of Palestinian landowners accepted the compensation, with the others insisting on their right to return to their lands and refusing to recognize any of these laws (Wakim 2002).

Constructing perceptions

In his classic study of Western perceptions of the Orient, *Orientalism* (1978), the Palestinian-American intellectual Edward Said describes the life cycle of a mindset in a graphic way. He observes that fictions have their own logic and their own "dialectic of growth and decline" (Said 1978: 62). Learned texts, media representations, and any supposedly authoritative body of knowledge have a reinforcing tendency. Having gained a certain perspective from something they have heard or read, Said maintains, audiences come to have particular expectations that in turn influence what is said or written henceforth.

In *Palestinian Refugees: Mythology, Identity, and the Search for Peace* (2003), Australian diplomat Robert Bowker emphasizes the pervasive influence of "mythology" and collective memory on the identity and consciousness of Palestinian refugees. Mythologies ought not to be dismissed as fictitious, folkloric tales, since they shape collective consciousness and national-cultural identity, which in the process "anchor the present in the past." Israeli commentator Meron Benvenisti, in *Intimate Enemies: Jews and Arabs in a Shared Land* (1995: 200), notes that national myths, made up of a mixture of real and legendary events, are "the building-blocks from which a society constructs its collective self-image" and, once absorbed, "become truer than reality itself."

Similarly, Malcolm Kerr (1980: 8–9), the late scholar of the modern Arab world, identifies "two elements as constituting the conventional wisdom relating to the Palestinian–Israeli conflict": the notion that Palestinian national claims are "artificially and mischievously inspired" and thus may be ignored; and the notion that the only real issue in the Arab–Israeli conflict is an unreasonable Arab refusal to accept Israel's existence – not, as Arabs contend, a real grievance against Israel arising from the Palestinians' displacement.

This perception that the Palestinians have no rational basis for their hostility to Israel and no legitimate national claim to the land of Palestine is fundamental to the misconceptions surrounding this conflict. The Palestinians have consistently contested the Jews' inherent right to exist in Palestine and maintain that they, as a native population with centuries of residence and title deeds to the land, have their own claim to patrimony in Palestine.

The assumption that the Palestinian position was "mischievously inspired" has constituted the frame of reference within which the conflict has been contained. This frame of reference defines and sets boundaries around thinking on Palestinian–Israeli issues. It is Israel-centered, approaching the conflict generally from an Israeli perspective and seldom recognizing the existence or legitimacy of a Palestinian perspective. As Edward Said (quoted in Lesch 1988: 214–216) wrote, "Palestinians long ago lost to Zionism the right even to have a history and a political identity," so the dispossession and dispersal of the Palestinians in 1948 remains to a great extent "an unrecognizable episode," particularly among the most informed Western scholars – "unrecognizable" not only in the sense that the dispossession has been forgotten but because it is seldom recognized to be the ultimate cause of the conflict.

Furthermore, terminology played a major role in shaping perceptions of the 1948 events. It has become basic for constructing the framework through which we view any situation, shaping our cognition and patterns of thinking. For instance, even the term "Palestine" is in dispute. Palestinians, among them historian Aref al-Aref, call the 1948 dispossession *al-nakba, al-karithah* – the calamity, the catastrophe, the disaster – in recognition of the national tragedy caused by their expulsion and flight from their homeland. On the other hand, the Israelis, and even third-party scholars such as Bernard Reich (1996), call the 1948 conflict the "War of Independence."

The well-known Israeli historian Avi Shlaim (1988) remarks that history is in a real sense "the propaganda of the victors," and because Israel won the contest for

Palestine, its version of that contest, of the rights and claims that underlay it, and of the justice of the outcome, has prevailed in most international discourse. For most Israelis, the Palestinians have never had a history, they have never had a just cause and they were responsible for all the tragedy they have suffered. Their conventional wisdom holds that the conflict originated in 1948, not because Palestinians lost land, homes and national identity, but because they hate Jews and do not want to coexist with them. Others, particularly the Arab states, were blamed for the fact that over 700,000 people were displaced from their homes and native land.

In his acclaimed work *One Palestine, Complete: Jews and Arabs under the British Mandate* (2000), Tom Segev asserts that Britain's promise to both Jews and Arabs that they would inherit Palestine set in motion the conflict that haunts the region to this day. No doubt, the horrors and ravages of conflict and the war psychology of fear are the principal causes of the Palestinian civilian population's search for safe haven in neighboring Arab countries. Palestinian political scientist Ibrahim Abu-Lughod states:

> In the case of Palestine, had the world not been confronted with a familiar yet bizarre interpretation – that which attempts to demonstrate the culpability of Arab leadership in the removal of the Palestinians . . . as well as the individual responsibility of the Palestinians for being refugees . . . it would be sufficient to call the attention . . . to the fact that a bicommunal war occurred and that, as in all such wars, some people were dislocated as a result.[6]

Two questions arise. Might an authoritative interpretation of the 1948 events emerge that would be acceptable to both Israelis and Palestinians? And why did Israel's "new historians" try to bridge the narrative? Ilan Pappe hopes that the "new history" can aid ordinary Israelis in "coming to terms" with the "original sin" of Israel's expulsion of the Palestinians in 1948 (Karmi and Cotran 1999: 54). Simha Flapan, in the introduction to *The Birth of Israel: Myths and Realities* (1987), indicates that his principal purpose is to "debunk a number of Israeli myths, not as an academic exercise but as a contribution to a better understanding of the Palestinian problem." He adds:

> I am restricting myself to an analysis of Israeli policies and propaganda structures. I choose to do it this way not because I attribute to Israel sole responsibility for the failure to find a solution . . . the Palestinians, too, were active players in the drama that brought upon them the calamity of defeat and the loss of their homeland. But review of the contributing Arab myths, conceptions . . . must be done by an Arab . . . Certainly the ideal way to fulfill this undertaking would have been a joint project by an Israeli–Palestinian Historical Society. I hope this is not wishful thinking, and that someday such a common effort will produce a study free of the deficiencies and limitations of this one.

However, as Abu-Lughod maintains, even with the best of intentions, control of the data, and skilled analysis, it is doubtful that Palestinian and Israeli scholars – as well as third-party scholars – will arrive at a consensus either on the facts or on their interpretation (Isacoff 2006).[7] The difficulties are not only those of national identity and perspective; nor are they of language and skills, or access. They are much more complex and relate simultaneously to values, beliefs, attitudes, and the national and historical experiences of both peoples.

The causes: Arab and Jewish narratives

Despite the fact that the Israeli new historians' narrative came somewhat closer to the Palestinian one, the Palestinian narrative of the Arab–Israeli conflict still contrasts very sharply with the Israeli classic narrative. Each holds the other responsible for launching the hostilities that evolved into the 1948 war, guilty of starting that war, and thus ultimately responsible for creating the refugee problem. The two narratives also diverge sharply on the original number of Palestinian refugees.[8] These two traditions therefore have very little in common and each reflects a passionately partisan perspective that it makes no effort to hide. Neither admits to a share of the guilt for the violent conflict in 1948. The most serious dispute relates to the establishment of Israel in 1948, the simultaneous uprooting and expulsion of the Palestinians, and the thwarting of their right to self-determination. While the birth of Israel, widely viewed in the West as a liberation struggle against British occupation, has been recognized and acknowledged by most nations, the destruction of Palestine and the creation of the Palestinian refugee problem that this birth required remain hotly contested, controversial issues.

From the start, Palestinian scholars, as well as others who are sympathetic to their perspective, have challenged the Israel/Zionist interpretation of what happened in 1948 and how the Palestinian refugee problem was created. The Zionist and Israeli scholars "subscribed to the notion that the Palestinian exodus in 1948 was either voluntary or largely instigated by the leaders of the neighboring Arab countries" (Zureik 1994: 19). Palestinians maintained that "the expulsion of the Palestinians was a clear goal pursued by the founders of the Jewish state" and that the Zionist goal was "to incorporate as much of Palestine as possible with as few Palestinians as possible" (PASSIA 2004: 1). Their efforts were rewarded in the revisionist history of 1948 published from the mid-1980s by such Israeli historians as Benny Morris (1987), Tom Segev (1986), Simha Flapan (1987), and Ilan Pappe (1994).

The 1948 Palestinian refugee exodus

The 1948 Palestinian exodus was used by Israel to demonstrate that the Palestinians' attachment to their land and homes was weak; that by clearing the way for Arab military forces to "drive the Jews into the sea," the Palestinians showed that they were bent on Israel's destruction; and that in the end Israel bore no responsibility for the Palestinians' displacement and homelessness. This raises the question: why did the Palestinians leave?

One major example of fiction becoming history through constant repetition is the widely believed (but contested) story that Palestinian civilians left their homes in 1948 because Arab governments and the Palestinian leadership broadcast instructions over the radio requesting them to do so in order that the Arab military forces might have a clear field to drive the Jews out of Palestine. In fact, there is no evidence that any orders were ever broadcast to the Palestinians to leave their homes.

The first major challenge to the conventional wisdom about Israel's birth and Palestine's destruction came from the Irish journalist Erskine Childers, in a classic article that appeared in the *Spectator* on May 12, 1961, which refuted the broadcasts myth. Childers asserts that he found no evidence of any broadcasts or blanket orders from Arab governments or of Palestinian leaders calling on Palestinians to leave their homes. Dan Kurzman, in *Genesis 1948: The First Arab–Israeli War* (1970), recounts the events of 1948 as seen by both Arabs and Israelis. He searched Israeli military archives and the British Broadcasting Corporation's radio monitoring files and found no record of either Arab military communications ordering a civilian evacuation or any broadcast radio instructions. Over a decade later, Walid Khalidi made a thorough investigation into the issue and similarly found no evidence of broadcasts.

Among the Palestinian scholars, Nafez Nazzal (1978) relates the expulsion narrative from the Palestinian perspective, asserting that, rather than leaving voluntarily, the Palestinians were expelled from their homes. Confirming this, Elias Sanbar (1984) views the eviction of the Palestinians as a logical consequence of the triumph of Zionism in Palestine. He asserts that, for Zionism to achieve its goal, it had to take Palestinian land without the Palestinian people and thus fulfill Israel Zangwill's premise of "a land without a people for a people without a land."

However, it was in 1987 that three detailed accounts appeared that truly challenged cherished myths of the 1948 events. One was by the American scholar Michael Palumbo, who demonstrates in *The Palestinian Catastrophe: The 1948 Expulsion of a People from Their Homeland* the absurdity of the myth. Palumbo tells the story of how the Zionist conquest of Palestine involved not only the occupation of the territory and the displacement of its people, but the widespread plunder and looting of Palestinian Arab land, shops, homes, and possessions. In the same year, Zionist sociologist Simha Flapan, in *The Birth of Israel: Myths and Realities*, concluded that Israel's assertion that Arabs and Palestinians were responsible for the refugee problem was false. Finally, in *The Birth of the Palestinian Refugee Problem, 1947–1949*, Israeli historian Benny Morris concludes that no Arab authority issued "blanket instructions, by radio or otherwise, to Palestine's Arabs to flee," that the Palestinian flight was induced to a great extent by a "general sense of collapse" that permeated the territory, and that a "small but significant proportion" of that flight resulted from explicit expulsion orders issued by Jewish forces. Using declassified Israeli archival material, Morris discusses Operation Dani, to take over Ramle and Lydda. He notes that when Allon asked: "What shall we do with the Arabs?" Ben Gurion made a dismissive, energetic gesture with his hand and said: "Expel them [*garish otam*]" (Morris 1987).

Palestinian scholars tend to focus on the brutal massacre of 240 civilians at the village of Deir Yassin when explaining the reasons for the Palestinian exodus

(McGowan and Ellis 1998). Some also give weight to the devastating impact of the death of Palestinian leader Abdel Qader Al-Husayni. (Here the two narratives collide: Palestinian historians maintain that Husayni died as he led a successful counterattack at Castel, while Israeli historians maintain that he was shot by a Jewish sentry as he approached Castel, which he apparently believed was already in Arab hands.)

The Arab invading armies

Palestinian scholar Walid Khalidi maintains that the Arab capitals did not have the will, or the intention, or the force to destroy the newly born Jewish state (Khalidi 1987). The long-awaited Arab states' "invasion" of Palestine began on May 15, but it backfired and resulted in further disastrous territorial losses. Among the invading armies, Transjordan had the largest, best-trained, and most strategically placed force, numbering about 4,800 men. In addition, there were roughly 4,000 Iraqis, 3,000 Egyptians, 2,000 Syrians, and 1,000 Lebanese. These forces had no unified command and they faced more than 50,000 troops of the Haganah. Consequently, attacking the Jewish state was inconceivable, so they concentrated on defending the territory allocated to the Arabs. But they proved inadequate even for this task, and a good part of the territory designated by UN Partition Resolution 181 for the Arab Palestinian state was wrested from the Jordanian Arab Legion and the Egyptian and Syrian armies.[9]

Moreover, the Arab armies at times undermined the Palestinian guerrillas. Avi Shlaim, in *Collusion across the Jordan: King Abdullah, the Zionist Movement, and the Partition of Palestine* (1988), maintains that a senior intelligence officer in the Haganah gained a tacit agreement from Fawzi al-Qawukji, commander of the Arab Liberation Army, not to intervene in Haganah attacks on rival Palestinian guerrilla forces. That agreement facilitated the Haganah offensives against Jaffa and the Jerusalem corridor in April 1948.

The refugee problem in international context

No doubt, a long-term solution for the Palestinian refugees should be consistent with international law and relevant UN resolutions. Most peace agreements that prescribe permanent solutions for refugees and displaced persons recognize their right to return and repossess their properties. Nevertheless, each refugee case is unique and so are the mechanisms set up to facilitate permanent solutions for refugees. But in most cases, the rights of refugees and displaced persons to return in safety and dignity to their homes, repossess their property, and choose their place of residence within the country of origin free from arbitrary interference are seen as important elements in finding durable solutions. Such agreements were reached, for example, in Macedonia, Kosovo, Croatia, Bosnia-Herzegovina, Tajikistan, Georgia, Burundi, Rwanda, Liberia, Sierra Leone, Mozambique, Cambodia, and Guatemala. In Guatemala, the government undertook to "ensure that conditions exist which permit and guarantee the voluntary return of uprooted persons to their places of origin or to the place of their choice" (in accordance with the Agreement on Resettlement of the Population Groups Uprooted by the Armed Conflict of June 1994). Under the 1994 Quadripartite Agreement in Georgia, "displaced persons/refugees shall have the right to return peacefully without risk of arrest, detention, imprisonment or legal criminal proceedings." The 1995 Dayton Agreement (Bosnia-Herzogovina) explicitly states: "Choice of destination shall be up to the individual or family. The Parties shall not interfere with the returnees' choice of destination, nor shall they compel them to remain in or move to situations of serious danger or insecurity, or to areas lacking in the basic infrastructure necessary to resume a normal life." Moreover, all parties are required to ensure "that refugees and displaced persons are permitted to return in safety, without risk of harassment, intimidation, persecution, or discrimination, particularly on account of their ethnic origin, religious belief, or political opinion." The 1995 Erdut Agreement on Croatia states: "The right to recover property, to receive compensation for property that cannot be returned, and to receive assistance in reconstruction of damaged property shall be equally available to all persons without regard to ethnicity." Under the 1999 Interim Agreement on Kosovo, the parties "recognize that all persons have the right to return to their homes," while "all persons shall have the right to reoccupy their real property, assert their occupancy rights in state-owned property, and recover their other property and personal possessions." The 2000 Arusha Peace and Reconciliation Agreement in Burundi states that return "must take place in dignity with guaranteed security, and taking into account the particular vulnerability of women and children."

Refugees' "right of return" (*haqq al-awda*)

More than five decades after their initial expulsion from their homeland, Palestinian refugees remain in forced exile. The Palestinians affirm that all refugees have the right to return to their homes and repossess their properties (Abu Sitta 1999; Aruri 2001). The Islamic movement Hamas defines the refugees' "right of return" to what is now Israel as "an inalienable right about which no political concessions should be made" (Regular 2006). Israel rejects the right of return of the Palestinian refugees in order to maintain the Jewish purity of the state of Israel and because it considers such a right to be a major demographic and security risk.

The right of return of the Palestinian refugees has been absent from Palestinian–Israeli agreements, such as the Oslo Israeli–Palestinian Declaration of Principles of 1993. The Interim Agreement of 1995 states that the issue of refugees displaced in 1948 will be covered at a later stage in the context of final peace negotiations, during permanent status negotiations. Solutions for Palestinians displaced from the West Bank and Gaza in the 1967 war were to be dealt with as a first step in the interim period. For this purpose, the Declaration of Principles establishes a quadripartite continuing committee to decide on "the modalities of admission of persons displaced from the West Bank and Gaza Strip in 1967." Similar provisions for Palestinians who became refugees or displaced persons as a result of the 1967 occupation by Israel of the West Bank and Gaza are found in the 1994 Gaza–Jericho Agreement and the 1995 Interim Agreement. During the Camp David summit of July 2000, Israel accepted a one-time family reunification of some 100,000 Palestinian refugees and the establishment of an international body to deal with compensation and resettlement issues.

Unofficial Israeli–Palestinian peace initiatives, such as the Nusseibeh–Ayalon, launched in September 2002, conceded that "Palestinian refugees will return only to the state of Palestine." The Geneva Accord, launched in December 2003, omits explicit reference to the right of refugees and displaced persons to return to their homes and repossess their properties. Instead, it presents the following five options to refugees: return to the Palestinian state; return to land included in the land swap with Israel; integration into present host countries; admission into a third country; or return to Israel.

Settling the Palestinian refugee problem

There is a wide spectrum of views on the refugee problem, with two traditionally conflicting positions at each end: the hard-core Arabist position that all refugees should be able to return precisely to their point of origin, under whatever circumstances; and the Israeli position that no Palestinians will be allowed to return to pre-1967 Israel but may return to the Gaza Strip and the West Bank. Whatever the moral merit of the first position, Israelis have argued that it is totally unrealistic and a dead end for any comprehensive peace negotiations. Consequently, many third-option initiatives have been proposed.

Although the Clinton Parameters (2000) made no specific mention of the right of return to Israel, they proposed five possible homes for refugees: the future state of Palestine; areas in Israel being transferred to Palestine in the land swap; rehabilitation in a host country; resettlement in a third country; admission to Israel. Return to the West Bank, Gaza Strip, and areas acquired in the land swap would be the right of all Palestinian refugees, while rehabilitation in host countries, resettlement in third countries and absorption into Israel will depend on the policies of those countries.

The Nusseibeh–Ayalon Statement of Principles (2002) proposes that Palestinian refugees will return only to the state of Palestine, while Jews will return only to the state of Israel. It states: "Recognizing the suffering and the plight of the Palestinian refugees, the international community, Israel, and the Palestinian state will initiate and contribute to an international fund to compensate them."

The Geneva Accord's Article 7 calls for an agreed resolution to the refugee problem for achieving a just, comprehensive, and lasting peace. It recognizes UNGAR 194, UNSC Resolution 242, and the Arab Peace Initiative (Article 2.ii.) concerning the rights of the Palestinian refugees to represent the basis for resolving the refugee issue. It states that refugees shall be entitled to compensation for their refugeehood and for loss of property. This shall not prejudice or be prejudiced by the refugee's permanent place of residence.

The Arab Peace Initiative, launched by the Arab Summit Conference held in Beirut on March 28, 2002, called for a comprehensive peace with Israel, recognition of Israel, and normal relations with all twenty-two Arab countries, in return for Israeli withdrawal from Arab territories occupied since June 1967. Beginning in 2006, the initiative assumed new importance, as Arab states tried to revive their endeavor. It was endorsed by the Arab League summit that took place in Riyadh in March 2007:

> The summit reiterated the adherence of all Arab countries to the Arab peace initiative as it was approved by Beirut summit 2002 with all its components based on the international legitimacy resolutions and its principles to end the Arab Israeli conflict and bring about fair and comprehensive peace that achieve security for all countries of the region and enable the Palestinian people to set up their independent state with eastern al-Quds as capital.
>
> (Dajani Daoudi 2009: n.p.)

Furthermore, it was endorsed by the fifty-seven member states of the Organization of the Islamic Conference.

Regarding the refugee issue, the Arab Peace Initiative states: "Achievement of a just solution to the Palestinian refugee problem to be agreed upon in accordance with UN General Assembly Resolution 194," departing from the text of previous communiqués, which insisted on demanding the return of all refugees to their homeland. Moreover, Israel had been blamed for the creation of the refugee problem and thus bore full responsibility for resolving it. It was left to future negotiations to determine how many refugees were to "return" to Israel and how many were to return to the future Palestinian state. The difference is that much less emphasis was placed on the right of return . A similar plan was offered by Arab states at the armistice negotiations in 1949. The number of refugees to be returned was not specified. One section "Assures the rejection of all forms of Palestinian repatriation which conflict with the special circumstances of the Arab host countries." This clause indicates that full return of the refugees and the literal implementation of return were not contemplated. UN Resolution 194 asserts the right of Palestinian refugees who are willing to live in peace with their neighbors to return to Israel. UN Security Council Resolution 242, passed in 1967, calls for Israeli withdrawal from territories occupied in the war of June 1967, but does not specify "all territories."

A series of studies have been conducted to identify possible ways of settling the Palestinian refugee problem (Thicknesse 1949; Cattan 1982; Tamari 1996a, 1996b; Rabah 1996). Some have looked at the possibility of evacuating Jewish settlements, the use of land transferred to Palestine in territorial exchanges, and the Palestinian urban structure. Others have studied the urban rehabilitation of existing refugee camps in the Palestinian territories, upgrading them and integrating them in the local urban and village structures of the West Bank and Gaza.

In *Palestinian Refugees: Mythology, Identity, and the Search for Peace* (2003: 233), Robert Bowker proposes concrete programs of "economic empowerment" to improve the well-being of refugees through job creation, immigration to third countries, acceptance by Israel of a "guest worker" program that would allow qualified refugees to return and work in Israel, and beefing up the family unification scheme by persuading Israel to allow older refugees to return.

Rashid Khalidi advances a controversial proposal for the resolution of the Palestinian refugee problem based on abandoning notions of "absolute justice" in favor of working toward a solution founded on principles of what he calls "attainable justice" (Khalidi and Cotran 1999: 238–239).

According to data presented by the FAFO Institute, a Norwegian research center that tracks the condition of Palestinian refugees, the absorption of 710,000 refugees into Palestine will enable the eradication of the refugee camps in Lebanon and Syria without a single refugee needing to fulfill their right of return inside Israel.

The Palestinian Authority conducted an in-depth analysis of conditions in the existing camps, classifying them according to the type of land, quality of construction, variety of social and economic levels and so on. A plan prepared by the Palestinian Ministry of Planning and International Cooperation (MOPIC) in 2003 points to a readiness to separate the rhetoric about the right of return from the reality on the ground. For planning purposes, the MOPIC plan assumed that some 450,000 refugees could be settled in the West Bank and 260,000 in Gaza by 2010. The ministry studied the impact these potential immigrants would have on the physical, social, and economic development of the new state of Palestine and concluded that national strategies and plans had to be developed to make the absorption process as smooth as possible.

Conclusion

It is worthwhile to look back on the traumatic events of 1948 from the standpoints of the victors – the Israelis – and the vanquished – the Palestinians. Otherwise, all potential solutions to the refugee problem will remain doomed to failure. The lessons we may learn from 1948 are that the tactical and strategic inflexibility of the Palestinians led to the catastrophic confrontation with Israel; and the tactical and strategic inflexibility of the Israelis destroyed any chance of peace with the Arabs.

The refugee issue revolves around two problems: Israel first has to accept the principle of right of return; and then agreement has to be reached on the geographic destination to which the Palestinian refugees should return. On the ground, there is a large gap between the insistence on the right of return to the old Palestine, meaning Israel, and a readiness to fulfill the right in the new Palestine, meaning the West Bank, the Gaza Strip, and any other territory that Israel concedes to the Palestinians in a land swap. It may be preferable for returning refugees to be part of the Muslim majority in the Palestinian state rather than part of the Muslim minority in Israel. For Palestinians currently living in Arab countries, granting them compensation and citizenship in their host countries may constitute a realistic solution to their dilemma. Others might be willing to return to the state of Palestine or to emigrate to other countries. International law provides a practical framework for resolving the refugee problem and should not be ignored or underestimated in any future settlement.

Notes

1 According to the UN, approximately 3.6 million of the 8 million Palestinians in the world – less than 50 percent – are registered refugees. In addition, there are non-UN-registered persons who are descended from the 1948 exodus.
2 While Nur Masalha and Norman Finkelstein argue that there was a transfer policy, Benny Morris (1987) states that there was no such policy. See Finkelstein (1991), Masalha (1991), and Morris (1991).
3 The disparity between the totals quoted by the Palestinians and UNRWA stems from the fact that not every refugee family was registered on lists used by UNRWA. Also, professional Palestinian refugees integrated in neighboring Arab societies were not listed by UNRWA.
4 The majority of Palestinian refugees are from villages, towns, and cities inside 1948 Palestine/Israel. They were denationalized under Israel's 1952 Nationality Law and prevented from returning to their homes of origin. The government of Israel expropriated land and properties belonging to these refugees.
5 Palestinian refugees from West Jerusalem, such as my family, lived a few steps away from the homes and lands from which they were uprooted in 1948.
6 This and the subsequent quote from Flapan (1987) are taken from Abu-Lughod's review article (Abu-Lughod 1989).
7 While such consensus may be unlikely, it is hardly impossible, as argued by some scholars, including Isacoff (2006), who wonders: "How do we know that one story is not just as good as the next?" He maintains that every historical school of thought purports to provide a "true" account of its subject matter, though contradictory schools of thought cannot all be given equal weight. What can be done to resolve the practical problem encountered by researchers faced with multiple narratives and historical bias? Isacoff develops a pragmatic method, which aims to evaluate historical narratives according to their utility in solving analytical and political problems. He illustrates the approach through the case of the Arab–Israeli conflict, where multiple, conflicting accounts of the "story" are vivid and copious. He concludes that while historical objectivity is elusive, some narratives are better than others at adjudicating both political science debates and "real-world" political problems.
8 Estimates vary from about 520,000 (Israeli sources) to 726,000 (UN sources) to over 800,000 (Arab sources) refugees. In June 1995, UNRWA estimated the total refugee population at 3.173 million, of which camp dwellers made up 1.044 million. However, both figures were strongly challenged by researchers from both sides.
9 Figures related to the conflict are difficult to confirm, though they may be checked and cross-referenced from numerous sources. For instance, the figures presented here for the relative strengths of the two sides are highly contested by Israeli authors: Nadav Safran (1969) maintains that the number of Arab troops was "about equal" to the well-trained Haganah and Jewish militias, and claims that it peaked at about 96,000 during late 1948/early 1949.

Borders, territory, and settlements

3

FROM BILATERALISM TO UNILATERALISM

The changing territorial discourses of Israel–Palestine conflict resolution

David Newman

Introduction

The purpose of this chapter is to trace and analyse the interplay of the tangible and symbolic dimensions of territory in the Israel–Palestine conflict. While the number of active territorial conflicts has decreased significantly during the past three decades, territory remains a major component in the political organization and ordering of society (Goertz and Diehl, 1992; Coakley, 1993; Lustick, 1993; Diehl, 1999; Kahler and Walter, 2006). The territorial configuration of the state remains an important component in the inter-state system of ordering, with the physical borders of the country continuing to determine the area within which the state exercises, or attempts to exercise, its control practices.

Territorial conflicts are not concerned only with the tangible dimensions of hard-core security issues traditionally understood as defensive, strategic and military postures. They are equally concerned with the symbolic dimensions of national identity and belonging, a sense of attachment to the "homeland" which, by its very definition, is exclusive to the "self" group (Sack, 1986; Paasi, 1996, 2002; Newman, 1999b). Other groups residing in the "self" territory are often perceived as being no more than alien residents, constituting a minority – in both the demographic and political senses. Territory provides the compartment within which much ethnic conflict occurs, often spilling over the border into neighbouring territories and spaces as ethnic and national groups attempt to change the existing territorial–demographic ratios in their own favour. During the past decade alone, we have witnessed the impact of ethno-territorial conflicts throughout the Balkans, in many parts of Africa, in Sri Lanka and, as almost a constant on the face of the world political map, in Israel–Palestine. In some cases, it has been the superficially imposed territorial configuration of past colonial periods which has been responsible for the conflict, given the mismatch between border location and ethnic/national dispersion; while in other cases territory has become the means through which the resolution of existing ethno-national conflicts is attempted. At the tangible level, territorial configurations can be moulded by conflict participants as a means of conflict management. Pieces of territory can be bartered and exchanged as a means of achieving conflict resolution. At the symbolic level, territory is so imbued with notions of attachment, affiliation and identity that it is seen as constituting an intangible good which can never be reshaped or divided.

Studies in conflict resolution have shown that the intangible and symbolic factors are the most difficult to resolve between belligerents. This is as true of territorial factors as it is of other political conflict characteristics. When territory is presented as a discourse about tangible goods, it can be resolved through a process of quantification, bartering and exchange, resulting in the contraction or expansion of state territory. Settlements can be dismantled, compensation can be offered to refugees, borders can be relocated, and territorial parcels can be offered in exchange for territory annexed by the other side. But it is much more difficult, in some cases impossible, to resolve conflicts around the symbolic dimensions of territory. Historical and homeland spaces are so tied up with the formation of national identities that the symbolic components of territorial conflict remain indivisible.

Territorial discourses in Israel–Palestine

Territorial discourses in Israel–Palestine have always been interlinked with two other political discourses – the security and the demographic. The former deals with the use of space as a means of defending the country, focusing on notions of defensible borders, buffer zones, topography and access routes (Horowitz, 1975; Allon, 1976; Newman, 1999a; Kam, 2003). The latter focuses on the relative demographic ratios between Jews and Arabs which enable each to retain a majority within a given territorial area, thus ensuring that the state is defined in terms of a single dominant national group. These two alternative discourses are concerned with the tangible dimensions of territory – border demarcation, size and shape of territory, and so on. Territory is no more than a means through which either security or demographic superiority is achieved. But territory also has its own internalized discourse, separate from a dependence on the other political discourses. Territory is not simply an output of the political, security and demographic situations, but constitutes an input in its own right. At its symbolic, non-tangible level, territory constitutes a special space, a homeland, determining the national identities and affiliations of the two peoples. While the conflict participants may be prepared to undertake territorial compromise in their attempt to achieve security or demographic compromise, they may not be prepared to make similar territorial compromise if it entails withdrawing from parts of the "historic homeland". Here I shall trace the interplay of these two factors through four alternative territorial discourses which have accompanied the Arab–Israel conflict throughout the past seventy years.

TABLE 3.1 Territorial dimensions of the political discourses in Israel–Palestine

	Partition	Homeland	Securitization	Binational/Demographic
Tangible/ Intangible (Symbolic)	*Tangible* Maximal territorial and demographic separation	*Intangible* Greater land of Israel requires exclusive national control of entire territory	*Tangible* Defensible borders (Jordan valley), buffer zones (Sinai peninsula, Jordan), strategic sites (Golan Heights, West Bank hills)	*Tangible/Intangible* Single territorial configuration of outer borders (Jordan valley and Mediterranean Sea) *Intangible* Each side has free access to historical, religious and mythical sites
Borders	Peel Commission, UN Partition Resolution, War of Independence – Green Line, Separation Barrier	Undefined, elastic borders within the framework of Greater Israel	Defensible borders in the east and on the Golan Heights	

The participation discourse

The partition discourse has been the tangible territorial discourse which has accompanied the Israel–Palestine conflict ever since the first ideas of partitioning Palestine between Jews and Arabs in the 1930s. Partition has been implemented once, following the establishment of the state of Israel in 1948 and the subsequent War of Independence.[1] The territorial configuration of partition was based on the armistice lines of that period and did not follow any of the previous partition proposals, not even that of the United Nations Special Committee (UNSCOP) which had been approved by the General Assembly in November 1947 (Klieman, 1980; Waterman, 1987; Galnoor, 1991). In effect, all attempts at conflict resolution during the past decade based on an eventual two-state solution have focused on the nature of territorial partition between separate Israeli and Palestinian states. While the outer territorial configuration of partition has remained the same throughout the seventy-year period (Mediterranean Sea to the Jordan River), the internal power, settlement and demographic relations have changed in such a way that it has become increasingly difficult to demarcate an internal boundary (Newman and Falah, 1995). As such, the default boundary for territorial configuration has been the Green Line boundary, not because it was an ideal functional line of separation (it was far from that), but because it has remained the single administrative boundary on the ground through which the territorial entity known as the West Bank is configured. Nevertheless, the tangible dimensions of the partition discourse are such that the boundary can be reconfigured, with small territories and land parcels being exchanged in an effort to meet, as far as possible, the changing demographic and settlement realities.

The homeland discourse

If the partition discourse reflects the tangible dimension of territorial management, the homeland discourse constitutes the symbolic, or intangible, equivalent. In this context, territory constitutes the historical and mythical *raison d'être* for the existence of the state on a specific site (Newman, 1998a; Yiftachel, 2000; Goemans, 2006). Contextually, the very notion of Zionism as the name of the national movement reflects an abstract attachment to space. Although the national territory was located in a specific region, its broader contours and configurations were vague, with undefined borders and attributes. Attachment to the homeland territory is an exclusive one – it has room for one group only. The social construction of knowledge, through disciplines such as geography, archaeology and history, is used in an attempt to prove the respective duration and/or priority rights of the contesting groups to the territory (Burghardt, 1973; Murphy, 1990, 2002; Castellino and Allen, 2003). The homeland is intangible since it lies at the heart of the respective Israeli or Palestinian identity and, as such, cannot be divided or bartered. As part of the state formation process, homeland landscapes are renamed in line with the exclusive historical experiences of the people laying claim to the territory. During the past century, the Israel/Palestine landscape has gradually been "Hebraized" as towns have been named and maps have been drawn (Cohen and Kliot, 1981, 1992; Falah, 1996; Benvenisti, 2000). When, as in the case of some irredentist claims, religion – a divine right to land – is thrown into the equation (such as in the case of the Jewish settlers' claims to the West Bank – Judaea/Samaria), the symbolic dimension is such that negotiations over territory cannot even take place. The homeland is indivisible.

The securitization discourse

Like the partition discourse, the securitization discourse is tangible. In this case, territory constitutes a strategic resource. As part of the process of territorial management certain areas must remain under Israeli control because they are perceived as providing safety and security to the inhabitants (Kam, 2003). The discourse is a tangible one in the sense that the areas required for "security purposes," such as borders (the Jordan valley), sites of topographic superiority (the western uplands of the West Bank, the Golan Heights), buffer zones (the Sinai Peninsula, the state of Jordan), or access routes (the trans-West Bank routes) can be quantified but, for the purveyors of the securitization discourse (the army and the defence establishment), these land parcels are indivisible. Other areas, lacking these same security attributes, can be exchanged for these sites, but the resulting territorial configuration does not allow for compactness or contiguity and, as such, creates new problems of territorial management resulting in potential political instability (such as that which occurred following the implementation of the Oslo Accords). It has been argued that the specific territorial security requirements of Israel have changed in an era of ballistic missile warfare, that the threat emanates from Iraq (prior to the American invasion of the country) and Iran, rather than from the neighbouring countries (Syria, Jordan and Egypt) and consequently the traditional securitization discourse is no longer relevant and the territories previously considered as being of strategic importance (such as the Jordan valley) can now be ceded as part of a political resolution of the conflict (Newman, 1999a), but this has been only partially accepted by the defence establishment. "In the name of security" remains a central motif underlying claims to territory, with the most recent expression of this being the construction of the Separation Barrier (see below).

The binational discourse

The binational discourse is essentially a non-territorial one in the sense that territory, power and governance would be shared between the two groups within a single set of external boundaries (Jordan River to Mediterranean Sea). It is, at one and the same time, both tangible and intangible, in that each side retains its attachment to its respective homeland places and spaces while there is no need for internal lines of separation or borders. Alternative versions of power and territorial sharing have been proposed over time, ranging from federalism (Elazar, 1979), to ethnocracy (Yiftachel, 1997, 2001) or binationalism in a "state of all its citizens" (Newman, 2002a; Ram, 2004). But such forms of power sharing within a single territorial space are the least likely of any political scenario to be implemented; they will be rejected by the majority of both populations, each of whom desires its own exclusive national space. Each perceives the "other" as constituting a threat to its own existence within a single space, using its respective demographic majority as a means of exercising future power hegemony rather than power sharing. Ironically, it is the spectre of a single territorial space in which the struggle for hegemony becomes focused around demography, rather than territory, that has resulted in the increased support within Israel for a two-state solution and even unilateral disengagement from parts of the Occupied Territories (see below), even among those who were opposed to any form of territorial compromise in the past. For Israelis, at least, the notion of a single, non-national state goes against the very *raison d'être* of the establishment and continued existence of the state of Israel as an exclusively Jewish homeland.

Border discourses

Border discourses are themselves contingent upon the way in which territorial configurations are perceived by the conflict participants and the way in which these relate to alternative discourses of political, demographic and identity hegemonies.

Borders are contingent of two separate, but related, discourses within the Israeli–Palestinian context. The first of these concerns the territorial demarcation (for Israel) of a line which will be secure and defensible and (for the Palestinians) territorial integrity and compactness for their future state (Horowitz, 1975; Allon, 1976; Falah, 1997; Newman, 2002b). At this level, borders are tangible territorial features which can be negotiated and redrawn according to the changing settlement, demographic and political realities, with territorial parcels being exchanged between the two sides (Cohen, 1986; Alpher, 1994; Newman, 1998b).

The second border discourse concerns the nature of territorial identities and the symbolic attachment to historic landscapes, as well as the desire to retain maximal separation between two conflicting national entities. At this level it is far more difficult to arrive at territorial compromise owing to the exclusive claims to homeland territories and mythical spaces which constitute an integral part of the national identity and existential *raison d'être*. Each side aspires to a "purified" and homogeneous ethnic space (Newman and Falah, 1995). As noted above, for conflict resolution to be achieved, this symbolic discourse based on territorial exclusivity has to be translated into a tangible process of negotiations, bartering and territorial partition.

At the tangible level, the demarcation of borders figures prominently in the territorial management of the Israel–Palestine conflict. Only two of Israel's boundaries, those with Egypt and Jordan (excluding the section of the Jordan valley bordering the West Bank), have the status of internationally recognized boundaries, while the borders with Lebanon, Syria and a future Palestinian state are yet to be determined. The Green Line boundary between Israel and the West Bank was demarcated as an armistice line following the 1948 Israeli War of Independence (the Palestinian Naqba) (Brawer, 1990, 2002) and has remained the default line for territorial negotiations ever since the Israeli conquest of the West Bank and the Gaza Strip in 1967 (Newman, 1993, 1995). The fact that this line was an artificial superimposition on the landscape at the time, causing significant economic and spatial dislocation for the Arab-Palestinian communities on each side of it (some becoming part of sovereign Israel, some becoming part of a stateless West Bank administered by Jordan, and others being divided into two parts on either side), does not change the *de facto* reality of the Green Line as an effective boundary from that time on. Even since the Israeli occupation of the West Bank, the Green Line has retained its administrative and political significance, by virtue of Israeli non-annexation of the region, and it remains strongly imprinted on the spatial and cartographic imaginations of all conflict participants, as well as the international community. The very use of the terms "West Bank" and "Gaza Strip" as constituting territorial entities assumes their enclosure within the boundary thus demarcated. That does not mean to say that a future Israeli–Palestinian boundary cannot be redrawn, but it would require bilateral negotiations and agreement between the two sides. Changes in the course of the line which are unilaterally superimposed by one side (Israel) and will involve territorial annexation will not be accepted by the Palestinian side or by the international community.

Following the signing and partial implementation of the Oslo Accords (see below) in the 1990s, negotiations and discussions aimed at reaching a final political agreement between the two sides took place. These negotiations were accompanied by a number of attempts to redraw the boundary in line with the changing territorial reality, based on three key factors:

- the Israeli securitization discourse and a desire for what it continued to perceive as "defensible boundaries";
- the Palestinian demand for territorial integrity and compactness rather than the dissected map of Areas "A", "B" and "C" they had received after Oslo;
- the Israeli attempt to include as many West Bank settlements as possible within the Israeli sovereign territory.

It was recognized, in retrospect, that one of the major factors resulting in the post-Oslo instability and renewed outbreaks of violence was the territorial non-contiguity which had emerged out of the Oslo Accords. This, in turn, had been the outcome of Israel's desire to retain certain areas perceived as being of strategic importance, including some west–east transportation arteries dissecting the Palestinian autonomy areas, as well as Israel's refusal, or inability, to consider the evacuation of Israeli settlements even when they formed isolated points on the map. Since transfer of control over settlements could not be handed over to the Palestinians, the Oslo maps configured territorial outliers, exclaves and safe-passage routes which would leave the settlements entirely under Israeli control.

While changing securitization concepts in an era of modern warfare have, during the past decade, resulted in a partial retreat from the Israeli demand for defensible borders and control of hilltops, the settlement issue has become a major factor preventing the demarcation of a clear and acceptable boundary between the two sides. All (Israeli) attempts to reconfigure the territorial boundaries have tried to include as many settlements as possible within Israel in an attempt to avoid the forced evacuation of tens of thousands of residents who are likely to resist their removal physically (Newman, 1998b). The establishment of settlements, in both pre-state Palestine and the post-1967 Occupied Territories, has constituted an important means through which territorial control is facilitated and expanded, influencing the eventual demarcation of boundaries (Kimmerling, 1983; Kellerman, 1993; Newman, 1989). While under international law the establishment of the West Bank settlements is illegal and they should be evacuated *in toto*, this does not take into account that their existence has changed the geographic realities of the region in such a way that they have become a major negotiating issue. This problem was partially recognized in the far-reaching Beilin–Abu Maazen Agreement of the mid-1990s.[2] This accorded the first public recognition of the principle of territorial exchanges in such a way that Israel would be allowed to retain some settlements *in situ*, in return for which small parcels would be transferred from Israel to the Palestinian Authority. Following the coming to power of the right-wing Netanyahu administration in 1996, this plan – like so many others – gathered dust in filing cabinets.

The issues of borders and settlements were revisited in the policies of the Sharon administration (post-2001) – the construction of the Separation Barrier and the proposal for Israeli withdrawal from the Gaza Strip. However, unlike the discourse of the 1990s, when Israelis and Palestinians at least attempted to undertake bilateral negotiations, the more recent proposals were unilateral, superimposed solutions undertaken by the Israeli government. As unilateral plans imposed by the dominant power, these plans (especially the Separation Barrier) are less acceptable to the Palestinians, but they were still implemented on the ground as they did not require the acceptance or agreement of any other partner.

The Separation Barrier, also known as the Security Fence/Wall, is intended to enclose the entire West Bank. Construction of this barrier, most of which consists of barbed-wire fencing, short sections of concrete wall and patrol roads, commenced in 2003 (Makovsky, 2004; Michael and Ramon, 2004).[3] It was seen by Israelis as constituting a security response to the increase in suicide bombings which had taken place inside Israel. The erection of a physical barrier was intended to prevent Palestinians from crossing into Israel, thus reducing the potential for further acts of violence. Its construction was supported by the vast majority of Israeli society, cutting across political loyalties, and it was erected with great haste. Understanding the longer-term political significance of the physical establishment of a barrier (in reality, a border), the government attempted to include as many Jewish settlements on the Israeli side as possible, and, as a result, effectively annexed parts of the West Bank. This also resulted in the creation of "spatial hostages", Palestinian villages on the West Bank (to the east of the Green Line) which nevertheless found themselves on the Israeli side of the fence, creating problems of access to places of employment, education and commerce. Subsequent rulings by both the Israeli Supreme Court and the International Court of Justice determined that the unilateral construction of the barrier on Palestinian land was illegal.[4] While this forced the Israeli government partially to redraw the route of certain sections, it did not deter it from continuing the construction of the barrier, not least because of the perceived reduction in suicide bombings which, it was argued, had resulted directly from this action.

The construction of the barrier gave rise to a renewed discourse inside Israel concerning the territorial dimensions and characteristics of a two-state solution to the conflict, the fate of the settlements and the functions of a border. The fact that, unlike all the other proposals of the 1990s, this plan was implemented on the ground resulted in the creation of new geographical facts which cannot be ignored in the final process of boundary demarcation. As in the case of the settlements, the powerful side (Israel) has been able unilaterally to impose new territorial realities, substantially weakening the Palestinian claim to a border corresponding to the Green Line boundary. But for Israelis seeing this physical barrier (parts of it are located parallel to the new trans-Israel highway), the notion of territorial and physical separation now took on a tangible and concrete dimension, in contrast to the previous vague mental images of what such separation would entail. This contributed significantly to the increased support for the implementation of a two-state solution, even among some groups who were opposed to it on ideological and irredentist grounds.

But the main reason for a renewed two-state discourse among the Israeli public was the gradual realization of what has been termed the "demographic problem". Here, too, what was previously perceived as an abstract idea – namely that continued occupation of the West Bank and Gaza Strip coupled with more rapid demographic growth among the Palestinian population would eventually lead to the loss of the Jewish majority in the "Jewish state" – was transformed into a tangible and real argument. The suicide bombings brought the Palestinians into the backyards of most Israelis, including those who had never previously had any contact with them. The spectre of a single binational state, rejected by the vast majority of Israeli Jews, was enough for many of them to fall back on the idea of territorial separation into two states as the "lesser of two evils".

This demographic argument was used by Prime Minister Sharon and his deputy, Ehud Olmert, in their proposal to disengage unilaterally from the Gaza Strip in 2004. In this region, the Palestinian population had reached 1.5 million, alongside no more than 7,000 Israeli settlers. The demographic ratio between the two, along with the concomitant dangers facing Israeli settlers when travelling to and from their settlements, partly precipitated Prime Minister Sharon's surprise policy turn (along with a desire to appease the US administration, which was critical of Israel for not following through with implementation of the Road Map; see below). The Gaza disengagement plan is also of great significance with respect to the settlement issue. If implemented, it would constitute a major precedent for settlement removal, an issue which has been discussed and proposed at great length during the past decade but has never withstood the actual test of implementation. Successful implementation of the Gaza disengagement would bring about a totally new territorial discourse relating to the bigger issue of the West Bank, based on a new reality of withdrawal and evacuation precedent.

From bilateralism to unilateralism: travelling the road (map) from Oslo to Geneva

The changing border and territorial discourses outlined in the previous section have resulted from the changing political, security and demographic realities, and, at the same time, they explain the various nuances which have been central to the main peace proposals during this period. In this section, we will compare four such proposals, one of which – the Oslo Accords – can be considered as the starting point for a tangible discourse of territorial negotiations, with the other three (the Road Map, the Geneva Accord and the Gaza disengagement) reflecting the changing power relations and political realities which have taken place since the breakdown of the Camp David peace negotiations in September 2000, the return of violence, the partial reoccupation of the West Bank by the Israeli army, and the suspension of all direct Track I bilateral negotiations between the two sides (Enderlin, 2003; Matz, 2003; Pressman, 2003).

TABLE 3.2 Territorial dimensions of recent political solutions for the Israel–Palestine conflict

	Oslo Accords 1993 and 1995	Road Map 2003	Geneva Accords 2003	Gaza disengagement 2004
Borders	Undefined; Areas "A", "B"and "C"; Israel retains control of Jordan valley	Undefined; minor deviations from Green Line; Jordan valley to be negotiated but with view to Israeli withdrawal	Green Line; Israeli withdrawal from Jordan valley	Withdrawal from Gaza Strip
Demography	Israel relinquishes direct control of 80% of Palestinian population	Separation into two states	Separation into two states; maximal demographic separation	Israel relinquishes direct control of inhabitants of the Gaza Strip
Settlements	To be negotiated at later stages with a view to partial evacuation and territorial exchanges	Evacuation of most settlements with appropriate territorial exchanges	Evacuation of all settlements	Evacuation of all settlements in Gaza Strip and a few outlying settlements in the West Bank

The Oslo Agreements

> The aim of the Israeli–Palestinian negotiations within the current Middle East peace process is, among other things, to establish a Palestinian Interim Self-Government Authority, the elected Council (the "Council"), for the Palestinian people in the West Bank and the Gaza Strip, for a transitional period not exceeding five years, leading to a permanent settlement based on Security Council resolutions 242 (1967) and 338 (1973). It is understood that the interim arrangements are an integral part of the whole peace process and that the negotiations on the permanent status will lead to the implementation of Security Council resolutions 242 (1967) and 338 (1973).
>
> *(Article I of the Oslo Agreements)*[5]

The Oslo Agreements constituted the first major breakthrough in the Israeli–Palestinian conflict since the 1967 war. Negotiated secretly between Israeli and Palestinian representatives in Oslo, the agreement was eventually signed in two parts, the first in 1993 and the second in 1995. It received much global coverage, culminating in the public signing of the agreement on the lawn of the White House by the respective Israeli and Palestinian leaders and the President of the United States.

Both Oslo Agreements were interim in nature, defining a period of five years during which further negotiations would take place, leading to a final resolution of the conflict. The implementation of the agreements resulted in major changes in the system of governance and demographic control, reflected through a reconfiguration of territorial control. The West Bank was divided into Areas "A", "B" and "C", with the Palestinian Authority taking over full control in Area "A" (containing most of the West Bank urban centres and hence most of the Palestinian population), joint security operating in Area "B" (containing many of the smaller towns and villages), and Israel retaining full security control in Area "C" (consisting of the whole Jordan valley in the east, and all Israeli settlements throughout the region). The territorial result was a map which consisted of non-contiguity between numerous exclaves and isolated territories, with checkpoints and safe passages required between each type of area. It was a recipe for political instability, as proved to be the case over the subsequent six-year period.

The Oslo Accords were followed by some additional agreements, notably the Wye and Hebron Agreements, signed and implemented by the right-wing Prime Minister Benjamin Netanyahu, but these only exacerbated the territorial non-contiguity between Israeli settlement enclaves and Palestinian autonomy areas. If one major lesson was learned from the Oslo territorial experience it was that any future political agreement must create a map of territorial contiguity, with a single clear line of separation between the two political entities. This has obvious implications for the evacuation of Israeli settlements which are located on the Palestinian side of wherever that line is drawn. They could not remain as isolated enclaves under an extra-territorial form of administration.

The implementation of the Oslo Accords was to be followed by a five-year period of continued negotiations aimed at reaching a final resolution to the conflict. However, the return of violence on the streets, along with the assassination of Prime Minister Yitzhak Rabin, resulted in a slowing down of the process. Under the auspices of President Clinton, a peace summit was held between Prime Minister Barak and Yasser Arafat at Camp David in September 2000, but they failed to reach an agreement. The breakdown of negotiations was followed by an increase in acts of terrorism and Israeli military retaliation, all but putting an end to the Oslo process. What had seemed to be the major glimmer of hope in the mid-1990s had now descended to a level of violence, and a new Intifada, of a degree which had not previously been experienced.

The Road Map

Following the American invasion of Iraq in 2003, the USA, the EU, the UN and Russia (known as the Quartet) placed a new peace plan on the table. This plan, known as the Road Map, was formally adopted by both the Israeli government and the Palestinian Authority as the way forward to the eventual establishment of a Palestinian state in the West Bank and Gaza Strip.[6] It was a performance-based and goal-driven plan, with three clear phases of implementation, timelines, target dates and benchmarks, based on reciprocal steps by the two parties in the political, security, economic, humanitarian and institution-building fields, all under the auspices of the Quartet. The destination was meant to be a final and comprehensive settlement of the Israeli–Palestinian conflict by 2005 (Lavie, 2003).

In Phase I (March–May 2003), the Palestinians were required to undertake an unconditional cessation of violence immediately. Palestinians and Israelis would resume security cooperation based on the Tenet plan to end violence, terrorism and incitement through restructured and effective Palestinian security services.[7] Palestinians would undertake comprehensive political reform in preparation for statehood, including drafting a Palestinian constitution, and the holding of free, fair and open elections. Israel would take all necessary steps to help normalize Palestinian life. It would also withdraw from Palestinian areas occupied after 28 September 2000, and the two sides would restore the status quo that existed at that time. Israel would also freeze all settlement activity, consistent with the Mitchell Report.[8]

In the second phase (June–December 2003), efforts would be focused on creating an independent Palestinian state with provisional borders and attributes of sovereignty, based on the new constitution, as a way station to a permanent status settlement. Progress into Phase II would be based upon the consensus judgement of the Quartet over whether conditions were appropriate to proceed, taking into account the performance of both parties. Furthering and sustaining efforts to normalize Palestinian lives and build Palestinian institutions, Phase II would start after Palestinian elections and end with the possible creation of an independent Palestinian state with provisional borders in 2003. Revival of multilateral engagement on issues including regional water resources, environment, economic development, refugees and arms control would take place. A new constitution for a democratic, independent Palestinian state would be finalized and approved by the appropriate Palestinian institutions. Further elections, if required, would follow approval of the new constitution. As part of this process, implementation of prior agreements, to enhance maximum territorial contiguity, including further action on settlements in conjunction with establishment of a Palestinian state with provisional borders, would also be implemented. There would be an enhanced international role in monitoring transition, with the active, sustained and operational support of the Quartet.

In Phase III (2004–2005) of the Road Map, the parties were meant to reach a final and comprehensive permanent status agreement that would end the Israeli–Palestinian conflict in 2005, through a settlement negotiated between the parties based on UN Resolutions 242, 338 and 1397. This would include an agreed, just, fair and realistic solution to the refugee issue, a negotiated resolution of the status of Jerusalem that would take into account the political and religious concerns of both sides, protection of the religious interests of Jews, Christians and Muslims worldwide, and the emergence of two states – Israel and a sovereign, independent, democratic and viable Palestine – living side by side in peace and security. Arab states would be required to accept full and normal relations with Israel, along with security for all the states of the region, in the context of a comprehensive Arab–Israeli peace.

The Geneva Accord

> The Permanent Status Agreement (hereinafter "this Agreement") ends the era of conflict and ushers in a new era based on peace, cooperation, and good neighborly relations between the Parties. The implementation of this Agreement will settle all the claims of the Parties arising from events occurring prior to its signature. No further claims related to events prior to this Agreement may be raised by either Party.
>
> *(Article I of the Geneva Accord)*[9]

The Geneva Accord was drawn up by a group of Israeli public figures and Palestinian politicians. It was a far-reaching proposal, going beyond the Road Map in terms of the issues it addressed, including the status of Jerusalem and an attempt to resolve the issue of Palestinian refugees. Within Israel, the proposal was criticized by the government since it was negotiated by politicians and public figures who were not members of the administration and, in some cases, had been voted out of power and were identified with the left-wing Labour and Meretz opposition political parties. The proponents of Geneva used the agreement to show the government that it was possible to negotiate conflict resolution with leading Palestinian personalities and to emphasize that it was essential to move away from the present (2003) stalemate.

Article IV of the Geneva Accord deals specifically with the issue of territory. It proposes that the international border between the states of Palestine and Israel be demarcated in accordance with UN Resolutions 242 and 338, based on the 4 June 1967 line, with reciprocal modifications on a one–one basis. This would be recognized as the "permanent, secure and recognized international boundary" between the two states. Moreover, the parties would "recognize and respect each other's sovereignty, territorial integrity, and political independence, as well as the inviolability of each other's territory, including territorial waters, and airspace".

Israel was expected to withdraw from the Occupied Territories, with control transferred to the Palestinian Authority. A Joint Technical Border Commission composed of the two parties would be established to conduct the technical demarcation of the international boundary. Settlements would be evacuated, with resettlement taking place inside Israel and any immovable property, infrastructure and facilities being transferred to Palestinian sovereignty. The state of Palestine would have exclusive title to all land and any buildings, facilities, infrastructure or other property remaining in any of the settlements on the date prescribed in the timetable for the completion of the evacuation of that settlement.

Provisions were also made for the creation of a territorial corridor linking the West Bank and Gaza Strip. This would be under Israeli sovereignty and would be permanently open, but Palestinian law would apply to people using it. Defensive barriers would be established along it, and Palestinians would not be able to enter Israel from it. (Similarly, Israelis could not enter Palestine from the corridor.)

Other articles in the Geneva Accord dealt with the complex and sensitive issues of Jerusalem, Palestinian refugees, security and border regimes. Concerning

Jerusalem, the city would be the capital for both states, with a clear territorial division separating the sovereign entities. The Old City and the holy sites would have separate religious administrations with free access to and from the sites. There would also be municipal coordination to ensure the most efficient management of the urban infrastructural systems, including planning, transportation, economic development, water provision and the environment.

Gaza disengagement

The Gaza disengagement plan was a unilateral Israeli plan implemented in the summer of 2005, involving the withdrawal of Israeli troops from the Gaza Strip, the dismantlement and forced evacuation of all Israeli settlements in the region, and the transfer of power there to the Palestinian Authority.[10] As an addendum, Israel also evacuated four settlements in the northern part of the West Bank, although this area remained under Israeli military control. This would enable territorial contiguity for Palestinians in this part of the West Bank. Israel, however, continued to control the external land perimeter of the Gaza Strip, maintained exclusive authority in Gazan airspace, and exercised security activity in the sea off the coast of the Gaza Strip. Although initially Israel had intended to maintain direct military control along the border between the Gaza Strip and Egypt (the Philadelphi Line), it eventually backed down and handed over control to Palestinian and Egyptian forces, thus enabling an open crossing for Palestinians into and out of the Gaza Strip, circumventing Israeli border restrictions and closures.

The plan met with much opposition inside Israel, especially among the settler movement and its supporters throughout the country. However, public opinion surveys demonstrated that the vast majority of the Israeli population supported the plan, not least because of the demographic imbalance between the 7,000 Israeli settlers and 1.5 million Palestinians, along with the fact that the human cost of defending these isolated settlements was not perceived, by most Israelis, as serving any significant defensive or security objective.

Ironically, it was a government led by Ariel Sharon, who had been responsible for the establishment of many of the settlements in the first place, that implemented this unilateral plan. Based on two premises – amid suicide bombings and terrorist activity, Israel did not have a negotiating partner amongst the Palestinian leadership; and Israel's long-term security was increasingly threatened by demographic imbalance between Israelis and Palestinians – the plan was implemented at great speed in August 2005.

The same plan formed the basis for further proposed limited disengagements in parts of the West Bank, following the election of the new Kadima government in the spring of 2006. (This party had been formed by Sharon in the face of right-wing opposition within his own Likud Party. He was succeeded as party leader and Prime Minister by Ehud Olmert after suffering an incapacitating stroke.) However, in the wake of the war between Israel and Lebanon in the summer of 2006, talk of further unilateral disengagements was put temporarily to one side.

The move towards unilaterally imposed territorial and political solutions was pushed forward by the growing public discourse surrounding the long-term demographic implications of continued occupation and the perceived threat that this posed to the essence of national identity inside Israel, not least the need to maintain a state within which the Jewish component constituted a clear majority. The translation of demography into a component of security, the ethos around which public discourse concerning the conflict is rooted and around which governments are elected, made it a more acceptable discourse for many Israelis who have traditionally opposed all forms of territorial withdrawal. The idea that the continuation of existing demographic trends would threaten the existence of the hegemonic Jewish state proved to be as significant in the security discourse as were the traditional military and defensive factors. The absence of a negotiating partner, as defined by the Israeli government, made it easier for the plan to be implemented along the lines chosen, although this resulted in asymmetry and a lack of preparedness on the part of the Palestinian Authority. But in terms of the internal Israeli discourse, the unilateral withdrawal from Gaza strengthened the national core identity in favour of the Jewish state and away from ethnocratic models of power-sharing (Yiftachel, 2006).

Conclusion

This chapter has addressed the changing territorial and border discourses in Israel/ Palestine during the decade following the signing of the Oslo Accords. The basic territorial question that faces Israeli and Palestinian negotiators today is no different to the one they have faced since the early twentieth century: how best to divide the small piece of real estate between the Mediterranean Sea and the Jordan River into two separate national territories. The debate over partition that began in the 1930s remains at the heart of all attempts to find a practical solution to the conflict, taking into account the changed geographic, demographic and power realities that have evolved on both sides of the boundary during the past fifty years. Where there was once a mandate territory, there is now a powerful state of Israel and an occupied territory. Where once there was a larger Arab than Jewish population, there is now clear demographic hegemony for the Jewish population within the pre-1967 boundaries, and near parity if the Occupied Territories are included.

The four territorial models discussed above are all based on the assumption that some variation of a two-state solution is the only means to resolve the conflict. Accepting this assumption requires the ultimate demarcation of borders separating the two territorial–political entities, an exercise which has been attempted by cartographers, planners, politicians and geographers over the past fifteen years. The basic parameters for boundary demarcation were presented at the 2006 Herzliya Conference (Newman *et al.*, 2006). These parameters included: the recognition of the Green Line as the default line from which it would be possible to implement territorial exchanges in areas of close proximity to the boundary; the requirement for territorial contiguity and compactness for the Palestinian state; the resultant evacuation of Israeli settlements (the extent of which would be determined by the nature of small-scale territorial exchanges); and the need for effective border management and cross-border passages as required by the two sides. The Separation Barrier could not be considered a legitimate political boundary in those places where it deviates from the Green Line, unless bilateral agreement was reached concerning territorial compensation for these areas.

Given the changing political realities and the breakdown of the peace process, proposals aimed at reaching a solution, even interim, to the conflict have been transformed from bilateral and negotiated to unilateral and superimposed. This has been most evident in the unilateral construction of the Separation Barrier and the disengagement from the Gaza Strip. The Israeli government has argued that, in the absence of a negotiating partner, it has no choice but to follow a unilateral path, rather than wait for the emergence of a new Palestinian leadership that would be prepared to talk. But whereas the bilateral plans (such as Oslo and the Road Map – which both sides formally signed) were never implemented, the unilateral plans (such as the Separation Barrier and the Gaza disengagement) were implemented on the ground, creating facts that would prove difficult (although not impossible) to rectify at a later stage.

The Israel–Palestine case study is a good example of the dialectic between contesting discourses of territorial partition (a two-state solution), on the one hand, and power sharing (a binational state), on the other. In the past, the two-state solution to the conflict has been perceived as a left-wing political position advocating ethno-territorial separation. More recently, it has been adopted by the centre and even the moderate right of the Israeli political spectrum in response to a perceived demographic "threat" to the Jewish state over the long term.

Notes

1 The Israeli War of Independence is known as the Naqba (Disaster) amongst the Palestinians.
2 Yossi Beilin was the architect of the Oslo Accords. He was later a cabinet minister, leader of the left-wing Yahad Party and instigator of the Geneva Accord. Abu Maazen was a senior Palestinian minister and became Prime Minister of the Palestinian Authority for a short period in 2003.
3 For detailed maps of the Separation Barrier see http://www.arij.org/ and http://www.stopthewall.com. For a PowerPoint presentation of the impact of the barrier in the Jerusalem region, see http://www.jiis.org.il/jiis-fence.pdf.
4 The ICJ ruling of July 2004 can be seen at http://www.icj-cij.org/icjwww/ipresscom/ipress2004/ipresscom2004-28_mwp_20040709.htm.
5 For the full text of the Oslo Accords (Declaration of Principles on Interim Self-Government Arrangements), see http://www.iap.org/oslo.htm.
6 For the full text of the Road Map, see http://www.un.org/media/main/roadmap 122002.html.
7 For the text of the Tenet cease-fire plan, see http://www.mfa.gov.il/MFA/Peace+Process/Guide+to+the+Peace+Process/Palestinian-Israeli+Security+Implementation+Work+P.htm.
8 For the text of the Mitchell Report, see http://www.bitterlemons.org/docs/mitchell.html.
9 For the full text of the Geneva Accord, annexes and maps, see: http://www.heskem.org.il.
10 For the full text of the Gaza disengagement plan, see http://www.mfa.gov.il/MFA/Peace+Process/Reference+Documents/Disengagement+Plan+-+General+Outline.htm.

4

A PALESTINIAN PERSPECTIVE ON THE ISRAELI–PALESTINIAN CONFLICT ON SETTLEMENTS, TERRITORY, AND BORDERS

Jad Isaac

Historical background

In 1922, the borders of Mandated Palestine were defined to include an area of 27,000 sq. km on which 660,641 Christian and Muslim Palestinians lived alongside 88,000 Jews. The British Mandate period witnessed mass emigrations of Jews to Palestine, encouraged and facilitated by the Jewish Agency and the World Zionist Organization, with support from the British authorities, to establish a Jewish homeland. Land acquired by the Jewish National Fund (JNF) was held in the name of the Jewish people and could never be sold or even leased back to Arabs (a situation that continues to the present day). The Palestinians became increasingly aware of the Zionists' intentions, which posed a real and imminent danger to their very existence. In 1937, the Peel Commission recommended that Palestine be divided into a Jewish state and an Arab one. In 1937, Jews owned only 7 percent of the land but they were designated a much larger area for the Jewish state. This obliged the Palestinians to reject the Peel plan and clashes erupted. It should be mentioned here that the Arab rejection of the Peel Commission's recommendations also originated from the Palestinians' belief that the commission had its mind made up and recommendations in place before it even set foot in Palestine. Certainly, the commissioners spent only sixty-eight days in Palestine, wholly inadequate to investigate the situation on the ground thoroughly, which suggests that a great deal of the report it published on July 7, 1937 had been pre-drafted. However, the Arabs were not the only ones to reject the commission's recommendations. The Twentieth Zionist Congress articulated its rejection by stating, "The partition plan proposed by the Peel Commission is not to be accepted."

Thereafter, the British Mandate authorities established the Woodhead Commission in 1938 to investigate why the earlier commission's recommendations had been rejected by both Arabs and Jews; and to come up with a more suitable partition plan. However, the Woodhead plan was strongly rejected by both Jews and Arabs.

This led to the 1939 St. James Conference (also known as the Round Table Conference), but once again its recommendations were utterly rejected by both Arabs and Jews.

On November 29, 1947, the UN General Assembly adopted Resolution 181, dividing Mandated Palestine into Jewish (56.5 percent) and Arab (43.5 percent) states (see Figure 4.1). The plan also declared Jerusalem (186 sq. km) to be a "Corpus Separatum": that is, a separate body to be run by an international administration (namely, the United Nations). The delineation of the boundaries of the two states was influenced essentially by hydrological considerations, as the Zionist movement wanted to control the waters of the Jordan River and divert them to the Negev. Palestinians rejected the plan because Jews, who at that time owned only 7 percent of the land, were given such a large share of it.

David Ben Gurion declared Israel an independent state and Eliahu Epstein, the agent of the provisional government, officially acknowledged that the state of Israel had been proclaimed as an independent republic within frontiers approved by the UN General Assembly. Thus, the partition plan map is still the only legally and internationally recognized boundary of Israel.

War erupted between Israel and the Arabs, and by 1948 Israel had gained control over more than 78 percent of Mandated Palestine. More than 750,000 Palestinians were expelled to become refugees and at least 418 villages were depopulated and/or demolished. Jordan and Egypt administered the 22 percent of Mandated Palestine that remained outside of Israel's control: the West Bank and Gaza Strip, respectively. West Jerusalem came under the control of Israel, while East Jerusalem ended up as part of the West Bank and so was administered by the Hashemite Kingdom of Jordan (see Figure 4.2).

In 1967, Israel occupied the West Bank, including East Jerusalem, and Gaza (hereafter referred to as the Occupied Palestinian Territories, OPT) in addition to Sinai and the Golan Heights. On November 22, 1967, UN Security Council Resolution 242 was issued, which emphasized the inadmissibility of the acquisition of territory by war and the need to work for a just and lasting peace in which every state in the area could live in security. It also called for the withdrawal of Israeli armed forces from territories occupied in the recent conflict and a just settlement of the refugee problem.

Initiation and development of settlements

Just hours after the end of the 1967 war, the Israeli government gave the Palestinian residents of Bab Al-Magharbeh in the Old City a few hours to evacuate their homes before it demolished the entire neighborhood. Furthermore, 2000 dunums of land were expropriated from the Old City. On September 24, 1967, three months after the war, Israeli Prime Minister Levi Eshkol announced his government's plan to build settlements in occupied Arab territories: East Jerusalem, Gush Etzion, and the Golan Heights. In the Latroun area, three Palestinian villages – Yalu, Beit Nuba, and Imwas – were demolished in 1967, forcing their inhabitants to leave and become refugees. A park was later established on their land.

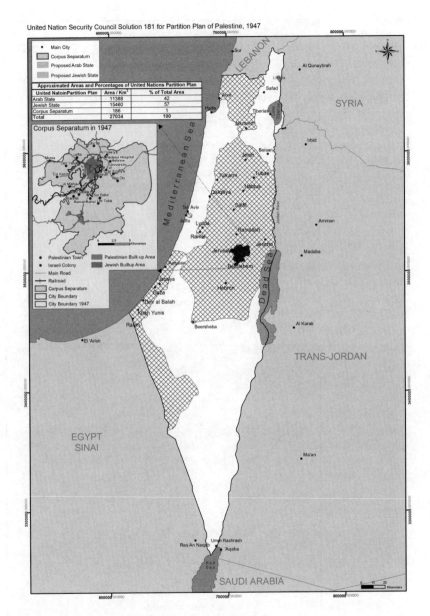

United Nation Security Council Solution 181 for Partition Plan of Palestine, 1947

FIGURE 4.1 The United Nations Partition Plan, 1947

Israel illegally expanded the borders of East Jerusalem from 6.5 to 71 sq. km to incorporate areas in the Ramallah and Bethlehem districts (Figure 4.3). These new borders included as much vacant land and as little Palestinian built-up area as possible. The Israeli Knesset formally annexed East Jerusalem in 1980, but the expansion of the municipal borders and the confiscation of private Palestinian property started soon after the 1967 war.

FIGURE 4.2
Status quo after
the 1948 war

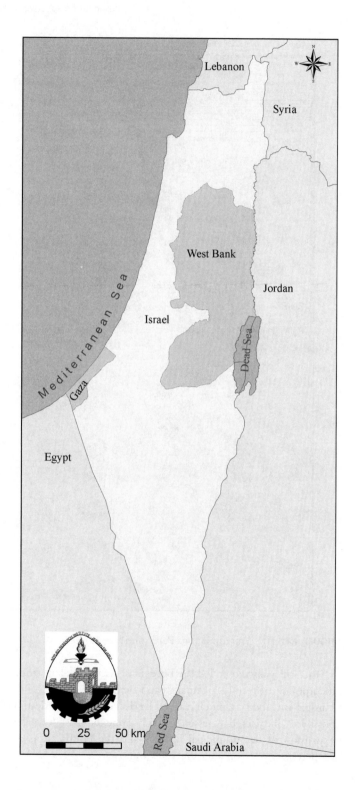

FIGURE 4.3
The changing boundaries of Jerusalem

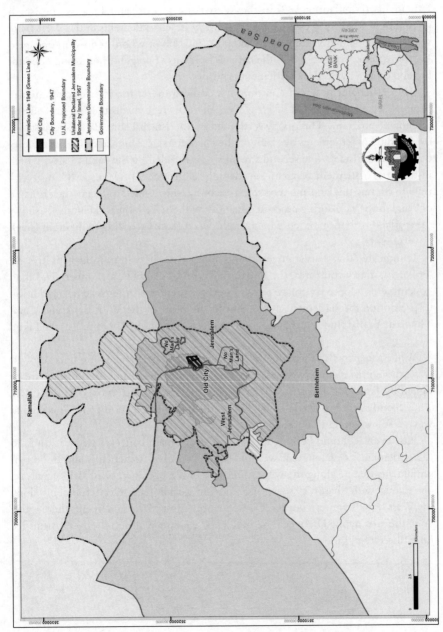

From that time on, the Israeli government nurtured hundreds of settlements in the OPT, which developed to become impediments to any peaceful resolution of the conflict. Since 1967, Israel has either confiscated or declared as closed areas or nature reserves over 55 percent of the OPT, thereby placing it out of Palestinian reach. Until September 2005, there were 21 Israeli settlements in the Gaza Strip housing approximately 8000 settlers; these were evacuated along with four settlements (population: 582) in the West Bank as a unilateral act by the Israeli government. By July 2009, there were still 199 Israeli settlements in the West Bank with a total population exceeding 580,000, 260,000 of whom resided in occupied East Jerusalem. Israel considers the latter as residents of neighborhoods and does not include them in its official settlements statistics.

The settlement program constituted a cornerstone of the Israeli government's plan to "Israelize" the OPT. However, there were two distinct streams in the settlement program. The first was adopted by the Israeli Labor Party and justified the building of settlements by claiming they had strategic significance for the security of the state of Israel. The second stream is spearheaded by the Likud Party, which justifies the settlement program on ideological grounds. It claims a "God-given" right to occupy this land and therefore has consistently refused to accept the principle of "land for peace" during peace negotiations with the Palestinians. Figure 4.4 shows the spatial distribution of settlements in the West Bank according to different Israeli governments.

It indicates that Labor governments focused their colonization activities on Jerusalem, the Latroun area, the Jordan valley, and Gush Etzion. Conversely, Likud governments adopted a policy of reinforcing settlements in Jerusalem, in addition to promoting the settlement movement in the heart of the West Bank and Gaza. The term Yesha' (Judea, Samaria, and Gaza) was coined in 1979 to reflect the Likud ideology.

While the growth of settlements has been progressively increasing since 1967, it was exponential during two eras. The first was after the Camp David peace treaty signed by Israel and Egypt in 1977, when settlers from Sinai moved to the OPT. The second started in 2001, coinciding with Israel's segregation plan. This second wave is still ongoing (Figure 4.5).

However, it should be noted here that Israel's main concerns when it came to the settlements' development were occupied Jerusalem settlements and the major settlements that lie along the western terrains of the occupied West Bank territory, correlating with Sharon's "seven star" plan to establish a line of settlements along the West Bank's western border. Consequently, most of the settlements there today lie in the area trapped between the Israeli Segregation Wall and the 1949 Armistice Line (the Green Line).

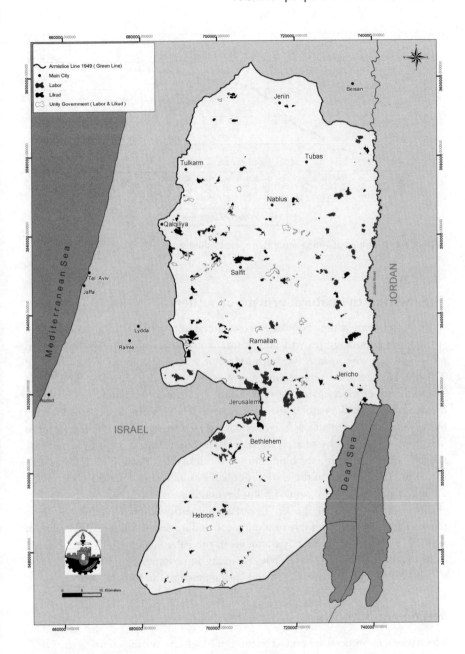

FIGURE 4.4 Israeli settlements in the West Bank and their master plans

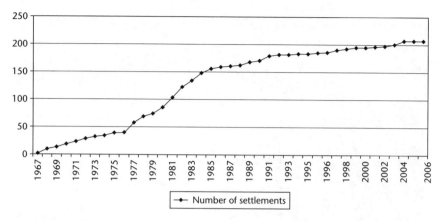

FIGURE 4.5 Number of Israeli settlements established since 1967

The myth of the natural growth of settlers

In Israel, the yearly natural population growth rate among Jews is 1.7 percent (2008). If the same population growth rate occurred in the Jewish population living in settlements, by the year 2004 the number of settlers should have been around 320,000. However, the actual figure was over 480,000 (see Figure 4.6), equating to a growth rate of more than 5 percent. So the increase in the number of settlers is incompatible with the natural growth rate in Israel. This can be explained largely by the Israeli government's policy of encouraging settlements by offering financial incentives to potential settlers. The anomalous population growth occurred primarily in the three largest communities: Modi'in Illit, Betar Illit, and Ma'aleh Adumim. The first two of these are about half a kilometer beyond the Green Line, while Ma'aleh Adumim is some 4.5 km beyond it.

Israel's settlements in the OPT violate numerous United Nations Security Council and General Assembly resolutions, including Security Council Resolution 446 (1979), which states that "settlements in the Palestinian and other Arab territories occupied since 1967 have no legal validity and constitute a serious obstruction to achieving a comprehensive, just and lasting peace in the Middle East."

Settlement outposts

The settlement outposts are crucial features of Israel's colonizing efforts in the OPT, which aim to annex as much land as possible before any final agreement with the Palestinians is reached. Israeli settlers, acting with the support of the Israeli occupation authorities, have established small settlement communities on Palestinian land in an attempt to take control of more land for the exclusive use of settlers. The outposts extend settlement lands deeper into Palestinian territory, placing more areas under direct settlement control and contributing to the fragmentation of the OPT.

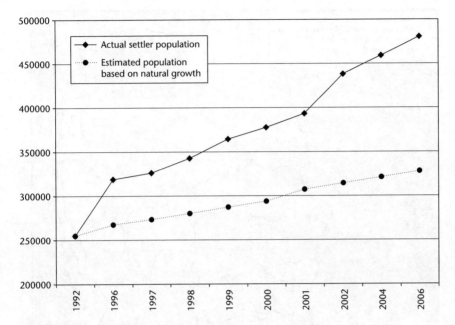

FIGURE 4.6 Actual settler population and growth rates during the years 1992 to 2006

Satellite image analysis conducted by ARIJ (Applied Research Institute-Jerusalem) in 2009 revealed that 232 settlement outposts had been established in the West Bank over the past thirteen years, of which 153 have been established since March 2001. According to the Road Map, Israel should remove all settlement outposts established since March 2001. In response, Israel has attempted to make a false distinction between "authorized" and "unauthorized" outposts to facilitate the development of the current outposts into permanent settlements. Despite Israeli leaders' promises to "dismantle" the outposts, they continue to increase in number throughout the OPT.

Settlements and bypass roads

The term "bypass road" was coined in the Oslo Accords to designate roads in the Palestinian territory that link Jewish settlements to military camps and Israel while circumventing Palestinian built-up areas. They are a central tool in Israel's creation of an apartheid system in the OPT. The Israeli occupation army has complete control of these roads and frequently forbids Palestinians to use them. The highways turn the Palestinian areas into isolated ghettos and deprive Palestinians of access to vital agricultural land. These practices have fragmented both land and people. The construction of the bypass roads, which requires the confiscation of a 75-meter buffer zone on each side of each road, has caused immense destruction to Palestinian land. There are now more than 820 km (120 sq. km) of bypass roads inside the West Bank (Maoh and Isaac, 2003; see Figure 4.7).

FIGURE 4.7 Israeli-controlled roads in the West Bank

The peace process

In 1987, the Intifada broke out to protest against the continuation of the occupation and to call for a resolution to the historic conflict between Israelis and Palestinians. Consequently, the Palestinian people, by and large, accepted the discourse of peaceful negotiations based on the grounds outlined at the Madrid Conference of 1991. The guiding principles of these negotiations were "land for peace" and United Nations Security Council Resolutions 242 and 338. The Palestinian negotiating team at Madrid demanded that Israel freeze all settlement activities in the OPT before the negotiation process could advance any further. The formal Israeli–Palestinian negotiations faltered thereafter mainly over this issue.

However, secret negotiations were held between Israel and the Palestinian Liberation Organization (PLO), which culminated in the signing of the Declaration of Principles (DOP) on September 13, 1993. The DOP called for an interim period of five years, during which representatives of the Palestinian people and the Israeli government would initiate negotiations over the final status of Jerusalem, refugees, settlements, borders, and water. It was also agreed that neither party should initiate any action during the interim period that might jeopardize the final status negotiations. The Palestinians interpreted this as an implicit agreement on the freezing of settlements.

A series of subsequent agreements, popularly known as the Oslo Accords, was signed in order to implement the DOP. In the Cairo Agreement of May 4, 1994, the Israeli government agreed to withdraw from Jericho and most of Gaza, where the newly formed Palestinian National Authority (PNA) would assume control. Yasser Arafat delayed the signing of the map of this agreement because it did not show the Armistice Line of 1949. The "Oslo II" Agreement, signed in Washington, D.C., in September 1995, set out the interim stage for Palestinian autonomy in the West Bank and Gaza, pending "final status negotiations" that were scheduled to begin in May 1996 and end by May 1999. The land was divided into Areas A, B, and C, which have varying levels of control. The Israeli military withdrew from Area A, where complete control was assumed by the PNA. In Area B, the Palestinians were granted full control over civil matters, but Israel retained overriding responsibility for security. In Area C, Israel retained full control over land, security, people, and natural resources.

The Interim Agreement states:

> the first phase of the Israeli military forces' redeployment will cover populated areas in the West Bank – cities, towns, villages, refugee camps and hamlets – and will be completed prior to the eve of the Palestinian elections, i.e., 22 days before the day of the elections. The further redeployments of Israeli military forces to specified military locations will be gradually implemented in accordance with the DOP in three phases, each to take place after an interval of six months, after the inauguration of the Palestinian Legislative Council, to be completed within 18 months from the date of the inauguration of the Council.

With respect to the third stage of redeployment, the Interim Agreement gives some guidance as to its extent. In particular, Article XI.2 states: "The two sides agree that West Bank and Gaza Strip territory, except for issues that will be negotiated in the permanent status negotiations, will come under the jurisdiction of the Palestinian Council in a phased manner, to be completed within 18 months from the inauguration of the Council." For the Palestinians, this meant that 95 percent of the West Bank and Gaza should have come under their control by July 1998.

On the ground, Palestinians gained initial control over 70 percent of the Gaza Strip and 3 percent of the West Bank as Area A, and 24 percent as Area B. In January 1997, the Hebron Protocol was signed in which 85 percent of that city (H1) came under PNA control. The remaining 15 percent of the city area was designated as "H2" and remained under Israeli control. H2 includes around 20,000 Palestinians and 400 Jewish settlers.

After an eighteen-month hiatus, the Israeli–Palestinian negotiations recommenced and the Wye Memorandum was signed in 1998. This included a detailed plan for implementation. It is important to mention here that the Oslo Agreement, referred not to percentages, but rather to areas. Percentages were introduced in the Wye Memorandum. Another important issue is that, after the Hebron Protocol, Israelis stopped negotiating details of withdrawals with their Palestinian counterparts. Instead, they informed the Palestinians of their decisions based on a letter of assurance that was sent by the American Secretary of State, stating that it was up to Israel to decide the scope and extent of further redeployment. The Israeli government under Prime Minister Netanyahu implemented the first phase of the Wye Memorandum but froze the rest. Elections then took place in Israel, which brought Labor's Ehud Barak into power.

In September 1999, the Sharm el Sheikh Memorandum was signed, comprising three phases of implementation with a final outcome identical to that stipulated in the Wye Memorandum. A new category of land classification was added: namely, the nature reserve, which covers 3 percent of the West Bank. At the time of writing, the nature reserve had not been officially passed into Palestinian hands. Table 4.1 outlines the stages of the interim agreements.

TABLE 4.1 The redeployment percentages according to the agreements

Agreement	Date	Area		
		A	B	C
Oslo II	May 1994	3%	24%	73%
Wye I	October 1998	10.1%	18.9%	71%
Wye II & III (not implemented)		18.2%	21.8%	60%
Sharm I	September 1999	10.1%	25.9%	64%
Sharm II (implemented with a delay)	January 2000	12.1%	26.9%	61%
Sharm III (implemented with a delay)	March 2000	18.2%	21.8%	60%

The jagged distribution of Areas A, B, C, H1, and H2 has fragmented the OPT into isolated cantons that are physically separated from each other and from Gaza. The safe passage between Gaza and the West Bank, which was written into the Oslo Agreement, was not put in operation. The stalling of negotiations and delays, as well as renegotiation of what had already been agreed, led to partial Israeli withdrawals, so that by March 2000 Area A comprised 1004 sq. km of the West Bank and a further 254.2 sq. km of the Gaza Strip, while Area B comprised 1204 sq. km of the West Bank. The rest remains under full Israeli control (see Figure 4.8). Israel ignored Palestinian demands to implement the third redeployment phase that was stipulated in Oslo, and decided instead to move toward the long-overdue final status talks.

In July 2000, US President Bill Clinton convened talks in Camp David between Israeli Prime Minister Barak and Palestinian President Arafat in which a framework for a final agreement was discussed. The Palestinian negotiators were presented with a map that outlined a discontinuous Palestinian state comprising the Gaza Strip and 62 percent of the West Bank in addition to 15 percent of the OPT to be leased to Israel for twenty-five years, while Israel will annex 23 percent of the OPT (Figure 4.9). The proposed state would be completely surrounded by Israel and would have no international boundaries, effectively eliminating its sustainability and sovereignty. The bulk of Jerusalem would remain under Israeli control. As negotiations proceeded, there was some progress but not enough to broker a deal on the historic conflict, despite the enormous pressure imposed on the Palestinian leadership by the American hosts. In sum, the Camp David summit opened a Pandora's box of final status issues in a hasty manner, with a "take it or leave it" approach that had no real chance of success.

On September 28, 2000, the second Intifada erupted. Israel imposed a strict curfew on the OPT and restricted the ability of Palestinians to travel and work to a degree unprecedented in the history of the occupation. However, during the first few months, negotiations about the final status continued. In December 2000, Clinton put forward his parameters for a final status agreement (Negotiations Affairs Department–PLO, 2001), which included the following regarding settlements, borders, and Jerusalem:

1 Territory. Based on what I heard, I believe that the solution should be in the mid-90 percents, between 94–96 percent of the West Bank territory of the Palestinian State. The land annexed by Israel should be compensated by a land swap of 1–3 percent in addition to territorial arrangements such as a permanent safe passage. The parties also should consider the swap of leased land to meet their respective needs. The parties should develop a map consistent with the following criteria:

   - 80 percent of colonists in blocks,
   - Contiguity,
   - Minimize the annexed areas,
   - Minimize the number of Palestinians affected.

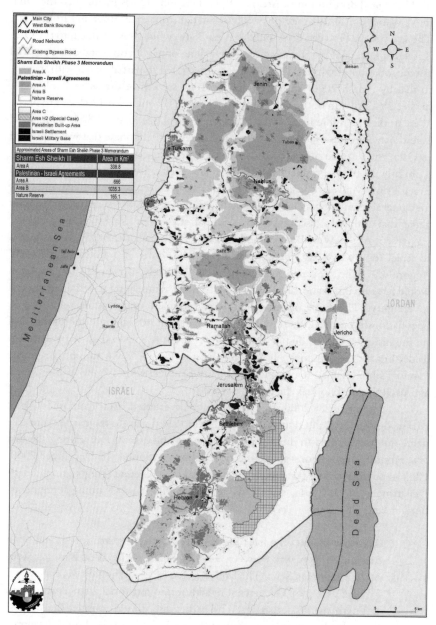

FIGURE 4.8 A geopolitical map of the Occupied Palestinian Territories

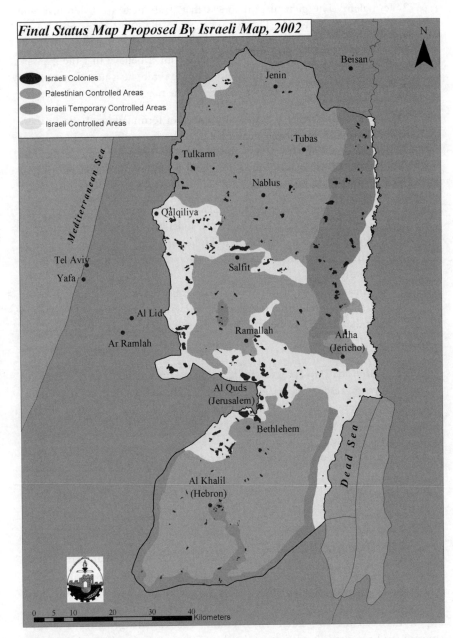

Final Status Map Proposed By Israeli Map, 2002

N

Legend:
- Israeli Colonies
- Palestinian Controlled Areas
- Israeli Temporary Controlled Areas
- Israeli Controlled Areas

Beisan

Jenin

Mediterranean Sea

Tulkarm

.Tubas

Nablus

Qalqiliya

Tel Aviv

Yafa

Salfit

Al Lid

Ramallah

Ar Ramlah

Ariha
(Jericho)

Al Quds
(Jerusalem)

Bethlehem

Dead Sea

Al Khalil
(Hebron)

0 5 10   20   30   40
                    Kilometers

FIGURE 4.9 The Israeli proposal at the beginning of Camp David talks

2 Jerusalem. The general principle is that Arab areas are Palestinian and Jewish ones are Israeli. This would apply to the Old City as well. I urge the two sides to work on maps to create maximum contiguity for both sides. Regarding the Haram/Temple Mount, I believe that the gaps are not related to practical administration but to symbolic issues of sovereignty and to finding a way to accord respect to the religious beliefs of both sides.

I know you have been discussing a number of formulations. I add to these two additional formulations guaranteeing Palestinian effective control over the Haram while respecting the conviction of the Jewish People. Regarding either one of those two formulations will be international monitoring to provide mutual confidence.

1 Palestinian sovereignty over the Haram and Israeli sovereignty over a) the Western Wall and the space sacred to Judaism of which it is a part or b) the Western Wall and the Holy of Holies of which it is a part. There will be a firm commitment by both not to excavate beneath the Haram or behind the Wall.
2 Palestinian sovereignty over the Haram and Israeli sovereignty over the Western Wall and shared functional sovereignty over the issue of excavation under the Haram and behind the Wall such that mutual consent would be requested before any excavation can take place.

The Palestinian leadership accepted the Clinton parameters but with reservations. In an attempt to rescue the peace process, Israeli and Palestinian negotiators embarked on serious and detailed negotiations, which included exchanges of ideas, plans, and maps. At Camp David, the Palestinians received Israeli plans, with the Americans attempting to promote them.

The Taba negotiations, which took place over a week in January 2001, were very intense and were conducted bilaterally between Israelis and Palestinians. At the onset of the negotiations, the two sides agreed that the June 4, 1967 border is the basis for the border between Israel and Palestine, and both sides accepted the principle of land swap but differed on the proportionality. The two sides then started addressing the gap in territorial base maps. The Palestinians calculated the areas of the West Bank and Gaza Strip that were occupied in 1967 to total 6210 sq. km. On the other hand, the Israelis deducted the following from this area: an area of East Jerusalem (71 sq. km), no man's land (52 sq. km), and the Dead Sea (195 sq. km). As the negotiations progressed, the no man's land in Latroun remained a source of dispute between the two sides. The Palestinians acknowledged Israel's security concerns and accepted that Palestine should not be a militarized state but insisted on Palestinian sovereignty over its territory, including borders and international crossings.

The Clinton parameters served as a guideline for the negotiations over territory. The Israeli side initially presented maps that involved the annexation of 12 percent of the West Bank for expanded settlement blocs. The Palestinian side rejected this proposal, as it would allow further development of settlements that would inflict significant damage on Palestinian land and the contiguity of their future state. As the negotiations progressed, the Israeli side presented a map detailing the annexation of 6 percent and leasing of an additional 2 percent of the West Bank. The Palestinians refused to discuss leasing land and presented a map that allowed for Palestinian territorial contiguity over 97 percent of the West Bank and at the same time consolidated the major settlements' annexation by Israel. Analysis of the two maps shows that settlements in Gaza, the Jordan valley, Hebron, and Jenin governorates will be evacuated as well as Har Homa, Ras al-Amud, Kedar, Teqoa, El David, and Nikodim. The Palestinian side rejected the Israeli proposal to maintain sovereignty over Ma'aleh Adumim and Givat Ze'ev and this issue was tabled for a decision by Arafat and Barak. Both sides agreed on establishing safe passage between Gaza and the West Bank through Tarqumia but differed on accepting the area as part of the land swap.

With regard to Jerusalem, the two sides accepted in principle the Clinton proposal of an open city with Palestinian sovereignty over Arab neighborhoods and Israeli sovereignty over Jewish neighborhoods. Both sides accepted that Jerusalem would be the capital of the two states: Yerushalaim, capital of Israel, and Al-Quds, capital of Palestine. However, the two sides had different perspectives on the open city issue. The Palestinians reiterated that their property claims in West Jerusalem had to be addressed. In return, they said they were prepared to address Israeli sovereignty over the Jewish Quarter of the Old City and part of the Armenian Quarter. By contrast, Israel presented the Holy Basin concept, which includes the Jewish Cemetery on the Mount of Olives, the City of David, and the Kidron valley. While the Palestinians expressed their understanding of Israeli interests, they insisted that these places were part of the territory occupied in 1967 and so should remain under Palestinian sovereignty.

Polls for the upcoming Israeli general election indicated that Labor was trailing Likud. Nevertheless, the Israeli delegation suspended the negotiations before they could reach agreement on the assumption that they would resume after the election. However, as expected, Likud won the election and the Taba negotiations never resumed. Nevertheless, a number of Israeli and Palestinian peace activists who were part of the negotiations continued to meet and eventually produced the Geneva Initiative, which allows for mutual and reciprocal territorial exchange (Map 4.8).

In September 2000, the Israeli government under Barak had first proposed the unilateral segregation (Hafradah) of Israel and the Palestinian territory. Foreign Minister Ariel Sharon had initially opposed the plan, but in June 2001, when he became Prime Minister, he established a steering committee to develop a comprehensive plan for segregation. A year later, the Israeli government established a Segregation Zone in the western terrain of the occupied West Bank. This covers a substantial and significant area that is rich in natural resources (specifically aquifers) and fertile agricultural land. The creation of the zone also isolated Palestinian communities in enclaves, undermining the territorial contiguity between Palestinian villages and cities. Most of the Israeli settlements are on the Israeli side of the zone.

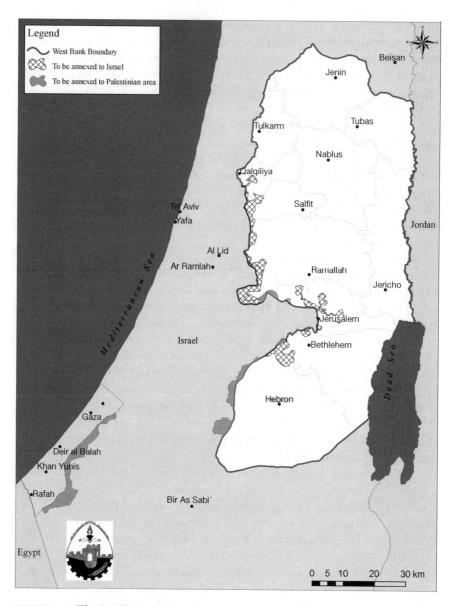

FIGURE 4.10 The Israeli Segregation Plan

The term "Segregation Wall" refers to the physical barrier that defines the zone, which consists of either 8–10-meter-high concrete partitions or fencing. The former type of barrier is used, along with military watchtowers placed 250 meters apart, in areas with sizeable populations generally close to the Green Line. The 4–5-meter-high fences are erected through agricultural land, which they devastate as they are double-layered (two fences, 40–100 meters apart) and reinforced with barbed wire, trenches, military roads and footprint-detection tracks.

TABLE 4.2 Status of the Western Segregation Wall as of April 2007

Current status	Length (km)	Percentage of the total wall length
Existing sections	428	55.6%
Planned sections	280	36.4%
Under construction	62	8%
Total	770	100%

On February 20, 2005, the Israeli government published a revised version of the Western Segregation Plan, with the Wall running for 683 km in the West Bank. Only 138 km of this route (20.2 percent of the total length) runs on the Green Line. If completed, this Wall would have isolated 576 sq. km of Palestinian land (10 percent of the total) from the remainder of the West Bank territory. It would also have separated 98 Israeli settlements, accommodating 83 percent of the settler population, from the Palestinian-controlled West Bank, as well as 55 Palestinian localities.

On April 30, 2006, the Israeli government published a revised version of the Western Segregation Plan, this time with the Wall running for 703 km, of which 128 km (18.2 percent of the total) would be along the Green Line. If completed, this Wall would have isolated 555 sq. km of Palestinian West Bank land (approximately 9.8 percent of the total) and would have separated 103 Israeli settlements (408,000 settlers; 85 percent of the total) from the rest of the West Bank. It would also have increased the number of isolated Palestinian localities to 59.

On September 12, 2007, the Israeli Ministry of Defense published yet another revised route for the Segregation Wall, which had been drafted that April. A total of 733 sq. km (13 percent of the total area of the West Bank) was now to be isolated behind the Wall, and its length was to be increased to 770 km.

The Israeli Segregation Plan

In September 2004, the Israeli Army issued military orders establishing a buffer zone averaging 150–200 meters on the Palestinian side of the Western Segregation Zone where new Palestinian constructions would be prohibited. As a result, an additional 252 sq. km of the West Bank (4.4 percent of the total) instantly became inaccessible to Palestinians.

In parallel, Israel has de facto created an Eastern Segregation Zone without walls or fences through its control of access points along the 200 km stretching from the Jordan valley in the north to the shores of the Dead Sea in the south and beyond. This zone has a total area of 1664 sq. km (29.4 percent of the total West Bank area), of which the Israeli Army controls 1555 sq. km (27.5 percent). It includes 43 Israeli settlements and 42 Palestinian localities.

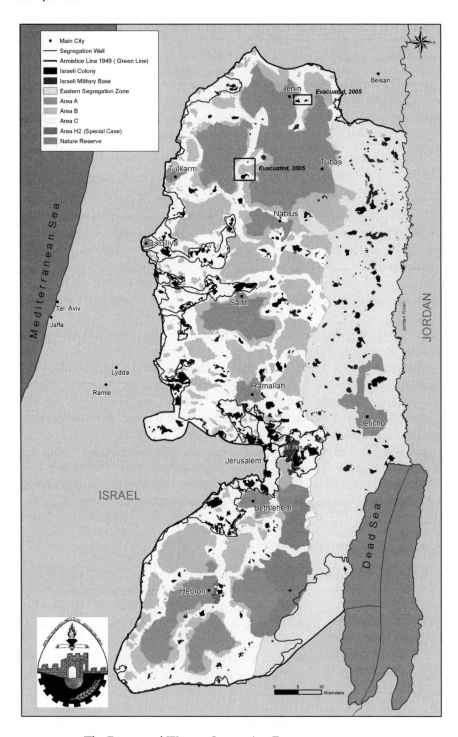

FIGURE 4.11 The Eastern and Western Segregation Zones

In an interview on April 5, 2004, Ariel Sharon responded to a question about whether there were plans for an "eastern fence" in the Jordan valley as follows: "I don't see a fence being built there today, unless we need to. Here and there we will block access points to the Jordan Valley" (Sussman, 2005). On September 7, 2004, the Israeli Agriculture Minister revealed plans to expropriate some 31,000 dunums of land to expand Jewish settlements in the Jordan valley; and on June 23, 2005, Israel announced plans to invest $50 million annually over the coming five years to strengthen its settlements in the Jordan valley. In September 2005, the Israeli Agricultural Ministry submitted development plans to establish new settlements in the Jordan valley to absorb some of the settlers who had been evacuated from Gaza. Map 4.9 shows the extent of the Eastern and Western Segregation Zones and the projected corridors to link them, which translate into Israeli control over 45 percent of the West Bank area. Israeli leaders insist that this whole area will remain an integral part of Israel: in 2005, Justice Minister Tzipi Livni stated publicly that the "Separation Fence" would serve as "the future border of the state of Israel" (Yoav, 2005).

The Disengagement Plan

The security buffer zone along Gaza's northern and eastern border was included as part of the 1994 Oslo Accord. This security zone accounted for 29 sq. km (8 percent) of Gaza's total area and was to remain under the Israeli Army's control. When the second Intifada broke out in September 2000, the Israeli Army expanded the area of the security zone unilaterally by a few hundred meters (with its width ranging between 800 meters and 1.3 km). The area was designated off-limits to Palestinians: they could not build, cultivate, or even merely be present there. In September 2005, the Israeli army evacuated 8000 settlers from Gaza and withdrew its forces to the outskirts of the Gaza Strip. However, the Israeli Army maintained a security buffer zone along the borders of the Strip, which meant that some 17 percent of Gaza's land area became inaccessible to the Palestinians. On June 28, 2007, the Israeli Army unilaterally expanded the buffer zone to a width of 1.5 km. Accordingly, the newly defined zone now occupies 87 sq. km (24 percent) of the Gaza Strip.

On June 18, 2005, Israel announced a plan to build an underwater barrier which now runs 950 meters out to sea and consists of a layer of cement surrounded by an iron fence. One hundred and fifty meters of the barrier comprises steel columns dug into the sea floor, while the remaining 800 meters consists of a "floating fence" sunk 1.8 meters deep into the water.

Exploiting the complaisancy of the international community, it seems that the current Israeli leadership will continue to act unilaterally with respect to Gaza and Areas A and B. The Israeli occupation authorities have devised a 500 km road system, including 18 tunnels, to link the isolated Palestinian areas with the main cities of the West Bank, in addition to high-tech checkpoint management systems. In total, it seems that the Israelis are unprepared to grant the Palestinians any more than 9 percent of historic Palestine. Certainly, such a plan is doomed to failure (see Figure 4.12).

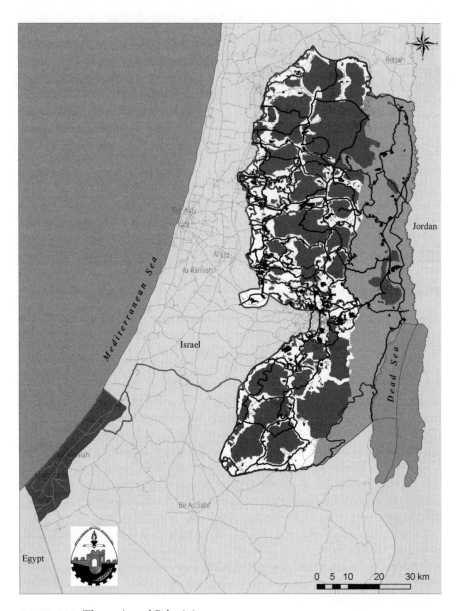

FIGURE 4.12 The projected Palestinian state

The Israeli military forces can still enter the Gaza Strip at any time they deem appropriate, seal all the borders to the outside world (and stop such essentials as food supplies from entering), devastate the infrastructure and guarantee that Gaza never achieves anything even resembling independence. This prolonged closure of Gaza, combined with the massive military assault in 2008–2009, has served to demonstrate that the area's occupation has not ended, but rather evolved.

Conclusion

The Palestinians accepted the peace process in the expectation that its ultimate goal was to end Israeli occupation and create a Palestinian state in the OPT. This was the historic reconciliation made by the Palestinian people and endorsed by their ratification of the Palestinian National Charter. But on the ground Palestinians found themselves subjected to a process of "peace in pieces." The peace process has failed to stop Israeli unilateral actions aimed at the de-Palestinization of Jerusalem, the expansion of settlements, the expropriation of ever more Palestinian land, the compartmentalization of Palestinian communities through the construction of bypass roads, and the Segregation Plan. Other failures include:

1   an extended interim period without an endgame;
2   no concrete dates for implementing agreements (permanent status should have been completed by May 1999);
3   a weak UN and international community;
4   absence of an arbitration mechanism;
5   lack of symmetry between Israelis and Palestinians;
6   violence adding to mistrust and increasing the gap between the two communities.

The Disengagement Plan is merely a diversion strategy to rid Israel of the pressures resulting from local, regional, and international initiatives. Attempts to link it with the Road Map are futile. Extended interim agreements have failed and most likely will fail in the future. The international community has a moral responsibility to stop Israel's continued defiance of UN resolutions. High-tech checkpoint management and transportation contiguity as well as quick-fix developmental projects will not make Palestine sustainable. What is needed is strong third-party intervention to ensure implementation of a permanent status agreement within a well-defined timeframe. The clock is ticking. Miserable living conditions, resource shortages and a lack of hope provide fertile ground for rising fundamentalism and/or voluntary transfer. Unless immediate action is taken, instability will continue and may well spread to the whole region.

Water

5

IS THE CONFLICT OVER SHARED WATER RESOURCES BETWEEN ISRAELIS AND PALESTINIANS AN OBSTACLE TO PEACE?

Hillel Shuval

Introduction

It is the goal of this chapter to propose a reasonable, just and equitable resolution of the water conflicts between the Israelis and the Palestinians which can meet the legitimate needs and interests of both peoples and will bring social and economic benefit to all. Such a resolution of these shared water problems can provide a major impetus to the peace process and might stop this issue being viewed as an obstacle to peace. Since I do not represent the official Israeli government position in any way, this proposal must be seen as the personal view of an academic who has studied the Israeli–Palestinian shared water issues for over eighteen years and has held discussions and dialogues on these issues with people on all sides, representing both official and unofficial points of view. The basic claims and concerns of the Palestinians and the Israelis will be presented in the following section.

Claims, counter-claims, fears, and concerns

In order to understand better the nature of the conflict and its intensity, it is essential to spell out the claims and counter-claims as well as the real and perceived fears and concerns of the sides in the dispute over shared water resources – mainly those concerning the Mountain Aquifer (ground water layer) centered in the West Bank.

Major Palestinian positions, claims, and concerns

The Palestinians' position is that while some 80 percent or more of the flow of the western and northeastern sections of the Mountain Aquifer are derived from rainfall over the West Bank areas slated, in their view, for inclusion in the future Palestinian state, 80 percent of the water is currently extracted from deep wells and springs mainly within the borders of Israel. The Palestinians' position is that these waters should be considered shared waters that should be allocated on an equitable basis. However, some Palestinian authors and officials consider them *Palestinian* waters derived from Palestinian land that should be allocated *totally* for their use and not shared.

The Palestinians, many of whom are farmers and villagers from families that have been living on these lands for hundreds of years, have a strong attachment to the land, and the water that falls as rain nourishes and sustains it and them. They feel keenly that they should not be deprived of the natural resources, such as water, that go along with the land (Haddad, 2007; Aliewi and Assaf, 2003). The Palestinians have strong feelings about the need for recognition of their just claims to their "water rights," particularly in relation to the ground waters of the Mountain Aquifer under the land that will form part of the future Palestinian state. They also have claims to a portion of the Jordan River, some of whose water they utilized prior to the Israeli occupation in 1967 and more of which would have been allocated to them in the West Bank under the proposed Johnston Plan of 1956 (Soffer, 1994; Wishart, 1990).

In general, the Palestinians claim priority rights to complete and total control of the "Palestinian waters" of the Mountain Aquifer. They reject expensive schemes to desalinate seawater in Israel for their use or to import water from other nations, as proposed by Israel, which would be under Israeli management and control. They fear that such projects would perpetuate Israeli control over vital water supplies, which would deprive them of true independence. The Palestinians hold that, if Israel wanted to, it could develop such projects as desalination on its own and in return should forgo claims to the local, easily accessible, "Palestinian" water sources to be found under the land of the Palestinian state which will be established in the West Bank. The Palestinians see the return of their *water rights*, together with the return of their land, as one of the most important issues in the establishment of their national identity and independence under the future Palestinian state.

At this point, a translation of a poignant quote from the Talmud might be appropriate to illustrate the Palestinians' strongly held position:

> The dove said to God on return to Noah's Ark – I would rather eat the bitter fruit of the olive branch I plucked myself from the bosom of God's earth than the sweet honey offered me by human hands which make me dependent on their good will.
>
> *(Eiruvin 18.2)*

The Palestinians would rather use the natural, "God-given" ground water that will be expensive to pump up from deep under their own land than receive desalinated water pumped to them through Israeli-controlled pipes.

Israel's major claims and concerns

Israel claims that it has legitimate riparian water rights to that portion of the Mountain Aquifer's natural water flow currently used within the recognized international borders of Israel, based on the principle of *prior or historic* use according to the spirit of international water law. It rejects the claim that it has "mined" or "stolen" the waters of the Mountain Aquifer from the Palestinians, and points out that major portions of that water have always flowed naturally underground into its territory and eventually into the sea. This flow has been developed by early Jewish residents and by the state of Israel at great expense and has been fully utilized over some 80–100 years. These waters are currently used to meet vital human, social, and economic needs in Israel. It is Israel's view that depriving its people of this water would cause significant and appreciable harm, which is against the principles and spirit of international water law.

Israel's official governmental position, as expressed publicly on a number of occasions, is that it will not relinquish to the Palestinians any of the natural waters of the Mountain Aquifer or other sources that it is currently using and has used historically. However, Israel has stated that it is prepared to offer the Palestinians significant options for additional water from its new desalination plants along the coast and other possible new sources of cooperatively developed water projects. In fact, Israel has already allocated some 50 million cubic meters per year (MCM/yr) of additional water to the Palestinians.

Many Israelis are concerned that if the Palestinians achieve independence, in all or part of the West Bank, they will, once they gain physical control of the territory, insist on making good on their claim that all, or most, of the water of the shared Mountain Aquifer that is derived from rainfall within the West Bank be allocated exclusively for their own use. Israelis are concerned that this will lead to unrestricted, unlimited, and dangerous over-pumping in the feed areas of the Western and Northeastern aquifers. This fear is compounded and exacerbated in Israel's eyes by the fact that after the transfer of the Gaza Strip to the administration of the Palestine Authority, some 1,000 or more new illegal wells were dug there by Palestinian farmers, resulting in serious, uncontrolled over-exploitation and pollution of the limited Gaza Aquifer. Also, in the past few years, Palestinians have dug several hundred new, unapproved wells in the Western Aquifer areas of the West Bank under their control. Israeli water supply managers are concerned that any reduction in Israel's ability to pump from the existing wells whose source is the Mountain Aquifer, which it has historically used within Israel, will seriously reduce its ability to manage, control, and regulate its water supply needs and cause it appreciable harm.

At this point I feel it appropriate to comment on some of the harsh criticism of Israel's water policies that has been made by several Palestinian authors. While some of their comments are justified, others are incorrect and misleading. My own thoughts and the responses of Israeli officials to some of the accusations made by Palestinian and other authors are briefly are summarized as follows:

- Jewish farmers, cities, villages, and water companies have legally developed the water resources of both the Mountain and Coastal aquifers within the current internationally recognized borders of Israel with the full approval of both the Turkish and British Mandatory government authorities going back some 80–100 years, well before the occupation of the West Bank in 1967. After the establishment of Israel in 1948, based on the United Nations' decision to partition Palestine into Arab and Jewish states, water resource development intensified within the internationally recognized borders of Israel. Under the letter and spirit of international water law, this historic or prior use provides Israel with rights for the legal continued use of these waters. They flow naturally into Israel and are extracted within the borders of Israel; they have not been "stolen" from the Palestinians. International water law does not recognize that the upstream country owns or can control the water that flows into a neighboring country. For instance, Turkey, as the source country, does not own the waters of the Tigris and Euphrates rivers; and Syria and Iraq have not "stolen" Turkish water. There were few or no restrictions on Palestinian farmers and villages developing their water resources from these same shared aquifers during the Turkish and Mandatory periods, or during the period of Jordanian administration of the West Bank from 1948 to 1967. There is no basis for the claim that Israel restricted development of Palestinian wells in the areas under Jordanian administration because Israel had no authority there.

- Israel also rejects the accusation that it has totally disregarded the principle of equitable sharing of the Jordan River and other shared waters. Just the opposite, Israelis claim that, under the sponsorship of the American negotiator Ambassador Eric Johnston in 1955–1956, Israel negotiated in good faith with Syria, Lebanon and Jordan for the fair and equitable sharing of the waters of the Jordan River Basin (Soffer, 1994), a portion of which, possibly as much as 100 MCM/yr, would have been allocated to the West Bank for the Palestinians. A draft agreement for equitable shared use was reached by Johnston with all the partners at the technical level, but was rejected and torpedoed by the Arab League on political grounds since they refused to recognize Israel's right to exist and therefore to withdraw any water from the Jordan. This position was against the spirit and basic principles of international water law of equitable sharing between all riparians on joint water resources. Israel then reached an informal agreement with Jordan, sponsored by the United States, for joint extraction of water from the Jordan Basin. Jordan extracted water for the irrigation of the Jordan Valley and made *out of basin transfers* similar to those made by Israel by transporting a portion to Amman (Israel transported a portion to the Negev). As is well known, Israel and Jordan have cooperated unofficially, but effectively, since the 1960s on the shared use of the Yarmouk River. There is nothing in international water law to prevent transfer of water outside the watershed. Israel's sharing of the waters of the Jordan River with Jordan was formalized in the 1994 peace agreement between the two countries.
- The claim that the Lower Jordan is polluted is sadly quite correct. However, Israeli officials reject the claim that only waste water from Israel pollutes the Jordan River. They point out that there are numerous sources of waste-water flow from Jordan and Syria, including, at times, the sewage of Amman, which pollutes the river.
- Israeli officials and hydrologists reject the claims of some Palestinians that after 1967 Israel imposed punitive and discriminatory requirements for the licensing of new Palestinian wells in the West Bank. Actually, according to the

independent estimates of expert hydrologists, the Mountain Aquifer was fully utilized to its maximum safe yield by wells within Israel well before the occupation of the West Bank in 1967. Israel did not allow further wells to be dug *in Israel* without a specific license being obtained, and the same regulation was simply applied to Palestinians in the West Bank.

• The claim that Israel has not recognized Palestinian water rights is incorrect. Article 40 of Annex III of the Oslo II Accord of September 1995 specifically declares that "Israel recognizes Palestinian water rights in the West Bank" and states that "These rights will be settled in the permanent status agreement after the final negotiations." On the basis of this accord, Israel has increased the Palestinian share of the Mountain Aquifer by some 50 MCM/yr. However, it was agreed at that time that the exact amounts to be allocated to the Palestinians would be determined in the framework of a final peace agreement. It has been reported (Chapter 6, this volume) that during the Israeli–Palestinian peace negotiations under the auspices of President Clinton in 2000 (Camp David II) Israel made unofficial proposals to increase the Palestinian portion of shared water resources by some 180 MCM/yr, almost doubling their presently available water resources and providing a significant improvement in Palestinian quality of life. Sadly, the Palestinians withdrew from those negotiations, which essentially put an end to the possibility of increasing their share of the water resources until a final status peace agreement is reached. The possibility of a peace agreement including a resolution of the water issue may seem distant today, after the election of the Hamas government and their armed takeover of Gaza, which totally rejects negotiation with, recognition of, or peace with Israel. However, there are new reasons for hope, based on the determined initiatives of US President Barack Obama and the 2009 declaration of Israeli Prime Minister Benjamin Netanyahu in support of peace with the Palestinians based on the concept of "two states for two nations." Israel still holds that, in the framework of a peace agreement, there is a basis for a significant increase in the Palestinian share of the water resources.

• The claim that Israel is responsible for many Palestinian villages having no piped water supply is knowingly misleading and basically incorrect. During the Turkish, British, and Jordanian administrations of the West Bank, very few Palestinian villages had home water-supply systems. The Palestinian institutions sadly did not have the organizational initiative or funds to sponsor development of village water supplies and neglected the existing water-supply infrastructure. During the Israeli administration of the West Bank, more than 100 new village water supplies were constructed, infrastructure improvements were made, and thousands of families were connected to water in their homes for the first time – much more than was done under the Turkish, British, and Jordanian administrations. It is sadly true that many Palestinian villages and homes still lack a proper water supply – but this is not Israel's fault.

• Some Palestinian authors report that Israel has dug deep wells near Palestinian shallow wells, causing them to dry up. While this may have happened in a few cases, Israel compensated the affected villages with new sources of external water supply. Moreover, independent hydrological investigations point out that most such deep Israeli wells tap a lower aquifer which is separated in most cases from the shallow aquifer used by Palestinians. Israeli officials also point out that most of the complaints and accusations were made during the severe drought of 1998–1999, which resulted in many Palestinian shallow wells drying up naturally. Most of these wells resumed their normal flow after the drought ended. However, accusations of Israeli malfeasance continue to this day. In 2009 many village shallow wells dried up as a result of the severe drought that had persisted for the previous three years. The population in such villages often had no choice but to use exorbitantly expensive drinking water that was delivered in unsanitary trucks and wagons. Again, this was not Israel's fault.

- Some Palestinians blame Israel for the serious degradation of the aquifer under Gaza. The water quality there is indeed very poor, but this dates back to the days of the Egyptian administration that was in control of the Strip prior to 1967. The Egyptians allowed over-pumping which led to the intrusion of sea water and serious pollution of the ground water. Under the post-1967 Israeli administration, attempts were made to reduce the over-pumping and prevent further pollution. However, within months of Gaza being handed over to Palestine Authority control under the terms of the Oslo Accords, over 1000 illegal wells were dug by Palestinian farmers. The result was even more severe over-pumping and ground water pollution. The Palestinian Authority (PA) then made little or no attempt to address this serious pollution problem.

- Some Palestinian authors claim that a major share of the flow of the Jordan River, amounting to many hundreds of millions of cubic meters each year, belongs to the Palestinians. It is true that prior to the 1967 occupation of the West Bank by Israel, Palestinian farmers pumped limited amounts of water from the river and thus can, under international water law, claim certain prior use rights. However, according to a study by Palestinian researcher Jad Isaac (ARC, 2001), the total amount of water pumped from the Jordan by Palestinian farmers prior to 1967 was about 30 MCM/yr, rather than ten times that amount, as is claimed by other authors.

In light of the above-mentioned claims, counter-claims, and fears of the interested parties, which at first sight seem irreconcilable, what can be done to resolve this conflict? Let us examine the issues in more detail and look for possible solutions.

The water resources of the area

Five riparians share the water resources of the Jordan River Basin: Syria, Lebanon, Jordan, Israel, and the PA. Based on my earlier estimates (Shuval, 2000), those from recent World Bank reports and other sources, the 2009 per capita availability of natural fresh water resources is approximately as follows: Lebanon: 1000 cubic meters/person/year; Syria: 800 cubic meters/person/year; Jordan: 200 cubic meters/person/year; Israel: 240 cubic meters/person/year; PA: 70 cubic meters/ person/year. Clearly, then, the Palestinians suffer from the most severe water shortages of the five riparians in the Jordan River Basin. As a result of the severe drought during 2006–2009, the availability of good-quality water resources in Israel has fallen by an estimated 20–30 percent. There has been a major cutback in water allocations to farmers. The same degree of reduction of water resources has affected the other riparians in the Jordan River Basin. This has had particularly severe effects on the already water-short Palestinians.

In my view, the issue of the final, rightful reallocation or redivision of shared water resources between Israelis and Palestinians must be resolved in a final peace agreement between the sides and involves the waters of both the Mountain Aquifer and the Jordan River.

I shall deal first with the question of the Mountain Aquifer (see Figure 5.1), the major portion of the recharge area of which lies under the occupied territories of the West Bank.[1] These waters flow naturally underground into Israeli territory both to the northeast and to the west, where major portions of the ground water have been utilized by Jewish/Israeli farmers through springs, and wells going back some 80–100 years, within what are now the internationally recognized borders of Israel.

Hopefully, on the resumption of the peace process, a Palestinian–Israeli agreement will be achieved based on the concept of "two states for two nations," which is a concept supported by the majority in both nations. Based on that hypothesis, I shall assume that an independent Palestinian state will eventually evolve in areas of the West Bank. It is apparent that the Mountain Aquifer will thus be considered, under the spirit of international law, as a shared body of trans-boundary ground water. There will be negotiations between the partners with claims and counter-claims by both sides, as detailed briefly above, as to its future utilization and control, which must be resolved if a lasting peace agreement is to be achieved. International law experts have pointed out that prior to the Israeli occupation of the Jordanian-administered areas of the West Bank in 1967, both the Jordan River and the Mountain Aquifer were considered to be trans-boundary water resources. Thus, neither partner can claim *total* control or ownership of these shared waters.

The Mountain Aquifer

The Mountain Aquifer covers the central area of the West Bank and portions of Israel on both sides of the mountain range, and extends generally from the Jezreal Valley (near Afula) in the north to the Beersheba Valley in the south, and from the foot-hills of the Judean Mountains near the Mediterranean in the west to the Jordan River in the east (see Figure 5.1).

Historic Palestinian use of the Mountain Aquifer waters

A detailed and accurate inventory of the historic Palestinian Arab use of the waters of the Mountain Aquifer prior to 1967 is beyond the scope of this chapter.

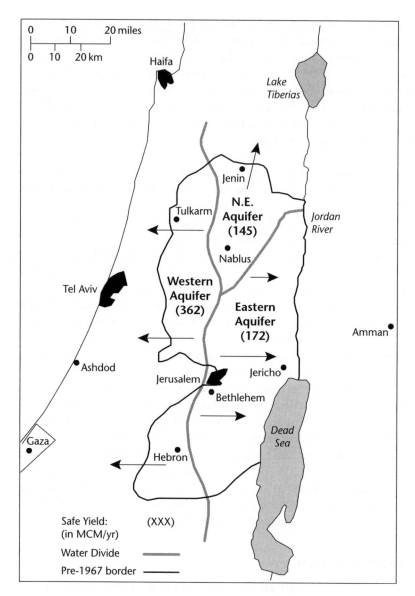

FIGURE 5.1 Schematic presentation of the Mountain Aquifer

Source: Shuval 1992a

However, some qualitative descriptions based on estimates of past use are presented (Shuval 1992a, 1992b).

The early use of the Western Aquifer by the Palestinian Arab population was limited to a part of the flow of springs, such as those at Rosh Ha-Ayin and the Tanninim, as well as some traditional shallow dug wells in the Qalqiliya and Tulkarm areas, estimated at some 25–30 MCM/yr. It is estimated that as a result of new wells dug by Palestinians in these areas in recent years, their total exploitation of the Western Aquifer in 2009 was about 40 MCM/yr. Other Palestinian Arab wells and springs prior to 1967 utilized some of the ground water in the Nablus, Bet-Shean area from the Northeastern Aquifer, amounting to about 25 MCM/yr.

The Palestinian use of the water from springs and wells in the Eastern Aquifer was relatively well developed prior to 1967, as is confirmed by the extensive Palestinian agriculture that developed in the Jordan Valley area. The total water withdrawal by Palestinians from the Eastern Aquifer is estimated at about 60 MCM/yr, of which 20 MCM/yr is brackish.

Prior to the 1967 occupation of the West Bank by Israel, Palestinian farmers also pumped water for irrigation from a number of sites along the Jordan River. This was ended by the Israeli authorities after the occupation. According to a study by Jad Isaac, prior to 1967 Palestinian farmers irrigated some 3,000 hectares with water extracted from the Jordan River (ARC, 2001). Based on the prevailing irrigation demands of agriculture at the time, that equates to about 30 MCM/yr of water extracted from the Jordan River by Palestinian farmers.

There is no evidence of major official constraints on the development and utilization of the natural water resources of the Mountain Aquifer or Jordan River by the Palestinian Arab population living in the West Bank under the Ottoman, British or Jordanian administrations from the turn of the twentieth century to the end of the Jordanian administration of the area in 1967. However, during this period, intensive Arab development of the ground water resources of the Mountain Aquifer would have required investment in hydro-geological investigation and modern deep well drilling technology costing more than was available to individual Palestinian landowners, farmers, villages or even municipalities. Thus, from a histori-cal perspective, it appears that the relatively limited Palestinian Arab development of the water resources of the Mountain Aquifer up to 1967 was mainly done by local farmers and villages who were restricted by lack of organization, planning and economic resources. This is one possible explanation for the fact that, up to 1967, prior to the Israeli occupation, the Palestinian exploitation of the waters of the Mountain Aquifer within the West Bank amounted to less than 20 percent of the potential.

After the occupation, Israel did not allow any significant further utilization of the aquifer by the Palestinians. This ruling was based on the Israeli hydrological perspective that, in effect, the aquifer was already being pumped and exploited to its full safe yield and that any further pumping in the West Bank or Israel itself would lead to a dangerous lowering of the water table and eventual intrusion of sea water along the coast, which would result in serious pollution of the water used by both peoples.

However, under the terms of the Oslo Agreement, Israel has supplied some 50 MCM/yr of additional fresh water exclusively for domestic and urban use to West Bank communities and some 5 MCM/yr to communities in the Gaza Strip.

Historic Israeli use of the Mountain Aquifer waters

Prior to the establishment of the state of Israel in 1948 and going back some 80–100 years, Jewish farmers in the Jordan Valley, Bet Shan, the Jezrael Valley, Hadera, Petach Tikva, the Yarkon River and other areas were already utilizing a significant portion of the safe yield of the Mountain Aquifer from springs, rivers and deep wells. These significant early water extractions were mainly made by private Jewish farmers, villages, the Mekorot Water Company and other locally organized initiatives, all of which had received official approval by the relevant governmental authorities of the period (Blass, 1960).

In 1921 the British Mandatory government granted Mr. Pinchas Ruttenberg, a Jewish engineer, an exclusive concession for the use of the waters of the Yarkon River – one of two natural outlets of the Western Aquifer. His company, which eventually became the Israel Electric Company, was also granted an exclusive concession on the waters of the Jordan and Yarmouk rivers in 1923, which led to the organized utilization of those waters for power generation and irrigation up to 1948. The intensive exploitation of the Mountain Aquifer was initiated by the early Jewish farmers, starting in about 1900, and included pumping from the Yarkon River to irrigate extensive orange groves in the area between Tel Aviv and Petach Tikva as well as numerous drilled wells in the Hadera area (Blass, 1960). The British Mandatory government also tapped the Rosh Ha-Ayin Springs as the source of the water supply for Jerusalem, populated by both Arabs and Jews.

The remainder of the aquifer's potential was developed mainly by Israel within its borders between 1948 and 1965. The main Israeli water project utilizing the aquifer was the Yarkon–Negev Pipeline, completed in 1954, which pumped some 200 MCM/yr to the south, which is essentially the total flow of the Rosh Ha-Ayin Springs. Today the Mountain Aquifer is tapped by about 300 hundred wells located to the west of the Green Line – that is, within the recognized international boundaries of Israel. In effect, by 1967, prior to Israel's occupation of the West Bank, Israel was utilizing some 80 percent of the potential of the Western and Northeastern aquifers within the borders of Israel.

Israeli exploitation of the Mountain Aquifer within the West Bank

Since the Israeli occupation of 1967, Israel has drilled numerous new wells in the Mountain Aquifer within the area of the West Bank, mainly to supply water to the new Israeli settlements but with some also going to Palestinian communities. Official, verifiable information on the exact amount of water withdrawn by Israel from within the West Bank Aquifer is not available, but unofficial Palestinian estimates suggest that it may be about 30–40 MCM/yr from the Eastern Aquifer and another 20–35 MCM/yr from the Western and Northeastern aquifers, for an estimated total of some 50–75 MCM/yr.

The Palestinians claim that *any* water extracted from within the West Bank for Israeli civilian settlements is illegal and in violation of the Geneva Convention concerning the rights and obligations of what is defined as the "belligerent occupier" (El-Hindi, 1990). Eminent Israeli law professor Eyal Benvenisti (1994) supports this interpretation of international water law.

From this rough analysis, based partially on some official sources from the Israel Hydrological Service (personal communication with Professor Amos Bein, 2005; Chaklai, 2004; Goldberger, 1992) and some unofficial estimates (Shuval 1992a, 1992b), it would appear that the estimated potential safe yield of the Mountain Aquifer is about 680–700 MCM/yr, about 500–550 MCM/yr of which is derived from the Western and Northeastern aquifers. Of this, some 350–400 MCM/yr (70–80 percent) is now and has been utilized within Israel's borders prior to 1967, with part of its use going back some 80–100 years. Some 150 MCM/yr is currently used by the Palestinians, while it is estimated that another 50–75 MCM/yr may be pumped by Israel from new wells drilled since 1967 within the West Bank for use mainly by the new Israeli civilian settlements there. It is estimated that there may be another 50–100 MCM/yr of unutilized water in the Eastern Aquifer, which might be tapped by the Palestinians as sweet water through deep wells. Some of these wells, such as those at Herodian, have already been drilled, albeit with mixed success. As mentioned above, the severe drought of 2006–2009 has resulted in an estimated reduction of some 20–30 percent in the available water resources.

The possibility of additional sources of untapped water in the Eastern Aquifer is specifically mentioned in the Oslo II Agreement and is estimated at 100 MCM/yr as potential supplemental water supplies for the Palestinians. However, the amount of water potentially available from this source remains unverified and may be only half that amount. In addition, Israel delivers some 50 MCM/yr to West Bank municipalities for domestic and urban use only, in accordance with the Oslo Agreement.

The Palestinians now pump some 100 MCM/yr or more from the Gaza Aquifer. However, this source has an estimated long-term safe yield of only 60 MCM/yr and consequently suffers from severe over-pumping and degradation. Much of it is unfit for use as drinking water. The Israeli settlements in Gaza pumped an additional 5 MCM/yr or more. These wells reverted to the Palestinians on the withdrawal of the Israeli settlements in the summer of 2005. This set an important precedent of Israel returning water resources to the Palestinians. In addition, Israel has offered to sell the water-short Palestinians in Gaza significant amounts of drinking-quality water derived from Israel's first major desalination plant in Ashkelon, a short distance north of Gaza, which was completed at the end of 2006.

The total estimated available water in the West Bank and Gaza for the Palestinians from the local aquifers in 2009 is thus estimated at about 250 MCM/yr. And there may be an additional 50 MCM/yr in undeveloped sources in the Eastern Aquifer. Due to the recent severe drought, though, these estimates are probably 20–30 percent too high. For the already water-short Palestinians, the effects of this drought have therefore been severe.

The role of international water law

International water law today is based primarily on the 1997 United Nations Convention: "Law of the Non-Navigational Uses of International Water Courses." However, relatively few countries have signed and ratified this convention, and it has not as yet been formally activated, since this requires ratification by thirty-five nations. It is therefore not binding in any way. Nevertheless, it is considered the main guiding spirit of international water law at this time. Many question whether this document applies to ground water, but Daibes-Murad (2005), an expert on international water law, points out that it does apply to some extent. International law experts and negotiators are also aware of the convention's principles and tend to refer to them when sitting at the negotiating table. Two of these principles merit further discussion:

- to assure *equitable utilization of the water resources among all the riparians on an international water course* with priority given to meeting *vital human needs*, particularly for domestic and urban water, above and beyond hydrological, geographic, prior use and geopolitical considerations;
- not to cause significant or appreciable harm to other riparian states.

The basic and overriding principle of *equitable utilization* of water resources among the riparians on an international water course is a deeply embedded principle of the spirit of international water law drawn from the earlier and widely accepted Helsinki Rules of 1976. It has also been reinforced by the recently drafted "Berlin Rules" of the International Law Association (2004), which have reconfirmed and expanded the *equitable utilization* concept. While Article 13 of the Berlin Rules ("Determining an Equitable and Reasonable Use") lists a number of relevant factors that should be considered, Article 14 ("Preference among Uses") specifically states: "In determining an equitable and reasonable use, states should first allocate water to satisfy *vital human needs.*" Here it must be emphasized that experts in international law have pointed out that the term "equitable utilization" of shared water resources does not mean *equal* utilization among the parties. It has been generally accepted that it means *fair and reasonable utilization*. Parties must negotiate and reach agreement on what is a fair, reasonable and politically acceptable allocation or utilization of their shared water resources. When such an agreement is reached and accepted by both sides, then it is considered fair and reasonable, as well as equitable, under law.

Experts in international law have come to the following conclusions. There is no legal basis in international water law for the claims of some nations that they have *sole and exclusive rights* over the use of water derived from sources within their territory. The upstream country merely has rights to an *equitable shared use* of the water. The Syrian and Iraqi claims for their continued use of the waters of the Tigris and Euphrates rivers that originate in Turkey are therefore fully accepted under international law. Similarly, the claim that Syria has absolute rights to all the waters of the Jordan River, which rises in Syria, and that Israel, one of the downstream users, has none would not be accepted as being in compliance with international water law. As one final example, Egypt has fully recognized rights under international law for its continued use of the waters of the Nile, which originate entirely in upstream countries.

Likewise, international law does recognize the legitimacy of *prior or historic use rights*, but the claim that prior and historic use assures immutable and sole water rights is also not absolute in terms of international water law. Modern concepts of international water law, which emphasize the requirement of *equitable sharing among all the riparians* with priority given to meeting *vital human needs* for domestic and urban water use in a trans-boundary water basin, mean both the upstream source countries and downstream historic users have obligations to their neighbors.

Thus, based on modern principles of international water law, both the historic riparian rights of Israel (as the downstream user) and the rights of the Palestinians (as the upstream party on a shared body of water) must be considered on the basis of equity, fairness and *vital human needs* (Shuval, 1992a; Daibes–Murad, 2005). Both parties to the conflict would be expected, in the first instance, to negotiate directly between themselves to arrive at a settlement based on the principles of equitable shared use rather than to enter a confrontational litigation in the expectation that some supra-governmental authority would enforce a judgment based on what each side views as its legitimate water rights. In the one case of this type, brought before the International Court of Justice by Hungary and Austria and based on their conflicting claims of water rights, the Court ruled that the dispute should be returned to the two sides, who should resolve it through direct negotiations (Wolf, 1997). In the final analysis, the Palestinians and the Israelis will therefore have to determine, through direct negotiations between themselves, what they consider to be fair, just, reasonable and equitable sharing of their common water resources in order to meet vital human needs. Their joint decision will then become a binding part of the final status peace agreement.

Estimating the legitimate water needs of the two parties: the minimum water requirement (MWR) needed for water security

In an attempt to determine the legitimate minimum reasonable water requirements of the parties to meet vital human needs, as called for in the Berlin Rules of the International Law Association, I have estimated the amount of water required to ensure an acceptable level of health and hygiene, sustainability and a reasonable standard of living in an arid area. It can be assumed that the parties in the dispute will each ultimately require, as a minimum degree of water security to meet vital human needs, access (mainly from within their territories) to adequate, reasonable, and equitable supplies of good-quality drinking water, which is required for human health and welfare.

In 1992 I formulated the concept of the minimum water requirement (MWR), which is an estimate of an optimum reasonable amount of good-quality water to meet vital human needs for drinking and domestic use, but also includes the good-quality water essential for all urban, commercial and industrial needs to ensure the welfare, survival and livelihood of the population in the arid Middle East, excluding agriculture (Shuval 1992a, 1994). Based on my studies, I recommended an MWR of some 125 cubic meters/person/year. This figure can be considered as a *long-term aspiration and goal* which should eventually be achieved by the Palestinians and the other riparians in the Jordan River Basin over the next twenty to thirty years, on an egalitarian basis, as economic development progresses and standards of living advance.

This water usage is the current level of water demand in the domestic/urban sector (including industry) in Israel, which assures a good, hygienic standard of domestic and urban life and sufficient water to assure a livelihood for *human survival and sustenance* of the population in commerce, trade and industry (Braverman, 1994). It is also the level of domestic/urban sector water use in several European countries that enjoy acceptably high standards of domestic hygiene, sustainability and economic life. (In the United States domestic/urban water demands are greater, averaging some 180–200 cubic meters/person/year.) In meeting vital human needs, as demanded by the spirit of international water law, the MWR includes water for domestic use as well as drinking-quality water for all other urban uses to assure a livelihood, including commerce, trade, services, industry and tourism, but excludes agriculture. It is reasonable to assume that this level of urban sector water consumption can be maintained long into the future if coupled with sound measures of water conservation.

Today, Palestinian domestic/urban use is generally at a much lower level than 125 cubic meters/person/year, due to water shortages and/or inadequate water supply infrastructure, as well as to such socio-economic factors as small, crowded homes that lack full-time water supply. In many cases Palestinian domestic water use does not even meet the minimum for hygienic standards recommended by the World Health Organization of 100 liters/person/day (about 37 cubic meters/person/year). Braverman (1994), in his report to the World Bank, estimated that, in the future, as Palestinian socio-economic conditions improve, the population's water requirements for domestic/urban and commercial use will be similar to that of Israel – about 100 cubic meters/person/year.

Some have claimed that it is naive and unrealistic to assume that the Palestinians will eventually achieve the same standard of living and the same level of domestic/urban water consumption as Israel. However, there is firm evidence that in well-established, middle-class Palestinian urban neighborhoods, such as Shoafat, near Jerusalem, they have *already* achieved a similar level of socio-economic development.

The MWR should be a goal and a target to be achieved, in phases, based on the assumption that all the nations in the Jordan River Basin will eventually reach similar socio-economic levels and will require at least the MWR on an egalitarian and socially just basis. A number of Israeli, Palestinian and international water experts have accepted the MWR concept as providing a fair basis for evaluating eventual vital human needs and for cooperation between Israelis and Palestinians and the other riparians in the Jordan River Basin (Assaf *et al.*, 1993; Braverman, 1994).

However, official Israeli and Palestinian authorities have, to date, not accepted the MWR formulation. In the drafting of a Palestinian–Israeli peace agreement, it would be socially and economically important to ensure that the Palestinians have available to them sufficient good-quality water resources at least to achieve the World Health Organization recommended minimum daily domestic/urban supply.

Water allocations for agriculture, nature, ecology and future urban–industrial development are not included in the MWR estimate, but significant additional quantities can be made available for these sectors from recycled, purified municipal waste water, which is estimated at 65 percent of the urban water supply (see Table 5.1). The Israelis do not have sufficient natural sources of water to meet their own long-term water needs and cannot be expected to meet those of the Palestinians. After the total utilization of all sources of local good-quality drinking water from natural sources, the further water needs of both the Israelis and the Palestinians will therefore have to be met by water recycling and reuse, desalination of brackish water or seawater, and development of regional projects for the importation of water in an era of peace, such as those proposed by Kally (1990).

Since it is difficult, if not impossible, to plan for all future developments and population growth, it is suggested that the estimated MWR needs of the riparians for a twenty-year period should be used as the basis for a peace agreement which will provide for rightful reallocations or redivision of resources that will assure a reasonable period of water security, economic development, sustainability and social stability. As an illustration, it might be estimated that in twenty years from the time of writing (the year 2030), Israel will have a population of about 10 million and the Palestinians about 6 million. On the basis of these estimates, Table 5.1 outlines how much water will be needed to meet vital human water needs. It is assumed that 65 percent of urban water supplies will be treated and recycled for use in agricultural, industrial, nature, ecology and urban non-potable reuse, providing extra supply of water from local sources.

Assuming that the Palestinians will ultimately be able to access and utilize some 300 MCM/yr from within the West Bank and Gaza, including the as yet unexploited water resources in the Eastern Aquifer, it is apparent that they will still fall

TABLE 5.1 Estimated Israeli and Palestinian minimum water requirements (MWR)

	A	B	C	D
	Population (millions)	MWR MCM/ yr fresh water	Recycled MCM/ yr (65 percent of B)	Total (B+C) MCM/ yr fresh + recycled
Palestinians	6	750	490	1240
Israelis	10	1250	810	2060
Totals	16	2000	1300	3300

Note: MWR = 125 cubic meters/person/year in 2030 for domestic/urban/commercial/industrial water supply.

a long way short of their projected MWR needs of 750 MCM/yr. So how might this potential disaster be averted?

Increasing the Palestinians' share of water resources

Equitable reallocation or redivision of water currently utilized by Israel

Without entering into the question of Israel's strong claims of water rights to that portion of the Mountain Aquifer that it has used historically, it will undoubtedly be urged to consider negotiating an agreement on the equitable shared use of the natural flow of that aquifer with the Palestinians in order to reach an accommodation and help meet some of the latter's vital human needs in the framework of the final peace agreement. Israel will be expected to find an appropriate way to meet the strong Palestinian demands and expectations for increased allocation or redivision of the natural waters of the Mountain Aquifer available within the borders of the future Palestinian state. At this time, however, Israel officially opposes any such reallocation. Likewise, the Palestinians claim water rights for all, or almost all, of the rainwater falling over the Mountain Aquifer and for a portion of the flow of the Jordan River, which was allocated to Palestinians living in the West Bank under the terms of the Johnston Plan (Shuval, 2003).

It would be prudent for both parties to accept the spirit of international water law, which calls for agreement to be reached through negotiation for equitable sharing to meet vital human needs, rather than to become embroiled in endless and irreconcilable arguments and litigations about whose claims to water rights are stronger, in the hope or expectation that some external body or court will rule in their favor.

The equitable reallocation or redivision and sharing of some of Israel's current use of the Mountain Aquifer water supply might be one way for the Palestinians to meet a portion of their MWR needs for drinking water and domestic/urban sector usage. Israel's official policy is not to share these waters with the Palestinians, but I have advocated that it is in Israel's best interests to share some of its current water resources, even though they are limited, with the Palestinians, so that the latter are able not only to survive but to thrive economically and socially (Shuval 1992a, 1992b). Promoting a fair and equitable resolution of the water conflict between Israel and the Palestinians should and must be a cornerstone of a permanent peace agreement. In addition, I believe that only an economically and socially strong Palestine can become a good neighbor, living in peace alongside Israel.

However, since I do not represent the Israeli government or the official water authorities, I can only offer advice. Without going into the details, I feel that, at best, reallocation of Israel's existing water use will meet only *part* of the Palestinians' MWR up to the year 2030. Israel does not have enough water to meet *its own* MWR for the year 2030, let alone that of the Palestinians. Since we are assuming a *fair* basis for water sharing, Israel's MWR must be considered equally with that of the Palestinians. So it is clear that *additional, external sources* will be required to meet Palestinian and Israeli MWR for 2030.

Nevertheless, I would recommend to the Israeli authorities that they should agree to relinquish some of their current use of the Mountain Aquifer, and agree to an increase in the *equitable reallocation or redivision* of the Palestinians' share of the water of the Western and Northeastern aquifers. In the first instance, Israel should relinquish all of the water it has been pumping since 1967 from those areas of the West Bank from which it withdraws under the terms of any final status peace agreement. That amount is unofficially estimated at some 75 MCM/yr. Israel will have a weak case if it claims prior or historic use of that water, and its legal "right" under international water law to continue such use is extremely debatable (Benvenisti, 1994). For example, an important precedent was set by the Israeli authorities on the withdrawal of the Israeli settlements from Gaza. The wells that Israel dug there for the settlers reverted to the Palestinians. In addition, I would recommend that Israel consider forgoing the exploitation of an additional 75 MCM/yr currently pumped from the Western or Northeastern aquifers, thus increasing the Palestinian share of the Mountain Aquifer by a total of 150 MCM/yr. Israel would have to reduce its own pumping, within Israel, from the Mountain Aquifer proportionately. Further, Israel should consider reallocating an additional 50 MCM/yr to the Palestinians in the Jordan Valley, directly from the waters of the lower Jordan River. This might be seen as a symbolic recognition of the Palestinians' prior use of Jordan River water up to 1967 (ARC, 2001), usage that Israel currently blocks. Thus, the total increase for the Palestinians from previously utilized or controlled Israeli sources would be 200 MCM/yr, or some 45 percent of the additional estimated amount needed to meet the Palestinian MWR for the year 2030. That additional water allocated for domestic/urban use would, however, go a long way toward alleviating the urgent Palestinian need for more water over the next ten–fifteen years, and would comfortably meet the World Health Organization's minimum water requirements.

This additional availability of good-quality water for the Palestinians might eventually be increased by water allocations from other neighboring countries that are prepared to share the waters of the Jordan River Basin, as well as by desalination, water recycling and regional water projects.

With the proposed reallocation or redivision of 200 MCM/yr of Israel's use of shared water resources, Israel itself will be left with just about its own MWR of 125 cubic meters/person/year. It therefore cannot be expected to reallocate any more than that.

Here, it should be noted that the official Israeli proposal for increasing the water resources of the Palestinians is to make available to them, at cost, the output of one or more of the major new seawater desalination plants located along the Israeli coast, such as the one planned for Hedera, which would produce some 150 MCM/yr.

However, during the Camp David II negotiations in 2000–2001, it has been reported (see Chapter 6, this volume) that Israel tentatively and unofficially offered to increase the Palestinian share of the Western Aquifer by 50 MCM/yr, the Northeastern Aquifer by 10 MCM/yr, the Eastern Aquifer by 80 MCM/yr and the Jordan River by 40 MCM/yr, meaning a total increase in the availability of water resources for the Palestinians of 180 MCM/yr. This increased water availability would have provided a significant improvement in the quality of life of the Palestinians. Regrettably, though, the Palestinians withdrew from those negotiations and no official documents have emerged to confirm that the above offer was ever made.

Proposed water sharing by Lebanon and Syria with the Palestinians, based on the principle of equitable sharing of water resources among the riparians in the Jordan River Basin

Figure 5.2 shows the estimated total water resources potential from all sources of the five Jordan River Basin riparians for the year 2000 as compared to Turkey, their water-rich contiguous neighbor, based on World Bank research, other sources and my own estimates (Shuval, 2003; Gleick, 1993). These are only rough estimates and not up-to-date; however, they more or less correctly represent the relative availability of water to each of the five riparians. It can be roughly estimated that the population of the five riparians in the Jordan River Basin will double over the next twenty–thirty years and their estimated MWRs to meet vital human needs for domestic/urban use required for a reasonable level of social and economic welfare based on 125 cubic meters/person/year will double as well.

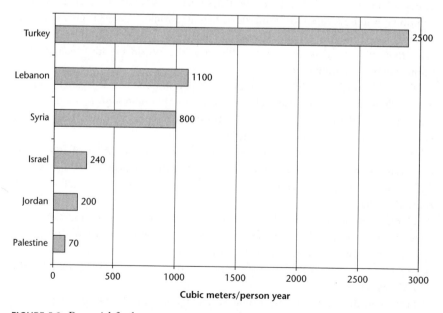

FIGURE 5.2 Potential fresh-water resources available in 2000

As previously stated, unless the Palestinians obtain significant additional water supplies, they will face the most severe water shortages by 2030, with only about 50 cubic meters/person/year for all uses, *including agriculture*. Both Israel and Jordan will be at or below the MWR red line as well. However, Syria and Lebanon, while far from water-rich countries, will, in 2030, still easily be able to meet their MWRs and will even have considerable quantities of excess water. My estimates of these excesses are 7000 MCM/yr for Syria and 3000 MCM/yr for Lebanon (Shuval, 2003). Even if only half of those amounts are available, giving a total excess of 5000 MCM/yr, there is little question that both the Syrians and Lebanese will have much more water available to them per person than will the Palestinians, and by a significant factor. As stated previously, the overriding principle of international water law is *equitable sharing of water resources among the riparians* on a shared international water course, giving priority to meeting *vital human needs*, in particular the urgent requirements for drinking water and other domestic/urban needs for human health and welfare.

Thus, in approaching the equitable allocation of the waters of the Jordan River Basin in the spirit of international water law, it is only right, socially just and correct first to evaluate the absolute minimum vital human needs to meet the requirements of social and economic welfare of *all* the riparians and to ensure that each receives a fair and equitable share, at least to meet their vital human needs. It can then be argued that those riparians faced with severe water needs should be assisted by those riparians with more plentiful reserves. From the estimates of MWR for the year 2030 (Table 5.1), it is clear that the Palestinians will be faced with the most severe water shortages and will not be able to survive without assistance from their neighbors, including those in the Jordan River Basin. Only two nations – Syria and Lebanon, the upstream Arab neighbors of the future state of Palestine – will have water reserves above and beyond those required to meet their own minimum MWRs. In the year 2030 Israel will be just able to meet its own MWR; it will have no water reserves to spare. The situation in Jordan may be even worse.

On the assumption that Israel will reallocate to the Palestinians some 200 MCM/yr, this will meet some 45 percent of the Palestinians' water needs for the year 2030. If Syria and Lebanon then agree that an increased share of the flow of the Jordan and Yarmouk rivers should be supplied directly to the Palestinians to meet the remaining 55 percent, that will necessitate an annual reallocation of some 250 MCM/yr – less than 1 percent of these two countries' total available water resources.

Surely it is reasonable to expect Syria and Lebanon to work toward assuring equitable water sharing to meet the vital human needs of the water-short Palestinians, a brother Arab nation, who are the least fortunate of the Jordan Basin riparians. Such a reallocation of water to the Palestinians from the upper Jordan River could be seen as a symbolic recognition of the water allocation to the Palestinians on the West Bank through the West Ghor Canal that was proposed by the Johnston Plan of 1956 (Soffer, 1994; Wishart, 1990). Lebanon and Syria could easily be even more generous, and could assist the Palestinians with their water needs well beyond 2030 in the framework of regional water development projects such as the Al Wachda–Unity Dam project being developed with Jordan or the utilization of water from the Litani and Awali rivers in Lebanon (Kally, 1990).

The ideas and concept presented above are, of course, personal and may indeed be a truly unconventional approach to the concept of equitable sharing of the water resources of the Jordan River Basin. However, in my view, it is entirely within the spirit and principles of international water law that those countries with more plentiful water resources come to the assistance of their less fortunate neighbors in the same international water basin. The basis for a just and lasting peace among the riparians of the Jordan River Basin must be based on accepting the legitimacy of each of the partners and their rights to an equitable share of the water. The reallocation of the water should be based on an objective analysis of the vital human water needs of each and the ability of those with more plentiful resources to assist those in need. Israel cannot do this alone; but together with a minimal reallocation of water from Lebanon and Syria, all of the most urgent Palestinian water needs up to 2030 *can* be met. This is not a utopian dream.

Can or will Israel agree to a reallocation of the natural water resources it currently uses?

The recently published study by Professor Frank Fisher of MIT and Israeli, Palestinian and Jordanian water experts and economists provides an insightful and persuasive economic approach to the issue of whether Israel will or should reallocate water to the Palestinians (Fisher *et al.*, 2005). The following quotes from that study need little elaboration:

> Water is a scarce resource. Scarce resources have value. And the value of water in dispute is bounded above by the replacement cost given by desalination . . . No matter how much you value water, you cannot rationally value it more than the cost of replacing it. Hence the availability of seawater desalination places an upper bound on what water can be worth on the seacoast . . . Such desalination costs roughly $US0.50–0.60/cubic meter at the seacoast. The cost of extracting water from the Mountain Aquifer and supplying it to cities on the seacoast is roughly $0.40/cubic meter. Thus it follows that ownership of Mountain Aquifer water can never be worth more than about $0.20/cubic meter ($0.60-$0.40). If the amount of Mountain Aquifer water in dispute between the Israelis and Palestinians is 100–200 MCM/yr then . . . It follows that 100–200 MCM/yr of Mountain Aquifer water can never be worth more than $20–$40 million per year . . . the sums involved are trivial when compared to Israel's gross domestic product of $100 billion per year. The value of the water in dispute is not sufficient to obstruct a peace treaty, nor is it large enough to be worth a war.
>
> (Fisher et al., 2005: xiii–xvii)

It should be noted that the water conflict is possibly more easily resolved than many of the other issues since it is one of the few issues (perhaps the only issue) in the

Israeli–Palestinian conflict where a concession by Israel can be fully compensated for by the purchase of an alternative. Israel, if it decides to do so, can replace any water reallocated to the Palestinians from unlimited sources of desalinated seawater at a reasonable price. Most of the other key areas of dispute – borders, the holy places, Jerusalem, refugees and so on – are much more intractable.

The much-needed resolution of the water issue can be obtained only in the framework of an overall peace settlement. Within the framework of an overall package deal for peace based on a two-state solution, I believe that there can be a just and equitable reallocation of water for the Palestinians. All recent surveys indicate that the majority of Palestinians and Israelis support a peace agreement based on a two-state solution for two nations, despite the many existing tensions. However, sadly, the leaderships of both nations at present seem either incapable or unwilling to fulfill their people's dreams for peace, perhaps because they know that these will involve painful compromises by both sides.

Note

1   The terms "occupied territories" and "West Bank" refer to areas formerly administered by the Hashemite Kingdom of Jordan, which were occupied by Israel in response to being attacked by Jordan in 1967. This area is called the West Bank by Jordan and the Palestinians who live there, since it was thought of as the west bank of the Jordan while the remainder of the Hashemite Kingdom of Jordan was the east bank of that river. It is known by its ancient biblical name of Judea and Samaria in official Israel government sources. In this chapter I refer to the area as the West Bank, in accordance with the terminology of the Oslo Agreements and international usage.

6

PALESTINE WATER

Between challenges and realities

Amjad Aliewi, Enda O'Connell, Geoff Parkin, and Karen Assaf

Introduction

The Millennium Development Goals, approved by 189 countries in September 2000, and the Johannesburg Plan of Implementation, adopted in 2002 by the World Summit for Sustainable Development, emphasize the need to reduce inequalities, to change unsustainable consumption, to protect and sustainably manage natural resources for economic and social development, and to safeguard health. However, in the case of Palestine, the historic balance between water demand and supply has been artificially constrained by non-market forces. Thus, it is necessary to plan for and develop more equitable, yet feasible, future water consumption rates and supply capabilities for needed social and economic development. The development and management of water resources in Palestine is complex due to the above-mentioned hydro-political constraints, scarcity of water, and the need to put in place sustainable development policies in the water sector. In this context, it is foreseen that the stability of the final status agreement on water between Israel and Palestine will be assured only if the Palestinians achieve their water rights. In addition to the scarcity of water resources under the political constraints imposed by Israel, the protection of the water resource environment is a constraint that makes it difficult to develop sustainable demand/supply scenarios in Palestine, which does not seem to be heading toward a clear socio-economic future. With additional Palestinian water rights and control over their own water resources in the West Bank, the quantities of water potentially available in the future could greatly alleviate the Palestinians' chronic water shortage. The current scenario that the Palestinians are following in the management and planning of their water resources is that there are water use arrangements that keep life moving – but that scenario is still unjust.

Historical background

Records show that pre-1948, Jewish and Palestinian communities in the region were consuming similar quantities of water for both domestic and agricultural purposes. With the establishment of the Armistice Line in 1949, Israel commenced restrictions on the development of wells in the area under Jordanian administration and in parallel Israeli exploitation of water resources accelerated and the water consumption gap between the Israelis and the Palestinians started to widen. In 1964, and without recognition of other riparian users' needs or rights in the Jordan River Basin, Israel implemented the first "out of basin" transfer (National Water Carrier System) of the Jordan River waters to the Negev and southern coastal areas of Israel (see Figure 6.1; Assaf, 2004). The diversion of the Jordan River possibly led to a change in the climate of the West Bank and a 50 percent reduction in the surface area of the Dead Sea, which constitutes a serious ecological, environmental, and economic problem as the lower Jordan is now only a flow of sewage and waste water from many sources of pollution.

After 1967, with the annexation of the Golan Heights and the occupation of the West Bank, Israel increased its control over both the headwaters and the lower Jordan River. This control was extended with the invasion of southern Lebanon in 1978 and the establishment of the "security zone" (which was returned to Lebanon in May 2000). Further exploitation of the resources of both the upper and lower reaches of the Jordan continued over this period with total disregard for other riparians until the peace treaty with Jordan was signed in 1994.

In recent years there have been many discussions about constructing a conveyance system between the Red Sea and Dead Sea to solve the problems created by diverting the Jordan River. At the Johannesburg Environmental Summit in 2002, the Jordanian Minister of Water suggested the Red–Dead Sea Canal project (the "Peace Canal"), with the following objectives: to protect the Dead Sea from disappearing; to desalinate some 850 million cubic meters per year (MCM/yr) of seawater; to generate 550 megawatts/year of electricity; and to develop new tourism and industrial zones.

The decline of the Dead Sea level to 417 meters below sea level and the shrinking of its surface area to 500 sq. km are serious problems that need to be addressed. Most important is the fact that this project would provide an inflow into the Dead Sea after the "unnatural" reduction of its historic flow. The total cost of this project is estimated to be US$5 billion, with $1 billion given as a grant and the remaining amount as a loan. The project would probably take nearly twenty years to implement fully, but it would provide new sources of water and energy, provided that all of its phases were completed. A pre-feasibility study has been prepared by the Jordanians, terms of reference have been prepared by the World Bank and discussed many times, and in the spring of 2005 the three parties (Jordan, Palestine, and Israel) agreed to conduct a joint feasibility study.

Meanwhile, colonization of the West Bank and Gaza was carried out through the construction of settlements. These settlements, in addition to utilizing a dispro- portionate amount of the available aquifers, discharged domestic, agricultural, and

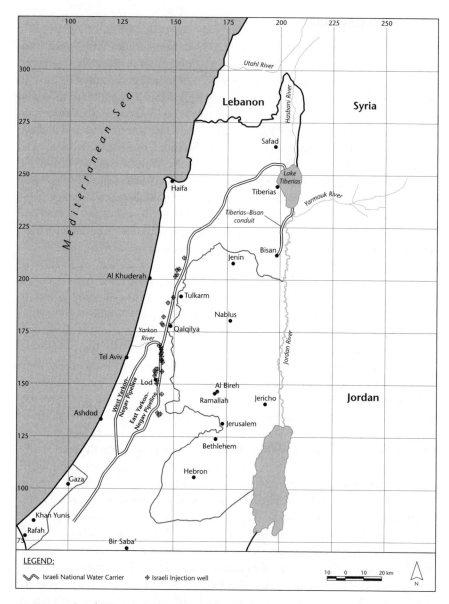

FIGURE 6.1 Israeli National Water Carrier System

industrial wastes into nearby valleys without treatment, resulting in significant harm to the environment, and creating a major threat to Palestinian water resources.

Post-1967 action was also taken to close some Palestinian wells and to place restrictions on pumping, accompanied by restrictive control through licensing, application of fixed operating quotas, and withholding of permission to deepen wells. Israel imposes facts on the ground to preserve the status quo with regard to the allocation of water resources without recognizing Palestinians' right to a greater share of these resources or compensation for consequences of inequitable allocation in the past. They do this by:

- Mining the West Bank aquifers by dense networks of wells inside the West Bank and alongside the Green Line (see Figure 6.2).
- Drilling wells to supply Israeli settlers. Unlike Palestinian wells, Israeli wells tap deeper aquifers and are equipped with more powerful pumps, and in general are more efficient than neighboring Palestinian wells. Thus, the Israeli wells have two advantages over the Palestinian wells: first, their pumping capacity is higher than that of the Palestinian wells; second, many are drilled to great depths to utilize the entire depth of the tapped aquifer (see Figure 6.3).
- The deep wells drilled by the Israeli authorities in the area have affected the level and quantity of water in Palestinian wells. The productive capacity of some of the wells has been reduced, and some springs have dried up. It is clearly shown (Figures 6.4 and 6.5) that abstractions from the Palestinian wells decreased gradually after 1968 and the wells stopped pumping altogether in 1980. This is due to the tapping of groundwater by Israeli wells.
- Putting obstacles in the way of the Palestinians to restrict their drilling of new wells to meet their future water demands.
- Controlling the utilization zones of the groundwater aquifers and openly confirming that by the recent construction of the Separation Wall.
- Intercepting groundwater before it reaches the Gaza coastal aquifer (Figure 6.2).
- Intercepting surface wadis flowing through Gaza.
- Drying up specific Palestinian springs and wells by drilling nearby deep wells for Israeli use.
- Polluting the groundwater aquifers, especially through waste from the Israeli settlements (SUSMAQ, 2001).

Progressive desertification has also taken place in the West Bank and Gaza due to the reduction of available grazing area by 50 percent, mainly as a result of the acquisition of land for settlements, military camps, and "nature reserves." Forestation programs in the West Bank and Gaza that existed during the British Mandate and Jordanian administration were stopped under the Israeli occupation and 25 percent deforestation has taken place over thirty years, mainly due to the establishment of the Israeli military camps and settlements.

The entire period from 1967 to the present day has been accompanied by the degradation of existing infrastructure and limited development in new infrastructure for water supply, sewerage, and solid waste. This has resulted in insufficient and unreliable service with poor quality and large losses in the systems. The Israeli "operator" also cut off supplies periodically, thereby discriminating unfairly between Palestinians and Israeli settlers when shortages or problems occurred, especially during periods of drought (Assaf, 2004). Consequently, the gap in water consumption between Israel and Palestine has widened from a similar utilization

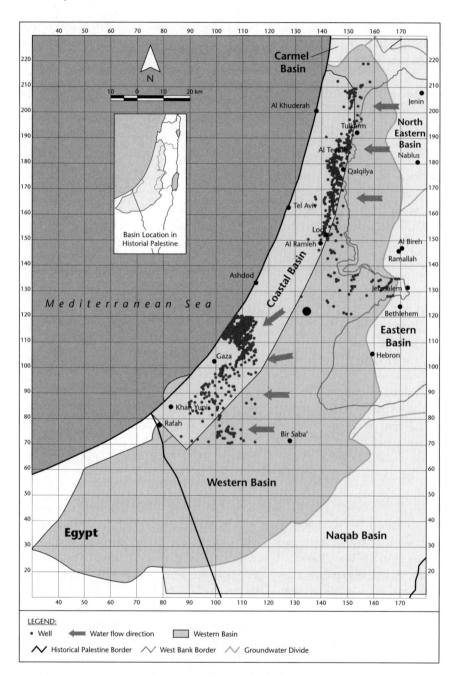

FIGURE 6.2 Israeli pumping of the West Bank and Gaza aquifers

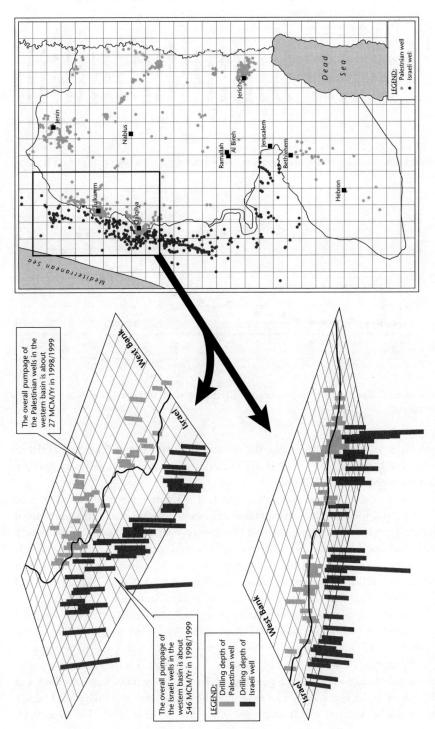

FIGURE 6.3 Deep Israeli wells and shallow Palestinian wells

Map labels:
Mediterranean Sea
Dead Sea
Jenin
Nablus
Tulkarem
Qalqilya
Ramallah
Al Bireh
Jerusalem
Bethlehem
Jericho
Hebron

LEGEND:
Palestinian well
Israeli well

West Bank
Israel

The overall pumpage of the Palestinian wells in the western basin is about 27 MCM/Yr in 1998/1999

The overall pumpage of the Israeli wells in the western basin is about 546 MCM/Yr in 1998/1999

LEGEND:
Drilling depth of Palestinian well
Drilling depth of Israeli well

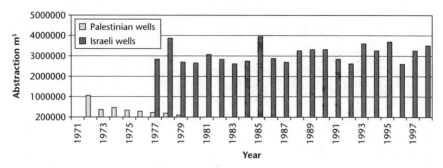

FIGURE 6.4 Abstraction from Palestinian wells compared with abstraction from nearby Israeli wells

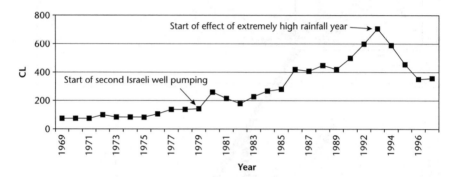

FIGURE 6.5 Water quality deterioration in Bardalah wells in response to Israeli pumping

pre-1948 to the three times-plus differential that exists today. The differential in water use between Israeli settlements and Palestinians is even more marked, being in the order of four to six times.

Not until the Declaration of Principles in 1993, ratified by the Oslo II Accord in 1995, did the principles of equitable utilization and the shared management of regional resources between Israel and Palestine receive official mention. It can only be hoped that these principles will once again become part of the negotiating agenda in the future. Effectively, Oslo II – like the Interim Agreement – permitted only a relatively small increase in the utilization of water resources by Palestinians and otherwise agreed (referred) to a status quo on other abstractions.

The two remaining areas of historical/geographical Palestine have a projected population of 3.6 million, with 2.3 million in the West Bank and 1.3 million in the Gaza Strip. These projections are based on a 1997 census that was undertaken by the Palestinian Central Bureau of Statistics. The overall natural increase or population growth in Palestine is 3.5 percent, based on 3.2 percent in the West Bank and 4 percent in the Gaza Strip. The latter may be the most densely populated region in the world, with over 3600 people per square kilometer in 2003. (The West Bank has 407 people per square kilometer.) Population increase is the fundamental para-meter affecting future water needs. This determines not only municipal demand, but agricultural demand (to feed the population) and industrial demand (to provide an economy to support the development of the population). In Palestine as a whole, more than 50 percent of the population lives in an urban environment, with 28.5 percent in rural areas and 15 percent in camps. In addition to the 3.6 million Palestinians "in" Palestine, there are over 4.5 million living outside, mostly in other Arab countries. Another 1.5 million Palestinians live inside Israel, as Israeli citizens.

Status of water resources and use in the West Bank and Gaza Strip

The existing water resources of Palestine are derived from four aquifer basins (Figure 6.6; Table 6.1) and a series of springs that emanate from the groundwater.

Tables 6.2, 6.3, and 6.4 represent the water use in Palestine for different purposes (Aliewi, 2005). Municipal, industrial, and agricultural water demands are presented in Tables 6.5, 6.6, 6.7, and 6.8. The gap between water supply and demand is presented in Table 6.9 and Figure 6.7.

Rainfall availability

The West Bank is a hilly area with variable elevations from 400 meters below sea level in the Jordan Valley to 1000 meters above sea level in the hills. The rainfall of the West Bank is strongly seasonal, mainly from October to May. Rainfall is orographic across the West Bank and generally varies from 700 mm/yr (millimeters per year) in the mountains to 100 mm/yr in the Jordan Valley. The Gaza Strip is located on the extreme edge of a shallow coastal aquifer with a total (small) area of 365 sq. km. The major source of renewable groundwater in the aquifer is rainfall, which is sporadic across Gaza and generally varies from 400 mm/yr in the north to about 200 mm/yr in the south.

TABLE 6.1 Reported aquifer basins recharge

Aquifer basin	Recharge rates (MCM/yr)
Eastern (EAB)	100–172
Northeastern (NEAB)	130–200
Western (WAB)	335–450
Gaza Coastal	55–65
Total	720–887

Source: Data based on several studies conducted by House of Water and Environment (HWE) and the Palestinian Water Authority (PWA)

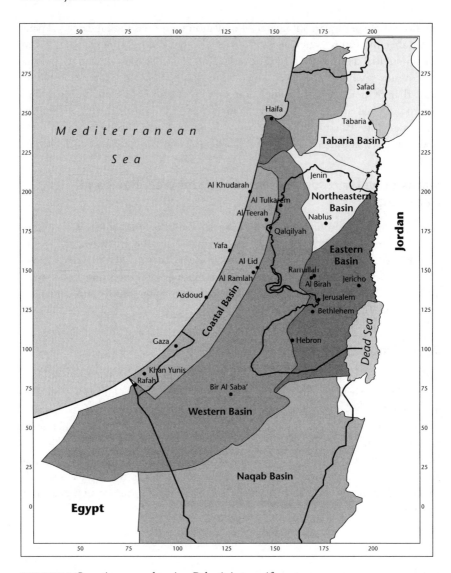

FIGURE 6.6 Location map showing Palestinian aquifers

TABLE 6.2 Estimated municipal and industrial total water use in Palestine (MCM/yr)

Region	Wells	Springs	Total
West Bank	55*	4	59
Gaza Strip	53**	–	53
Total	108	4	112

Notes: * 22 MCM/yr are purchased from Israeli sources; ** 48 MCM/yr are abstracted from wells in the Gaza Aquifer and 5 MCM/yr are supplied from the Mekerot Israeli water company

TABLE 6.3 Estimated total water supply for irrigation in Palestine (MCM/yr)

Region	Wells	Brackish wells	Springs	Total
West Bank	40	0	49	89
Gaza Strip	43	42	0	85
Total	83	42	49	174

Source: Data based on several studies conducted by the PWA

TABLE 6.4 Estimated total water supply in Palestine (MCM/yr)

Region	Wells	Springs	Total
West Bank	95	53	148
Gaza Strip	138	0	138
Total	233	53	286

Source: Data based on several studies conducted by the PWA

TABLE 6.5 Projected municipal water demand (MCM/yr)*

Year	2000	2005	2010
West Bank	127	159	187
Gaza Strip	77	96	115
Total	204	255	302

Note: * Assuming 100–150 liters/person/day; physical losses 8–12%

TABLE 6.6 Projected industrial water demand (MCM/yr)*

Year	2000	2005	2010
West Bank	5	25	30
Gaza Strip	3	16	18
Total	8	41	48

Note: * Assuming 8–16% of total municipal demand

TABLE 6.7 Projected agricultural water demand (MCM/yr)

Year	2000	2005	2010
West Bank	177	205	233
Gaza Strip	102	121	140
Total	279	326	373

TABLE 6.8 Estimated total water demand in Palestine (MCM/yr)

Region	Municipal			Industrial			Agricultural			Total		
	00	05	10	00	05	10	00	05	10	00	05	10
West Bank	127	159	187	5	25	30	177	205	233	309	389	450
Gaza Strip	77	96	115	3	16	18	102	121	140	182	233	273
Total	204	255	302	8	41	48	279	326	373	491	622	723

TABLE 6.9 Estimated gap between supply and demand in Palestine (MCM/yr)*

Region	Supply			Demand			Gap		
	00	05	10	00	05	10	00	05	10
West Bank	148	148	148	309	389	450	161	241	302
Gaza Strip	138	138	138	182	233	273	44	95	135
Total	286	286	286	491	622	723	205	336	437

Note: * The gap is estimated on the basis that the water supply of 2000 remains the same until 2010.

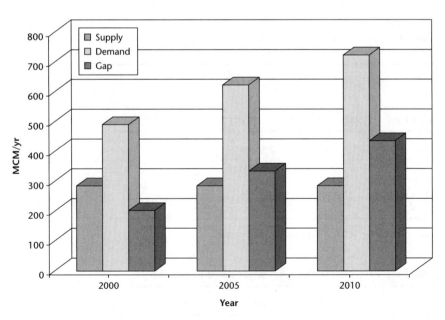

FIGURE 6.7 Water supply/demand gap in Palestine

Runoff

There are two surface catchment areas in Palestine: the western catchment area that drains into the Mediterranean Sea, and the eastern catchment area which drains into the Jordan River and the Dead Sea Basin. The total quantity of surface runoff which originates from the Palestinian territories in the western catchments is 72 MCM/year, with the total surface area equal to 2950 sq. km inside the Palestinian territories. The eastern catchment is all presented as part of the Jordan River and Dead Sea basins. The total catchment area of the eastward-draining wadis of the Dead Sea and the Jordan River Basin (including Wadi Araba) is 40,650 sq. km, of which Wadi Araba is 11,300 sq. km. The total area inside the Palestinian territories is 2750 sq. km, or 6.8 percent. The total average flow from the West Bank is 17.4 MCM/yr.

Wadi Gaza is the major wadi (as surface water) in the Gaza Strip, originating in the Naqab Desert in a catchment area of 3500 sq. km and with an estimated average annual flow of 20 to 30 MCM/yr. In addition, Wadi Gaza at present is diverted by the Israelis toward reservoirs for artificial recharge and irrigation. Due to these Israeli practices, only a little, if any, water from huge floods may reach the Gaza Strip.

The Jordan River Basin is the most important surface water resource in the region. The total natural flow of this river, in the absence of extraction, ranges from 1485 to 1671 MCM/yr at the entrance to the Dead Sea. The total area of the basin covered by isohyetes over 300 mm is 14,847 sq. km. Of this area, 1638 sq. km (11 percent) is within Palestinian territories. Israel is the greatest user of the Jordan River water, with its present use at around 59 percent of the total flow. It transfers huge quantities of surface water (420 MCM/yr) through the National Water Carrier from the upper Jordan to Naqab. At the same time, Palestinians have been denied use of Jordan River water since the Israeli occupation following the 1967 war. In addition, Jordan uses 23 percent of the natural Jordan River flow, Syria 11 percent, and Lebanon around 0.3 percent. It must be noted that the Palestinians had used and developed the water resources in the Jordan River Basin before 1967. Around 150 pumps on the river had been used for irrigation of land in the Jordan valley, pumping 10 MCM/yr. This fact alone supports the argument that Palestinians have a right to use Jordan River water under international water law.

Based on the above, Palestinian surface water rights are 270 MCM/yr, distributed as follows: 181 MCM/yr from the Jordan River, 17.4 MCM/yr from the Dead Sea Basin, and 72 MCM/yr from western wadis (SUSMAQ, 2001).

Challenges to the sustainable development and management of the Palestinian water sector

Technical and environmental challenges

At present, water demand in Palestine exceeds the available water supply (Figure 6.7), which has led to low consumption. On average, the per capita consumption in the West Bank is about 70 liters/day and water losses from conveyance systems can reach 40 percent; thus the actual water consumption per capita amounts to just 42 liters/day – about one-third of what the World Health Organization deems a minimum for good health. In the Gaza Strip, a total of only about 8.9 MCM/yr of the water supplied by municipal wells may be considered acceptable on health grounds. This figure corresponds to approximately 18 percent of the total supply, and translates to an acceptable per capita supply rate for domestic use of only about 13 liters/person/day (Aliewi and Assaf, 2003).

The water gap in 2005 for all uses was 336 MCM/yr (Table 6.9). The main causes of increased water demand in Palestine are agriculture (59 percent of total demand), demographic growth and urbanization. Urbanization reduces aquifer replenishment and increases the risk of flooding. Climate change is expected to result in less regular and lower rainfall, creating major constraints for agriculture and water supply for other purposes. It could also lead to higher rates of evapo-transpiration, lower soil moisture content, growing desertification, falling water levels in aquifers, and saline intrusion into coastal aquifers. Desertification has already taken place in Palestine as a result of losing 50 percent of the grazing area to Israeli settlements, military camps, and "nature reserves." This has had an impact on climate patterns in the region.

Some of the Palestinian aquifers, such as the Western Aquifer Basin, are mismanaged, and in some drought years this aquifer has been over-exploited by the Israelis: in 1999 they pumped 572 MCM from this aquifer while its replenishment, according to the Oslo II Agreement, is 362 MCM/yr. Other aquifers, such as the Coastal Aquifer, suffer from saline intrusion, also due to over-pumping.

The poor sanitation services, poor management of sewage and solid waste and over-application of fertilizers and pesticides in the agricultural sector can all cause pollution in the Palestinian aquifers. In Gaza, aquifer quality is an important issue, with high levels of nitrates and chlorides arising from over-extraction and reduction in storage volumes leading to a continuous degradation of water quality. There are also some areas where seawater intrusion has been detected. Furthermore, in areas of intensive pumping, saline water has been drawn upward from underlying water or from saline geological formations. Contamination of water will minimize the already limited quantities of water resources in Palestine, thereby widening the gap between water supply and demand.

Socioeconomic challenges

Over the last few years, as a result of Israeli security measures, the Palestinian economy has suffered a 38 percent decline in Gross National Income (GNI), unemployment has reached at least 37 percent, real per capita income is 46 percent lower, poverty affects 60 percent of the population, imports and exports are down by a third, and investment by 60 percent (SUSMAQ, 2005a). In these circumstances, agriculture plays the most important role in providing essentials for survival. However, this sector is constrained by limitations on land and water resources.

A lack of reasonable access to water and the consequent limitations imposed on the use of agricultural land are certainly harming the Palestinian agricultural economy. At the social level, there is a need to emphasize the principles of access to essential water supply and sanitation services (40 percent of the Palestinian communities are not served in this respect), financial resources, information, gender equality, approaches based on actor participation, consultation and partnerships. The participation by local people and other stakeholders in decision-making and management are major elements in this context. It is important to adjust unsustainable consumption of water and to support the promotion of reforms and strengthen water institutions within integrated approaches and improved governance. The Palestinian citizen pays about $1.25 per cubic meter of water. This is a high cost in relation to the average Palestinian income. It is due to the high costs of electricity, fuel, spare parts, and maintenance for wells and systems that are normally imposed by Israeli companies. The necessary financial investment to develop water resources in Palestine to bridge the supply/demand gap are estimated at $2.5 billion for the period 2005–2015.

Political challenges: negotiations versus Palestinian water rights

Within the overall Israeli–Palestinian conflict, water is a key issue. The negotiations between Palestine and Israel have so far occurred in four stages.

First stage

The Declaration of Principles, signed on September 13, 1993 (Oslo I), was the first bilateral agreement between the Palestinians and the Israelis and the first step on the long road to peace. According to this agreement, water resources would be discussed by the permanent Palestinian–Israeli Committee for Economic Cooperation. The parties agreed to prepare plans for water rights and equitable use of water resources. However, the agreement did not identify or establish any explicit water rights for the parties.

Second stage

Article 40 of Annex III of the Oslo II Agreement, signed on September 18, 1995, formed the basis for water sector planning, and for project implementation during the interim period (1995–2000), at the end of which a final agreement was supposed to be reached. Below are some details and comments about Article 40:

1   It specifies that 70–80 MCM/yr are available for Palestinian utilization from the Eastern Aquifer Basin and other agreed sources. The Palestinians will have the right to utilize this amount for their needs – domestic and agricultural. A quantity of 28.6 MCM/yr was agreed for immediate needs. Israel committed to supply 5 MCM/yr to the Gaza Strip (this still has not been supplied), and

4.5 MCM/yr to the West Bank (this is currently being supplied). The immediate Palestinian commitment was to develop 19.1 MCM/yr in the West Bank. The remaining quantities (between 40.6 and 50.6 MCM/yr) were supposed to be developed by the year 2000. However, by 2006, the implemented quantity was only about 30 MCM/yr. The Israelis restricted the major development of these quantities to the Eastern Aquifer Basin, specifically from the southern part of this basin, due to the widespread presence of Israeli wells in the middle and northern parts of the basin, and the presence of Israeli settlements, buffer zones, military and training areas, and nature reserves, which cover large portions of the basin, thus restricting its sustainable utilization. It should be noted that two independent studies carried out by two American engineering companies in the Eastern Aquifer Basin (CDM/Morgant, 1997; CH2MHILL, 2002) conclude that 70–80 MCM/yr are not available there, and that Article 40 ignores important practical realities for water exploitation. On the basis of engineering feasibility and cost criteria, both studies state that only about 30–40 MCM/yr can be accessed and developed from this basin.

2   It considers that both the Western and Northeastern aquifer basins are fully or over-exploited by the Israelis, with no further access or development potential for Palestinians. The latter have repeatedly attempted to obtain approval to drill wells in these basins, with little or no success to date. The majority of permit applications have been rejected outright by the Israeli side, even when they merely wished to develop existing wells. The Sustainable Management of the West Bank and Gaza Aquifers project, implemented by the Palestinian Water Authority and the University of Newcastle-upon-Tyne, found that the Palestinians could utilize more than 100 MCM/yr of additional water from the Western Aquifer Basin without causing significant harm to existing Israeli wells along the Green Line.

3   Its first principle is the most significant part of Article 40. It states – for the first time – that "Israel recognizes Palestinian water rights in the West Bank." These rights will be settled in the permanent status agreement after the final negotiations. The Israeli government therefore explicitly acknowledged the Palestinian sovereign right to water in the West Bank. Due to the complexity and significance of water to both sides, further discussion of the water issue has been postponed to the final status negotiations, together with other critical issues, such as Jerusalem, borders, refugees, settlements, and security, all which have yet to be resolved.

4   It fell far below fulfilling Palestinian water rights and needs. Although it recognized Palestinian water rights, the terms were broad and there was no elaboration on the nature of these rights or the principles governing the rights and obligations of both sides.

5   Since 1995, the implementation of Article 40 has been restricted and extremely slow. Decision-making within the Joint Water Committee was mostly unilateral and dominated by Israel. The dominant factor in the Israeli evaluation and rejection of Palestinian projects was the "no harm principle."

6   Water is inherent in each issue to be discussed in the permanent status nego-
     tiations, be it borders, settlements, Jerusalem, or the viability of the Palestinian
     state. It should be decided and made clear that if the issue of Palestinian water
     resources is not put on the agenda as a separate item in these negotiations, then
     each issue that is discussed will not be finalized until the water resources issues
     associated with that item are clarified and resolved.

Third stage: Camp David II

The interim period finished in 2000. The following year, Camp David II marked
the start of the final status negotiations, but these discussions collapsed without reaching any agreement. In this round of negotiations, the Israeli side offered additional
water quantities to the Palestinians, as follows:

- 50 million cubic meters from the Western Aquifer Basin;
- 10 million cubic meters from the Northeastern Aquifer Basin;
- 80 million cubic meters from the Eastern Aquifer Basin;
- 40 million cubic meters from the Jordan River.

However, when the talks collapsed, Palestinian water rights had not been discussed.
The essentials of Israel's Camp David II proposals have been well documented.
Under the component entitled "Palestinian Statehood and Conditions," the Israelis
agreed that a Palestinian state could be established in most of the West Bank and all
of the Gaza Strip, but only if they, the Israelis, retained management of water sources
in the West Bank and allowed a limited quota to the Palestinians. In other words,
Israel would control the Palestinian state's water resources. Some "water quotas"
were discussed during these meetings, but no official agreement was reached.

Fourth stage: the Road Map

Although Israel had already recognized the water rights of the Palestinians in the
West Bank in the Oslo II Interim Agreement, the proposed Road Map mentions
water resources in the Palestine region just once, and only in a vague manner and
in a regional context. The Road Map does not emphasize water as a specific issue
for negotiation. Rather, it states only the following as one of its aims or tasks:
"Revival of multilateral engagement on issues including regional water resources,
environment, economic development, refugees, and arms control issues." In the
Road Map, all statements were about regional cooperation to solve the problems of
water allocation; there was no mention of Palestinian water rights. It must be
emphasized that "regional water" – as stated in the Road Map – does not in any
way mean *bilateral* negotiations, that is discussion or negotiation with Israel with
regard to the recognition of the rights of Palestinians to their own water resources.
Also, there is no reference at all in the Road Map to international law with respect
to water rights.

Ten important points relating to Palestinian water rights

1 The available water resources are shared through transboundary aquifers, the Jordan River and wadi runoff.

2 None of the agreements to date have come close to fulfilling Palestinian water rights and needs, or meeting the Palestinian call for the implementation of international law to solve such a dispute. The overall control of all water resources and utilization in the West Bank and Gaza Strip by Israel since 1967 have constrained the development of Palestinian water resources, and thereby suppressed dependent socioeconomic growth.

3 The Oslo Accords opened a window of opportunity for the Palestinians to gain control of an equitable share of the available water resources, but no progress has been achieved toward restoring Palestinian water rights.

4 The instability of the political environment in Palestine has caused delays in both private and donor investments in the water sector. There remains great reliance on Israeli approval, customs, and laws for Palestinian water projects. There is a clear suppressed water demand due to Israeli water policies in Palestine.

5 The Oslo II Agreement allowed the Palestinians to develop some 70–80 MCM/yr during the period 1995–2000. Although there are 720–887 MCM/yr of groundwater resources in the Palestinian lands of the West Bank and Gaza Strip, only around 112 MCM/yr are available for domestic and industrial use to Palestinians (less than 13 percent of the sustainable yield of the Palestinian aquifers, although most of this yield originates in Palestinian lands).

6 In 1996, under the terms of the Oslo II Agreement, the responsibility for and authority over the West Bank Water Department (WBWD) should have been transferred to the Palestinian Water Authority (PWA), but the Israelis refused to do this, partly because they did not want to give up thirteen deep wells in the West Bank that are administered by the WBWD (their production is 12 MCM/yr).

7 Utilization of the West Bank aquifers occurs through both wells and springs. Table 6.10 provides estimates of Israeli and Palestinian utilization for the water year 1998/9, where it is immediately apparent that total utilization (1010 MCM/yr) exceeded the estimated total average recharge for the three aquifers (679 MCM/yr, according to Oslo II Agreement) by almost 50 percent. This level of abstraction is clearly not sustainable in the long term, if the estimated recharge figures of Oslo II are reliable (they may not be) and also using the figures presented in Table 6.1 above. Furthermore, rainfall and recharge fluctuate annually, so, depending on the capacity of the aquifers to recover, some over-abstraction might be possible, if balanced temporarily by above-average recharge. Table 6.11 shows the estimated percentage shares for Israeli and Palestinian utilization in 1998/9, with a breakdown of Israeli utilization both within and outside the West Bank. It can be seen that only 14 percent of overall utilization is Palestinian; for the Western Aquifer Basin (WAB), it is only 5 percent. In 2000, 572 MCM was pumped (mainly by Israel) from the WAB,

compared with the Oslo II quoted recharge figure of 362 MCM/yr. This was achieved through a large concentration of wells on the western side of the Green Line (see Figure 6.2). In addition to issues relating to quantities of water, the *quality* of abstracted Palestinian water is frequently poor. This problem has reached crisis proportions in Gaza, where over-abstraction has led to large-scale saline intrusion in the Coastal Aquifer, which, together with pollution from sewage and agriculture, has resulted in serious health problems in the population. Only 18 percent of the total quantity of water supplied in Gaza can be considered acceptable on health grounds.

8 The water resources of the Jordan River are shared among the riparian countries as follows: Israeli, 59 percent; Jordan, 23 percent; Syria, 11 percent; Lebanon, 0.3 percent; Palestine, 0 percent. The corresponding catchment areas are: Israel, 12 percent; Jordan, 36 percent; Syria and Lebanon, 41 percent (combined); Palestine, 11 percent. Of the total natural flow of the Jordan River, which ranges from 1485 to 1671 MCM/yr, only about 7 percent reaches the Dead Sea. This has led to the shrinking of that sea over a period of years, with serious economic and environmental consequences.

9 Syria, Lebanon, Palestine, Jordan, and Israel are all legal riparians with legitimate rights. The West Bank (as part of Palestine) is therefore a watercourse state, as its territory is part of an international watercourse. In reviewing the various proposals and plans for developing and solving the water conflicts over the Jordan River, the 1956 Johnston Plan still seems the most significant. It gives Palestinians rights to 270 MCM/yr of the water in the Jordan River Basin.

TABLE 6.10 Israeli and Palestinian aquifer utilization through wells and springs, 1998/9 (MCM/yr)

Aquifer	Israeli share	Palestinian share	Overall
EAB	132.9	71.9	204.8
NEAB	147.1	36.9	184.1
WAB	591.6	29.4	621.0
Total	871.6	138.2	1009.9

TABLE 6.11 Percentage shares of Israeli and Palestinian aquifer utilization, 1998/9

Aquifer	Israeli share			Palestinian share
	Inside the West Bank	Outside the West Bank	Total	
EAB	60%	5%	65%	35%
NEAB	7%	73%	80%	20%
WAB	1%	94%	95%	5%
Overall	14%	73%	86%	14%

10   The overall utilization of water resources by Israel and Palestine is shown in Table 6.12, where it can be seen that 89 percent of the total resource is under Israeli control. This is expressed in terms of per capita consumption in Table 6.13 for 1999, which shows that the ratio of Israeli to Palestinian consumption is 4:1. Table 6.14 breaks down consumption into agricultural, domestic, and industrial use per capita; here, the Palestinian domestic water consumption, at 83 liters/person/day, is less than the World Health Organization recommended minimum of 100 liters/person/day. *It is therefore evident that there is a major equity issue concerning the sharing of Israeli and Palestinian water resources.*

TABLE 6.12 Israeli and Palestinian utilization of water resources (MCM/yr)

Resource	Natural flow/ Recharge	Total utilization	Palestinian utilization		Israeli utilization	
			Volume	% of total utilization	Volume	% of total utilization
Groundwater	1454	1503	251	17%	1252	83%
Jordan River	965	870	0	0%	870	100%
Runoff	215	197	20	10%	177	90%
Total	2634	2570	271	11%	2299	89%

TABLE 6.13 Israeli and Palestinian per capita water consumption, 1999

Community	Population	Consumption for all purposes (MCM/yr)	% of allocation	Consumption (liters/person/ day)	Ratio of Israeli to Palestinian consumption
Palestinian	2,895,683	252.4	11%	239	1
Israeli settlements	172,200	54.8	2%	872	4
Israeli	5,869,200	2074.0	87%	968	4
Total*		2381.2	100%	2079	

Note: ★ Total consumption excludes wadi runoff.

TABLE 6.14 Israeli and Palestinian agricultural, domestic, and industrial water use, 1999 (liters/person/day)

	Israeli use	Palestinian use
Agricultural	574	140
Domestic	334	83
Industrial	58	16

Sustainable management and development of Palestinian water resources

The sustainable development of Palestinian water resources should be based on economic growth, social equity, protection of the water resources and their environment, and improved governance. This should also include encouraging democratic processes, strengthening institutional capacities, administrative and legislative capabilities, and consolidating the Palestinian–Israeli peace process.

The PWA has formulated a number of plans, policies and strategies for the development of the water sector, including a National Water Plan and Palestinian Development Plan. Legislation has been drafted to keep pace with these plans, especially the Water Law of 2002. This establishes that all water resources are public property and that the PWA is responsible for managing both water resources and wastewater. The other main elements of the law are as follows:

- Pursue Palestinian water rights.
- Strengthen national policies and regulations.
- Build institutional capacity and develop human resources.
- Improve information services and assessment of water resources.
- Govern water and wastewater investments and operations.
- Enforce pollution control and protection of water resources.
- Promote public awareness and participation.
- Promote regional and international cooperation.

Within the water sector, the establishment of the National Water Council (NWC), another element in the Water Law, was an important step. It allowed a wider group of stakeholders to become involved in water sector planning, and its prestige was assured by the fact that the Chairman of the Palestinian Authority (later the Prime Minister) also served as Chairman of the NWC. The Water Law decreed that water service delivery would be provided by three regional utilities in the West Bank and another in Gaza. These regional utilities were tasked with coordinating their activities with the local government network and provision was also made for the establishment of joint service councils (JSCs) to ensure that the interests of smaller communities are upheld. A separate bulk utility is also planned. This will assume responsibility for the development, collection and transportation of bulk supplies to, from, and between the regional utilities. The PWA will retain responsibility for strategic planning and coordination, policy and planning, integrated resource management, standards, and regulation.

In order to develop and manage the Palestinian water sector sustainably, a process of identifying and assessing suitable management options to address the gap between water supply and demand is required. This should take into consideration the social, economic, and environmental impacts of all possible water management options. In the SUSMAQ project, detailed analyses of the various management options were made and their sustainability was evaluated (see SUSMAQ, 2005b for more details).

The SUSMAQ study was based on numerical groundwater flow and transport models of the aquifers, which were formed by field data analysis and modeling studies of geology, hydro-stratigraphy, pollution sources and groundwater quality, and of the rainfall distribution in current and future climates, and how this might affect groundwater recharge. The socioeconomic aspects of water management were studied through a series of institutional analyses, household surveys, village-level case studies and local stakeholder workshops. These detailed studies formed the basis for development of an integrated sustainability assessment methodology, based on a multi-criteria analysis (MCA) approach, which brings together the different aspects of sustainability and allows an open and transparent means for stakeholders to engage in a dialogue to develop the most appropriate water resources management options related to various potential socioeconomic, hydro-political, and climatic futures for Palestine.

The Pressure–State–Response (PSR) framework for policy analysis was adopted. This is based on the use of indicators which can measure the economic, social, and environmental performance of a country, sector, or system in terms of sustainability. The framework proposed for the evaluation of management options within SUSMAQ (Figure 6.8) is closely aligned with the PSR framework (Figure 6.9). In the PSR context, three categories of indicator can be identified:

- pressure indicators, which focus on changes in the main drivers that create pressure on water resources;
- state indicators, which focus on describing the state of the system in economic, environmental, and social terms; and
- response indicators, which measure the actions taken to improve the state of the system, and the resulting impacts.

The responses are the management options. Provision is made for iteration and feedback within the PSR framework. For example, if the responses do not lead to more sustainable system performance, then alternative responses need to be considered, and the system reevaluated. Similarly, the socioeconomic pressures might need to be altered, for example by reducing the amount of water allocated to agriculture. However, this could lead to increased imports of food (virtual water) with a loss of self-sufficiency and a negative impact on foreign exchange. A comprehensive sustainable water resources management plan for a country or region must be sustainable from each of the social, environmental, and economic standpoints. However, conflicts can arise if, for example, socioeconomic development is to be prioritized at the cost of degradation in environmental quality. An acceptable balance between conflicting objectives must be established which reflects the overall preference of a society. To support the decision-making process in arriving at such a balanced position, MCA techniques have been developed which enable different preferences to be expressed (for details, see SUSMAQ, 2005b).

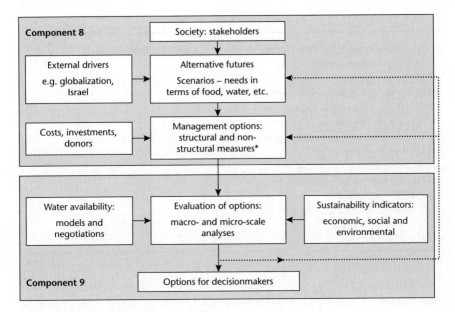

FIGURE 6.8 Framework for assessing SUSMAQ management options

Note: * Management options include: structural measures – wells, pumping, desalination, etc.; non-structural measures – virtual water, legislation, regulation (environmental and economic).

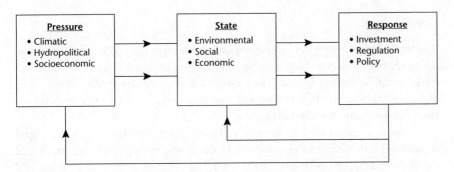

FIGURE 6.9 The Pressure–State–Response (PSR) system with feedbacks

Management options and the water supply/demand gap

The management options (MOs) are the generic potential water management solutions for each of the scenarios. The MOs agreed for the SUSMAQ demonstration studies are listed in Table 6.15 (SUSMAQ, 2005b).

In this study we present only analysis of how much each management option will impact the gap between supply and demand, using ceiling values and working in three scenarios of the development of the socioeconomic futures of Palestine: the *current scenario* when the situation remains as it is (under the difficulties of Israeli

TABLE 6.15 SUSMAQ management options

MO1: Groundwater supply development (including associated infrastructure)
MO2: Rainwater harvesting
MO3: Tanker supply
MO4: Direct connection to Mekerot
MO5: Desalination (including associated infrastructure)
MO6: Demand management
MO7: Environmental protection/conservation
MO8: Wastewater reuse
MO9: Sectoral reallocation
MO10: Changes to agricultural policy
MO11: Water transfer
MO12: Administrative and institutional structures
MO13: Surface water development
MO14: Importation

---

occupation); *consolidating scenario*, when the peace process advances considerably; and *future scenario*, when Palestine is an independent state with full water rights. In addition to Gaza, these scenarios consider three geographic zones for the West Bank: North, Central, and Southern.

The allocation of ceiling values and other stages of water availability are summarized in Table 6.16 (SUSMAQ, 2005b).

Conclusions

This study has provided an in-depth analysis of the challenges facing the Palestinian water sector, including those of a technical, environmental, socioeconomic, and hydro-political nature. Unless Israeli control is eliminated and Palestinian water rights are fulfilled, the Palestinians will continue to face a water crisis within both the West Bank and the Gaza Strip.

There is a great need to protect and sustainably manage the existing (and dwindling) Palestinian water resources in order to advance economic and social development and to safeguard health. We have discussed how to plan for and develop more equitable, yet feasible, future water consumption rates and supply capabilities in support of social and economic development under current, consolidating, and future scenarios in Gaza and the West Bank.

The water situation in Palestine is in a critical state predominantly as a consequence of Israeli occupation, but it could be somewhat alleviated through management options in both the supply and the demand side. We have outlined a number of management options that could be implemented for the sustainable management of the water resources in Palestine and have shown how these options might reduce the gap between supply and demand.

TABLE 6.16 Water available (ceiling values) for SUSMAQ management options (MCM/yr)

MO ref.	Brief Description	Total	Gaza	West Bank	West Bank		
		(MCM)			North	Central	South
Baseline Scenario (2002)							
CUR01.1	GW supply	243.0	145.0	98.0	49.0	43.0	6.0
CUR02.1	Rainwater	8.0	2.0	6.0	2.3	1.2	2.5
CUR03.1	Tanker supply	9.8	0.8	9.0	4.0	1.0	4.0
CUR04.1	Mekerot	43.6	3.6	40.0	10.3	17.0	12.7
CUR05.1	Desalination	0.8	0.8	0.0	0.0	0.0	0.0
CUR06.1	Demand management	1.5	0.0	1.5	0.5	0.5	0.5
CUR07.1	Protection/conservation	1.0	0.5	0.5	0.0	0.5	0.0
CUR08.1	Reuse	1.0	0.5	0.5	0.20	0.10	0.2
CUR09.1	Sectoral reallocation	5.0	2.0	3.0	3.0	0.0	0.0
CUR10.1	Changes to agriculture	25.0	5.0	20.0	6.0	8.0	6.0
CUR11.1	Transfer	22.0	0.0	22.0	0.0	0.0	22.0
CUR12.1	Admin/Institutional	N/A	N/A	N/A	N/A	N/A	N/A
Baseline supply		296.4	151.9	144.5	61.8	61.3	21.4
Demand reduction		26.5	5.0	21.5	6.5	8.5	6.5
Cumulative value		322.9	156.9	166.0	68.3	69.8	27.9
Reallocation		5.0	2.0	3.0	3.0	0.0	0.0
Current Scenario							
CUR01.1	GW supply	268.0	145.0	123.0	61.5	54.0	7.5
CUR02.1	Rainwater	9.0	2.0	7.0	2.7	1.4	2.9
CUR03.1	Tanker supply	10.8	0.8	10.0	4.4	1.1	4.4
CUR04.1	Mekerot	48.6	3.6	45.0	11.6	19.1	14.3
CUR05.1	Desalination	0.8	0.8	0.0	0.0	0.0	0.0
CUR06.1	Demand management	3.5	0.0	3.5	1.2	1.2	1.2
CUR07.1	Protection/conservation	1.5	0.5	1.0	0.0	1.0	0.0
CUR08.1	Reuse	2.0	0.5	1.5	0.5	0.5	0.5
CUR09.1	Sectoral reallocation	5.0	2.0	3.0	3.0	0.0	0.0
CUR10.1	Changes to agriculture	25.0	5.0	20.0	6.0	8.0	6.0
CUR11.1	Transfer	22.0	0.0	22.0	0.0	0.0	22.0
CUR12.1	Admin/Institutional	N/A	N/A	N/A	N/A	N/A	N/A
Cumulative supply		328.4	151.9	176.5	76.3	75.0	25.2
Demand reduction		28.5	5.0	23.5	1.2	1.2	1.2
Cumulative value		356.9	156.9	200.0	77.4	76.2	26.4
Reallocation		5.0	2.0	3.0	3.0	0.0	0.0
Consolidating Scenario							
CON01.1	GW supply	385.00	150.00	235.00	109.00	112.00	14.00
CON02.1	Rainwater	15.00	4.00	11.00	4.22	2.20	4.58
CON03.1	Tanker supply	8.00	2.00	6.00	2.67	0.67	2.67
CON04.1	Mekerot	60.00	10.00	50.00	12.90	21.30	15.90
CON05.1	Desalination	25.00	25.00	0.00	0.00	0.00	0.00

TABLE 6.16 Continued

MO ref.	Brief Description	Total	Gaza	West Bank	West Bank		
		(MCM)			North	Central	South
CON06.1	Demand management	15.00	5.00	10.00	3.00	3.00	4.00
CON07.1	Protection/conservation	7.00	5.00	2.00	1.00	0.50	0.50
CON08.1	Reuse	35.30	23.20	12.10	6.10	3.00	3.00
CON09.1	Sectoral reallocation	25.00	20.00	5.00	3.00	1.00	1.00
CON10.1	Changes to agriculture	50.00	10.00	40.00	12.00	16.00	12.00
CON11.1	Transfer	54.00	20.00	34.00	4.00	8.00	22.00
CON12.1	Admin/Institutional	N/A	N/A	N/A	N/A	N/A	N/A
CON13.1	Surface water	10.00	2.50	7.50	3.50	4.00	0.00
Additional supply		530.30	214.70	315.60	135.69	142.45	37.46
Demand reduction		65.00	15.00	50.00	15.00	19.00	16.00
Net additional		595.30	229.70	365.60	150.69	161.45	53.46
Reallocation		25.00	20.00	5.00	3.00	1.00	1.00
Future Scenario							
FUT01.1	GW supply	552.0	150.0	402.0	194.0	173.0	35.0
FUT02.1	Rainwater	27.0	8.0	19.0	7.3	3.8	7.9
FUT03.1	Tanker supply	4.0	1.0	3.0	1.3	0.3	1.3
FUT04.1	Mekerot	10.0	10.0	0.0	0.0	0.0	0.0
FUT05.1	Desalination	105.0	55.0	50.0	0.0	0.0	50.0
FUT06.1	Demand management	40.0	15.0	25.0	8.0	8.0	9.0
FUT07.1	Protection/conservation	28.0	20.0	8.0	3.0	2.0	3.0
FUT08.1	Reuse	97.4	62.8	34.6	13.0	14.0	7.6
FUT09.1	Sectoral reallocation	50.0	40.0	10.0	3.0	4.0	3.0
FUT10.1	Changes to agriculture	80.0	20.0	60.0	18.0	24.0	18.0
FUT11.1	Transfer	86.0	40.0	46.0	12.0	12.0	22.0
FUT12.1	Admin/Institutional	N/A	N/A	N/A	N/A	N/A	N/A
FUT13.1	Surface water	133.0	5.0	128.0	80.0	48.0	0.0
FUT14.1	Importation	20.0	10.0	10.0	3.0	4.0	3.0
Additional supply		944.4	300.8	643.6	297.3	242.8	103.5
Demand reduction		120.0	35.0	85.0	26.0	32.0	27.0
Net additional		1064.4	335.8	728.6	323.3	274.8	130.5
Reallocation		50.0	40.0	10.0	3.0	4.0	3.0

PART II
Concepts

Democratization and the domestic political environment

7

THE EFFECTS OF CONFLICT

National security, UNSC Resolution 1325, and women in Israel

Galia Golan

Relative to the neighborhood, Israel is a robust and thriving democracy. Judged by the standards and parameters of the Western concept of liberal democracy, Israel has all the necessary institutions, processes, laws and practices: rule of law, due process, pluralism, freedom of speech, association, and movement, free and democratic elections, institutionalized transfer of power and so forth. Yet large portions of its population consider themselves under-represented, second-class citizens and discriminated against, be they of the Palestinian minority inside Israel, Bedouin Arabs, Jews of Eastern origin, Ethiopian or even Russian immigrants. Women, a far broader group, are also treated as a minority, at the bottom rank of even these minorities as well as among the population at large. A majority of the population, women are grossly under-represented (if not entirely excluded) from major decision-making bodies and leadership positions and have no equality in most sectors of society. While the women's movement in Israel has indeed succeeded in improving the situation of women over the past twenty years, following feminist models developed in various Western democracies, it achieved at least a formal (legislative) victory aimed at the pinnacle of democratic rights: the right to be a part of decision-making with regard to national security. Inasmuch as Israel is a country engaged in a long, ongoing and often violent conflict, decision-making on matters of national security holds a critical and venerated place in Israeli society and the Israeli body politic. This regard for – one might even say obsession with – national security may itself be misplaced, eclipsing many critical social, economic and political matters, but for many it serves as a litmus test for Israeli democracy.

Responding to UN Security Council Resolution 1325 (2000), which called for women world-wide to be part of decision-making and negotiations connected with peace and security, in 2005 the Knesset of Israel approved an amendment to its 1951 and 1998 Equality of Women's Rights Law.[1] This amendment stated that women were to have "appropriate representation on public committees and on national policy-shaping teams"; namely, bodies "established for the purposes of shaping national policy on any matter, including foreign or security matters or for the purpose of preventing, managing or resolving a state of international dispute, *inter alia* the conduct of negotiations, including with a view to the execution of an interim agreement or peace agreement." Upon the insistence of the women's movement and in response to other lacunae in Israeli democracy, the law added that "appropriate expression" be accorded for "representation of women from a range of population groups."

In this chapter, I shall discuss the logic behind the UN resolution upon which the Israeli law was modeled and the importance of the law itself for Israeli democracy.

The two justifications generally cited for including women in peace-making efforts are the principle of universal rights and the women-as-victims claim. In the first, the justification is simply the fact that women constitute at least half of the population, and therefore they have a right to a role in determining their fate, especially if their life or death might be at stake. Indeed, the principle of equality is further trampled by the generally increased marginality of women in time of war or acute conflict. At such times, national decision-making bodies contract, and military "experts" assume precedence over civilian expertise, excluding the few women who may have penetrated the broader political scene. This is often accompanied by a more general reversion to traditional gender roles, with women limited to the home, coupled with support for the menfolk doing the fighting. (This, by the way, is no easy role, but it is invariably considered secondary to that of the fighting men.) Here the second justification may be raised: women are in no way peripheral to wars or armed conflict. Increasingly, and especially in armed conflicts today, civilians, mainly women and children, have become the major victims. The majority of refugees are women; the majority of displaced persons are women. In the First World War, the percentage of civilian victims was 5 percent; in the Second World War it was 48 percent; in the conflicts of the 1990s; and thereafter it has been 90 percent. Women are viewed as "property" of the enemy, to be punished, violated or conquered, increasingly with rape being used as a weapon. They are particularly vulnerable in war – without weapons, without training in warfare, without the means, competence or confidence to defend themselves, control their fate, or protect their loved ones. Thus, they are vulnerable physically, emotionally, mentally and materially. Yet, if not condemned to total helplessness, they are called upon to sustain daily life, meeting daily needs in the face of the hardships of war and conflict.

Prolonged conflict may produce additional disadvantages for women as societies become militarized. Gender relations are clearly affected by the elevation, adulation and privilege accorded the "male protector" in a militarized society. The male is viewed as playing a vital role for society, for the nation, leaving the women in subordinate, auxiliary positions, at best as "helpers." In the best of times, what are considered male attributes tend to be more highly valued by societies than those associated with women. In militarized society these male attributes – strength, power, aggressiveness, cold reason – become the revered norm. They inspire far more confidence and are deemed more important than women's "soft" attributes: empathy, understanding, sensitivity, emotionalism. Further, in these situations, men have an advantaged position by virtue of their expertise or experience in the one area that is most highly valued and needed: security, defined as warfare. Almost by definition, this is an area far less accessible to women or associated with women. At the same time, societies engaged in prolonged violent conflict tend to have increased rates of family violence, including murder of wives. There are clear connections between national, societal and domestic violence, apparent as militarization, with its legitimization of violence, engulfs a society (Enloe, 1983; Jacobs *et al.*, 2000; Adelman, 2003; Yang and Lester, 1997; Cambell, 1992).

Implicit in the UNSC resolution championing the rights of women to be part of peace-making, however, is the suggestion or even assertion that women may have something to offer in such a role. This is certainly not a requirement but rather an added value; beyond the right to a role, there is the positive and different contribution women can make. The attributes generally associated with women (due to a large extent to the socialization of women and the gender division of roles within the family and society, among other factors) are indeed qualities that could make for more sensitive negotiating skills. Women's ways of thinking and acting are said to be expressive, men's instrumental, leading to different perceptions of social relations and power, for example. Thus, while men may think in instrumental, hierarchical terms, tending to competition, clear borders and absolute justice, viewing power as power *over* someone or something, women are said to be more associational, contextual, taking into account relationships and circumstances, associating power with cooperation or joint efforts (Gilligan, 1982; Chodorow, 1978; Belenky *et al.*, 1986). In negotiations, therefore, women might seek a non-competitive, win–win outcome rather than a zero-sum "victory." If men's gender identity is defined by the attributes of strength, power, and aggressiveness, a failure to demonstrate these attributes might be perceived as weakness, threatening gender identity. The failure of an adversary to demonstrate these attributes may likewise be regarded with suspicion, as deception, while compromise may be seen (or believed will be seen) as weakness.

Women, on the other hand, may be more sensitive to the interests, particularly the human interests, of the other side, not only because of their more empathetic, associational attributes, but because they themselves are usually "the other," the "minority." Women may therefore have greater appreciation and consideration for difference, may be more inclusive, and may seek greater transparency, given their own lack of access and exclusion from information and decision-making. Since women have had to rely on persuasion rather than strength, they may bring entirely different qualities to the negotiating table, including communication skills and a willingness to listen: that is, to hear the other side. Women also might carry less "baggage" to the table – they are not perceived as combatants, as directly responsible for the loss of life and suffering, as the oppressor. Even as the enemy, they may be perceived as less threatening or hostile, providing a somewhat more conducive atmosphere for conflict resolution.

It is this and many of the qualities mentioned above that render women suitable for bridging between hostile sides, crossing the divide, not only because they are less stigmatized than men (as warriors) but because they have less to lose personally than men do. Indeed, women have been engaged in peace-making, bridging, not only in the family but between conflicting sides, as part of civil society. Bringing to the negotiating table their experience in civil society and their appreciation of civil society (perforce the major arena of their activities), women may well be expected to allot greater attention to reconciliation, cooperation, and education for peace, as part of any agreement, so as to bring along the public – an objective that is essential to sustainable peace.

All this – and more, presumably – is the logic behind Resolution 1325. And, with the possible exceptions of the Nordic countries, most likely every country needs this resolution. It is, however, of particular importance for countries involved in conflict situations, where questions of war and peace are often immediate and central elements of daily life. Israel is certainly one of these. It has been involved in armed conflict throughout its brief history, indeed even before statehood, and militarization has steadily crept into its political and social culture as a result.

By many standards, Israel is a relatively advanced country in terms of women's rights. Approximately half of the workforce is made up of women; women have had the right to vote for almost eighty years and have served in the nation's parliament from the earliest days of the state; they work in virtually all professions and trades, and are conscripted into the armed forces; virtually 100 percent of them are literate and they have long constituted the majority of university students and graduates. Israeli women also enjoy, on paper, some of the most progressive gender legislation in the world, including paid parental leave, single-parent family assistance, equal pay for equal worth, affirmative action in civil service appointments, protection from abuse and from sexual harassment, and more. Thus, the status of women in Israel is comparable to that of many industrialized countries, with a similar standard of living.

However, as in these countries, patriarchy is still the norm in Israel. This is reflected in pre-school education, textbooks, advertising, films and literature, political parties, senior government and private sector offices, academia, and the media. Similarly, particularly with the advent of globalization, women constitute the majority of part-time and non-standard employees, the majority of the unemployed and the poor, and on average they earn 30 percent less than men. Only 15 percent of the Knesset are women, an even lower proportion serve in local government, and only two women have ever been elected to the office of mayor of a city in Israel. In addition, unlike most of the industrial countries to which Israel may be compared, Israeli women are still subject to the exclusive rule of the religious courts in matters of marriage and divorce (Israel Women's Network, 2007).

It is difficult to determine to what degree the above aspects (positive or negative) of women's situation in Israel are directly related to the existence of armed conflict, but there has certainly been an impact of militarization of society on the status of women and gender relations (Golan, 1997). The primary but not only reason for this is the centrality of the military as an institution in Israel, because of the conflict. Ostensibly, the Israeli army (or IDF – Israeli Defense Forces) is a "people's army" based on compulsory service for almost all citizens, male and female, at the age of eighteen. All Jewish citizens (80 percent of Israel's total population) are subject to the draft, as are the males of some of the minorities who are either drafted or able to volunteer (for example, Bedouin, Druze, and Circassians). There are increasing (albeit still not large) numbers of Jewish youths who do not serve for various reasons, but the army is still perceived as a "people's army" and induction is still a virtually automatic part of the life-cycle for most Israeli youth. For the new immigrant, the army is a major vehicle for education and integration into society; for the vast majority of Israelis, it is almost the last stage of socialization as they emerge from adolescence into adulthood. But this socialization is not conducive to gender equality, for the army is the quintessence of a patriarchal institution.

There have been changes in recent years in the role of women in the IDF, some due to feminist action leading to court decisions,[2] some due to the need for more qualified personnel in combat-related positions (a phenomenon that has broadened the role of women in the military forces of a number of countries). As a result, in today's IDF women may opt for certain combat positions, for which they will train and serve alongside men. This is an important change, inasmuch as the value of a soldier's position is generally gauged by his (or her) proximity to actual combat. Nonetheless, for the vast majority of women inductees, there has not been a great change; and more importantly, there has been virtually no change in the gender-related attitudes or norms in the IDF, at least so far. Even the fact that women's duty in a combat capacity is voluntary while for men it is not indicates the persistence of gender-related attitudes. Women in the IDF are still not considered of equal value or utility. They also obtain exemption from serving far more easily than men do: women who are religiously observant, married, or parents are not obliged to serve at all. Thus, only a third of conscripts are women. They also serve less time than men, and do virtually no reserve duty after their obligatory service. (Men do active reserve duty annually for most of their adult lives.)

While there has been improvement, and a positive trend may be discerned, the traditional approach to women continues, to a large degree: they are seen as subordinate, auxiliary, marginal, even inferior; more often than men, they serve in undervalued, stereotypically female positions, such as clerical or support roles. Even with the official opening of 88 percent of types of position to women, some 63 percent of roles in the IDF are filled exclusively or almost exclusively by men (Israel Women's Network, 2007). On a more subjective level, for a male recruit in training to be called "a woman" is the supreme humiliation. Even for women in the professional army, there is a glass ceiling, with only 10 percent of higher ranks held by them (Israel Women's Network, 2007). The simple explanation is that the highest positions, and especially the highest rank, that of general (with only two or three exceptions), are linked to combat experience: specifically, moving up the ladder of field commands – which are closed to women. Thus, albeit of a different degree, the message even in the professional army is one of women's inferiority to men. Moreover, young recruits are exposed to a steady stream of male role-models from all walks of life in the form of reservists on active duty – engineers, psychologists, artists, writers, lawyers, architects, professors, doctors. Women recruits have no such exposure to female role-models, since women very rarely do reserve duty (and then only briefly, immediately after their compulsory service, if they are unmarried).[3]

All of these distinctions, and more, deliver a most important message about the worth of women in comparison to men. The message is amplified many times over during the period of service, both by the nature of the tasks permitted or accorded women and the attitude, and behavior, exhibited towards them. Indeed, even women in the army themselves internalize the message. Recent research has shown that they often adopt male attitudes and behavior (even tone of voice) with regard to other women, referring to them or treating them as contemptuously as do the men (Sasson-Levy, 2003). Thus, while military service has been demonstrated to build more self-confidence in women (in comparison with those who do not serve) and still more self-confidence and assertiveness in those serving in command positions, it would appear that this is accompanied by a reinforcement of stereotypical – negative – gender attitudes among women and men alike.

Aside from this relatively direct way in which militarization, in the form of the centrality of the army, impacts upon gender attitudes in Israel, there are other, no less problematic effects. A country in a state of war will, by necessity or custom, particularly value the male child. Mothers of male children in Israel (certainly in the Jewish majority) invariably carry with them an apprehension about the inevitable role that their child will most likely be asked to play. In Israeli society, he is regarded as the potential defender, a hero who may well be called upon to make the ultimate sacrifice for our benefit and safety. He has a special, critical role to play in and for our society. The somewhat excessive self-confidence and sense of entitlement of the average Israeli male may have something to do with this conscious or unconscious appreciation of his value to society. Such appreciation may indeed be positive in cultivating a sense of self-worth and pride in boys and young men, but what message does it send out to Israeli girls? As in the period of army service, so too earlier, girls may internalize this valuation of the male, regarding him as more important to society, with greater entitlement because of his future obligation to the nation. There have been some research findings to the effect that women feel guilty in time of actual war in Israel, because their husbands, partners, and boyfriends are fighting and risking their lives, while they are not (Kriegel and Waintrater, 1986). We shall see below what happens to Israeli women in time of actual war, although both terrorism and the nature of missile-led warfare equalize dangers somewhat.

The importance of the army and the issue of the country's security also create advantages for the Israeli male beyond his service. The "old boys' network," created usually through army service, whether in the professional army or via reserve duty throughout most of a man's life, often provides advantages that are totally lacking for women in almost every walk of life. More prominently, the presumed superior qualities developed by the professional soldier often (and, in the case of generals, virtually always) secures him a privileged position once he enters civilian life – another advantage unavailable to women. Coming out of the professional army, high-ranking officers are very often "parachuted" into senior positions in business, administration, government, education,[4] and especially politics. Thus, the ex-general (or ex-colonel) is extolled not only for his devotion to the nation, but for his presumed qualities of leadership, organization, assertiveness, and any number of other traits associated with leading large groups of people in difficult situations. He is considered an expert, with experience and knowledge, on the subject that has priority over all others in Israel, due to the ongoing conflict: security. It is the subject of national security, upon which women cannot have either the expertise or the experience of the Israeli male, that makes the ex-officer valuable to a political party, to the parliamentary committees that are considered important, to the tasks that are considered crucial by the media and public at large. Thus, an inordinate number of ex-generals have been chosen to serve as prime minister or to head a government ministry, including ministries ostensibly unrelated to military matters. Particularly after the failure of the civilian leadership in the 2006 Israeli war in Lebanon, but also well before, a common demand has been to choose an ex-general to head a political party. Israeli media clearly favor such a background when it comes to discussions of security and often even when security is only indirectly the topic. During the 2006 war, the media were totally dominated by military or ex-military commentators and interviewees, while the rare women who appeared were worried mothers/wives of soldiers, victims of bombardment, or (even more rarely) opponents of the war.[5] The only notable exception with regard to the media during the war was the military spokeswoman, selected perhaps to present a reassuring image.

While the presence of the military in the media and particularly in the political world contributes significantly to the militarization of Israeli life, with its negative effects on gender equality, a possibly more alarming phenomenon is the growing presence of professional army veterans in the education system. In recent years, retiring officers have been offered a course to prepare them as school principals. This has led to an influx of such personnel into the school system, most likely bringing with them the military values and hierarchical modus operandi so rigorously developed in the army. This is not to say that every ex-officer is a warmonger or inhumane person; many have learned from the horrors of war the need for a shift to peaceful means of conflict resolution.[6] The problem, though, is in the influence of military thinking and customs on their approach to the education system – what they bring to the students, the faculty and even the parents, in the way of values and outlook, perceptions of citizenship and decision-making, and of strength or weakness – all of which affect and are affected by attitudes toward gender relations.

Ironically, the participation of ex-officers and fighters even bestows legitimacy on the peace movement in Israel. It may be the only country in the world where a mass peace movement was founded (Peace Now, in 1978) by reserve officers and soldiers from combat units. Later, in the 1980s, a peace organization (the Council for Peace and Security) was created by and for ex-security officers – mainly very high-ranking IDF veterans – and more recently a peace organization of "combatants" (both Israeli and Palestinian) was formed. In each case the message of these virtually all-male groups (originally) was that those who fight, by definition men, have a better understanding, but also a greater right, to object to conflict and propose peace. It is not only that their loyalty is above suspicion but that their views should and do carry more weight than those of others. Women's peace groups, of which there are many in Israel, as well as the women who are involved with the above groups, are accorded far less media coverage and far less respect (if, indeed, they are even known) than the men's, precisely because they are not perceived as having the same knowledge, and therefore legitimacy, to speak out on these subjects. The one and only women's peace group that gained public support was the Four Mothers. They used the "mother" motif, an acceptable (traditional and non-threatening to men), emotional appeal as mothers of soldiers, rather than "rational" security arguments, when urging Israeli withdrawal from Lebanon in the late 1990s and 2000.

An additional conflict-related problem is the number of weapons floating around in time of crisis, for example during the Intifada of 2000–2003. The effect on women was clearly demonstrated by the sharp rise (of 50 percent) in the number of women shot and killed, as compared with the period 1997–2000 (Aharoni, 2005). Regarding Israeli women themselves in time of war, as noted above, they tend to feel guilty that they are safe while their husbands or sons are fighting "for them." This was the case in the first Lebanon war (1982). During the second Intifada, between 2000 and 2003, there were 75–90 percent fewer calls to rape crisis centers and reports of violence against women because, it was found, women did not feel it was "legitimate" to complain when everyone was suffering from the fighting and terror attacks (Isha l'Isha, 2005). Similarly, in the second Lebanon war, there were fewer than average calls reporting rape or sexual attacks, due, it was found, to the feeling among women that they had no right to complain about their personal problems (lack of legitimacy) when the men were fighting and the country was subject to missile attack (Isha l'Isha, 2007). After the war, however, the number of calls to trauma centers and women's counseling centers was higher than usual, as women who had been violated or abused relived their trauma during the stressful time of war and subsequently sought help (Isha l'Isha, 2007; Gild, 2008). In the second Lebanon war, despite the decline in reporting, research found that there had been violence in the home, particularly among those who had reported violence in the past, since battered women's shelters were closed because of the rockets and women found themselves confined to their homes with their violent husbands (Aharoni, 2006; Isha l'Isha, 2007). The women hit hardest by the war itself were those in the weaker sectors: the poor, single parents, and the unemployed (and it should be remembered that women comprise the majority of the poor, single parents, and the unemployed in Israel), along with new immigrants, Arabs, and the elderly. The reason for this is that most people with means fled the northern areas of the country to hotels, relatives, or friends in areas not subjected to the rocket attacks. The rest, the weaker sectors – mainly women – were left behind and shut in for twenty-four hours a day in their homes or shelters, responsible for the welfare of their children and often of extended family members who shared their shelter with them. Thus women suffered not only added mental strain but severe economic hardship. If they had employment, many simply could not get to their jobs because they had to care for their children, while many places of employment (like the schools) were closed, causing loss of income. Particularly affected were those in non-standard work – housekeepers, nannies, cleaners, and those in hourly service positions – the majority of whom are women, and by definition from the minority groups in society. At the same time, expenses tended to rise for these women, for they had to provide for the needs of their extended families, all day and night. In a study of the effects of the war on women in the north (mainly in the city of Haifa), it was found that, of 130 women interviewed, only 24 were able to escape altogether from the region where the rockets were falling (traveling to friends or relatives in the south of the country) during the whole 33-day war; 31 others managed to get away for a few days' respite. Moreover, 80 percent reported that they were in a worse economic situation after the war than before (Aharoni, 2006; Isha l'Isha, 2007).

Arab women in Israel, subject to the same economic and much of the same mental stress as other women in time of war, also suffer from the militarization of Israeli society, albeit in somewhat different ways. The relationship of Arab citizens to the state of Israel is very complicated – the differences in traditions, customs, and cultures compounded many times over by the history of hostility, subjugation, and deprivation suffered by the Palestinians with and since the creation of the state. This matter is too complex to delve into here, but it is relevant to an understanding of the effects of militarization in Israel on Arab women. For example, because of the conflict, Israeli police tend to regard all Palestinians in the country with suspicion, even as potential security threats, and, as a result, according to one study, they tend to treat Palestinian women's complaints of abuse less seriously (Shalhoub-Kevorkian, 2004). Their attitude is far less sympathetic or empathetic, even disregarding them entirely (Working Group . . ., 2005) Because of their historic/political relationship to the state, Palestinian women are also more reluctant to turn to state institutions for assistance (in itself a step of greater difficulty for the Palestinian woman than the Jewish because of the traditional structure and customs of Palestinian society; Shalhoub-Kevorkian, 2004). A reluctance to turn to the authorities for assistance for a family matter becomes a major impediment when the authorities represent the oppressor or the enemy. For example, there was a very significant decline in the number of women willing to report their cases of family violence to the police following the October 2000 incidents of police violence when thirteen male Palestinian citizens were killed in Israel. This mistrust affects reporting of child abuse as well as cases of honor killings, placing Palestinian girls and women in an even more vulnerable situation than their Jewish counterparts.

There are many other ways in which the ongoing conflict affects the lives of Palestinian Arab women in Israel as they find themselves with all the economic, social, and political disadvantages of being Arabs compounded by the priority given to men in both Arab and Jewish Israeli society. The conflict has led to discrimination in state funding: for example, there are fewer services for Arab women – such as shelters and crisis centers – and national budget cuts affect them even more severely (Shalhoub-Kevorkian, 2004; Working Group . . ., 2005; Adva Center, 2004; Israel Women's Network, 2007). A more recent, direct, and particularly harmful result of the conflict is the ban on non-Israeli-citizen Arab spouses of Israeli Arabs obtaining permanent resident status, or citizenship, or sometimes even temporary entry to Israel. Thus, an Israeli Arab woman who marries an Arab from abroad, be he Moroccan, Palestinian, or the citizen of any Arab country, cannot live legally with him permanently (if at all) in Israel. This is a temporary law that requires periodic renewal, but the Israel Association for Civil Rights failed in its bid to have it overthrown by the Supreme Court. The law obviously affects Israeli Arab men as well, but, according to the report to the UN by the Working Group on the Status of Palestinian Women Citizens of Israel (2005), the more frequent cases are those of women marrying a non-Israeli Arab spouse rather than the other way around.

Thus, the violent conflict in which Israel has been engaged for so long and the accompanying militarization clearly have profound effects on women in the country, be they of the Jewish majority or the Arab minority. This fact alone would justify women's participation in negotiations to bring about an end to the conflict, as called for in Resolution 1325 and Israel's own 2005 law. Beyond this, though, would Israeli women bring something different to the table? Are they more able than men to bridge the gap between the hostile negotiating partners? Are they similar to women in North America and Western Europe – those of similar standard of living, education, and so on who have been found to be generally more dovish than their male compatriots? Or have Israeli women internalized the gendered messages of militarization, or remained bound by traditional attitudes toward gender, to the extent that they would be no different from men with regard to the issues of peace, violence, and war?

The answers to these questions are not easy to determine. Looking at the general population in Israel, whether through small surveys or broad studies, few if any differences may be found between men and women in their attitudes on these matters. In the past, conservative (hawkish) views were characteristic of both, although there was a greater tendency among women than men to favor negotiations over the use of force. The absence of difference was attributed both to the socialization that resulted from the presence of prolonged conflict and the influence of religion. Today, however, the absence of gender differences may mean something else, for opinion polls in Israel over the past decade and more have shown both men and women to be in favor of compromise regarding the Arab–Israeli conflict and, today, they favor negotiations rather than the use of force (or *only* the use of force). In an older study, Israeli women were more likely to perceive war in terms of suffering, loss, and pain, while men tended to see it in terms of strategy and necessity. Women also had greater fear of "the enemy" (identified as the Palestinians in the poll) than did the men.[7] Regarding the means for dealing with this, recent surveys have indicated that Israeli women as well as men perceive security in terms of a strong army, even as they both support the idea of negotiation.[8] Of course, one needs to break down all of these findings in terms of age, education, religiosity (a particularly important factor in Israel), and socio-economic and ethnic background. Two of the variables that continue to be important are education (which generally makes for greater willingness to compromise and less support for the use of force) and religiosity (which has the opposite effect – the more religious a person is, the more "hawkish" they tend to be). However, there are no *consistent* gender differences for any of the variables.

There has not been a study of gender difference in attitudes at the leadership level in Israel, possibly because there are so few women at that level. Inasmuch as the sparsity of women is often accompanied by their adapting to male norms and values, one might not expect to see significant gender differences. Their views on these questions would most likely be a reflection of their party's ideology, as would be expected at any point on the political spectrum. From that point of view, there are more women in left-wing than right-wing parties in Israel. If, however, we look to civil society – the arena in which people, especially women,[9] take an active role on these and other issues – one discerns a slightly clearer picture. Looking at civil society organizations or activism around issues of security in the Israeli context – war and peace, occupation, settlements – we find more women (and possibly even more men) active on the left (pro-peace), than on the right. Thus it is here, perhaps, that one would find the women who would bring something different to the negotiating table, more prone to seek a win–win result and bridge the gaps; for here, presumably, one would find the women who had not accepted, adapted, or internalized the gender effects of militarization.

As noted above, there are many women's peace groups in Israel, and women tend to dominate (in numbers, if not necessarily power) the mixed-gender peace groups. As might be expected, it is from the ranks of the women's peace groups, but also from the ranks of the feminist movement, that the demand for women's participation in peace negotiations has come most strongly. For, in keeping with general belief in Israel that only men understand and are qualified to deal with security matters, all of Israel's peace negotiations have been conducted exclusively by men (with the brief exception of Golda Meir), and quite often by military men still in uniform.[10] Therefore, the organizations Isha l'Isha (Women to Women), coming from the feminist movement, and Bat Shalom (Daughter of Peace),[11] from the women's peace movement, have led the Israeli struggle for women's participation in discussions and negotiations regarding the Arab–Israeli conflict, pushing (ultimately successfully) for the adoption of Resolution 1325 and playing a role in the creation of the International Women's Commission (IWC) for a Just and Sustainable Palestinian–Israeli Peace. The IWC is explicitly a concrete implementation of Resolution 1325 and is a coalition of Palestinian, Israeli, and international women under UNIFEM, with the honorary chairs President Taja Halonen of Finland, President Ellen Johnson Sirleaf of Liberia, and Prime Minister Helen Clark of New Zealand. The major purpose of the IWC is to bring women's voices – from a range of population groups – to the negotiating table, in the pursuit of a just, sustainable peace in the Middle East, in the belief not only that women have a right to sit at the table, but that they will bring to that table greater consideration for human rights, the daily needs of people, and concern for reconciliation, along with greater transparency and openness.

Notes

1 Equality of Women's Rights Law (Amendment No. 4), 5765–2005 (05/12/2005).
2 Most notably the "Alice Miller Case," brought to the Supreme Court by the Israel Women's Network and the Association for Civil Rights in 1995 (Bagatz 4541/94, Miller vs. Defense Ministry *et al.*). Alice Miller held a civil aviation pilot's license from South Africa and a degree in aeronautics but was refused permission to apply for the pilots' course when she was inducted into the IDF. The Court ruled that the IDF had to make appropriate arrangements to permit women to become candidates and, if qualified, enter the pilot training courses. Since then a number of women have taken the course and qualified.
3 A number of years ago, the head of the women's corps (which has since been dissolved), Brigadier-General Amira Dotan (the first woman to be promoted to such a high rank, subsequently a member of Knesset), sought to remedy this by having older women volunteer for reserve duty. This never became a custom, however.
4 Retiring officers are offered a course to prepare them as school directors, leading to an influx of ex-military personnel into these positions.
5 Noteworthy, possibly typical, was an interview on the government channel during the war with a woman protestor juxtaposed with an interview with the worried mother of two sons fighting in Lebanon – shifting the topic to the emotional issue of protesting while "our boys" are dying, and from a discussion of the goal or legitimacy of the war itself. The latter was left for the men, if at all.
6 Most notably, there have been highly significant protests by military personnel regarding the occupation, refusal to serve, and the creation of peace movements; see below.
7 Part of unpublished research conducted by Galia Golan and Naomi Chazan on the attitudes and behavior of Israeli women with respect to peace and war, with the support of the MacArthur Foundation, 1989–1992.
8 Monthly polls of the Tami Steinmetz Center, Tel Aviv University, 2008–2009.
9 Women tend to be more active in informal political activity than men, in part perhaps because of women's near exclusion from or blocked opportunities in formal party politics.
10 Camp David 2000, for example, excluded women altogether. Sarai Aharoni of Isha l'Isha is conducting a broader gender study of Israeli–Arab peace talks.
11 Bat Shalom is the Israeli component of the Jerusalem Link – A Women's Joint Venture for Peace, created in 1994.

8

DEMOCRATIZATION IN PALESTINE

From civil society democracy to a transitional democracy

Walid Salem

Although the research on democracy development in Palestine is new, hundreds of studies (books and research papers) were produced about it in the fifteen years that followed the signing of the Israeli–Palestinian Declaration of Principles for Interim Self-Government, the so-called "Oslo Agreement," in 1993. Four schools of thought can be discerned in these studies about Palestinian democracy. The first feels that liberation should be achieved first, as a precondition for democratization, and that the call for democratization during the occupation will divert eyes from resisting that occupation (Hilal 1995, p.83). Some Fatah leaders, for instance, subscribe to this idea. The second school sees a process of de-democratization taking place in Palestine, starting in 1993 when "Palestinian political and civil society [was deprived] of the benefits of the legitimate associations and parties that had served them hitherto, on both local and state levels" (Nabulsi 2003, p.117). The third school of thought feels that "the PNA was clearly not set up through the Oslo agreements primarily to deliver democracy to Palestinians. Its primary objective was to negotiate the territorial and constitutional limits of a Palestinian quasi-state in the context of an extreme asymmetry of powers and resources vis-à-vis Israel. To get anything at all, it had to demonstrate its ability to deliver security to Israel on terms determined by the latter" (Khan and Giacaman 2004, p.43).

Different from all three of these schools of thought, a fourth tried to study the Palestinian democracy created after Oslo as a "transitional democracy." One young Fatah leader (Ahmad Ghniem) said that it was a "transitional democracy within an agreed upon jurisdiction with Israel," while Qais Abdelkarim Abu Laila, one of the leaders of the Democratic Front for the Liberation of Palestine (DFLP), called it a "transitional democracy within an imposed jurisdiction by Israel" (Salem 2000, p.182). So it seems that there is an agreement between Palestine Liberation Organization (PLO) factions on the left and right that a transitional democracy began in Palestine after Oslo. Hamas showed that it concurred through its involvement in the Palestinian elections at the beginning of 2006, and through earlier writings by its leaders in support of Palestinian democracy.[1]

This chapter aims to present the debate on democratization in Palestine in the framework of this fourth school of thought. The term "transitional democracy" is used hereafter to refer to that type of electoral pre-state democracy that was and still is practiced in the Palestinian occupied territories during the long transitional period to statehood that began with the establishment of the Palestinian Authority in 1994 (one year after the Oslo Agreement). What are the characteristics of such a transitional democracy? Where is it positioned historically in the development of Palestinian democracy? How was it established? What are its components? And what are the steps ahead toward state democracy? This chapter will analyze the answers of the policy-makers and practitioners in Palestine to these questions, but it will begin with a short historical overview in order to shed light on the roots of Palestinian "democracy."

Historical overview: civil society democracy

Until Oslo in 1993, and in the absence of a Palestinian state, Palestinian democracy was in general a civil society democracy. There were just two short exceptions to this: when a Palestinian government was elected by a national council in Gaza in 1948 and acted for two weeks before being dissolved by the Egyptians;[2] and when the Palestinian Gazans elected a special legislative council for Gaza in 1963. The term "civil society democracy" refers to the types of democratic practice that were observed in Palestine in the absence of a state, with civil society organizations obliged to carry out some tasks that would normally be performed by the state.

Palestinian civil society democracy began in the Mandatory period (from 1917) and continued until 1994, when the Palestinian Authority was established to assume responsibility for governance in parts of the West Bank and Gaza Strip for the first time in Palestinian history. This civil society democracy was characterized by three components: political pluralism, participation, and elections (Abu-Lughod et al. 1993). During the Mandatory period, these three components operated within the semi-elected Christian and Islamic societies that existed in the 1920s, and combined with civil society organizations comprised mainly of women, laborers, youth, and students. In the 1930s, six political parties emerged. The structure of these civil society organizations was patrimonial and post-patrimonial, so some writers said they comprised a "domestic society" more than a new, modern civil society.[3]

Between 1948 and 1967, Palestinian civil society democracy declined because of the Nakba and the refugee crisis. Palestinians who fled to Arab countries joined political parties there, and those who stayed in the new Israel lost their previous organizations and generally joined the Israeli Communist Party, or established new national organizations such as the Al-Ard (Land) Movement, which was outlawed by the Israeli government in the early 1960s. Those in the West Bank joined secret political parties and participated in municipal elections. In Gaza they also participated in the 1963 legislative council elections.[4]

The PLO was established in 1964 by an Arab Summit resolution, and both represented a semi-civil society organization and at the same time built a quasi-state structure. Membership in the PLO was given to all Palestinians. As the PLO bylaws stated, "The Palestinians are natural members in the PLO," so the PLO became "a homeland to the Palestinians and an alternative to the real one" (Hourani 1980, p.77). PLO structures were supposed to be elected by all Palestinians, as the Iraqi government suggested in 1964 (Salem 2000, p.57), but the other Arab regimes refused, and a special type of PLO democracy was established which included representatives elected by factions (the so-called "popular unions" of women, laborers, and others who were elected by Palestinian communities around the world) and independent representatives selected by the PLO National Council. This type of "democracy" included a lot of compromises, and distribution of shares, quotas, and profits not only for the political factions but for sectarian and client groups. The PLO also claimed legitimacy on the basis of its revolutionary history.[5]

Along with the PLO form of democracy, the civil society developed in the West Bank and Gaza Strip during the Israeli occupation promoted post-patrimonial relationships that helped support citizenship rather than tribalism, sectarianism, and clientelism. It also built relatively transparent, accountable systems and modern types of pluralism and participation that were built on professionalism. Some grassroots organizations that are part of this new civil society held elections and rotated their leaderships.[6] With the Oslo Agreement achieved and the PLO returning to the West Bank and Gaza Strip, the PLO type of democracy collided with the West Bank and Gaza Strip brand of civil society democracy.

The move to "transitional democracy"

Democracy is practiced by a people in their independent state and homeland. In Palestine, beginning with the formation of the Palestinian Authority (PA) in 1994, the process has been different: democratic institutions developed in the absence of statehood and independence, and Israel continued to control external security, movement of the Palestinian people in the West Bank, and Palestinian trade. This is why Palestinian democracy is called a "transitional democracy" – expressing a Palestinian democratic route with serious internal and external constraints, rather than a Palestinian process of democratization. It is a democratic route that is not sufficiently deep to become an internal process with its own motives and mechanisms toward democratization. On other hand, it was built and practiced under international supervision and monitoring, as will be analyzed in more detail later.

The Palestinian debate in the last decade, among both decision-makers and researchers, has two main components: whether this democratic route is the outcome of an internal process, or has been imposed from outside; and whether it is a route for peace-building more than a route toward democratization. After the eruption of the Al-Aqsa Intifada, a new dimension has been added, concerning whether democracy can act as a vehicle for state-building in Palestine.

The debate about internal and external factors in regard to Palestinian democrat-ization in the last decade focuses on whether Israel aimed, through the Palestinian elections stipulated in the Oslo Agreements, to promote democratization in Palestinian society, or whether it merely wished to create a Palestinian elected body that had the legitimacy to implement the agreement (Shikaki 1996, p.32). Others argue that the Palestinian 1996 legislative council and presidential elections were products of two wills: the "Israeli will to have elections as a tool to give legitimacy to the Oslo agreement, and the PA will to have elections as a tool in order to get constitutional legitimacy" (Barghouthi 1997, p.232). An echo of this discussion came from the well-known Israeli, Natan Sharansky, who stated:

> The logic of Oslo was simple, we need peace and security in the Middle East. We are tired from all of these wars. Take a dictator from Tunis, bring him to West Bank and Gaza, give him control over 98 percent of all the Palestinians, offer him territory, legitimacy, and economic tools and as a result, he will be so interested in playing the role of a leader to his people that he will become our partner. That was the idea.
>
> *(Sharansky 2002, p.8)*

Sharansky continued by quoting the late Israeli Prime Minister Yitzhak Rabin, who said in 1993, "Arafat will deal with terrorists without a supreme court, without B'tselem [a human rights organization] and without all kinds of bleeding heart liberals" (Sharansky 2004, p.152).[7] Many others agree with Rabin: "it is better for Israel to deal with an individual" (Shikaki *et al.* 1997, pp.13–14), rather than with an elected Palestinian government that is guided by the will of the Palestinian people. Moreover, in negotiations over the Palestinian elections, the Israelis lobbied for the election of an executive council of 25 members, while the Palestinians insisted on 100-member legislative and executive councils. In the end, the two sides agreed that the Palestinian people should elect a council of 88 members, in addition to the Ra'ees (the President).[8] The Palestinian position during these post-Oslo negotiations was similar to that which they had adopted in the pre-Oslo negotiations that took place in Washington in the early 1990s between Israeli and Palestinian–Jordanian delegations. Here the Palestinians had presented their plan to establish a Palestine Interim Self-Governing Authority (PISGA) and a 180-member legislative council that would elect the executive.[9] Thus the various opinions range from those who see the external factor aiming to create peace rather than democracy, and those who see Palestinian will as a factor in securing both legislative and executive elections in 1996 while Israel insisted on electing only an executive body.

But did these elections really help to create democracy in Palestinian society after 1996? Or did they merely represent a process that aimed to promote nation-building? Such questions emerged as a result of the behavior of the PA from the elections until the eruption of the 2000 Intifada. While there is no space here to detail all of the developments that took place in this period,[10] the four years between 1996 and 2000 witnessed the hegemony of the executive over the legislative and judicial branches of government. It acted in the absence of any law prescribing a democratic framework for the security apparatuses, while its civil structures were built upon sectarianism and clientelism in the absence of democratic, transparent, and accountable institution-building. Moreover, Yasser Arafat was leader of both the PLO and the PA at this time, which meant there could be no separation of authority between the two structures.

One of the most significant aspects of the Oslo Agreement was that it gave the PLO responsibility for negotiating with Israel, while the PA was given the internal roles of preserving security, building the economy, and developing the institutions of Palestinian society. If this division of tasks had been genuinely implemented, the Palestinians might have seen better results, but in the absence of any separation between the PLO and the PA there was a centralization of all authority in the hands of Arafat. He used the PLO's "revolutionary legitimacy" to deter and prevent any unwanted developments in the PA. Under the structure that Arafat created, the elected PA (representing Palestinian people in the West Bank and Gaza Strip) is supposed to work under the authority of the PLO (which supposedly represents Palestinian people throughout the world). On that basis, the Palestinian Legislative Council (PLC)'s 88 elected members were added to the existing membership of the PLO Palestinian National Council (PNC), which included more selected than elected members. Moreover, the PA Cabinet was told that it should act under the supervision of the PLO Executive Committee. So Arafat would meet with the two executives together, without any separation between the two bodies, meaning he was the sole decision-maker in both the PLO and the PA.[11]

This "Arafatism phenomenon" resulted from the centralized nature of the PLO and from the fact that all of Arafat's major competitors had either died or left the PLO prior to Oslo.[12] In addition, agreements with Israel gave Arafat the role of inaugurating all laws passed by the PLC, as well as authority over the bank accounts of the PA, allowing him to keep all PLO monies in his hands. He used these monies for direct payments to almost anybody who asked for money in order to buy loyalty. He also kept as much authority as possible in his hands, and headed all the security apparatuses, which operated under his sole authority. Moreover, he postponed the inauguration of the PA Basic Law from 1997 until 2002, while the Law of Judicial Authority was released by him only in May 2003.

During Arafat's period in power, the PA was effectively a one-party system: Fatah, which had 66 of the 88 members of the PLC.[13] These Fatah PLC members did not bother to monitor or restrict the activities of Arafat, which was hardly surprising as he was their party leader as well as head of the executive.[14] One other reason why Arafat enjoyed such powerful central authority was the boycott by the PLO's left-wing factions and the Islamists of the 1996 elections, which they felt aimed "to approve and legitimize Oslo" (Majdalani 2002, p.25). This gave Fatah, and by extension Arafat, full authority.

Furthermore, Arafat was elected by all the Palestinian people of the West Bank and Gaza Strip, while PLC members were elected by their individual districts, so he naturally had more power than the PLC members. And the PLC members hardly helped their cause by getting involved in executive issues, including extracting financial support from Arafat, rather than concentrating on their legislative role (Salem 2000, p.72).

During the Arafat period, the PA became the second-largest employer (after Israel) of Palestinians, and Arafat himself oversaw all appointments to the PA's civil and security structures. This "contributed to keeping democracy far from the agenda of Palestinian political society and its main factions" (Hilal 2006, p.50).

Last but not least, Arafat was hailed by both Israel and the international community as a man of peace; neither paid particular attention to his undemocratic practices inside Palestinian society. This allowed him to use the electoral process as a tool to promote his personal authority, rather than build democracy.

The period 1996–2000 was similar to the period 1994–1996 (when the PA was appointed by Arafat) in the sense that patrimonial and neo-patrimonial processes occurred in both, at the expense of institutional democratic processes. In the latter period, Palestinian democracy remained "far more impressive in theory than in practice" (Brown 2005, p.3). Some PLC members played a limited role in monitoring the work of the executive,[15] but the citizens who elected those members saw their democratic power decline. Members used the votes of the citizens merely to gain legitimacy, but then immediately followed the orders of the one person who ruled both the PLO and the PA. The heritage of PLO political practice proved so powerful that the 1996 elections could not shift the Palestinian political leadership toward new modes of operation. Consequently, there was failure in both democratic transformation and in peace-building between 1996 and 2000.

Theoretical studies into the relationship between peace and democracy show that democratic states do not tend to initiate wars against each other.[16] In the Palestinian context, under occupation, it seems reasonable to suggest that the Intifada of 2000 (if it had erupted at all) would have been nonviolent if the institutions of the PA and the Palestinian political parties had been built up during the preceding period of relative peace (1994–2000). Unfortunately, the PA failed in terms of both peace-building and democratization, so the Intifada *was* violent.[17]

But was this failure temporary or permanent? Analysis of the period that followed (2000–2005) should help us find an answer.

Democratization as a vehicle for state-building?

The eruption of the Intifada in 2000 precipitated a debate among Palestinians and others about what went wrong in both peace-building and democratization. Some concluded that it was not enough to work for peace while ignoring democratization. Therefore, the discussion turned to whether democratization might act as a vehicle to bring the Palestinians full statehood. This reversed the earlier argument that most effort should be put into ending the occupation and establishing a Palestinian state *before* attempting to build democracy in Palestine. After 2000, Palestine's donor countries moved to the idea of building up the PA's democratic structures as a precondition to moving politically. The new idea was that, without democratic, transparent PA institutions, any international funding for the PA might find its way into the hands of terrorists. Alternatively, a dictatorship might seize power and promote violence and conflict, rather than peace, between the two sides. The Palestinians felt the donor countries should concentrate on building up the PA and its strong police force until 2000, but this meant that promoting democratization and fighting corruption within the PA were neglected. Some Palestinian civil society actors criticized the donor countries for allowing this state of affairs to develop.[18]

The donor countries, mainly the Quartet,[19] monitored the 1996 elections and supported the PA thereafter. Their response to the 2000 Intifada and the impasse in democracy and peace-building was a "Performance Based Road Map to a Permanent Two-State Solution to the Israeli–Palestinian Conflict," first proposed in May 2003. In contrast to the Oslo Agreement of 1993 and the Taba Agreement of 1995, the Road Map was not (from a democratization perspective) only about elections. It spoke about reform in the PA, including building transparent, accountable security and civil administrations, preparing a constitution, appointing a prime minister, and other institutional components. That said, the joint international–Palestinian civil society democratization project in Palestine could be seen as having begun with the elections of 1996 and then moved to developing Palestinian democratic institutions through the Road Map, which was based on previous Palestinian and international studies regarding reform in the PA.[20] How did Arafat respond to this new international and Palestinian civil society approach to democratization?

Around the period of the Road Map, Arafat was obliged to release the Basic Law (in 2002) and the Judicial Authority Law (2003), to appoint a prime minister (2003), to decide a date for PLC elections (January 2002, although ultimately these were not held because of Israeli objections), to appoint a professional minister of finance, to release information about PA monopolies, to transfer responsibility for payment of the security apparatuses from himself to the Ministry of Finance, and to transfer control of part of the security apparatuses to the Ministry of the Interior.[21] All of this was done to give the impression of improving institutional democracy, but in reality the whole system was moving in the opposite direction: no real moves were made to build open, transparent security apparatuses that operated under the rule of law; no real moves were made to restructure the judicial system; only the Ministry of Finance was restructured to any significant degree, and even this was done against Arafat's wishes.

Arafat continued to resist the building of democratic institutions until his death on November 11, 2004. However, it should be noted here that the PLC finally started to call for reform, institution-building, and an end to corruption after 2000. Increasing in maturity and encouraged by the Palestinian civil society and the donor countries' strategies for democratization, the PLC developed its own plan for reform of the PA and obliged Arafat to change the government in 2002 in order to avert a vote of no confidence. Five governments followed over the next two and a half years, indicating the degree of internal instability amid increasing calls for reform, as well as the external pressure resulting from the impasse in the peace process and deteriorating relations with Israel.[22]

With the election of Mahmoud Abbas Abu Mazen as Palestinian President on January 25, 2005, a new window opened for deepening democratization in Palestine. Abu Mazen was elected with just 62.5 percent of the vote (compared with 87 percent for Arafat in 1996) and he did not have the consensus in Fatah that Arafat enjoyed. These two facts made it much more difficult for him to concentrate authority in his own hands, more willing to compromise with rivals inside Fatah, and more prepared to seek dialogue with emerging powers in Palestinian society, such as Hamas. Moreover, he accepted the Quartet's assumption that "The build up of democracy will improve the Palestinian image externally and also in Israel," and as a result will help the PA to achieve statehood, as Nabil Amre, a Fatah Central Committee member, wrote. Amre added: "For the first time in history, national independence is conditional on good performance" (Amre 2005, p.62).

In his first three months in office, Abu Mazen delegated authority to the Prime Minister, transferred the chairmanship of various committees from himself to the relevant ministers (including the "Jerusalem Committee," which Arafat had insisted should come under his authority), made new appointments to all the senior positions in the security apparatuses, and brought the Palestinian factions together for a summit in Cairo (March 2005), where all parties agreed to suspend hostilities with Israel until at least the end of the year. Abu Mazen also stopped signing checks made payable to individuals that Arafat had routinely supported, and established committees to investigate what had become of missing funds. He did all this even though he knew his power both within Fatah and outside the party was far weaker than Arafat's had been: six candidates had run against him in the presidential elections, while only one had run against Arafat in 1996.[23]

The main challenge for Abu Mazen, however, was to move from the electoral democracy of 1996 to an institutional democracy, as demanded by the Road Map. Operating within the heritage of PLO patrimonial and neo-patrimonial practices, he failed in this respect in the first year of his presidency. He had assumed that Legislative Council elections in which all of the main Palestinian political factions (with the exception of Islamic Jihad) participated would give him the power to initiate discussions with those factions about democratization, peace-building with Israel, building united security forces and dismantling the Palestinian factions' militant groups. However, during his first year in office, Abu Mazen had to deal with a conflict between three "legitimacies": the old "revolutionary legitimacy" of the PLO's left-wing factions and the Al-Aqsa Brigades of Fatah, who claim legitimacy because they are working for liberation; the emerging "jihad legitimacy" that is based on such slogans as "Islam is the solution"; and electoral legitimacy, which has failed to develop truly democratic institutions. With the weakness of the third legitimacy, the first two still have powerful claims, and continue to demand that an end to occupation is the precondition for building democratic institutions. With that being the case, the strategy of using democratization as a vehicle for statehood is under threat.

From democratization to democratic transformation?

One pressing question is whether it will be possible to move from democratization of just a few individual aspects of Palestinian political life to a full process of democratic transformation that is motivated by internal factors. Those who believe that this is feasible argue that "The time of historical legitimacy ended with the passing away of Arafat" (Giacaman 2005, p.125), and "The motivation for working outside [Palestinian] official institutions will decrease, and efforts will focus on the design of public policies inside these institutions, which means that the second PLC will be a vital, active institution" (Shikaki 2005, p.21).

However, despite this optimism that the main Palestinian factions will be persuaded to work within the PA institutions, other challenges will continue to be present in respect to building the institutions of Palestinian democracy. The first of these is the future relationship between the PA's democratically elected institutions and the PLO's non-elected institutions. This could be resolved by involving the PLO in a full electoral process in which Palestinians all over the world will have a vote. In this way, the PLO will continue to be the center of the Palestinian political system.[24] Others have an alternative solution, suggesting that the "leadership of the Palestinian people should be left to the PA, while the PNC of the PLO should be transformed to a conference for all Palestinians to be held from time to time" (Al-Shu'aibi 2005, p.94). Regardless of which course is taken, the PLO is far weaker than it once was. During his last three years, Arafat was obliged to establish a Ministry of Foreign Affairs to oversee PLO embassies and representative offices around the world and was forced to allow all PLO monopolies to be scrutinized by the Ministry of Finance. Moreover, the PLO's PNC ceased meeting after its summit with American President Bill Clinton in Gaza in 1998, when the organization's charter was modified.[25] When Abu Mazen was elected, he separated the PLO meetings chaired by himself from the PA Cabinet meetings, which were chaired by the Prime Minister. It is not yet clear whether this separation will lead to a resurgence in the PLO after its paralysis during the late Arafat period, or allow it to resume its role as the champion of Palestinian refugees both outside and inside Palestine.

The second challenge concerns building Palestinian security apparatuses to operate under the supervision of the PLC and the remit of Palestinian law, and simultaneously disbanding the armed groups of the factions. One logical outcome of the inclusion of the political factions in the PLC after the January 2006 elections should have been the inclusion of all those factions' armed groups within the PA security apparatuses. But it remains unclear whether all of these factions welcome such inclusion or would rather adopt the Lebanese Hezbollah model: having a political party *and* an armed group, with the justification that the continued Israeli occupation demands retention of the latter.

The third main challenge relates to the Palestinian Islamists' view of democracy. Until 1993, they "concentrated on pluralism, not democracy" (Abu Amre 1993, p.22), but they also accepted the will of the people. Ahmed Yassin, the founder of Hamas, said in 1993: "I will respect the free choice of the Palestinian people. Even if the Communist Party won in free democratic elections, I will respect the people's choice" (Abu Amre 1993, p.123). However, some questions remain far from resolved. For instance, will the Palestinian Islamists accept the concept of rotation of authority if they suffer electoral defeat having held power? One of Hamas's leaders, Jamal Mansour, spoke in support of this concept at the end of the 1990s, but it is far from clear whether this view is shared by all leaders of the organization. There are also issues of public rights, women's rights, and minorities' rights which require an open and frank dialogue throughout Palestinian society and within Hamas. Only then might we get a brand of Palestinian political Islam that fully accepts democratic principles.

Other challenges facing Palestinian democracy include: fighting corruption effectively; creating regimes of accountability and transparency in the PA and civil society organizations; ensuring the independence of the judiciary and establishing a constitutional court; safeguarding an independent media; building vertical decentralization to give freedom to local governments and civil society organizations; building citizens' participatory structures; and promoting freedom in economic investment while ending monopolies.

These are some of the challenges in the path of moving from democratization that is merely imposed from outside to a full process of democratic transformation that is motivated internally. To overcome them, the Palestinian political system must abandon pre-democratic patrimonial and neo-patrimonial structures and build truly democratic institutions and political parties.

Conclusion

Moving from Palestinian civil society democracy to political electoral democracy began in 1996. The electoral aspect of Palestinian democracy was laid down in 1996 within a transitional period. This was part of the implementation of an agreement with Israel and enjoyed international sponsorship. So building Palestinian democracy began as a Palestinian–Israeli–international commitment that included obligations for all three sides.

The electoral aspect of democracy created hope among the Palestinian people living in the West Bank, Gaza Strip, and East Jerusalem that they were moving toward democracy, and that the elections were "an opening, not a crowning of the stage of building a people's democracy" (Nussiebeh 1993, p.187). Moreover, this electoral process created a route to democracy that had never existed in the Arab region, and made Palestine relatively democratic in comparison with other Arab regimes. The Palestinian elections could boast genuine democratic competition (they were conducted fairly under the watchful eyes of international observers), pluralism, and the right of women to participate as both voters and candidates.[26] Freedom of speech was also guaranteed before, during, and after the elections (with the exception of a few activists whom Arafat imprisoned).[27]

All of this created a "Palestine paper democracy," but the 1996 elections were followed by a return to pre-democratic patrimonial and neo-patrimonial practices, including sectarianism, nepotism, clientelism, and every other aspect of individual authoritarianism. This caused the "democracy index" in Palestine to move from 567 in 1996 to 430 by the end of 2004 (Shikaki *et al.* 1997, 2005). After the eruption of the second Intifada in 2000, attempts were made to move from electoral democracy to institutional democracy, but the pre-democratic revolutionary and jihad legitimacies in a period of struggle against occupation halted this process.

It can only be hoped that, with the inclusion of all the main Palestinian political groups in the Palestinian political system, it will be possible to create a democratic political system in Palestine for the first time in its history. This would enable the PA to move from democratization to a process of democratic transformation that will also help to secure freedom from Israeli occupation.

Epilogue

More than four years have passed since the preceding text was written, and significant developments have occurred with respect to the Palestinian democratization process. From 2006 until the end of 2009, these developments can be summarized as follows.

Palestinian electoral democracy received a boost in the January 2006 elections that witnessed the participation of those factions that had boycotted the 1996 legislative elections. Participation in the electoral democracy process widened as the elections included all factions, with the sole exception of Islamic Jihad, which boycotted the poll. The momentum gained in 2006 was halted, however, by the bloody takeover of Gaza by Hamas in June 2007. This led to full paralysis of the PLC, and Hamas started ruling the Gaza Strip by executive order. At the same time, the West Bank was ruled by decrees released by the Palestinian President. A deep rift emerged between the West Bank and Gaza, and at the time of writing it was unclear whether this could be bridged, given the difficulties of reaching a Palestinian reconciliation agreement. The paralysis of the PLC was accompanied by paralysis in the PLO until August 2009, when Fatah's Sixth Conference was held (it had been twenty years since the Fifth Conference). This was followed in the same month by an extraordinary meeting of the PNC of the PLO, which elected six new members to the PLO Executive Committee, to replace those who had died.

With these developments, the era of Abu Mazen as leader of all the Palestinian people began. As we have seen, after Arafat's death in 2004, Abu Mazen became President, but he was not yet a leader of the PLO. However, with his election as leader of Fatah at its Sixth Conference, coupled with the revival of the PLO Executive Committee that he chairs, he has started to enjoy the status of leader in both the PA and the PLO. He has therefore finally filled the leadership vacuum caused by the death of Arafat.

Despite this, though, Hamas has continued to question his legitimacy. In January 2009 it claimed that Abu Mazen's period as President had legally expired, since he was elected in January 2005 for a four-year term. In June 2010, the PLC's governing period also expired. Nevertheless, both continue to rule, exploiting a weak point in the PA Basic Law that states that they may continue to govern until a new President and a new PLC are elected. This added to the paralysis of the Palestinian democratization process, which will continue until an (unlikely) agreement on a date for elections can be reached. The challenges of Palestinian democratization became more pronounced in this period due to the conflict between the two big parties, Fatah and Hamas. All other groups are very weak in comparison. This conflict, being a strategic one, included political issues relating to peace with Israel and internal issues, including a restructuring of the PLO to give Hamas representation in the organization that is equal to the percentage of votes it won in the PLC elections. Hamas may well utilize its new power in the PLO to change the organization's political line. Other internal issues include restructuring the PA's security forces and the security agenda.

The challenge associated with the role of Islamists in the democratization process in Palestine also deepened in this period. As has been mentioned, the Islamists (Hamas) perpetrated a coup in Gaza after they had been elected, so it is far from certain that they will accept routine elections and the rotation of authority. Moreover, there are still some questions relating to their positions in respect to minorities' rights and women's rights. Currently Hamas is reluctant to agree with Fatah on a date for elections because public opinion polls do not guarantee them success, so they are concerned they might lose their authority. It is not yet known whether this reluctance to face the ballot is temporary or permanent. Either way, it exacerbates the paralysis in the Palestinian democratization process.

The role of the international community in the Palestinian democratization process also changed in this period. The international community no longer has the authority to control developments in Gaza. The likes of Syria and Iran are the players which now have a say there. In the West Bank, however, the international community still plays a big role. However, rather than pressing for democratization, it now seeks to enhance the viability of Palestinian statehood by supporting Prime Minister Salam Fayyd's plans to develop infrastructure and transparent institutions over a two-year period (August 2009 to August 2011). This strategic change expresses a spirit of realism since the democratization process has been paralyzed.

The irony is that this paralysis occurred just after the democratization process had deepened and widened in terms of participation. This paradox remains, since most of those who came to power in 2006 will continue to call for the revival of the democratic process. They will do so in the hope that their pressure will force agreement on a date for new elections that will revive the democratically elected institutions.

Notes

1 Several Hamas leaders, such as Jamal Mansour (1999) and Maha Abdel Hadi (1999), expressed support for democratization in Palestine in the late 1990s.
2 See the story of the emergence and collapse of this government in Sakhnini (1986).
3 For Palestinian "civil society" (domestic society) during the Mandatory period, see Salem (1999), Budieri (1995), Muslih (1993).

4 For more about 1948 to 1967, see Salem (1999), Hourani (1980).
5 For more about the PLO type of democracy, see Hourani (1980), Hilal (1995, 2006), Salem (1999).
6 These new civil society organizations in the West Bank acted beside other organizations that were established earlier (including those established during the Jordanian administration and before). These previous organizations, such as those of the Federation of Charitable Societies, formed in 1958, and the various Waqf (Endowment) Charities, have the characteristics of domestic society more than the characteristics of civil society organizations. Moreover, some of the new civil society organizations formed during the Israeli occupation retreated to neo-patrimonial structures and practices by abandoning elections and becoming dominated by a single leader. Dennis Sullivan, Jamil Hilal, Izzat Abdelhadi, and Walid Salem have all analyzed these developments.
7 While Sharansky and Shikaki agree that the Oslo process was about peace and security rather than democracy, they differ in other respects. Shikaki concluded that democracy should be built along with the process of ending occupation, while Sharansky made peace with the Palestinians conditional on Palestinian success in building democracy, a view that this chapter will discuss later.
8 Details in Salem (2000, pp.58–63).
9 See Panorama Center (1994, pp.86–94).
10 For elaboration, see the Arab Thought Forum's annual reports about democratic transformation in Palestine, the Palestinian Center for Human Rights' reports evaluating the performance of the Palestinian Legislative Council, the annual human development report of Birzeit University Development Studies Center, among others.
11 Arafat held weekly meetings of "the Palestinian leadership," which included PLO Executive Committee members, government ministers, and the security departments' leaders. There were no separate meetings for the PA Cabinet, or separate meetings of the PLC Executive Committee. It was a "hodgepodge" without any separation of authority, and none of the participants in these meetings had any real authority. They acted more as advisers to Arafat, who retained all the authority in his own hands.
12 The previous competing personalities included such personalities as Khalil Al-Wazir Abu Jihad and Salah Khalaf (Abu Iyad), both killed, and the leaders of PLO left-wing factions, such as Nayef Hawatmeh of the DFLP and George Habash of the Popular Front for the Liberation of Palestine (PFLP), who left the PLO after the signing of the Oslo Agreements.
13 The other 22 seats were distributed as follows: 1 for the Democratic Building Movement of Haidar Abdel Shafi, 3 close to the PFLP, 7 Islamists, 1 from Fida, and 10 completely independent. Such PLO organizations as the People Party, the Popular Struggle Front, the Palestinian Liberation Front, and the Arabic Liberation Front failed in the elections, as did ten very small new lists (Salem 2000, pp.67–68).
14 On a few occasions PLC members tried to challenge Arafat. The biggest challenge came in 1997, when they asked for the resignation of the government after reports of corruption involving some ministers. But after several meetings with Arafat, the PLC Council voted to give him the authority to solve the issue. Arafat formed a new government in 1998 but retained the ministers who had been accused of corruption.
15 This monitoring did not lead to a no-confidence move until 2002, when a Palestinian government was obliged to resign in order to avert a PLC no-confidence vote. Before then, the PLC had always been prepared to compromise with Arafat.
16 See, for instance, Doyle (1986).
17 Peace-building for the Palestinians was a process to gain individual and collective freedoms. In this sense it goes with democratization, because the latter cannot be achieved without freedom. The PA failed to promote nonviolence and effective negotiation, so failed to gain freedom for its people. It failed with respect to democratization for the reasons outlined in this chapter. Any Israeli responsibility for this failure is outside the scope of this chapter.

18 For instance, Shikaki wrote that the donors gave priority to peace and nation-building at the expense of democratization (Shikaki 1996, p.32).

19 A committee for Israeli–Palestinian peace that includes the United States, the UN, Russia, and the EU.

20 These studies and reports include the Rocard Report, prepared in 1998 in cooperation with several Palestinian academics and civil society activists, the Birzeit University Development Studies Center reports on human development in Palestine, and the "One Hundred Days" reform plan of the PA of 2002, among others.

21 Specifically the police, the civil defense, and the preventive security apparatuses.

22 The details of this period of instability can be found in the annual reports on democratic transformation in Palestine released by the Arab Thought Forum.

23 A women's movement public figure, Samihah Khalil, ran against Arafat in the 1996 election, while Bassam Salhi (People Party), Tayser Khalid (DFLP), Mustapha Bargouthi (Independent), Abdel Karim Shbeir (Independent), Sayyed Barakeh (Independent), and Abdel Halim Al-Ashkar (Independent) ran against Abu Mazen. Others withdrew from the race before the vote: Abdel Sattar Qassem, Majeda Al-Batsh (the only woman to run in the election), and Marwan Bargouthi, a rival of Abu Mazen from within Fatah.

24 For this view, see Hilal (1995, p.98).

25 The PLO charter was modified for the first time at a PNC conference in Gaza in April 1996, when all the articles denying Israel's right to exist and calling for armed struggle were deleted. Later, the Netanyahu government in Israel claimed that the modifications to these articles had not been made properly, and it was agreed to convene the PNC again in order to rectify the problem.

26 Out of 672 candidates in 1996, 25 were women; 5 were elected to the PLC.

27 Among them the human rights activist Iyad Sarraj and Raji Sourani from Gaza, and the journalist Maher Al-Alami from Jerusalem.

Human rights

9

MERGING THE HUMAN RIGHTS DIMENSION INTO PEACE-MAKING

Is it good for the Jews?

Edward Kaufman

Introduction

Connecting the paradigms of human rights and conflict has been a growing global concern among international and civil society organizations, and academics, but it had no major consequence within the majorities in the Israeli and Palestinian societies. The search for a better understanding of this issue is timely, given the collapse of the Israeli–Palestinian Oslo peace process and the last Gaza war (Kaufman and Bisharat 1998, 1999, 2002),[1] not taking into account the importance of ensuring human security on both sides. With the nature of conflict worldwide changing from predominantly international to intranational, as is the case of Israel, now facing only terrorist or non-state actors, the question of rights for the members of communities involved in asymmetrical wars arises at a more significant level. The fact that the victims of these "civil wars," these acts of terrorist movements and state repression, are increasingly civilians themselves makes it clear that a resolution is required in addressing acute forms of suffering that are not covered by the rules governing uniformed combatants. Without codes of conduct, a most negative slippery slope descends from extra-judicial executions to massacres and genocide, and the heavy price in human lives exacerbates the original, tangible roots of conflict.

Just to make sure that we share a similar understanding of the term, let us consider relevant to intrastate peace processes the human rights coined within the "International Bill of Rights," namely the 1948 Universal Declaration of Human Rights, and the Covenants of Civil and Political Rights, and Social, Economic and Cultural Rights, both coming into force in 1976. Most countries in the Middle East, including Israel, have ratified both covenants (Donnelly 2002).

Normally, the underdog is more predisposed to accept human rights as a standard for resolving conflict, appealing to the support of the international community to redress the lack of balance in the conflict. As a result, expectations grow that the international community will intervene on their behalf as they appeal to powerful nations and kinship neighbors, and refer to international laws principles – regardless of the fact that the weak side could also violate such norms. Within this context, it is no wonder that universal human rights are perceived by dominant actors to play a role for the benefit of the other side. But is it possible to make a case where the enlightened or long-term interests of the stronger side – in this case Israel – can factor in the acceptance of human rights principles as an important variable in its decisions?

In this chapter, the main purpose is to elicit fresh second thoughts from sub-scribers to the realpolitik school among Israelis and their supporters worldwide. Hence, points of argumentation and counter-points are advanced with the explicit purpose of being plausible and realistic in the perception of the "top dog" side of the conflict. Rather than using heavy, academic jargon and denser theoretical assumptions, our[2] priority is to speak loud and clear about a dimension that is most likely perceived negatively by the Israeli establishment.[3] A legitimate debate is emerging, with human rights considerations perceived as an irritant but also as a yardstick. On the one side, there are those who advocate the introduction of human rights codes as guiding principles during the negotiating process and as integral to the texts of peace agreements. On the more conservative side, there are those who suggest deferring justice until a later stage of post-negotiation, if it is to be introduced at all. Overall, there is a growing consensus that raising human rights issues at a later stage can consolidate the tenuous and often minimalist peace accords. But we have posited earlier that including fundamental rights, such as the right to life, civil rights, such as freedom of movement, political rights, such as the right to elect and be elected, and socio-economic rights, such as the satisfaction of basic needs, are relevant at the different stages of the peace process. We will test this, enlisting first the main arguments in favor – gradually moving from the realist to the liberal outlooks, recognizing that while stressing its analytical aspect, the normative aspects are hard to be totally disaggregated in a context where "ideapolitik" is increasingly showing the sense of progress of the international community (Kaufman and Bisharat 2003);[4] next acknowledging the existence of counter-arguments and attempting to address them; then introducing a brief discussion of how the human rights dimension was salient in the consensus reached on the refugees issue in Palestinian–Israeli track two diplomacy. (It may be necessary to disclose that the current author has been deeply involved in the work of human rights organizations, and while trying to be as objective as possible, other points of view may be underplayed.[5]) In our concluding remarks, we express our wish that the antagonistic reader at least acknowledges the validity of the argumentation.

Argumentation

Argument 1: Understanding the limits of power

In the changing international system, the supremacy of military power does not ensure a peace "diktat," when the issue is not a regime change but a deep-rooted conflict of entire nations versus states. On the one hand, the leadership replacement after Arafat's death did not result in a renunciation of national goals; on the contrary, the surprising electoral victory of Hamas has only increased the will to resist unilateral moves by Israel. On the other hand, although Israeli military tactics have evolved with the ever-growing challenges of defeating modern terrorism, it has become evident that force alone cannot ultimately guarantee personal security for the Israelis. The most advanced weaponry, ingenious strategy, and superior training will not empower Israel to prevent every terrorist attack. An enemy that wears no uniform, hides among civilian populations, and preys on the fears of the innocent cannot be totally eradicated by conventional means. This adversary can still inflict massive physical, and more importantly psychological, damage on the intended target, thereby achieving the terrorists' goals of disrupting society and sowing fear. A superior military might cannot ensure the absence of violence – allegorically, Israel may be "the lion [of Judah], king of the [Middle East] jungle," but it cannot crush the swarms of bees emerging from countless hives, ready to die while inflicting severe pain. Although the bees may not knock the lion out, their persistent attacks may cause him to change direction.

This line of thinking helped Hamas, after approximately fifty suicide bombings, to be perceived as "victorious" in the battle for Gaza, subsequently to win an election, and to continue shelling over the border fence with Al Qassam rockets. Even if such acts cannot threaten Israel's national security, the stamina needed to keep the territories at all costs has dramatically diminished among its citizens, especially since the badly run Second Lebanon War. Furthermore, we should take into consideration that the correlation of forces can change over time and the currently factionalized enemy forces in the Arab world could one day unite. Last but not least, domestic ethnic, social and political strife, including the reluctance of a significant minority to continue to fight in "wars of choice" rather than "wars of survival," might erode the current superiority of the top dog. Hence, while the military advantage should not be relinquished, a more balanced approach must be undertaken. The short-term gains of the severe restrictions imposed on Palestinian society must be weighed against the long-term effects they will have on future Israeli and Palestinian generations. Seemingly minor when examined individually, measures such as restricting freedom of movement coalesce, creating an unbearable situation for the Palestinian people residing in the West Bank and a humanitarian crisis in Gaza.

Argument 2: Differences between inter- and intra-state conflict

We consider it is best to disaggregate the Israeli–Arab conflict and consider its Zionist–Palestinian component within the global context, and consequently search for remedies based on universal standards. This component shares many attributes with other ethno-political conflicts, including those in Sri Lanka, Northern Ireland, the former Yugoslavia, Cyprus, and Nagorno Karabakh. Granted, there is a salient regional dimension, with the Palestinians part of the Arab world that united in the early stages against Israel's existence as a state and is now pressing for its withdrawal to pre-1967 borders. Nonetheless, the Palestinian accumulation of past and current grievances of a non-territorial nature brings them closer to the other war-torn states. The individual and collective rights of nearly two million Palestinians are central to settling the future of the West Bank, as was also the case in Gaza before the pullout. In the past, the "Israeli–Arab" confrontation was also called the "Middle East" conflict, without regard for the many other violent disputes in the region. Israel has now signed peace agreements with Egypt and Jordan, respectively the strongest Arab nation and the one with the longest borders with Israel. It withdrew from southern Lebanon and there has not been any significant international pressure on Israel to reach an agreement with Syria (there has been not one casualty in the Golan Heights for forty-four years). In retrospect, if it was difficult for Israel to negotiate on more than one front, the Assad dynasty should not have been the next in line to be engaged in negotiations. Even if more than one Israeli government opted to engage in this track first, it was for tactical reasons – to isolate Palestinian claims.

However, concern for human suffering rather than intervening in disputes over sparsely populated borders has increasingly become a priority for the international community. This is evidenced by its greater concern for the Palestinians' destiny than for that of the Syrians. In the Golan Heights, we have a boundary dispute where the territorial dimension prevails over the human element – a few thousand people, Jewish settlers and Druze, who were given perhaps unwanted, but nevertheless equal, Israeli citizenship. Kunnetra, the main urban center of the Golan, was handed back to Syria following the 1975 Kissinger-brokered disengagement agreement (Quandt 2001).

The conflict facing Israel today is significantly different from that of decades ago. Through its short history, the Israeli–Arab conflict has gone through a full cycle of war. It escalated from seven decades of a confined, protracted communal dispute in Palestine, to a regional war declared by seven Arab states in 1948, to a North–South conflict (with French and British forces helping Israel fight Egypt in 1956), to an East–West conflict in 1967 (with the USSR supporting the Arabs and the US alliance with Israel). The peak of armed confrontation occurred at Yom Kippur (the Jewish Day of Atonement) 1973, when the struggle reached global proportions with the first oil crisis and the United States going on nuclear alert to deter the Soviet Union from sending troops to its cornered ally, Syria. Since then, the conflict de-escalated, back to a complex, regional war in 1982, when Israel, initially in collusion with the Lebanese government, attacked Fatherland, the Palestinian-controlled enclave in the south, and planned to expel the Palestinians via Syria to Jordan. The 1991 Gulf War saw a US-led coalition that included several Arab countries fighting the Iraqi invasion of Kuwait, with Israel – for once – not responding militarily to a missile attack by Saddam Hussein's regime. Now back to its original dimension, the Israeli–Palestinian dispute became a low-intensity conflict during the first Intifada. The blood of today's conflict is being shed almost exclusively by Israelis and Palestinians, with thousands of innocent civilian casualties in the past decade.

Making peace with the Palestinians is now a precursor to a negotiated lasting peace with the rest of the Arab world. With the balance of power strongly in Israel's favor, there is a golden opportunity to resolve matters with the Palestinians. There was an expectation that a hawkish and determined government, like that of Prime Minister Sharon, could lead the people to grant human rights concessions and restrict the settlers' illegal and extra-parliamentary actions. But that dream evaporated when Olmert, Sharon's weak successor, assumed power.

Argument 3: The quest for equal citizenship

From an individual rights perspective, principles would have been respected if Israel's Knesset had annexed "Judea and Samaria" (as it did with the Golan Heights and East Jerusalem), giving the West Bank Palestinians equal rights; then the Jewish settlers could remain in the Occupied Territories, which had become part of Israel. What is not acceptable is to maintain a long-lasting, dual legal system for Arabs and Jews in the Occupied Territories. As in Gaza, Israeli Jews must understand that annexing "Judea and Samaria" can be done only at the "cost" of providing the Palestinians with full citizenship, or through reprehensible "ethnic cleansing." This latter option, although the platform of an extreme party and perhaps quite popular among more than a few in Israel, is rejected by most on grounds of morality and expedience. On the other hand, the denial of the right to vote and to be elected to one's own government cannot be maintained for over two generations. After four decades of the longest contemporary military occupation, a reminder of the principle "no taxation without representation" is needed. While in many protracted communal conflicts, the parties expect to coexist under the same government when peace is finally achieved (as in South Africa and Northern Ireland), the consensual arrangement anticipated for the Israeli–Palestinian conflict is a two-state solution in which full citizenship can be secured to all in each separate unit. The ideal of resolving the conflict through establishing one joint and harmonious Jewish–Arab binational state has been set aside by most as unrealistic and not respecting the strong self-determination preferences of both nations. At times, reference is made to other post-colonial situations, comparing the need to pull settlers out of the Palestinian Occupied Territories to the exodus of the *pieds noirs* from Algeria to France. However, many supporters of the same formula accept that the foreseeable outcome of our conflict is a good relationship between separate Israeli and Palestinian states. While the relevance of human rights principles may be greater for integrated solutions than for the cases of separation, in our reality, people's lives remain interwoven (like those of divorced couples who continue to live in adjacent houses with some of their children in each house, living with the non-preferred parent due to a court ruling). It should be noted that about 20 percent of the Israeli population comprises its original Arab inhabitants, and the settlers might well refuse to be evacuated from the Jewish holy places that would come under full Palestinian authority. Hence, even if issues of individual rights are to be considered the domain of each sovereign state, it will be important to redress the violations of the past, protect rights during the lengthy peace process, and address the likelihood that the population of each state may include a substantial number of the other's nation. The ideas of "pushing the Jews into the sea" or forced "transfer of Palestinians to Jordan" are simple extremist fantasies. As a Palestinian colleague reminds us, the two peoples are "doomed to coexist."[6]

It is in both parties' best interests to start building strong ties now, so that when the day for Palestinian independence finally comes, there will be a basic foundation for cooperation. It would be prudent, from the Israeli perspective, to make the initial steps in this process by placing greater emphasis now on matters of human rights. It is impossible to predict exactly how long it will take for that vision to be realized. However, the sooner Israel begins the transition from occupier to neighbor, the better.

Argument 4: Pragmatism and respect for humane principles

Clearly, protection of its citizens is Israel's number-one concern, which is why the reduction of Palestinian hatred of Israel, at the grassroots level, must be made a top national security priority. For far too long, the policy of the powerful was aimed at "teaching a lesson" of submission, particularly when the weak side advocated and used extreme violence. As a Jewish Jerusalemite taxi driver might say: "We will beat them and beat them till they stop hating us." Paradoxically, the mirror image arose within Palestinian organizations at the outbreak of the militarized Al-Aqsa Intifada.[7] The tendency in asymmetrical conflicts to show "who is the boss" is very tempting. By now, though, it should be evident that modification of behavior is not going to happen by punishment alone. The main attacks now come from individual volunteers, mobilized by fanatical organizations such as Jihad Al Islam, often brainwashed by irresponsible clerics, but also motivated by overcoming misery and humiliation with the spirit of vengeance and martyrdom. Although a great deal of disdain toward Israel is spawned by incitement in the Palestinian Authority (PA)-controlled media and in Palestinian schools, it is undeniable that many of Israel's security tactics perpetuate and increase the already strong enmity.

Respect for the "human dignity" of the individual is of universal relevance, but in our Middle East, humiliation and dishonorable treatment carry an additionally strong cultural weight that needs to be factored in. The impossibility of reigning over millions of Palestinians over the long term – with negative repercussions for the Arabs in Israel – was recognized publicly by the former hard-liner Sharon. Still, the facts on the ground – the innumerable road-blocks, the sleepless lines of Palestinians waiting mostly in vain to gain access to the Ministry of Interior's offices in East Jerusalem, and countless other examples of inhuman treatment – have a most negative and perhaps lasting impact on practically every Palestinian.

Re-evaluating and removing security procedures within the West Bank that were established to provide protection for Jewish settlements would not only improve life for the Palestinians but lead to greater security for Israelis, as people would be less willing to sacrifice themselves in order to harm Israel. A simple cost–benefit analysis of such procedures as home demolitions, carried out by the military units that are now performing policing duties in the territories, will help determine whether they are doing more harm than good with respect to their traditional functions as a defense force. Terrorist leaders prey on the impressionable and desperate, manipulating their fears and perceptions into a desire to become suicide bombers. Decreasing Palestinian hardship will reduce the recruitment base of the likes of Hamas and Islamic Jihad.

Recognizing human rights as entitlements could help humanize Israelis in the eyes of Palestinians, as happened when Arab satellite TV broadcast live footage of the sensitive and patient eviction of Jewish settlers from Gaza. A lack of human contact between the two peoples has led to a complete de-humanization of each in the eyes of the other. Younger Israelis see Palestinians as terrorists, while Palestinians view Israelis as aggressive settlers and soldiers. Human rights entitlements work as confidence-building measures and can go a long way to disprove the negative stereotypes of Israelis which Palestinians hold, and they will pave the way for a positive relationship in the future.

Argument 5: International standards as an imperative

Paradoxically, democratic governments often face domestic constituencies that perceive the implementation of specific international resolutions as a source of weakness, concessions granted solely due to pressure from biased international organizations and world powers. Examples include the UN Committee Against Torture (CAT) equating "moderate physical pressure" in interrogations with torture, and the International Court of Justice's declaration that the Separation Barrier/Security Fence/Apartheid Wall in the West Bank is illegal. Public antipathy toward such rulings can be overcome if they are presented as accepted universal principles, rather than specific criticism. Then there is a good chance that they will be accepted as a "cost of democracy." Israeli citizens perhaps now understand that the cost of being a member of the family of nations requires them to accept principles that translate into required concessions that do not emanate from the weakness or strength of leadership, but rather from contractual obligations.

Being accepted and fully integrated into the international community has been an important and long-term aim of Zionist and then Israeli foreign policy. The fact that Israel faces undeserved negative bias, and sometimes even blatant discrimination at the United Nations[8] and other international forums, does not make it automatically immune to all international covenants. Whereas the majority of UN General Assembly condemnations of Israel take the form of biased resolutions drafted by an authoritarian and/or Muslim regime, many of the international covenants governing human rights were drafted in order to prevent situations like those faced by Jews before the state of Israel existed. The persecution and oppression of Jewish minorities worldwide and the Holocaust would probably not have been on the same scale had these covenants been in place at the time. International public opinion toward Israel was actually quite positive for the two decades following independence. Since

1967, however, its international standing has been in decline. This may be linked to the West's growing dependence on Arab oil, or to a resurgence of global anti-Semitism. But it also undoubtedly reflects the fact that Israel is no longer viewed as a defenseless underdog but as an aggressive and trigger-happy occupier.

Lately, Israel has routinely been tagged as one of the world's grossest violators of human rights. Often this is a case of double standards, as those making the accusations are frequently authoritarian Arab/Muslim regimes. And yet severe human rights violations *do* take place in Israel and contribute to the country's negative global image. Judge Goldstone's inquiry into war crimes committed by both Israel in Gaza and Hamas in southern Israel cannot be dismissed as anti-Semitic, as its chair is a highly respected expert and indeed a Zionist Jew who has previously been honored by the Hebrew University. Israel must uphold current standards in terms of protection of human rights, even for those it considers terrorists, and must be prepared to be held accountable to them.

Argument 6: Enlightened self-interest and the propaganda of the deeds

By advocating and trying to adhere to human rights principles, such standards can also be invoked for the sake of the citizens of the stronger party. They often enjoy more daily rights than the oppressed minority, but their right to life has been challenged over the years by acts of indiscriminate terror. Each side should be held accountable to such standards. On collective rights grounds, given that Israeli Jews demand recognition and acceptance from Arabs, why not recognize Israel's right to exist rather than merely accept its *de facto* presence in the region? The Arab world in general and even some realists in Hamas are willing to accept that Israel is a reality that cannot be erased. Pragmatically speaking, this may be good enough. But it also means that acknowledgment of Israel's existence is based solely on its present strength, underpinned by its long-term military superiority. It will be in the Jewish state's best interests to seek not merely recognition but its neighbors' acceptance of Israel's "right to exist." Recognition of Palestine as a Muslim state and a member of the Arab League leads to reciprocity in the legitimate demand of Israel as a Jewish and democratic state, connected to its diaspora through common institutions.

Furthermore, by showing goodwill now, at the apex of its power, Israel might establish a better starting position for future territorial negotiations. If Palestinians are granted more rights now and consequently become more flexible, that may signal that compromises over territorial requests will be reached when the time for final status negotiations finally arrives.

By stressing its respect for the right to life (Article 3 of the Universal Declaration of Human Rights, UDHR), which is obviously the most fundamental one, Israel can benefit just as much at its adversary. By refraining from extra-judicial executions (institutionalized as "targeted elimination" in Hebrew) of Palestinian suspects, and the consequent imperiling of bystanders – so-called collateral damage – we can denounce suicide or homicide bombings as the worst of all human rights violations, since they are specifically targeted against innocent civilians. The human rights organizations around the world, the UN, and other international actors should be challenged to take an active stand against such crimes, but we can expect them to respond only when our hands are clean of deliberate killings without any legal procedure. The Israeli authorities have arrested and prosecuted – rather than assassinated – several Palestinians suspected of planning suicide bombings, as in the case of Marwan Barghouti. They must continue on this course, rather than revert to the extra-judicial one.

In addition, the constant state of conflict has had a negative impact on Israeli society. The environment of fear resulting from indiscriminate acts of terror has led to many instances of post-traumatic stress disorder among Israeli youth (Herzog Hospital 2001). Even more disturbing, however, is that Israeli schoolchildren are among the most violent in the world, a phenomenon believed to be the result of force being an accepted societal means of dispute resolution.[9] An astonishing 43 percent of Israeli children have admitted to bullying others, while one in four Israeli boys admitted to carrying a knife to school for protection (Maxwell 1999). It is only to be expected that Israel's use of overwhelming force to deal with the Palestinians has had a trickle-down effect on society. The culture of violence prevalent in Israel has had a dramatic impact on the most impressionable members of the community: children. They grow up learning that physical force is an acceptable and even successful means of response in a dispute. An asymmetrical Israeli response to a Palestinian attack surely encourages a youth to respond to a school bully by such rash means as carrying a weapon.

The legitimate use of force should not be abandoned altogether; however, it must be utilized only as a last resort. As Israel's Supreme Court made clear in historic rulings in relation to the Security Barrier, specific threats to Israeli security must be taken into account but balanced with minimizing human rights restrictions on the neighboring Palestinians. The rights of the other party cannot be sacrificed simply to secure our own. This message must be embedded in the minds of Israeli youth.

Argument 7: Getting fewer carrots and more sticks

The image of Israel as "David versus Goliath" is fading. World sympathy with Jewish suffering was an important element in the recognition of Israel after the Holocaust. Nowadays, active support emanates predominantly from the dwindling, but well-organized, Jewish diaspora and fundamentalist Christian lobbies. Despite their continuing support, Israel itself must take steps to avoid being seen around the world as a pariah state. Over recent years, the world community has increasingly applied sanctions to states and has prosecuted individuals that it feels have violated human rights. Systematic gross human rights violations (as detailed by Amnesty International 2007a, 2007b, among others) eventually result in falling investment, restrictions in preferential trade and scientific agreements, and reductions in foreign aid. The universal jurisdiction of crimes against humanity is not only accepted by a small number of judges in a few countries but is part and parcel of the International

Criminal Court. While still not fully functioning, legal action initiated in a number of European countries has generated apprehension among leaders and the rank-and-file in military and security services. In the long run, sanctions may deter Israelis from being party to repressive policies.

Argument 8: Reducing the parties' asymmetry

In the distant past, the victor's imposed solution would hardly have come under international scrutiny, and the top dog could administer the outcome at its convenience. More recently, however, the principles of justice have raised the expectations of the weaker side, increasing their willingness to fight and sacrifice. The stronger party is now responsible for restraining the weaker side, even if it has to grant concessions to achieve this. The "big brother" paradox is that he cannot use his extra strength to placate his sibling, and he often has to find ways to reduce the asymmetry to induce the other to relax. By narrowing the gap through confidence-building, the dominant actor's measures can persuade the weak to feel empowered to negotiate acceptance of other claims.

For example, the willingness to release a significant number of Palestinian political prisoners in exchange for an Israeli soldier kidnapped near Gaza may have positive implications. If we switch the paradigm from demanding full payment for a crime committed in the *past* to avoiding endorsement of violence in the *future*, parole boards should focus on the conditional release of individuals who take an oath of nonviolence. This will then shift responsibility for the implementation process to the Palestinian Authority, which should take control of both the released prisoner's entry into the job market through training in new skills and his psychological readaptation. The PA should also monitor his progress to minimize the risk of recidivism (Kaufman and Hassassian 2006).

With overwhelming military and economic superiority over the Palestinians, Israel sets the "rules of the game" in any negotiations or deals. The asymmetry of having an overwhelming advantage may appear to be extremely helpful in terms of attaining one's preferred outcome, but that is not necessarily true. When negotiating with those who have known nothing but powerlessness for nearly forty years, empowerment is the name of the game.

The Palestinians have little incentive to abide by agreements that are reached through imposition rather than negotiation, and such settlements often perpetuate the desire to fight to attain something more acceptable. By showing more willingness to concede, especially on security issues that affect Palestinians on a daily basis, it might be proven to the Palestinians that diplomatic dialogue is far more profitable than violent uprising. In effect, a concerted effort to demonstrate sincerity in negotiations will likely yield a more positive result for Israel than a hard-nosed, stubborn approach. For a durable peace, the agreements must meet the minimal needs and expectations of both parties. Only about half of the peace agreements have been fully or even partially implemented after five years. But it need not be that way: Israel's peace treaties with Egypt and Jordan have lasted for many years without collapsing, amid difficult regional ups and downs. We, Israelis and Palestinians, need to put ourselves in the shoes of the "Other" to achieve similar success again.

Argument 9: The human rights language and its impact

Words are as important as acts in improving relationships, especially when violence and loss of life have brought emotions to a high pitch. A case can be made through effective communication as long as one is paying attention to semantics and believes in the acceptance of shared universal principles, including the acknowledgment of the rights of the "Other." Even at the levels of protocol and declaratory statement, this message can establish an atmosphere of mutual respect which is more conducive to successful negotiation. Take the first line of the UDHR preamble: "The inherent dignity and the equal and inalienable rights of all members of the human family is the foundation of freedom, justice and peace in the world." Just repeat that, and the atmosphere may change. Sadly, in spite of the lobbying of Human Rights Watch in 1991 in Madrid at the inaugural meeting of the Middle East Regional Peace Conference, we found no "rights basket" or mechanisms or working group in the early stages of designing the bilateral and multilateral tracks that followed. It seemed that the "new world order" excluded Middle Eastern leaders from compliance with the yardstick that measures all other regions of the world. The more eclectic Israeli–Palestinian 1993 Oslo Agreement implicitly covers some UDHR principles, such as conducting elections (Article 21) in the Occupied Territories, but the pragmatic outlook of the agreement kept even this clause from being framed within a broader context of human rights. The Oslo II Cairo Agreement of September 1995 contains a short reference to human rights, but the Wye Agreement of 1998 has no reference to the human rights obligations of Israel and only a vague mention in relation to the Palestinian Authority. The later "Road Map to Peace" suggested by the "Quartet" (led by the US) has no mention of human rights at all. At the leadership level, no reference to "human rights" or "rights" was found in the forty-five speeches of Prime Minister Ariel Sharon after he took office as late as May 2003 – with the exception of one in Aqaba in 2003 at a meeting with Mahmoud Abbas. On the other side, Yasser Arafat repeatedly mentioned the term "rights," but he was exclusively referring to the Palestinian people (Kaufman and Abu-Nimer 2007). And the aforementioned Goldstone Report on Gaza has been dismissed as biased without answering its numerous allegations of blatant human rights violations.

A language of dignity and respect carries a lot of weight for persecuted people. For the losing side, rejection, negativity and boycotts – even suicide bombings – are often perceived as their only remaining sources of strength. Mention of "entitlements" by the strong is therefore expedient, since it may elicit a more constructive attitude from the underdog. Rather than conceding that they will "give up" territories in "Judea and Samaria," the Israeli authorities should stress that the Palestinians have an inherent "right" to a state in part of historic Israel or Palestine. Granted that inclusion of a human rights provision may not guarantee its execution, but without referring to it explicitly there would be little chance for implementation at all.

The Dayton Agreement on Bosnia and the Good Friday Accord on Northern Ireland, in contrast, feature human rights clauses throughout the text, and the European Convention on Human Rights is incorporated into a new agreement to set the standards for domestic law. We strongly feel that a similar commitment would have contributed not only semantically but psychologically to promoting goodwill on the part of the Palestinians and awareness about the importance of acting according to set international parameters on the part of the Israelis. Due to the deep-rooted nature of protracted communal conflicts, it is not sufficient merely to ensure the cooperation of leaders in the peace-making process; peace-building is also required among the sectors of civil society that will eventually be expected to legitimize and support the historic compromise.

Furthermore, it is expedient to demand that textbooks embrace the basic principles of universality and equality between all peoples and nations, including Arabs and Jews. The decision of the UNRWA to include in the human rights curriculum in Hamas-ruled Gaza the teaching of the Holocaust as the worst form of genocide is justified, albeit difficult to implement. Paradoxically, this came at a time when the Knesset was legislating to forbid the teaching and remembrance of the Palestinian Nakba (Catastrophe) of 1947/8, when three-quarters of the Palestinian nation suddenly became refugees in foreign lands. From an educational point of view, planting the seeds of tolerance toward the "Other" is a long-term investment in securing a lasting peace.

Argument 10: Negative domestic repercussions

The still-undefined borders and the presence of an Arab minority in Israel have blurred the distinction between their citizenship rights and their brethren in the Occupied Territories. The lack of respect for human rights in the Occupied Territories has had a negative impact on democratic values within Israel, particularly toward its Arab citizens, as shown in the excessive use of violence while curbing the October 2000 riots. Human rights violations against Palestinians across the Green Line lead to a slippery slope back home, first by discriminating against "our own" Arabs who identify themselves as Palestinians with Israeli citizenship. Not many Jews differentiate between their shared identities across the Green Line divide, as they see Jewish settlers in the Occupied Territories as full citizens of Israel. Nonetheless, on the slippery slope, Jews who support equal rights for Arabs are viewed as even worse than them, traitors to their own ancestry. B'tselem, the Israeli information center on human rights in the Occupied Territories, is viewed by hate-mail senders not as a watchdog but as an "Arab lover" (Podeh 2001). The proudly independent Israeli newspapers that report human rights violations are perceived by most Israelis as publishers of self-hatred journalism. The slippery slope continues, and people come to view judges who reject double standards as anti-Jewish. From there, the law enforcement agencies are labeled "Nazi."

Paradoxically, the Jewish settlers and their allies called for a popularly supported referendum in Israel before the pullout from Gaza, demanding the people's right to choose. Why did these Israelis fail to understand that the principle of self-determination should apply to *all* those affected by the decision, including those living in Gaza (at that time 1.5 million Arabs and just 8000 Jews)? The inhabitants of the territory in question should be allowed to express themselves first; only if they express a wish to be incorporated into Israel should its inhabitants be able to express their acceptance or rejection. This is only one example of the occupation resulting in increasing support in Israel for the principle of limiting the right to vote to "Jews only."

Argument 11: The Jewish autochthonous roots

In its Declaration of Independence, the state of Israel grants "complete equality of social and political rights for all its citizens," stressing its democratic nature, yet it also adheres to the vision of a "Jewish state," inspired by its prophets. The notion of human rights takes root in the Talmud, and goes as far back as the Ten Commandments (Cohen 1992, 1984). The Jewish covenant with God dictates that the people of Israel are to be a light to all nations, an example to the rest of the world of how to live in the correct way. Human rights are not a foreign imposition, or a punishment imposed by the international community. The values are rooted in the Jewish religion and books, which reveal the message of the prophets during the Jewish people's early experience of statehood more than two thousand years ago, and surely as a persecuted minority in exile. The struggle against discrimination in the Dreyfus case in France led Theodore Herzl to establish the World Zionist Organization and to the formation of the first International League for the Rights of Man. René Cassin – a Nobel Peace Laureate, proud Jew and president of the Alliance Israélite Universelle – when preparing the draft text of the UDHR, understood that it should reflect the Ten Commandments (Agi and Cassin 1998). The state of Israel was formed so that the Jews would have a refuge where they could escape from constant discrimination and the denial of their rights and dignity. But Jews cannot claim this moral right while simultaneously denying it to others. The Old Testament states: "Justice, justice you shall pursue."[10] Scholarly consensus argues that the word "justice" appears twice in order to signify that a just cause must be pursued only by just means. The security of the Jewish state and the safety of its people are undoubtedly just causes. However, as Jewish people defending a Jewish state, the tactics Israel uses in pursuit of these causes must be dictated by and kept in accordance with the principle of justice that is so embedded in the Jewish faith.

Whereas human rights are often viewed as the adversary's weapon, it is important to understand that by endorsing them and claiming some contribution to their shaping, we will be recognized as promoters of higher standards of human behavior. Jews have to accept that the widespread acceptance of honorable principles will lead to justified demands being made on Israel.

Rather than overstating our adherence to human rights standards in times of conflict, it may be best to stop here and go on to debate the arguments that are often used to dismiss such principles. But let us first only mention other positive points that may require further coverage: the importance of respect for human rights in democracy, and the hope that Palestinians and Israelis will not fight each other in future if they both achieve democracy; the corrosive effect of not respecting the rights of the Palestinians on ignoring the entitlements of the weaker sectors of Israeli society; the corruptive practices of occupation tending to arbitrary rule and its domestic impact; and more.

One last point: introducing human rights as a relevant dimension may result in a paradigm shift and open new avenues for imaginative and creative solutions. Stressing the uniqueness of this conflict makes people feel that there is no solution. Rather than confining ourselves to boiling in our own pot continuously, it is better to look at how other combatants around the world have managed to end their conflicts. We are not so naive as to expect that merely showing governments the right texts will be sufficient to get them to comply. However, human rights clauses emanating from declarations and covenants are drafted in broad terms and subject to different interpretations, which can allow room for some "constructive ambiguity." Overall, the learning experience from "best practice" elsewhere is that including the rights issues in the peace-making process ensures a more durable outcome and general satisfaction with a new status quo. Rather than continuing our "tunnel vision," why not fully explore lateral thinking? We are not running away from the burden of evidence. We will try to illustrate this argument in the section dealing with permanent status issues later.

Counter-arguments

Counter-argument 1: An insurmountable conflict of rights

We need to acknowledge that the contending rights of the parties in a conflict make it very difficult to make wise judgments about the prevalence of one claim over another, especially when these claims come from two nations that have been subjugated throughout most of their history. Clearly, absolutist, unilateral claims to territory for one nation deny the full rights of the other group, and if both have similar but contending rights, compromises must be reached.

Let us take the right of return to the land of their ancestors for Israelis and Palestinians as a matter of principle. One can argue for ever about who has more rights to be in Israel/Palestine – Jews, who were expelled from the "Holy Land" twenty centuries ago, or Arabs, who were expelled from Palestine more than six decades ago – but since human rights codes do not specify a time limit for such a right, we can concur that both nations have a legitimate presence here. The primary issue is how to satisfy the greatest number of core needs for the individuals of both communities with the least negative results. But let us remind ourselves that not all claims necessarily form a zero-sum game – that if it's good for me, it must be bad for the "Other." Sometimes immediate gratification may not be more useful in the long term than granting rights to the historic enemy and then jointly harvesting the fruits of peace, as happened at the end of the Israeli–Egyptian conflict. There are many parameters that can allow rights to be shared – the time factor, expanding the cake by receiving compensation from third parties (notably the international community providing generous funds to meet basic needs), etc. Furthermore, not all needs are material and tangible, and sometimes we can generate more resources by cooperating with, rather than confronting, one another. Unfortunately, this is easier said than done. But let us see how specific ideas apply to refugees, water, settlers and Jerusalem (to be discussed in the following section).

Counter-argument 2: Human rights as maximalist propositions

Advocates of realpolitik have argued that demanding human rights clauses may delay the formulation of an accord when the window of opportunity to conclude it is relatively brief. Furthermore, it could be argued that there have been many instances when clauses of agreements in asymmetrical situations seem to violate universal standards explicitly or implicitly. At times of emergency the survival of the peace process dictates harsh policies toward its opponents, including deportation or imprisonment without due process. The danger, however, is that long-term institutionalization of such human rights violations will weaken "law and order" within and across the contending nations, making reconciliation much more difficult at a later stage. If it is considered worthwhile to stick to the "cost of democracy," deviations have failed to conclude a deal and may in fact hinder reaching a long-term stable solution. Relating to human rights as a paradigm does not necessarily mean that all outcomes must be congruent with such principles. It is mostly a reminder of an expectation that higher standards should be achieved insofar as this is feasible. In many countries in the West, it became clear after September 11, 2001 that security considerations may clash with individual freedoms. Yet universal laws are respected as overall binding principles, and departures from them are hotly debated.

Furthermore, as a democratic nation that remembers its own people's victimhood, Israel is expected to cling closely to human rights values, and it is expedient to prevent the deterioration of this image. Without minimizing the impact of violent acts, as time goes on, not only will Israel's counter-terror strategy become more refined, but its strong democratic process should eventually bring an end to those practices that infringe on human rights. One Supreme Court ruling ordered the end of the demolition of the homes of suicide bombers, deciding that this was an unjustifiable collective punishment (Associated Press 2005). The security services accepted the ruling, and finally acknowledged that the practice had never succeeded as a deterrent. So in this case a combination of the evolution of Israeli military tactics and action by its democratic institutions helped address at least one of the human rights concerns of the Palestinians.

Many who work in the field argue that respect for human dignity is a universal concept, as well as a confidence-building measure. The Israeli–Palestinian example would seem to be a case in point. In the Oslo Agreements, it was considered that the nature of reaching agreements in protracted communal conflicts and the need for gradualism have often resulted in partial agreements prior to the final treaty, prior to the ultimate target being reached. In such cases, human rights serve as confidence-building measures until the process can be completed. Such improvements are often presented as offering "peace dividends," but their allocation as entitlements provides the element of justice needed to redress the sense of asymmetry of the oppressed. In other words, one of the main reasons for the failure of the Oslo process was the sense of "relative deprivation," the deterioration of human rights standards at a time of growing expectations – including the right to life of both Arabs and Jews (see Gurr 1967). Then, too late for the Camp David summit, shared solutions to the permanent status issues seem to have been formulated in what have been called the "Clinton parameters" (International Crisis Group 2002). The challenge now is how to move from polarized views about the legitimacy of violent means of action to the common ground relating to ends, goals and objectives. This transition could be facilitated by increased declaratory and hopefully practical respect for human rights.

Counter-argument 3: Cultural relativism versus universal standards

Much has been said about the Middle East being an exceptional region and about the many contradictions of Arab Islam with respect to human rights standards, although voices have increasingly been emphasizing points of convergence (Dwyer 1991). This complex issue has several aspects. First, in some Western cultures (Israel included), there is a fear that commitments of principle will bring about demands for exhaustive implementation. However, it is often argued that in high-context cultures, where behavior is often determined by ceremonial and ritual declarations, the minority or weaker side expects some symbolic recognition of its rights, even if this falls short of full implementation. The extraordinary value of acknowledging injustice has been increasingly recognized as distinguished political leaders around the world have apologized in recent years for historical wrongdoing perpetrated by rulers, peoples or nations. Nations that have been oppressed for decades or centuries may find comfort in such statements, even though they are often merely symbolic and scarcely redress past violations. Many of the issues that pile up relate to dignity rather than, say, the land and homes that may have been lost forever.

Second, in the context of a protracted and highly violent conflict, gross human rights violations against the "Other" tend to be popular, and our case is no exception. As mentioned, the conventional wisdom in Israel has been "force is the only language the Palestinians understand." Hence, skeptics have predicted that human rights norms are far from the attitudinal prism of the Arab masses, as they have not been socialized into such practices. The Palestinians may argue that the same could be said of the Israelis, with the added dimension that the victims of past persecution now have the chance to occupy the vindictive position of victimizer. However, human rights principles can be found in both Islam and Judaism and should be explicitly mentioned in the peace process as part of a common heritage. Over the centuries, cooperation between Arab and Jew was more the rule than the exception. Tolerance towards the "Other" and nonviolence can be found through-out their histories. At least, at present, their rhetoric, if not their actual adherence to international human rights standards, makes the Arab states and the Palestinians no less accountable than Israel. Arguments have been advanced that some basic human rights lack universal validity, but the debate has died down since globalization has made it necessary to disaggregate what were once considered monolithic communities. Each country now has a civil society that professes shared values across the divide, and those of us who work with our peers across the national divide know that these are not false claims.

The best way to fight against double standards is not through a defensive justification of our excesses, but by demanding that the various UN agencies and other mechanisms force our neighbors to be judged by the same yardstick. Should they pursue this, Israeli Jews will find many allies in the Arab world, whom they will empower to criticize their own regimes. Even if the world's expectations of Israel are high, given the Jewish contribution to the concepts of human rights and the fact that its people have suffered horrendous violations in the past, the inter-national organizations should have equally high expectations of the Arab regimes and be as firm with them as they are with Israel.

Counter-argument 4: The Palestinian struggle as part of an insoluble, existential conflict

For many in Israel, the Palestinian struggle is still a part of an existential conflict. It is well documented that Palestinian terrorist groups are not alone in fighting for Israel's destruction. Syria is still technically at war with Israel, and it has played a major role in providing funding, training, and arms for the terrorist cells of Hezbollah and Hamas. Together with contributors from other Gulf states, some members of the royal family in Riyadh have been funneling millions of dollars to fanatical anti-Jewish Islamists, while simultaneously presenting themselves as peace brokers through the "Saudi peace initiative" (Podeh 2001). In effect, the conflict has not contracted in scope to involve only the Palestinians, but rather has expanded to include other Muslim state actors. The non-Arab Islamic Republic of Iran, the world's biggest state sponsor of terror, not only supports Hezbollah and other terrorist organizations but has repeatedly reaffirmed its own commitment to the complete destruction of the state of Israel. So this argument calls for all effort to focus on stopping terror against Israel, and for any concessions on the human rights front not to occur beforehand. While fighting extremism, one should not cease to isolate such forces through the use of positive incentives, including recognition of the Palestinian right of self-determination and rejecting oppression of them. Pushing for the isolation of political Islamist terrorism places Israel in the same camp as other Western democracies *and* alongside Arab regimes that fear Iranian-inspired Shi'ite and al-Qaeda Sunni terror. This unusual coalition must think long and hard before condoning any action that threatens the right to life. Fundamentalist terror will eventually be defeated by the nearly unanimous self-defense of the enlightened world. Israel must and will be a part of that process, but it should also refrain from any actions that could be classified as state terror.

Counter-argument 5: Israel must learn from its past mistakes

Some have argued that kind, noble gestures toward the Palestinians always yield disastrous results for Israel. Many of the arguments in this chapter have been presented before by peaceniks, and they are almost identical to those which justified the concessions made following the 1993 Oslo Accords, and those offered in 2000 at Camp David. It was hoped that by making life easier for the Palestinians, and giving them some limited autonomy, a negotiated peace settlement would be more appealing to a large segment of the Palestinian population. As history shows, though, rather than peace, these two examples of Israeli generosity and optimism led to the murder of thousands of innocent Israelis at the hands of Palestinian terrorists. The lesson to be learned was that Israeli concessions, on any level, could not come before a complete cessation in Arab aggression. Only after the Palestinians demonstrate that they are willing and able to crack down on terrorist organizations can Israel let its guard down and worry about anything other than its own security. At times, Israel has moved forward considerably since the outbreak of the second Intifada. Jumping the gun now and making foolish concessions before a Palestinian leader takes significant action against terror will only entangle Israel in a process that has repeatedly failed miserably in the past.

Being aware of this populist criticism, our reservations about the Oslo process and its aftermath were that any concessions that were offered fell short of the declaratory policy, were implemented too late, and were not framed within the wider context of the human rights paradigm. Our argument of "too little" refers not only to the small number (or complete absence) of human rights clauses in the agreements, but in qualitative terms to the lack of a different discourse from the prevailing arrogance of power. No one argues that Israel should not retain a strong security presence on its side of the fence when it withdraws from the West Bank. However, at the same time, it is imperative that Israeli policy does not infringe on full Palestinian control of their destiny in Gaza, including the freedom to communicate with the rest of the Arab world through the Egyptian border and the rest of the world by air and sea links. Yet such respect of Palestinian sovereign rights also implies that there is no obligation to allow their free passage into Israel, or through Israel to the West Bank. Any such special dispensations can be negotiated for equivalent concessions from the Palestinian side.

The withdrawal from Lebanon following mounting Israeli casualties sent a strong signal to terrorist organizations that Israel was sensitive to heavy Jewish loss of life. This perceived weakness motivated Palestinian terrorists to increase attacks on Israeli civilian targets, as was evident in the outbreak of the second Intifada shortly after the start of and during the Second Lebanon War. To avoid appearing weak and thereby encouraging future terrorism, Israel should not opt for the easy route of imposing collective punishment. The answer is not to create extra hardship for the

Palestinians simply in order to display Israeli strength. Generating more oppressive conditions will not convince the Arab masses to dissociate themselves from the terrorist organizations.

The bombing of the Baghdad nuclear reactor, the rescue of passengers at Entebbe airport, the capture and bringing to trial of one of the killers of two Israeli reservists in Ramallah, the bombing of Jihad Al Islam training camps in Syria and many other missions have displayed the heroism and professionalism of the Israeli Defense Forces and Israel's intelligence network. Even if Hamas could claim to have had some influence in persuading the Israelis to pull out of Gaza, the effective and sensitive evacuation of the Jewish settlers was much more significant because it showed the true nonviolent future potential of the Israeli Defense Forces.

Human rights in final status issues: strengthening legitimacy through consensual alternatives

There has been a significant human rights element in some of the Palestinian–Israeli workshops that have addressed the refugee problem. Other civil society projects have discussed other final status issues, such as Jerusalem, water, settlements, borders and security, and have adopted a similar rationale that has proven useful for consensus-building. These final status issues, postponed for discussion by the Oslo process until the last stage of negotiation, have been the most divisive points between the two nations, and we suggest introducing the human rights norms as additional criteria in a bid to generate innovative solutions. It is crucial to remind ourselves that universal rights apply to the protection of *any* individual, be they a terrorist, a refugee or a settler.

Palestinian refugees

Our premise is that any agreed solutions should, as much as possible, take into account the preferences of the refugees themselves, reviewing the options available according to the principles of international law and humanitarian precedents (Zureik 1996). UN General Assembly resolutions, such as Resolution 194 on the right to return to their homes, carry little weight when compared with Security Council resolutions and the likelihood of implementation. But what makes a UN document international law is its codification in a covenant, treaty or pact, duly endorsed and later ratified by a majority of member states. Hence, the return to "homes" or the "homeland," as the country of origin, could be interpreted in different ways. Furthermore, the complexity of the problem in terms of "rights" and the additional claims from Jews who fled from Arab countries is discussed extensively by Quigley (1998).[11] Yet the problem can be prioritized by the international community – Israel and the wealthy Arab states included – providing compensation and/or reallocation above all to those who need their basic needs to be met, especially those still living precariously in refugee camps who are secondary citizens in their countries of residence. In other words, the refugee options should always improve their socio-economic rights and their access to opportunity (UDHR, Articles 22–27).

As a matter of principle for a sustained peace, the refugees' choices should be accommodated as much as possible, and they should be allowed to choose between the following five options:

- return as a full citizen to the new Palestinian state;
- if requested, citizenship in the Arab country in which they have resided;
- transfer to a third country that expresses humanitarian goodwill in resettling a fixed number of those who have lived in refugee camps;
- negotiation with the Jewish state authorities regarding specific cases of family reunification in Israel; or
- remain where they are if none of the previous four options are deemed acceptable.

In a workshop including Israelis and Palestinians, mostly refugees from the Deheishe Camp, which took place in Jericho in early September 2000, the participants looked at this issue from an equal rights perspective, with consensus-building leading to greater understanding. The discussion raised the following points:

- The right to leave and return to one's own country is guaranteed by the Covenant of Civil and Political Rights, ratified by Israel and endorsed by the Palestinian institutions. On this basis, it is not easy to draw a dividing line between the Jewish Law of Return (Khok Hasvut) and the Palestinian Right of Return (El Awdah) to come back to the land of their respective ancestors. At face value, this principle therefore seems to be a conflict of rights which needs to be addressed.
- This basic reading of the covenants suggests that the right of return is a given, regardless of the refugees being expelled, escaping through fear or entering exile of their own volition. Hence, the expectation of a humane recognition of the Palestinian refugees' suffering and even the assumption of responsibility may be more of a moral duty than a legal obligation, which exists regardless of the intentionality of their departure or expulsion. To make it safer for Israel, it has been suggested that any text outlining this should be drafted and then put aside until all the concrete points of the agreement in terms of returning refugee numbers and overall compensation undertakings by the world community are worked out, without carrying irreversible consequences. Only then would the statement be brought back onto the table and even put at the top of the section of the agreement that deals with the issue of refugees. Once the process is agreed on, without further delay a compassionate text should be jointly drafted. It should be an expression of humanity, a sensitive declaration by Israel of its sorrow for the plight and suffering caused to more than two-thirds of a nation who were forced to become refugees.
- Once the above has been agreed, anyone who relinquishes their right of return to their place of origin in what is now Israel should be offered adequate

compensation and alternative solutions by all parties to the conflict, and they should be able to count on the goodwill of the international community.

- There is a consensus in the interpretation that the right of return to their "homeland" should be respected, but the issue becomes more controversial when dealing with their "homes" when these are no longer located in their own soon-to-be-established state of Palestine. Before dealing with this issue, we may reach one more point of agreement by introducing the concept of self-determination.

- In both societies, there has been a large majority over a long period of time who accept the concept of two separate states: an Israeli (Jewish) state living side by side with a Palestinian (Arab) state. Respect of the principle of self-determination would imply that the decision to accept any other resident or citizen has to be delegated to the democratically elected government of each nation.

- The issue of Palestinians returning to their former homes is problematic as many of their homes no longer exist or are occupied by other families, and a fair compensation scheme will have to be devised. The most pressing issue is to find a solution for the 250,000–300,000 Palestinian refugees who have been in Lebanon since 1948 in the most restrictive conditions and without citizenship. According to a survey conducted in 2004 by Dr. Khalil Shikaki, only 19 percent wish to go "back to their homes," and this figure halves when they are told that they will have to become citizens of Israel.[12] As suggested by the International Crisis Group (2004), a sizeable number of refugees could be settled in what is currently Israeli territory in the expectation that they will soon become part of the new Palestinian state as a result of land swaps outlined in the peace accord.

- While any compensation should prioritize those Palestinians living in refugee camps or adjacent to them, as additional monies become available they should be shared with those who require most assistance, depending on income and wealth.

- While focusing on the Palestinians in refugee camps, and without denying that they are real victims, the Arab countries from which Jews fled or were expelled (Iraq, Libya, Egypt, etc.) should be asked for contributions to help those who have not been fully rehabilitated. This is a negligible number, but any contribution would nevertheless be a goodwill gesture in recognition of equal rights.

There is no perfect solution to the refugee problem, but framing it as suggested in human rights terms is the best alternative to a non-mutually agreed outcome.

Conclusions

Peace is sustainable when security and justice go hand in hand. Sacrificing one for the other has always proven to be self-defeating in the long run, so every effort must be made to uphold both principles. We highlighted the relevance of human rights as the operational expression of "justice," a concept that UN Security Council Resolution 242 coined together with "lasting" to qualify the meaning of "peace" ("a just and lasting peace"). We can look upon this resolution as a diplomatic compromise between contending positions behind the two terms. But we can also see the wisdom of a combination which is not a zero-sum outcome but rather a win–win proposition in which both sides have more to gain. The territorial element which Palestinian and Israeli leaders may be calling an "historical compromise" for the underdog and "painful concessions" for the top dog brings many other tangible and intangible elements whose resolution can immensely improve the quality of life for both sides. If we could look upon individual aspirations in terms not only of our own "people" but of our "peoples," we could move a long way toward stable peace and reconciliation, which can add to the precarious diplomatic agreement the essential peace-building dimension.

At this time, many Israeli political parties and the majority of its citizenry have recognized the collective right of the Arab Palestinians to statehood, while the newly elected Hamas has had difficulty amending its "all or nothing" charter to accept the Israeli Jewish right of self-determination. Clearly, the world has criticized the latter's position and has applauded the Israelis' support of the concept of Palestinian self-determination, but the challenge is to translate this future collective right into respect of their individual freedom.

Many of us are tired of trying to decide who has more rights: the Jews or the Arabs? For quite some time, Palestinian and Israeli civil society organizations, academics, writers and people of goodwill have agreed that both nations have enough rights, and that it is short-sighted for the stronger side to try to dispossess the weaker. Any solutions should take care to satisfy minimal core needs, without which no nation will stop fighting.

Realist and liberal Zionist writers stress that, after centuries of suffering, Jews are now collectively committed to be the subjects rather than the objects of history. This protagonism can best be fulfilled not by the sword alone but by the pen, too. The texts of Judaism are part and parcel of the contemporary human rights canon, by which we are now being judged, as our prophets were throughout history.

Adopting a humane approach allows the Israelis to feel good about themselves, but we also know that in the twenty-first century, the principle of legal equality is advancing globally. Even if the United Nations maintains double standards and bloc politics often determine the wording of its General Assembly resolutions, the texts of human rights covenants and treaties are becoming the international rule of law, and its implementation now has enforcement mechanisms (Kaufman 1999). Israel wants to be a member of the "family of nations," so it must adhere to these rules. It should take note of how adherence to human rights standards has been made a precondition of Turkey's entry into the prestigious "club" of the European Union. Israel tends to look West rather than East, too, so this lesson should be learned from Turkey's experience. However, Israel also wishes to be accepted in the Middle East, which will require securing the goodwill of the Palestinians. If the latter can be persuaded to open doors to the Arab states, or at least not to block the Israelis' advances, recognition and acceptance should follow.

Although not a panacea, adherence to human rights principles can help in the pre-, mid- and post-negotiations stages of any peace process. As members of a democratic nation that remembers its traumatic past, and still has millions of its people scattered around the world in the diaspora, Israeli Jews should be fully aware of the value of human rights. Often, the security situation on the ground seems to clash with these principles, as is often mentioned by Israel's Supreme Court. However, as time goes on, Israel's strong democratic process should eventually bring an end to all practices that are not within the bounds of human rights.

So far, preliminary considerations have been advanced in the tenuous hope that they will make sense to the Israeli government and public. To what extent do the different points of argumentation make sense to those within the "establishment"? After so much error and little trial, is it not worth including this ingredient in the recipe for peace? We invite readers to reflect and enrich the list, make it even more accessible to the top dogs' minds. Even if we fail to connect with Israel's political leaders, perhaps the policy-makers of the world (and of the United States in particular) might be convinced that the Israeli–Palestinian conflict will be resolved only if the same principles that have helped end other disputes are adopted in this case, too.

Notes

1 This article often uses the term "we" instead of "I" when discussing an idea shared with a Palestinian colleague.

2 I use the plural (we, us) when presenting this article, since its main assumptions are the products of a team of Palestinians working with me. These colleagues include Ibrahim Bisharat, Mohammed Abu Nimer and Walid Salem.

3 I would like to express my gratitude to Simon Dinits and Sahar Sattarzadeh at the University of Maryland and Sonia Martinez at the Hebrew University for their assistance in researching and editing this chapter. And to my friend and colleague Patricia Weiss Fagen for her valuable advice.

4 I have paraphrased, amended and expanded some of our findings, so, hopefully, they will be better understood by the Israeli public at large and the political leadership in particular.

5 The author is one of the longest-serving members of Amnesty International's Executive Committee, a founder and former chair of B'tselem, and currently a member of the Advisory Board of Human Rights Watch/Middle East.

6 Prof. Manuel Hassassian, who teaches the course "Conflict Resolution: The Israeli/ Palestinan Experiment" with the author at the University of Maryland.

7 The militarized second Intifada was called an "unmitigated catastrophe" and "self-defeating" by Sari Nusseibeh in his book *Once upon a Country* (quoted in a review by Amos Elon (2007) "Hard Truth about Palestine," *New York Review of Books* 54 (7):28).

8 In 1975, the UN General Assembly adopted Resolution 3379, condemning Zionism, the ideology upon which the state of Israel was founded, as racist. The resolution was valid for sixteen years before it was finally repealed. Though Secretary-General Kofi Annan characterized the resolution as the United Nations' darkest hour, today a multitude of similarly anti-Israeli and anti-Semitic attitudes continue to plague the organization.

9 In 1999, a year before the eruption of the second Intifada, a World Health Organization survey found that Israel was the eighth worst out of twenty-eight countries surveyed on school violence.

10 Deuteronomy, 16.20.
11 They should also be provided with full citizenship rights, be compensated for their lost properties, and, if they desire, be granted the right of return to their countries of birth.
12 Khalil Shikaki, reporting on a poll held in Jerusalem, December 29, 2004. See <http://trumannews.huji.ac.il>.

10

FATAH AND HAMAS HUMAN RIGHTS VIOLATIONS IN THE PALESTINIAN OCCUPIED TERRITORIES FROM APRIL 2006 TO DECEMBER 2007

Bassem Eid

Introduction

On January 26, 2006, Hamas won control of 74 out of the 132 Legislative Council seats that serve Fatah leader and Palestinian Authority President Mahmoud Abbas, elected in January 2005 (*Electronic Intifada* 2006). The shocking Hamas triumph was attributed to Palestinian dissatisfaction with the Fatah Movement's corruption and complacent attitude toward Israel. As a result of increased Israeli military control over the Occupied Territories and, more specifically, the construction of a 700-kilometer concrete barrier separating the West Bank from Israel, Palestinian resistance sentiments had heightened (Abunimah 2006). Resistance to the Israeli occupation had reached the forefront of concern for a Palestinian majority. Consequently, Fatah's appeasing, conciliatory efforts were voted out of the Legislative Council.

Following the 2006 parliamentary elections, internal turmoil ensued. The shift in governmental control triggered a treacherous power struggle between Fatah and Hamas that continued at the expense of Palestinian civilians. The two movements failed to uphold various peace agreements constituted in 2006 and 2007, and conflict continued into June 2007, when Hamas initiated a rapid military conquest of the Gaza Strip. In a single week of escalated fighting in which 161 Palestinians were killed, including 41 civilians, Hamas took control over every Fatah stronghold and governmental office throughout the Gaza Strip (Palestinian Center for Human Rights 2007a). President Abbas immediately dismissed the Hamas-led government, formally dividing the Palestinian territories.

The governmental split has widespread implications for the future of the Palestinian people. Hamas and Fatah have violated international humanitarian law and the United Nations Declaration of Human Rights on numerous occasions and continue to threaten the safety of the Palestinian people. The continued fighting has killed hundreds of Palestinian men, women, and children throughout the Gaza Strip and the West Bank since June 2007. The Hamas takeover devastated civilian lives throughout the Occupied Territories, and resulted in absolute Hamas control over the Gaza Strip. The inter-factional violence between June 7 and 14, 2007 followed fifteen months of mounting tension and conflict between the two primary Palestinian political actors. This chapter will focus on violations of Palestinian rights from April 2006 through December 2007, which marks the official break between Hamas and Fatah, culminating in their bloody battle over Gaza, and thus marking a decisive moment in the history of the Palestinian people.

This author believes that both parties are equally complicit in human rights violations in Palestine and as such takes no position on which should lead the Palestinian people.

Hamas's human rights abuses during the seizure

Since its victory in the January 2006 parliamentary elections, Hamas has violated the human rights of numerous people throughout the Palestinian territories. From April 2006 through December 2007, it committed various international war crimes against Fatah members. It engaged in the capture, torture, and murder of Fatah members and leaders in the Gaza Strip and the West Bank. Members of Hamas stormed the homes of Fatah members with guns and other weapons, wounding and sometimes killing selected targets and civilians during the months following its parliamentary victory (Palestinian Center for Human Rights 2007a).

During the last week before Hamas's seizure of Gaza, violence against Fatah members escalated and numerous targeted attacks took place. For example, on June 11, Hamas captured and killed Jamal Abu El Jidian, the Secretary General of the Fatah Movement. El Jidian's home, located in the town of Jabaliya in northern Gaza, was shelled. His family and that of another Fatah member were also killed in the attack (Xinhua 2007). Hamas forces also captured Beit Lahiya of Jamal Abu al-Jadiyan, a senior Fatah official, during its seizure of the Gaza Strip. Lahiya was removed from his home and shot many times in the street (Human Rights Watch 2007).

Additionally, in seizing Fatah strongholds throughout the Gaza Strip, members of the Izzedine al-Qassam Brigades, the militant wing of Hamas, killed dozens of Fatah members and leaders. On June 12, in capturing the Fatah security forces' headquarters in northern Gaza, Hamas was reported to have executed several Fatah members and witnesses, killing over ten people in the raid (Issacharoff 2007). Hamas also threatened the families and affiliates of Fatah members, carrying weapons into their homes throughout the deadly week. The fundamentalist Islamic movement also broadcast hit lists of Fatah leaders across the Hamas–controlled airwaves and threatened to infiltrate Palestinian Authority media outlets.

Hamas militants brutally executed dozens of individuals who were working for President Abbas, including many who were not politically active. For example, Hamas security forces bound the legs and arms of Muhammad Swairki, Abbas's cook, then pushed him from the fifteenth story of an apartment building in Gaza City (Issacharoff 2007).

The human rights of civilians were also gravely violated throughout Hamas's takeover of Gaza. Between June 7 and 14, 2007, rampant gunfire in the streets and indiscriminate attacks throughout the Gaza Strip halted civilian life. In particular, according to customary international humanitarian law, medical personnel and hospitals must be protected at all times (Issacharoff 2007). However, Hamas directly targeted hospitals, endangering patients and medical staff, and obstructing healthcare access for thousands (Amnesty International 2007a, 2007b).

A general state of lawlessness emerged during Hamas's siege of Gaza. Rampant gunfire on the streets, attacks on targeted Fatah members, bombings, kidnappings, and the lack of consolidated and effective law enforcement heightened feelings of insecurity among the Palestinians. The fear that emerged among the Gazan people perpetuated the culture of violence that still pervades the region. Hamas celebrated violence as an acceptable tool for conflict resolution, which led to the increased misuse of firearms among civilians. During its takeover of Gaza, Hamas committed severe human rights abuses against Fatah members and civilians, ultimately failing to ensure the security and protection of the Palestinian people.

Hamas's human rights abuses following its seizure of power

After Hamas gained control over the Gaza Strip in June, the Izzedine al-Qassam Brigades continued to commit human rights violations against the Palestinian people. Attacks on Fatah members and institutions continued after Abbas's dismissal of the Hamas-led government. Almost immediately following Hamas's seizure of the Gaza Strip, President Ismail Haniyeh and his senior officials halted Gazan access to Fatah-controlled media outlets. On August 1, Haniyeh terminated the broad-casting of Palestinian public television, directed by Mahmoud Abbas, throughout the Strip. Later that week, he also shut down a pro-Fatah radio station and news agency (*Gulf News* 2007).

In addition to limiting freedom of the press and freedom of speech, the Hamas government violated the rights of Fatah supporters to assemble peacefully in protest against Hamas rule. Fatah rallies throughout Gaza sparked inter-factional violence. For example, during the first week of August 2007, over 300 pro-Fatah Palestinians rallied in Gaza City for about twenty minutes before Hamas dispersed the group with clubs and rifle butts. Hamas security forces halted dozens of buses transporting Fatah supporters to the rally, seizing Fatah flags and beating up passengers (Associated Press 2007).

In addition, Hamas has committed abuses against local and international media reporters in Gaza. During the early August pro-Fatah rally, Hamas security forces attacked television reporters and journalists and confiscated their cameras. They also infiltrated media agency offices based in Gaza City, taking recorded and written material from the rally (Associated Press 2007). Following the raids, the Palestinian Journalists' Union proclaimed a three-day boycott of Hamas-organized events to protest against their maltreatment in Gaza.

On August 31, security forces forcibly dispersed Fatah supporters protesting against Hamas control over Gaza at Friday prayers, injuring at least eight people, including two foreign journalists (Reuters 2007). The following Friday, Fatah supporters again gathered for open-air prayer in protest against Hamas's military takeover. In response, Hamas broke up the prayer meeting, beat and arrested dozens of participants, and, once again, targeted representatives of the media who were reporting on the clash (Abu Alouf and Ellington 2007).

On November 12, thousands of Fatah supporters assembled at the Qatiba Grounds near Al-Azhar University, Gaza City, to commemorate former PA President Yasser Arafat. Gunmen dressed in civilian apparel and Hamas security forces were heavily deployed in and around the grounds and used guns and batons in their attempts to disperse the rally. The security forces indiscriminately shot into the crowd, killing six participants and injuring over eighty men and women. In addition, twelve-year-old Ibrahim Mahmoud Ahmad was shot in the neck by Hamas forces at the demonstration. That evening, Hamas called for the arrest of dozens of Fatah activists throughout the city. Additional Fatah supporters in the Gaza Strip were summoned over the following two days (Palestinian Center for Human Rights 2007b). The Hamas Executive Force has also conducted numerous raids on Fatah offices, institutions, and events supporting the political party. Hundreds have been arrested and detained. The unpredictable violence against Fatah supporters throughout the Gaza Strip has driven them into a perpetual state of insecurity and fear.

Another string of brutal attacks against Fatah members commenced on December 28, 2007. Hamas police forces arrested thirty-five students at al-Azhar University who were organizing an event to celebrate the anniversary of the Fatah Movement. Upon release, the students claimed that they had been forced to sign a document swearing not to partake in Fatah anniversary events under the threat of a $4000 fine and a fifteen-day detention (Palestinian Center for Human Rights 2007c).

On December 29, Hamas police raided a Fatah office located in the al-Remal neighborhood of western Gaza City. They confiscated several pieces of equipment, including a computer and a photocopier, and arrested six individuals at the office. One released detainee declared that officials would have forced him to pay a $4000 fine to the Hamas authorities if he had not signed a document declaring that he would not participate in events celebrating the anniversary of the Fatah Movement (Palestinian Center for Human Rights 2007c).

Also on December 29, masked gunmen raided another Fatah office located in the al-Daraj neighborhood in eastern Gaza City. Hamas militants confiscated office equipment, photographs, and Fatah flags. The following day, police and masked gunmen stormed the Fatah headquarters near the Ansar security compound in western Gaza City and the Palestinian Liberation Organization Executive Committee office, from which they confiscated more equipment (Palestinian Center for Human Rights 2007c).

In addition to committing human rights abuses against Fatah supporters, the Hamas Executive Force prevented civilians from peacefully assembling throughout the Gaza Strip. On Saturday, November 24, Hamas militants detained Wa'el Ahmed al-Salmi, a member of the Palestinian General Intelligence, and transported him to an unknown destination. In response to the detention, fifty civilians living in al-Shati refugee camp rallied toward the home of Ismail Haniyeh. His security forces stopped the demonstrators with sticks and later arrested several of them, including a fourteen-year-old youth. In investigations conducted by the Palestinian Center for Human Rights, the detainees claimed that they had been beaten during their confinement (Palestinian Center for Human Rights 2007d).

Numerous human rights violations have also been committed against the Palestinian Christian community. Due to Hamas's desire to implement Shariah, strict Muslim law, many Christians in the Gaza Strip have considered fleeing to avoid forced conversion (*Spero News* 2007). After June 2007, a string of anti-Christian attacks heightened fears among the Christian citizens of Gaza. In late June, attacks on the Rosary Sisters' School and the Latin Church caused over $500,000 of damage. The masked gunmen responsible for the attacks stormed the school and church, using grenades to blow the entrances. The gunmen destroyed desks, chairs, and beds, and set curtains and other materials ablaze. Furthermore, sacred images and religious books were desecrated (*Asia News* 2007). While several Hamas officials visited the convent and the school following the attack, continued strikes reflect Hamas's failure to protect members of the Christian community and their institutions in the Gaza Strip.

At the end of September 2007, Claire Farah Tarazi, an eighty-year-old Christian Palestinian woman, was assaulted in her home during a targeted robbery. A masked gunman forced his way into Tarazi's home during the night and demanded money. When Tarazi returned with some gold jewelry, a cellphone, and a few hundred shekels, the gunman beat her with a tool, then locked her in a bedroom. He proceeded to ransack the home before leaving (Toameh 2007). The gunman referred to Tarazi as an "infidel," implying that the attack was religiously motivated (Cole 2007).

On October 7, the body of a prominent Christian bookstore owner, Rami Ayyad, was found beaten, mauled, and shot outside his store, the only Christian bookstore in Gaza City. The murder reflects the increasing threat to the Christian community in the Gaza Strip under Hamas leadership (Martine 2007). Muslim extremists also bombed his bookshop. While the Christian community has sought additional protection under the Hamas government, continued attacks threaten the community's stability and security under fundamentalist Islamic control.

On November 5, prominent Christian leaders throughout the Gaza Strip, including Artinious Alexious, a priest at Gaza's Greek Orthodox Church, and Emanuel Salum, an influential Catholic in the territory, were coerced into attending an event in which Ismail Haniyeh discussed the spread of Islam throughout the world. The security forces for the event comprised hundreds of gunmen, including members of the militant group Jihadia Salafiya, responsible for attacks against the Gazan Christian community over the previous months. Haniyeh forbade international media coverage of the event, except by Hamas-accredited journalists. According to attending journalists, Haniyeh explicitly mentioned Alexious and

Salum when he discussed the "excellent" conditions of Christian life in the Hamas-controlled Gaza Strip. However, Christian community members claimed that the two leaders were threatened into attending the event and believed that Hamas has failed to protect them from militant Islamic groups. Jihadia Salafiya has widely warned Christians against engaging in any missionary activity and has stated that Christian schools and institutions throughout Gaza will be publicly monitored to prevent proselytizing and the conversion of Muslim students. The Islamic outreach movement has consistently called for the strict imposition of Shariah throughout Gaza in order to enable Hamas's effective control over the territory (Klein 2007).

Intimidation of the Christian community and its religious institutions has not diminished. With a growing proportion of Hamas calling for the Islamization of the Palestinian Occupied Territories, the Christians have become increasingly uncertain of their current or future safety in Gaza. Once Hamas seized control, protection for the Christian community plummeted. Thus far, Hamas has continued to rule with a complete disregard for human rights. Until it progresses toward more moderate, peace-oriented positions, Gazan Christians will continue to live in fear and desperation.

Fatah human rights violations in June 2007, immediately after the state of emergency decree

During a week of heightened inter-factional fighting, between June 7 and 14, 2007, Palestinian National Authority President Mahmoud Abbas declared a state of emergency in the Palestinian Occupied Territories. Tension between Fatah and Hamas had been mounting since Hamas's victory in the January 2006 parliamentary elections, but this was the most brutal violence yet between the two political powers. Following Abbas's decree, based on the seventh chapter of the amended Palestinian Basic Law, there was a series of arrests of Hamas affiliates and individuals in possession of firearms throughout the West Bank (Palestinian Independent Commission for Citizens' Rights 2007).

During the month of June, Fatah flagrantly violated Palestinian law and committed numerous human rights abuses in its illegal detention and arrest of Hamas supporters, their families, and members of local media agencies. For example, Article 111 of the Palestinian Basic Law outlines the following regulations for arrests under a declared state of emergency: any detention must be reviewed by the Attorney General or a competent court within a fifteen-day period of the arrest; and the defendant has the right to select and appoint a lawyer (Palestinian Independent Commission for Citizens' Rights 2007). In addition, according to the Penal Procedures Code under the Palestinian National Authority, no individual can be arrested or detained without the consent of a competent party. Holding security forces cannot induce physical or psychological pain to the detainee. Finally, the detained individual cannot be subjected to house searches at night, unless absolutely necessary (Palestinian Independent Commission for Citizens' Rights 2007). Fatah security forces in the West Bank defied the penal procedures and Basic Law as soon as the state of emergency was declared, and thereafter their illegal arrest and abuse of detainees continued unabated.

Throughout June, Fatah security forces throughout the West Bank displayed a shocking disregard for Palestinian Basic Law and customary human rights standards. Many detainees were held in detention centers for more than fifteen days without review by the Attorney General. Some detention centers violated health and safety regulations and were not inspected by the Attorney General (Palestinian Independent Commission for Citizens' Rights 2007). The detention centers often lacked proper ventilation, lighting, and a sufficient number of bathroom facilities. They were also usually subject to severe overcrowding. While appropriate medical services were available for detainees, some reports indicate that certain medicines were unavailable at the detention centers' medical facilities (Palestinian Independent Commission for Citizens' Rights 2007).

Many individuals detained during the initial period following the decree, in which Abbas outlawed the Executive Force and Hamas militia, were tortured, both physically and emotionally. Many others testified that excessive force was used during their arrest. Some reported that they received death threats and that their families were threatened with violence as well. Others claimed that they had been blindfolded for extended periods of time and transported in the trunks of vehicles (Palestinian Independent Commission for Citizens' Rights 2007).

Some families and friends of detainees claimed that they had never received official word about the detaining or arrest of their loved one. Many individuals were also prohibited from establishing contact with friends or family during their detention and, therefore, could not secure the services of a defense attorney. Withholding a detainee's right to appoint a lawyer constitutes a fundamental violation of human rights (Palestinian Independent Commission for Citizens' Rights 2007).

Arrests were often conducted by parties who were not authorized law enforcement officers. In the majority of cases, the forces involved in the arrests refused to identify themselves and, as previously mentioned, used extreme force during the arrest process. Detainee reports indicate that the arresting parties often failed to show either an arrest or a search warrant. They were sometimes responsible for the destruction of the detainee's property and conducted house searches at night (Palestinian Independent Commission for Citizens' Rights 2007).

Fatah human rights violations, July–December 2007

Fatah's violent arrest and unwarranted detention of Hamas supporters and media representatives persisted with appalling frequency throughout the West Bank. In particular, Fatah security forces continued to torture Hamas affiliates. On September 30, Rasem Khattab Hasan Mostafa, from Nablus, was transferred to Rafedia Hospital with severe bruises on his head after interrogation by the Military Intelligence Service. The MIS had captured Mostafa on September 26, when gunmen had raided the Andaleeb Nursing School in the Women's Union Hospital in Nablus. The force used gunfire to disperse the students, then took Mostafa to an undisclosed location (Palestinian Center for Human Rights 2007e).

On September 5, four school principals in Nablus were summoned by the Palestinian General Intelligence and taken with sacks over their heads to J'neid Prison. On September 13, only three of the four principals were released. On September 14, three men in a village near Nablus were detained and tortured by the Palestinian General Intelligence. One released detainee claimed that he was severely beaten, blindfolded, bound, and terrorized with sounds of gunfire. On September 17, five teachers were detained at a checkpoint while traveling to school. They were taken to the Military Intelligence Compound in Nablus, and then to J'neid Prison. Three of the teachers were released that night, but two remained in the prison (Palestinian Center for Human Rights 2007f).

On September 17, M.K., from Nablus, was also taken by members of the PA security forces to their Nablus headquarters. The officers interrogated the man about his connection to Hamas and his possession of a firearm. The detainee was subjected to various methods of torture, including beating with sticks. M.K. was not released until October 11 (Palestinian Center for Human Rights 2007g).

In addition to the violence committed against arrested individuals, the families of detained and/or imprisoned Palestinians in the West Bank have also been threatened and physically abused by Fatah security forces. While this category of abuse is not well documented (due to victim fear and their understandable desire for anonymity), there have been numerous cases of family abuse. On August 21, during the arrest of his son Mohammad Ali (age 30) from his home, Ahmad Taher Ahmad Mohsin (age 92) and several other relatives were beaten while attempting to prevent the arrest. The security forces also riddled the home's interior with gunfire during the operation. On August 28, members of the Preventive Security Service attacked Fawwaz Hisham Hussein El-Tarada's family in their home. Tarada was then tortured during his interrogation on account of his ties with Hamas and the Executive Force (Palestinian Center for Human Rights 2007h).

There has also been an increase in media arrests and torture cases in the West Bank. For example, on October 7, members of the Iqra TV channel media crew were arrested in Ramallah by the Preventive Security Service on the charge of reporting to an enemy entity. Once taken to the security service's headquarters, the crew was beaten and tortured during interrogation. These attacks constituted violations of the rights to freedom of the press and freedom of speech stipulated in the Palestinian Basic Law and international law (Palestinian Center for Human Rights 2007i).

On November 7, two journalists, 'Alaa' Mohammed al-Titi and Asyad 'Abdul Majid 'Amarna were arrested and detained in Hebron by the Preventive Security Service. Both journalists had worked for al-Aqsa TV in Ramallah, a station that was affiliated with Hamas, and had then become freelancers when al-Aqsa was terminated by the Palestinian Authority government in the West Bank after Hamas's seizure of the Gaza Strip (Palestinian Center for Human Rights 2007j). Their arrest reveals the continued assault on freedom of expression and the persecution of Hamas affiliates by Mahmoud Abbas's Fatah-controlled government in the West Bank.

In addition to targeted attacks on Hamas supporters and members of the media, Fatah obstructed the Palestinian right to assemble peacefully, dispersing various politically oriented rallies. On August 22, the Public Relations Department in the Palestinian Police Nablus Directorate stated that Colonel Ahmad El-Sharqawi had banned all public assembly, except with the permission of a party formally recognized by Palestinian law. El-Sharqawi's declaration is in blatant violation of the Palestinian Basic Law, which permits citizens to assemble peacefully. The decision has also had threatening implications for the rights of Palestinian people in other parts of the West Bank (Palestinian Center for Human Rights 2007k).

On September 9, Palestinian security forces dispersed a rally organized by Hebron University's Student Council (controlled by the pro-Hamas Islamic Bloc) on a main street in front of the university. Male and female police officers used sticks to disperse the students, injuring several participants. Security forces also attacked photographers and journalists, and some were detained while trying to cover the rally (Palestinian Center for Human Rights 2007l).

On September 22, dozens of wives of political prisoners and female members of Hamas marched from Jamal Abdel Naser Mosque toward El-Manara Square in Ramallah. Just before they reached the square, the police used tear gas to disperse the crowd (Palestinian Center for Human Rights 2007m). At least one woman was also detained. The forced dispersion reflects a dangerous shift toward the elimination of free speech and the right to assemble peacefully in the West Bank.

Following the Annapolis Peace Summit in November, Fatah security forces again suppressed politically motivated assemblies throughout the West Bank. On November 27, despite a ban on public demonstrations issued by Abbas's government, hundreds of students of various political parties and civil society organizations gathered in Hebron, Nablus, Bethlehem, and Ramallah to protest peacefully. The security services used excessive force to control the crowds. Open gunfire, beating, and batons were used to break up the demonstrations. Hisham Na'im Yusef Baratha'a, from Hebron, was shot in the chest, and died as a result (Palestinian Center for Human Rights 2007n). In Ramallah, thirty protesters were injured due to the extreme force used by the security forces. In addition, eight participants were arrested, including Jamal Juma, the coordinator of the Palestinian Grassroots Anti-Apartheid Wall Campaign. While covering the Ramallah protest, several members of the media were assaulted by the security forces. Mu'ammar Urab, of Watan TV, and Wael Shuyokhi, an Al-Jazeera correspondent, were seriously wounded (Ma'an News Agency 2007).

Another protest against the Annapolis Conference on the following Tuesday resulted in additional arrests and violence. Up to 200 protesters of the pan-Islamist Hizb ut-Tahrir were detained by the Preventive Security Service. Other men, women, and student participants were arrested and beaten. Event organizers also claimed that the heavy deployment of PA forces surrounding Ramallah prevented fourteen buses from traveling to the protest (Ma'an News Agency 2007).

On November 28, the funeral of Hisham Baratha'a, who was killed on the first day of the anti-Annapolis protests, generated heated turmoil in Hebron, West Bank.

Islamist protesters rallied at the funeral. While the Palestinian Authority police denied responsibility for the death, witnesses claimed that Abbas's security forces at the first anti–Annapolis protest had shot him. When protesters began throwing rocks at the security forces, they fired gunshots into the air to disperse the crowds. Three people were treated for gunshot wounds, and over twenty others were hospitalized after suffering other injuries (BBC News International 2007).

Statistics

Table 10.1 shows the deaths of Palestinians killed by other Palestinians in Palestine between December 29, 2000 and October 15, 2009. The Palestinian Authority can be held accountable – morally and judicially – for all of these murders, either because its officers committed them or because it neglected to tackle the problem by investigating such crimes fully.

International attempts to resolve the conflict

Most of the Arab countries have been involved in trying to reconcile Hamas and Fatah. Some of them support the reconciliation – for example, Egypt, Jordan, and Saudi Arabia. Others – for example, Syria and Iran – have worked to make the separation permanent. Others – for example, Qatar – have been unwilling to show support for either Fatah or Hamas. However, neither Hamas nor Fatah has shown much interest in reconciliation, and it seems that the Occupied Territories have been divided into two separate states: Gaza is ruled by Hamas and the West Bank is almost ruled by Fatah. Few ordinary Palestinians believe that reconciliation will take place.

President Abbas tried to foster a reconciliation by declaring that an election would take place in January 2010, but he failed for two reasons: the Election Central Committee felt there was insufficient time to organize an election; and Hamas rejected the idea and started warning people in Gaza not to enter polling stations.

Additionally, Israel and the USA have not been interested in fostering a reconciliation as the split should help them achieve their aims for Palestine.

TABLE 10.1 Number of Palestinians killed by Palestinians in Palestine, 2000–2009

Beating	15
Capital punishment	65
Death in custody	26
Gunfire	935
Honor killing	48
Stabbing	71
Unclear causes	271

Source: <http://www.phrmg.org>

Consequently, Israel is trying to ease daily life in the West Bank in support of Abbas's leadership.

Conclusion

From January 2006 through December 2007, both Fatah and Hamas brazenly violated the Palestinian Basic Law and international human rights standards throughout the West Bank and the Gaza Strip. Since the Fatah–Hamas clashes peaked in June 2007 and Mahmoud Abbas decreed a state of emergency in the Palestinian Occupied Territories, the two sides' security forces have committed grave offences against supporters of the opposing party, their families, and media representatives. These violations are still continuing.

The Palestinian Human Rights Monitoring Group (PHRMG) recommends that Mahmoud Abbas and his government uphold the Palestinian Basic Law and the Palestinian Penal Code and abide by international human rights standards. Fatah must halt the illegal detention, arrest, and torture of Hamas affiliates and their families and restore essential legal procedures to ensure the proper representation of defendants and just trials. Arrests should be conducted by legitimate law enforcement parties that are authorized by the Attorney General. The PHRMG also calls on Abbas and his government to prosecute individuals for previous breaches of the Palestinian Penal Code.

Additionally, the Preventive Security Service must halt its attacks on domestic and international media representatives. The working rights of journalists, photographers, and reporters located in the territories must be universally respected, as stipulated in Palestinian Basic Law and international human rights agreements. Finally, Palestinians must be guaranteed the right to assemble to protest peacefully throughout the West Bank.

Meanwhile, Ismail Haniyeh and his government must halt the use of violence against Fatah members and supporters, Christians, and other Palestinian civilians in the Gaza Strip. Hamas will achieve legitimacy only once it reforms its policies to reflect tolerance for minorities.

Hamas's offenses should be brought to justice with the help of an outside arbitrator. There must be just prosecution of the movement's war crimes and a move away from the use of gunfire and violence throughout the Gaza Strip by the Hamas Executive Force and Palestinian civilians.

The focus in Gaza and the West Bank must be on upholding international human rights standards and promoting peace throughout the Palestinian Occupied Territories. The two primary political powers in Palestine must be held accountable for their violations and work with the support of Israeli and international actors to restore order and foster a culture of human rights. The Palestinian people can begin to work towards a successful, independent state only once the leaderships of Hamas and Fatah assert and prove their commitment to human rights.

Peace culture
and education

11

CHALLENGES FOR CONSTRUCTING PEACE CULTURE AND PEACE EDUCATION

Daniel Bar-Tal

Introduction

The relations between Israeli Jews and Palestinians will not change until both societies go through major socio-psychological transformation. This is because both societies have developed a socio-psychological infrastructure that stands as a major obstacle to the peace process and constitutes the cornerstore of the culture of conflict. This culture continuously feeds the animosity and hatred that plague the relations between these two societies.

This chapter will first describe the societal psychological repertoire that has developed in the intractable conflict and serves as a basis of the conflict culture. Then it will outline the nature of the necessary peace culture that has to replace the dominant culture of conflict in order to change the relations between Israelis and Palestinians dramatically. Next, the chapter will elaborate on the peace education that is an important means for this essential change. Finally, a few conclusions will be drawn.

The intractable Israeli–Palestinian conflict: development of conflict culture

The Israeli–Palestinian conflict, in much the same way as other intractable conflicts that have continued for a long time,[1] deeply involves the members of the society, who develop a socio-psychological repertoire of beliefs, attitudes, and emotions about their goals, causes of the conflict, its course, their rival, and the desired solution (Bar-Tal, 1998, 2007a; Coleman, 2003; Kriesberg, 1998a). This repertoire consists of three elements – collective memory of conflict; ethos of conflict; and collective emotional orientations – which are in interrelation and constitute a socio-psychological infrastructure. They serve as foundations for the developed culture of conflict. The developed infrastructure is functional during the climax of the conflict as it allows adaptation to the very demanding, stressful and prolonged conditions that challenge the societies involved. It facilitates satisfaction of basic individual and collective needs, helps people to cope with chronic stress, and creates effective conditions for withstanding the enemy (Bar-Tal, 2007a, 2007b).

Socio-psychological infrastructure of conflict

Collective memory

Collective memory is defined as representations of the past remembered by society as the history of the conflict (Kansteiner, 2002). It presents a coherent and meaningful, socially constructed narrative that has some basis in actual events (Cairns and Roe, 2003; Halbwachs, 1992), but is biased, selective and distorted in ways that meet society's present needs. It focuses on at least four themes: first, it justifies the outbreak of the conflict and the course of its development; second, it presents its own society in a positive light; third, it describes the rival society in delegitimizing ways; and fourth, it portrays its own society as the victim of the opponent. Nevertheless, Israeli and Palestinian society members treat their collective memory as the true history of the conflict.

Ethos of conflict

In addition to the narrative of collective memory, during prolonged intractable conflict, Israelis and Palestinians, and other societies involved in intractable conflicts, have developed a particular ethos: the ethos of conflict (Bar-Tal, 1998, 2000a). Ethos is defined as *the configuration of shared central societal beliefs that provide a particular dominant orientation to a society at present and for the future* (Bar-Tal, 2000a). The ethos of conflict provides a clear picture of the conflict: its goals, conditions, requirements, images of one's own group and of the rival. It represents a coherent picture of society, provides a particular orientation for society members, indicates a direction and goals for individual and societal behavior, imparts legitimacy to the social system, and explains and justifies leaders' decisions.

An ethos of conflict consists of eight types of societal beliefs[2] (Bar-Tal, 1998, 2007a):

- *Societal beliefs about the justness of one's own goals* support the goals in conflict, indicate their crucial importance and provide justifications and rationales for them.
- *Societal beliefs about security* refer to the importance of personal safety and national survival, and outline the conditions for their achievement.
- *Societal beliefs of positive collective self-image* concern the ethnocentric tendency to attribute positive traits, values and behavior to one's own society.

- *Societal beliefs of victimization* concern self-presentation as a victim.
- *Societal beliefs delegitimizing the opponent* concern beliefs which deny the adversary's humanity.
- *Societal beliefs of patriotism* generate attachment to the country and society by propagating loyalty, love, care and sacrifice.
- *Societal beliefs of unity* refer to the importance of ignoring internal conflicts and disagreements during intractable conflict in order to unite one's forces in the face of the external threat.
- *Societal beliefs of peace* refer to peace in general and amorphic terms as the ultimate desire of the society (see also Bar-Tal, 2007b; Rouhana and Bar-Tal, 1998).

Collective emotional orientation

In addition, during the intractable conflict Israeli and Palestinian societies have developed collective emotional orientations because the shared context together with information, models and instructions arouse a particular set of emotions shared by society members (Bar-Tal *et al.*, 2007). The most notable is the collective orientation of fear (Bar-Tal, 2001), but it can be assumed that hatred and anger also appeared (Halperin, 2008; Halperin *et al.*, 2010).

Functions

The above-described infrastructure of collective memory, ethos of conflict and collective emotional orientations fulfill important functions, especially when the conflict reaches its climax and no signs of possible peace appear. First, it provides a meaningful and coherent picture of the conflict for society members. Second, it serves to justify the society's acts toward the enemy, including violence and destruction. Third, it prepares the society's members for threatening and violent acts by the enemy, as well as for difficult life conditions. Fourth, it encourages solidarity, mobilization and action. Finally, it creates a sense of differentiation and superiority.

Institutionalization

As a result of the important functions of the socio-psychological infrastructure during intractable conflict, institutionalization takes place. This is characterized by four features:

1   *Extensive sharing.* The beliefs of the socio-psychological infrastructure and the accompanying emotions are widely shared by society's members, who acquire and store this repertoire, as part of their socialization, from an early age. It becomes a lens through which society's members interpret new information and explain their experiences.

2   *Wide application.* Institutionalization means that the repertoire is not only held by society's members but is put into active use by them in their daily

conversations, because it is so accessible. In addition, it appears to be dominant in public discourse via societal channels of mass communication. Moreover, it is often used for justification and explanation of decisions, policies and courses of action taken by the leaders. Finally, it is also expressed in institutional ceremonies, commemorations, memorials and so on.

3   *Expression in cultural products*. The institutionalization of the socio-psychological infrastructure also takes place through cultural products, such as books, TV programs, films, plays, the visual arts, monuments, etc. It becomes a society's cultural repertoire, relaying societal views and shaping society members' beliefs, values, attitudes and emotions. Through these channels it can be widely disseminated and can reach every sector of the public.

4   *Appearance in educational materials*. The socio-psychological infrastructure appears in the textbooks used in schools and even in higher education.

These socio-psychological dynamics are found in mirror-image in both Israeli and Palestinian societies (see Rouhana and Bar-Tal, 1998). But while there is a great deal of literature charting their existence on the Israeli side, there has been much less study on the Palestinian side. (For the Israeli side, see, for example, Firer, 1985, and Podeh, 2002 (analysis of school textbooks), Cohen, 1985 (children's literature), Ramras-Rauch, 1989 (adult literature), Shohat, 1989 (films), and Urian, 1997 (plays). For the Palestinian side, see Brown, 2003 (analysis of Palestinian school textbooks) and Firer and Adwan, 2004 (Israeli and Palestinian school textbooks).)

Evolution of the culture of conflict

Given the above-described processes, societies that live through prolonged experiences of intractable conflict with the dominant socio-psychological infrastructure evolve a *culture of conflict*. This develops when societies integrate into their culture tangible and intangible symbols which are created to communicate a particular meaning about the prolonged and continuous experiences of living in the context of conflict (Geertz, 1993; Ross, 1998). Symbols of conflict become hegemonic elements in the culture of societies involved in intractable conflict: they provide a dominant meaning about the present reality, about the past, and about future goals, and serve as guides for practice.

   Culture of conflict indicates that the above-described socio-psychological infrastructure has become part of the political, societal, cultural and educational context in which Israelis and Palestinians live. Thus it is stable and easily available. In essence, the culture of conflict encompasses all the domains of individual and collective life of the Israelis and Palestinians. This culture contains the repertoire that facilitates adaptation to the condition of conflict, but at the same time it fuels its continuation, as it is rigid and resistant to change. Moreover, with time, the beliefs of collective memory and ethos of conflict serve as the basis for the formation of the social identity of both societies (Oren *et al.*, 2004).

This was the situation up to the 1980s, when the Israeli and Palestinian societies engaged in intractable conflict and there was no sign on either side of a willingness to move to a peaceful resolution. However, when both societies openly embarked on the road to peace in 1993, the shared psychological repertoire, and especially the culture of conflict, constituted the major obstacle to political transformation. With the movement toward a peaceful resolution of the conflict, which has been carried forward by leaders, political parties and NGOs, there was a need to gain the support of a significant part of Israeli and Palestinian society and mobilize it for the cause. But such mobilization can take place only if members of both societies begin to change their dominant psychological repertoire of conflict and start to adopt an alternative repertoire. The new psychological repertoire provides the seeds for the emergence of a new culture, the culture of peace. But since 2000, with the failure of the Camp David conference, the conflict has escalated again, as is reflected in the second Palestinian Intifada, reconquest of the West Bank in 2002, the second war in Lebanon in 2006, and the war in Gaza in January 2009. These developments have led to a strengthening of the socio-psychological repertoire supporting the conflict (Bar-Tal and Sharvit, 2008; Bar-Tal, Halperin, and Oren, 2009; Sharvit and Bar-Tal, 2007).

Without a significant movement toward peace culture, which requires a fundamental change in the socio-psychosocial infrastructure, it will be very difficult to resolve the conflict peacefully and move toward reconciliation between the Israeli Jews and the Palestinians. Therefore, I would like to elaborate on the elements of peace culture.

Development of peace culture

A culture of peace must focus on new goals for both societies and new relations between the rivals, the Israelis and the Palestinians. Peace culture, in general, can be seen as a phenomenon with a very wide scope that encompasses many different elements. Nevertheless, the present conception concerns only the construction of peaceful relations between former rivals who have been dominated by a culture of conflict that perpetuates animosity and violent confrontation.

Reconciliation and peace culture

The process through which societies form their new repertoire during a peace process is called reconciliation and it aims to achieve mutual recognition and acceptance, vested interests and goals in developing peaceful relations, mutual trust, positive attitudes as well as sensitivity to and consideration of the other party's needs and interests (Bar-Siman-Tov, 2004; Bar-Tal and Bennink, 2004; Maoz, 1999; Kelman, 1999; Lederach, 1997). The psychological essence of reconciliation is change of motivations, goals, beliefs, attitudes and emotions by the majority of society's members (Bar-Tal, 2000b). Psychological change is vital because, without it, the rival parties do not establish lasting peaceful relations. Reconciliation is then the necessary condition for establishing a culture of peace,[3] in which an ethos of peace is the core foundation. It provides epistemic foundations, which are vital to the maintenance of stable peace.

Ethos of peace

The ethos of peace contains the following themes of societal beliefs.

1   *Societal beliefs about peace as a goal.* The new beliefs about peace must embody the new goals of the Israeli and Palestinian societies that have been shaped by minorities in them and center on constructing and maintaining peaceful relations between them. In addition, these beliefs have to provide rationalization and justification for the new goal of peace, including new symbols and myths. They have to outline the costs and benefits of achieving peace realistically, connote the meaning of living in peace, and specify the conditions and mechanisms for its achievement (for example, use of compromises), and especially for its maintenance. The new goals indicate that both societies have abandoned some of their old dreams and visions and accept goals that are achievable and also satisfy the needs and aspirations of both societies.

2   *Societal beliefs about the peaceful resolution of conflicts.* These beliefs provide a new way of life, as they suggest new ways of dealing with conflicts, which are inseparable parts of human inter-group relations. They indicate that conflicts should always be resolved via peaceful negotiation and mediation. There is a need to evolve beliefs and attitudes that negate the use of violence. During the intractable conflict violence was the preferred way to deal with disagreement and the new culture has to make clear that its use is now absolutely illegitimate. In this ethos, peace stands as an alternative to violence and war. Therefore, there is a need to develop institutionalized means of resolving the conflicts that may appear in the relations between Israelis and Palestinians. Any possible disagreements should be dealt with by the institutionalized mechanisms of conflict resolution. Israeli and Palestinian societies have to understand that conflicts cause damage to both of them, and the peaceful resolution of conflict is in the long run always rewarding for both of them.

3   *Societal beliefs about the erstwhile opponent.* Another determining condition for reconciliation is changing the very negative images that the Israelis and Palestinians have of each other. It is important to legitimize and personalize the erstwhile opponent: legitimization grants humanity to members of the opposing group, after years of its denial. It allows one to view the opponent as belonging to an acceptable group, with which there should be a wish to maintain peaceful relations. Personalization enables one to see members of the rival group as humane individuals who can be trusted and have legitimate needs and goals. In addition, equalization needs to take place, so that the rival becomes an equal partner with whom it is possible to establish new relations. This requires recognition of the principle of status equality between the groups, a principle

that is brought to bear first in negotiations and later in all types and levels of inter-group interaction. Finally, the new beliefs should make it possible to see the other group as a victim of the conflict as well, since its members have also suffered. These new beliefs should contain a balanced stereotype consisting of positive and negative characteristics and a perception of the other group that acknowledges its heterogeneous composition.

4   *Societal beliefs about one's own group.* The change must also include the societal beliefs that Israelis and Palestinians carry about themselves, which formerly propagated self-righteousness, self-glorification and self-praise. In this change, each society must take responsibility for its involvement in the outbreak of the conflict, as well as its contribution to the violence, including immoral acts and refusal to engage in peaceful resolution of the conflict. Thus, the new societal beliefs present the Israelis and Palestinians in their own societies in a more objective light – more critically, especially regarding their past behavior. In addition, within the framework of own presentation and the presentation of the erstwhile opponent there is a need to stress commonalities between Israelis and Palestinians after years of stressing only differences. This should go beyond emphasis on common goals of achieving lasting peace to encompass common values and especially similar and common lines of culture.

5   *Societal beliefs about the relationship between the Israelis and Palestinians.* There is a need to form new societal beliefs about the relations between the Israeli and Palestinian societies that have been engaged in an intractable conflict for many years. These beliefs should stress the importance of cooperation and friendly relationships with the erstwhile rival. Of special importance is the stress on equality of relations and mutual sensitivity to each other's needs, goals and general wellbeing. That is, both sides need to recognize that for lasting peace the wellbeing of the two sides is in the interests of both, so peaceful relations require ongoing sensitivity, attention and care for the needs and goals of the other group. In this vein, developing trust between the Israelis and Palestinians is of special importance in building peaceful relations. These new beliefs about the relationship should also present past relations in a new framework that revises the collective memory and forms a view of the past that is compatible with that of the former rival.

The above psychological framework focuses almost entirely on the changes in beliefs and attitudes of the Israelis and Palestinians. But reconciliation also requires positive affects and emotions about peaceful relations with the erstwhile opponent. Positive affects should accompany the described beliefs and indicate good feelings that the parties have toward each other and toward the new relationship. These good feelings should be reflected in mutual acceptance, recognition, and caring about the other side's wellbeing. This kind of caring does not develop out of altruistic considerations, but in response to interdependence and common goals. With regard to emotions, reconciliation requires a change in the collective emotional orientations of fear, anger and hatred, which often dominate societies in intractable conflict. Instead, societies at peace should develop an emotional orientation of hope, which reflects the desire for the positive goals of maintaining peaceful and cooperative relations with the other party. This emotional orientation indicates a positive outlook for the future, an expectation of a pleasant life, without violence and hostility (Jarymowicz and Bar-Tal, 2006).

The above description outlines the ultimate goals of the reconciliation process between the Israeli and Palestinian societies, but it should be noted that the process of changing attitudes and beliefs is under way and both societies have come a long way in the last thirty years from complete negation of each other to mutual recognition, legitimization and more. This is very well documented, at least on the Israeli side, by Oren (2005).

Methods for facilitating the development of a peace culture

A culture of peace does not evolve without explicit efforts to achieve it, which include designing policies, planning, and execution of those plans. Many different methods have been proposed to engender reconciliation between erstwhile rivals and develop a culture of peace (e.g., Bar-Tal and Bennink, 2004; Kriesberg, 1998b; Norval, 1998), and some of these have already been employed by the Israelis and Palestinians. Among them are:

1   *Joint projects* develop common interests and goals in the two societies and foster links between members of the two groups at different levels, including elites, professionals and grass roots (e.g., Barnea and Abdeen, 2002, described joint Israeli–Palestinian projects in medicine).

2   *Non-governmental organizations* from both societies may spread the message about the importance of constructing peaceful relations, help establish cooperative and friendly relations with the erstwhile adversary or provide economic assistance to members of society and thereby show that peaceful relations have important benefits. In this vein, of special importance are people-to-people NGO projects which try to enhance dialogue between the two erstwhile rival societies and remove obstacles to the peace process. Since 1993, various people-to-people projects via NGOs have been carried out – see, for example, Baskin *et al.* (2004).

3   *Cultural exchanges*, such as translations of books, visits of artists, or exchanges of films, TV programs and exhibitions, provide opportunities to learn about the erstwhile opponent in human cultural terms. (For example, in 1994, Shakespeare's *Romeo and Juliet* was staged in a joint production by the Israeli Chan theatre group and the Palestinian Al Kasaba theatre group.)

4   *Mass media* can be a very powerful tool for promoting change in the psychological repertoire as it can transmit information to a wide public about the new peaceful goals, the erstwhile rival group, developing relations, and so on. (Wolfsfeld, 1997, showed that in the first stage, after the Oslo Agreement of

1993, the media played an important role in providing the frame "give peace a chance.")

5   *Writing a common history* involves recreating a past that can be agreed upon by the groups involved in the conflict. The first steps in this direction were taken by the Peace Research Institute in the Middle East (PRIME), which through its Israeli–Palestinian cooperative efforts published a brochure that presented to Israeli and Palestinian students the two narratives of the history of the conflict (*To Teach the Historical Narrative of the Other*, 2003).

6   *Truth and reconciliation commissions* reveal the truth about the past to both nations and serve as mechanisms for perpetuating justice (Albeck, *et al.*, 2002).

7   *Payment of reparations* takes place when one or both sides accept responsibility for the misdeeds perpetrated during the conflict and are willing to compensate the victims. (This possibility was raised with regard to settling the Palestinian refugee problem; see Klinov, 2002.) But of special importance in creating a culture of peace is the evolution of peace education within schools (Abu-Nimer, 2000; Bar-Tal, Rosen, and Nets, 2009; Bekerman and McGlynn, 2007: Iram, 2006).

Peace education

Any major societal change requires that schools play an important role, as they are a major agent of socialization (Dreeben, 1968). First, education in schools is sure to reach a whole segment of a society (i.e., the young generation), since school attendance is compulsory for all children and adolescents. Second, the young generation, which is still in the process of acquiring a psychological repertoire, is least affected by the dominant conflict culture and is more open to new ideas and information. Third, in comparison with other socialization agents, society has maximum control over the messages transmitted in schools. Educational authorities, such as the Ministry of Education, can decide on curricula, educational programs, and textbooks. Fourth, the young generation is required to learn the messages and information transmitted in schools, and, therefore, it is possible to ensure that students will at least be exposed to them.

Peace education has been used in other societies as a major method to advance peace processes (see, for example, the compulsory curriculum in schools called "Education for Mutual Understanding" (Gallagher, 1998) or the Education for Peace program in Bosnia and Herzegovina (Clarke-Habibi, 2005)). It is thus not surprising that attempts to develop peace education have occurred on a strategic level, as the Israeli Ministry of Education tried to initiate in 1994, while various NGOs – for example, PRIME, the Adam Institute, the Middle East Children Association (MECA) and the Israel–Palestine Center for Research and Information (IPCRI) – have also tried to implement it on a more local level.

The objective of peace education is *to construct a mindset that includes beliefs, values, motivations and behavioral tendencies among children and adolescents that facilitate conflict resolution and the peace process and prepares them to live in an era of peace and reconciliation* (see Bjerstedt, 1993; Salomon and Nevo, 2002). To achieve this objective, the educational system needs to make major preparations. It is not enough merely to declare a new educational policy which supports peace; active steps must also be taken to implement it. Curricula must be developed, textbooks written, teachers trained, experiential programs constructed, proper learning climates created, and so on (see Bar-Tal, Rosen, and Nets, 2009). Peace education requires a systematic, well-planned and holistic approach that comes from the top down in the educational system, with ideological and pedagogical preparations for all the educational staff in the system.

It should be noted here that peace education can evolve when there is well-publicized and continuous movement toward conflict resolution that includes negotiation between the rivals. Peace agreements obviously legitimize this important educational venture and enable its considerable extension. Legitimization also depends on at least majority support for the peace process, including from major political parties and organizations. It has to be acknowledged that some segments of the society may object to the peace process and could thus jeopardize peace education (Bar-Tal and Rosen, 2009).

Moreover, in order for peace education to succeed, three conditions must prevail in the educational system. First, there should be unequivocal public support from the highest educational authority (the Minister of Education in the Israeli and Palestinian cases). Second, the formulated policy should be well defined and decisive, including detailed planning of how to implement peace education. Finally, the relevant bodies must be given the authority to implement peace education, as well as the necessary infrastructure and resources (Bar-Tal and Rosen, 2009). Determination, perseverance and a reasonable allocation of funds are all essential, too.

Principles of peace education

Peace education should be guided by a number of principles:

1 *Peace education is not a short-term plan or a one-off project, but a reorganization of the whole education system to adjust it to the peace process, and reflect it.* It is a substantial transformation that should provide students with the ability to deal with the transition from conflict to peace.
2 *Peace education should be community-oriented* because it cannot be separated from the experiences of the community in which the school is embedded. Schoolchildren and adolescents are part of the community in which they live and are greatly influenced by the views expressed in it. It is thus important for the schools to reach and involve the community in the program of peace education.
3 Peace education cannot exist as a separate program, but must be *incorporated into the curriculum of the subjects taught in schools.*

4   Peace education should *begin at an early age*, when children are especially open to absorbing new values, knowledge and attitudes.

5   Peace education should be *performed in coordination and combination with other educational programs* initiated by the Ministry of Education, such as education for democracy, the prevention of violence, multiculturalism, etc.

6   Peace education must *include experiential aspects of social life in a school*. Experiential aspects should be integral parts of the atmosphere in school, in order to nurture refraining from violence, resolving conflicts, mediation, negotiation, tolerance and more.

7   Peace education should *include all students in the education system in the state of Israel and Palestine, of all grades and all sectors.*

8   The success of peace education depends, to a large extent, on the teachers. They have to carry the weight of this task. *Therefore, it is extremely important to train them* so that they can handle the challenges that peace education presents.

9   It is worth mentioning that peace education could be *accelerated if other countries in the Middle East that have joined the reconciliation process cooperate in planning, supporting and implementing it.*

Practically, applying peace education means conveying knowledge, creating experiences and developing the skills that are relevant to the reality of the peace process, and will allow students to develop positions, values, motivations and behavioral tendencies that will aid the emergence of a culture of peace.

Knowledge

With regard to knowledge, there are many different topics that can extend the perspective and provide the epistemic basis for peace. This knowledge has to be based on newly reconstructed facts, without bias or selectivity, but with critical analysis. This knowledge should cast new light on the issues that during the conflict served to downgrade the opponents and glorify one's own society. Thus, it should be possible to present one's own society critically and not distort the other society. A few examples for topics are suggested below.

Conflict and peace

Topics of conflict and peace should demonstrate, in a concrete and detailed manner, the essence of the conflict, the reasons for its occurrence, the different categories of conflict (especially the violent ones), their results (including atrocities and genocide), the significance of wars and their costs, conflict resolution methods, the nature of the peace and reconciliation process, the meaning of peace, the different kinds of peace, methods for and obstacles to achieving it, ways of sustaining it, the roles of international institutions in promoting it, international treaties prescribing conduct in war, international courts and human rights.

History of the conflict in the Middle East

The history of the conflict in the Middle East should be presented and analyzed in an unbiased and unselective way, based on facts that do not present the Israeli or Palestinian societies in a flattering light. The background to the Israeli–Palestinian conflict, its psychological foundation, its course, the causes of the wars and their results, the heavy price that both societies have paid, mediation attempts that have failed, the violence that has occurred, atrocities that have been carried out and violations of human and civil rights that have been perpetrated by both sides should all be covered.

The peace process

The peace process, with all its difficulties and achievements, should be covered. It is especially important to discuss the meaning of peace for nations, the entire Middle East and the wider international community. It is essential to present the agreements that have been signed, describe the obstacles to the peace process and analyze the reconciliation process, which is crucial to lasting peace.

Israel, Palestine and the Middle East

This topic should provide knowledge for Israeli and Palestinian students about the other society's country, society, culture, history and religion. It should extend the knowledge beyond the two societies to all the states and societies of the Middle East.

Multiculturalism

This topic should include knowledge about awareness of multiculturalism, tolerance, minorities, the nature of ethnicity, nationality, social identity, stereotypes, discrimination and ethnocentricity.

Attitudes and skills

The aforementioned examples do not cover all the topics that are relevant to peace education, and other topics will be no less important in clarifying the new reality. The knowledge that is conveyed should create the infrastructure for creating *positive attitudes* toward peace in general and specifically toward the peace process being conducted with the erstwhile enemy. Finally, peace education should develop behavioral tendencies that are not only compatible with the peace climate that is emerging in the Middle East but will contribute to improving the quality of life in Israeli and Palestinian society. This means *developing skills* of communication and negotiation, tolerance, self-restraint, dialogue, cooperation, empathy and sensitivity toward the other, empathy and sensitivity toward different religious and ethnic groups, open-mindedness and critical thinking.

It is important to emphasize that conveying the contents of peace education should be done in an open way – through comprehensive discussion in which all views can be presented. Topics should be presented in all their complexity, while examining all the relevant perspectives. Ideally, students should gather the data and facts themselves in preparation for the discussion of different topics.

Mechanisms

There are several mechanisms that may be used for conveying knowledge, values, positions, motivations and behavioral tendencies within the scope of peace education. The most prominent ones are outlined below.

Curricula and textbooks

In principle, peace education should not exist as a separate educational program, but should be embedded in various subjects taught in all school grades. Subjects such as history, geography, literature, sociology, economics, citizenship, national studies and languages are the most obvious candidates for a significant peace education component to be incorporated in the curriculum, and to appear in the textbooks.

Special programs

In addition to including peace education in the subjects already taught in school, there should be room for special programs on various elements of peace education that have been developed, and will be developed, by both Ministries of Education and various educational organizations.

Atmosphere in the classroom

Peace education, as presented above, is not only aimed at conveying knowledge and ideas through teaching but encompasses behavior patterns in schools. It should emphasize a life of peace, cooperation, social sensitivity, tolerance, dialogue and conflict resolution. It is about creating an atmosphere that allows the students to experience values of peace and practice skills that are required for such a life. Such an atmosphere will assist in improving the quality of life at school, will contribute to democratic education and will reduce tension, conflict and violence (Goldenberg, 1998).

Ceremonies

The education system conveys messages to students through ceremonies that aim, among other things, to commemorate meaningful events from the past. It is appropriate to commemorate events that are related to the peace process and have dramatically changed the reality in Israel and Palestine, such as signing peace agreements, in school ceremonies.

Peace centers

Peace education requires gathering textbooks, activity plans, curricula, films and training material for teachers. Pedagogical centers and schools can gather such material in order to set up "peace centers" for headmasters, teachers and students.

Educational television

Educational television can produce programs on various subjects relating to peace education. It is an important educational resource that can convey much knowledge in an accessible and interesting way. Television programs can inform students about the geography, culture and history of both countries, the history of the conflict, the essence of peace, and the price of conflict and war. These are examples of the great potential that television possesses for peace education. An excellent example is a version of *Sesame Street* co-produced by Israelis and Palestinians and featuring friendly contacts between Israeli and Palestinians children (Cole *et al.*, 2003).

Additionally, meetings between Israeli and Palestinian students and various other activities should be initiated. Such meetings, given the right preparation, will allow the exchange of knowledge and the creation of positive attitudes toward each other's nation and peace. Such meetings can take place either in Israel or Palestine (see, for example, Maoz, 2000).

Language

Finally, it is important that Jewish students learn Arabic, from elementary school onwards, because the state of Israel is located in the middle of an Arabic-speaking region.

Conclusion

Constructing a culture of peace is not an easy task in transitional societies such as Israel and Palestine – societies that are moving from life under conditions of intractable conflict to conditions of tractable conflict, and are hoping to build stable and peaceful relations with each other. For many years, amid the reality of an intractable conflict, the conflict culture, with its ethos of conflict, dictated the dominant orientation for Israeli and Palestinian societies. Furthermore, this culture was required to deal with a reality of continuous, violent and seemingly insoluble conflict. Almost all Israelis and Palestinians held these beliefs and attitudes during the years of intractable conflict and believed that they defined their uniqueness.

The new reality that is evolving requires the abandonment of some central beliefs in the ethos of conflict, transformation of the content of other beliefs, and the creation of many new societal beliefs as a foundation for the development of the peace culture. This is a difficult process that faces many obstacles. It must be tackled gradually and will take many years to complete. During this process, Israeli and

Palestinian societies will be in the transitional phase in which, on the one hand, the changes that have been described will take place, and, on the other hand, some groups will hold on to the beliefs of the intractable conflict ethos and resist any progress. These groups will view the described changes as an existential danger to their respective nations and will therefore make every effort to stop the peace process and the process of transforming the conflict culture.

During this transitional phase, peace education must be developed in the education system, to reflect the new reality that has evolved and prepare the next generation for life in a reality of peace. In much the same way as a society has to learn to live in an intractable conflict, it must now learn to live in a non-violent conflict that can be resolved through negotiation, and, eventually, how to live in peace.

A society that goes through a peace process without developing peace education will only lengthen the conflict. It must prepare the future generation for life in the new developing context. The role of education is to reflect the emerging reality of the next generation and prepare it for life in the evolving future. A society that fails to do this commits a sin against the younger generation. Therefore, peace education, as part of peace culture construction, should be a part of the educational enterprise in the states of Israel and Palestine.

Notes

1 Intractable conflicts are defined as: fought over essential and existential contradictory goals, prolonged (at least twenty-five years), violent, perceived as zero-sum in nature and insoluble, central to the lives of the participants and demanding great investment (Bar-Tal, 2007a; Kriesberg, 1998a).
2 Societal beliefs are cognitions shared by society's members on topics and issues that are of special concern for their society and contribute to their sense of uniqueness (Bar-Tal, 2000a).
3 Based on the definition of Geertz (1993), a culture of peace is defined as a significant accumulation of symbols that communicate a society's desire to live in peace.

12

CULTURE OF PEACE AND EDUCATION

The Palestinian context

Salem Aweiss

Introduction

Education has been recognized by all countries in the region as the cornerstone of sustainable social and economic development. It is also gaining a similar status in the peace-building process. As today's children and youth become increasingly desensitized to violence, schools and curricula are assuming greater importance, and their role is increasingly coming under scrutiny. There is a widespread belief that schools play a major role in shaping the attitudes and skills of children and young people toward peaceful human relations. Through teaching young children values of tolerance, respect, cooperation, and empathy, and by equipping them with the necessary communication and cognitive skills and strategies to resolve conflict in a non-violent manner, they are provided with the tools they need, now and in the future, to foster peaceful relations at home, at school, in their country, region, and around the world.

Education as the path to development and peace

There is a consensus that a strong, efficient, and relevant educational system is one of the main roads to human-centered development. The past decade or so has witnessed an interest in the concept of such a relationship. This relationship is best exemplified in the "education for sustainable development" (ESD) movement. ESD is a lifelong learning process that has the power to affect the general public as well as current and future decision-makers. It challenges individuals, institutions and societies to view tomorrow as a day that belongs to all of us, or it will not belong to anyone (for example in the UN Decade for Education for Sustainable Development, 2005–2014, initiative). This goal is achieved through improving the quality of education by means of integrating new fields of knowledge and disciplines into educational curricula and practices at all levels and in all sectors of education. Theorists and educators alike believe that ESD has the power and capability to produce an educated, creative, flexible workforce, characterized by technological competencies and marketable skills, able to adapt to fast-changing technologies, economies, and innovations. Although content and methodologies differ from one country to another, there are a number of basic principles and values that should govern any educational system whose aim is to achieve holistic, sustainable, individual, social and economic development.

There is also consensus that creating a culture of peace and tolerance through peace education and multicultural education programs is one of the major pre-requisites for reinforcing and sustaining human-centered development. Indeed, there is a widespread realization within the countries of the Middle East today that the region stands at a critical juncture in its history. This realization is shared by both Israelis and Arabs, at the governmental and civil society levels. It stems from the state of the region's human development and the barriers and deficits that continue to hinder the attainment of the potential of the peoples of the region and of a compre-hensive and just peaceful solution to the Arab–Israeli conflict.

Over the last decade, much work has been done by local, regional, and inter-national organizations and by the private sector and civil society institutions to identify the challenges that the region is currently facing and recommend a path for addressing those challenges. Theoretically, this work has been initiated and executed out of the conviction that education has a duty to become involved in the resolution of conflicts; that it builds the foundations for good citizenship, respect for self and others, democratic values and tolerance of opinions; and that it has a far-reaching effect on promoting reconciliation and peace. Empirically, educational research indicates that training young people in civics, mediation, ethnic tolerance, and conflict resolution decreases the likelihood that they will resort to violence later in life. History, however, tells us that education is no guarantee against hatred, intol-erance, aggression, belligerence, and war, even though it broadens people's horizons and breaks down stereotyping and prejudice. Education, moreover, is sometimes blamed for being part of the problem. It therefore must be part of the solution.

Creating a culture of peace

The year 2000 was declared by UNESCO the "Year of the Culture of Peace" in an effort to make children worldwide aware of the practical meaning and benefits of nonviolence in their daily lives. Since the mid-1980s, and signifying a departure from the more pacifist peace education, UNICEF has supported what is called "education for peace."[1] The former emphasizes knowledge about peace issues, whereas the latter is a more active approach that involves understanding, reflecting, giving young people tools, teaching values and skills.[2]

Peace educators look to peace theory that incorporates three ways to promote peace and reconciliation: peacekeeping, peacemaking, and peace-building (Berlowitz 1994). Peacekeeping is a response approach to the problem of violence that attempts to prevent violence by the threat of punishment. Peacemaking involves teaching conflict resolution skills and implementing peer mediation programs that use a third party, a mediator, to help the parties resolve their differences. Proponents of conflict resolution also teach positive communication skills to young people. Peace-building involves teaching children and youth how to live peacefully. It assumes that the problem of violence resides in the culture surrounding them. The goal is to give young people insights into the sources of violence and empower them to avoid and transform it. Part of the teaching process in schools and counseling agencies is helping children and young people recover from post-traumatic stress disorders.

In the early twenty-first century, politicians, educators, civil society activists, and other concerned individuals and institutions are looking for peace education and education for peace projects and programs to create a new, more tolerant world order based on mutual respect, nonviolence, justice, and environmental sustainability. But before we attempt to promote the principles and practices of peace education via regional and international institutions, it is important to start the peace education process at a national level. More specifically, we must begin the peace-building process as a bottom-up as well as a top-down process in our own homes, communities, and schools before we can aspire to be effective or successful at the regional and international levels.

What is peace education?

In the present context, "peace education" is defined as the process of promoting knowledge, skills, attitudes, and values to bring about changes that will enable children, youth, and adults to prevent conflict and violence, both overt and structural; to resolve conflict peacefully; and to create the conditions conducive to peace, whether at an intra-personal, interpersonal, inter-group, national, or international level. This definition is reflective of the thinking of a number of theorists in the field as well as a convergence of ideas that have been developed through practical experiences of different international organizations, mostly UNICEF.[3]

A variety of terms is used by different organizations to describe the various initiatives known as peace education, including: "peace-building in school," "education for peace," "global education," "peer mediation," "education for conflict resolution," and "values for life."

Goals, aims, and objectives of peace education/education for peace

Education for peace seeks to equip children and youth with knowledge and skills, to promote key universal and peaceful values and conceptions, and to effect changes in their beliefs, attitudes, and behavior that would result in increased tolerance, reduced prejudice, less stereotyping, changed conceptions of both self and the "other," and a reinforced sense of collective identity (see, e.g., Bar-Tal 2002; United Nations 1999). It also aims to attain the legitimization of the other side's perspective, its collective narrative, fears, dreams, and experiences (Salomon 2002).

In particular, peace education seeks to provide learners with an understanding of the nature and origins of peace, conflicts, and violence and their effects on both the victim and the aggressor/perpetrator, to sharpen their abilities to recognize injustice, bias, and prejudice, and to enhance their awareness about the existence of non-peaceful relationships between people and within and between nations. It also aims to equip children and youth with personal negotiation, social interaction and communication, conflict analysis and conflict resolution and peer-mediation skills, alternative or possible non-violent skills as well as active listening skills.

At the personal level, peace education aims to enhance children and youth's faculty of self-awareness (awareness of their own strengths, weaknesses, and needs), knowledge of community, awareness of heritage, understanding of their rights and responsibilities, and understanding of the interdependence between individuals and societies. The goals of peace education also include the creation of frameworks for achieving peaceful, compassionate, just, and creative societies by establishing mechanisms for building peace and resolving conflicts constructively.

At the practical level, peace education research investigates the causes of conflicts and violence embedded within perceptions, values, and attitudes of individuals as well as within the social and political structures of the society.

Creating a culture of peace: the Palestinian context

A new vision for Palestinian education in the twenty-first century

Upon the transfer of responsibility for the Palestinian educational system to the Palestinian National Authority, the Ministry of Education and Higher Education (MoEHE) formulated a new strategy with a new vision for the future of Palestinian education potential, challenges, and objectives. This strategy was translated into the Five-Year Plan focusing on five key areas: access to education for all children; quality of education; formal and non-formal education; management capacity in planning, administration, and finance; and human resources of the education system.[4]

In addition, the plan included five major principles that reflect the ministry's vision of the learning–teaching process:

1 *Education as a human right.* All children between the ages of six and sixteen have the right to receive free basic education, regardless of social or economic status, gender, or religious belief.
2 *Education as the basic component of citizenship.* Together with the family and the community, the school shall be a main catalyst for developing the Palestinian citizen's character, moral values, and social responsibilities.
3 *Education as a tool for social and economic development.* Education must meet the political, social, and economic challenges of Palestinian society.
4 *Education as the basis for social and moral values, and democracy.* Education shall be the cornerstone for building a Palestinian society with strong commitment to ethics, principles, and openness to the global culture.

5   *Education as a continuous, renewable, participatory process.* Education is a life-long activity, in and out of school, fueled by classroom learning, social relations and communications, community activities, and the mass media.

Along the same lines, the MoEHE has identified some principles of human development strategy in Palestine. These are summarized as follows: "creation and reinforcement of good governance based on democratic values, pluralism, transparency, accountability, respect of human rights . . . Palestinian education strategy focuses on education as a basis for democracy and values and as a vehicle for building a democratic society characterized by equality."[5]
    The same document also recommended that:

> The Palestinian educational system is urged to stay away from politicization and submission to political and social ideologies of the ruling parties. It is also required to promote readiness on the part of the future generations to resolve conflicts on the bases of respect for pluralism and mutual understanding, acquiring and teaching the new generations to take rational and clear positions and perspectives vis-à-vis the problems they encounter.

> The role of the future Palestinian educational system is to assist the new generations in their quest to understand themselves, identify the best alternative open for their communities, and to develop the potential for creativity in each member of the society. Moreover, the Palestinian educational system is expected to contribute to social solidarity in the age of globalization. The success of these goals is contingent on the citizens' cognitive maturity, openness, flexibility, tolerance, and awareness.

Curriculum development: internal needs and political pressures

There is widespread agreement regarding the importance of developing a national Palestinian curriculum to respond to the spirit of the age and its accelerating developments. The Palestinian MoEHE has begun to evaluate the Palestinian curricula within the framework of national plans to develop the entire educational process. The requests for the development of national curricula have, for some time, been merely confined to educationalists and education officials. However, this demand has acquired a new political dimension and has turned out to be, in part, guided by the ensuing security and political developments in the region.
    The MoEHE believes that creating a Palestinian curriculum devoted to serving and reflecting the Palestinian particularity is crucial for meeting the aspirations of the Palestinian nation, and placing it in a respectable position among other nations of the world. Creating a Palestinian curriculum is considered the means to establish the national identity and sovereignty of the Palestinian people, and a basis for fostering democratic values and human rights, and an instrument of sustainable human development, as emphasized by the Five-Year Plan.

The importance of the Palestinian curriculum emerged from the fact that curriculum is the main medium through which learning occurs and the objectives of society are achieved. As a result, the MoEHE gives due care to producing the school textbook as a major component of the curriculum, as the main source of knowledge and learning in the educational process. This tool is always available to the teacher and learner, in addition to other media, the Internet, computers, society, and family.

The first Palestinian Curriculum Plan

The first Palestinian Curriculum Plan of 1998 stated:

> the principles of the Palestinian curriculum are that Palestine is a democratic state, ruled by a democratic parliamentary system; Palestine is a peace-loving state, working towards international understanding and cooperation based on equality, liberty, dignity, peace and human rights . . . social justice, equality and the provision of equal learning opportunities for all Palestinians . . . to develop all Palestinians intellectually, socially, physically, spiritually and emotionally, to become responsible citizens, able to participate in solving problems of their community, their country and the world.[6]

To achieve these goals, a number of significant improvements have been introduced in the new Palestinian curriculum. One relevant subject is civic education that focuses on helping develop a democratic citizen. There are also serious attempts to introduce and teach universal values by encouraging respect for other cultures, promoting peace values and universal values, and themes such as human rights, freedom of speech, social justice, democracy, respect for law, diversity, tolerance, pluralism, and global environmental awareness.

Pedagogically, and according to publications of the MoEHE (e.g., the Five-Year Plan, curriculum framework, position papers), the new Palestinian curriculum promotes students' faculties of critical thinking, creative thinking, decision-making, and problem-solving.

A position paper published by the MoEHE notes that the curriculum is also politically sound in the sense that it adopted an approach that avoids any reference to animosity toward others in order to create an ambience conducive to peace in the region.[7] Moreover, according to an update issued by the MoEHE, the curriculum is tentative and should be viewed as a transitional attempt to account for the complex political situation in the region.[8]

What do Palestinian textbooks teach?

Although far from perfect, Palestinian textbooks represent a step forward in the evolution and design of a school curriculum for Palestinians that is essential to the development of á national identity.

Across the curriculum, and across grade levels, observers and reviewers note that

> the Palestinian textbooks of civic education . . . convey visions of society in which tolerance of other religions, human rights, peace, pluralism, democracy and other values are encouraged and fostered . . . Civic education textbooks . . . very much foster Western values: democracy, human rights, individual rights, education for peace and tolerance of all religions.
>
> *(Reiss, 2004)*

Other reviews (e.g., IPCRI, 2003, 2004, 2006) note that the textbooks promote an environment of open-mindedness, rational thinking, modernization, critical reflection, and dialogue.

On the other hand, generally speaking, and across all school subjects and grade levels, there is a lack of reference to, or positive acknowledgment of, the state of Israel. Several texts prize martyrdom and jihad (or struggle). In addition, there are multiple references to religious and social tolerance toward other Muslims and Arab/Palestinian Christians in present-day contexts and toward "the People of the Book" (Christians and Jews) in historical contexts. No references are made to political tolerance in relation to Israel and Jews. Historical geography is dealt with across the curriculum; political geography of the region, on the other hand, is avoided altogether.

In addition, there is little in the textbooks about the peace processes between the Arab countries and Israel. In the book *History of the Arabs and the World in the 20th Century* (grade twelve), for example, there is great detail about the wars, the British Mandate period and Israel's establishment, but only a minor reference to the peace process with Egypt and Jordan. The Oslo Accords are not mentioned in that textbook at all, and receive only a passing mention in the *Contemporary Problems* textbook (also grade twelve).

From an administrative standpoint, we know that the same books are taught at public and private schools (religious and secular). Private schools, for their part, are also free to take part in programs not included in the formal curriculum. These programs and projects include, among others, interfaith dialogue, conflict resolution, peer mediation, psychological counseling, and social communication. Religious schools run by Christian institutions and those run by the Islamic Waqf and other Islamic organizations and societies (e.g., Hamas) supplement the formal curriculum with themes and materials that promote their policies and agendas. It should be noted in this context that, although the Palestinian Authority controls the education system, there is reason to suspect that certain religious schools go beyond their mandated materials and teach materials that do not necessarily conform to the rules and regulations set by the MoEHE. In this context, one also needs to invoke the concept of the "hidden curriculum" that is reflected in the school environment or the school culture (what goes on inside the classroom, the playground, staff room, athletic activities, etc.) – a curriculum that cannot be supervised or controlled.

Under agreements made with the host authorities, UNRWA has to use the curricula and textbooks of the countries/territories where it operates. However, it also creates educational enrichment materials to supplement the local curriculum. One of UNRWA's key programs is aimed at the promotion of nonviolent conflict resolution and human rights. These systematic efforts, which have included translations into Arabic of relevant textbooks, the creation of special manuals, and the involvement of UNRWA pupils in cross-community summer camps, have reached every Agency school in the West Bank and Gaza and are to be expanded to the other fields.

Hamas, for its part, carries out a number of civilian activities in the fields of welfare and education. It has diversified educational activities and programs (schools, summer camps, and clubs) that, in certain geographical regions (the Gaza Strip) and particular subject matter (religious studies and language arts), compete with the PA's education system. This said, not much is known about the nature and content of instruction inside schools run by Hamas. Few outside individuals, mostly foreign and Israeli journalists and correspondents, reported their findings. For example, in an article written by CNN's Matthew Chance, the reporter who had access to a kindergarten in the Gaza Strip, noted: "In the classrooms of Islamic kindergartens in Gaza, the young are drilled in religious beliefs. Teachers, their faces covered by veils, say they don't preach hatred. But, they say, all the children here already know Israel as their enemy. Israel, for its part, says Hamas schools lead the way in inciting hatred in Palestinian youngsters toward Israelis" (CNN report, June 26, 2006).

Another example is taken from an Israeli newspaper. According to the principal of a Hamas school in the Gaza Strip (Mr. Nufal) interviewed by Avi Issacharoff, of the *Ha'aretz* newspaper, the curriculum barely differs from that taught at government (public) schools, and the kids in Hamas schools study the textbooks published by the MoEHE. But there is one difference: "Our children get supplementary Koran classes," Nufal says. However, the big questions of what precisely the children are taught from the Koran, and with what interpretation, remain unanswered (Issacharoff, 2006).

Other Israeli and international organizations (e.g., the Intelligence and Terrorism Information Center at the Center for Special Studies, and the Center for Monitoring the Impact of Peace) claim that Hamas's educational institutions teach violence and hatred and cultivate young generations of Hamas members who, according to these reports, are educated to continue pursuing terrorism as a means to resolve the Israeli–Palestinian conflict. The education system, these organizations stress, is used to incite young Palestinians to become martyrs. "The children of the kindergarten are the shaheeds [martyrs] of tomorrow," read signs in a Hamas-run school, while placards in classrooms at al-Najah University in the West Bank and at Gaza's Islamic University declare: "Israel has nuclear bombs; we have human bombs."

It is to be hoped that the textbooks, in their final versions, seize the opportunity to educate future generations of Palestinians to live in peace with Israel. In particular, Israel, as a political entity, should be recognized as a legitimate state and a neighbor to negotiate with and live beside in peace rather than an enemy to be hated, fought, and destroyed. Moreover, the Jewish tradition should be reported in historical contexts that relate to the region, especially those of historical Palestine. Themes on tolerance should be inclusive in nature in the sense that they should be directly related not only to non–Muslim Arabs and Westerners but to Israel and the Jews. Peaceful dimensions of jihad should also be emphasized and the Arab–Israeli conflict should be addressed in pragmatic terms that view it as political rather than existential and religious in nature.

One has to note, however, that although textbooks and syllabuses are important ingredients, experience has shown that they are not necessarily the most important elements in the fulfillment of a meaningful peace agreement between societies and nations in conflict. More important elements are "the sincere will and commitment of both parties for achieving such an agreement, and the environment the population has to live in."[9]

Initiatives related to peace education: the Palestinian context

Educators and other stakeholders alike try to promote peace, tolerance, and reconciliation by implementing the principles and practices of peace education, formally and informally, through school curricula, joint school-based programs, joint teacher training, publication of instructional materials, learning projects, weekend workshops, summer camps, community-based seminars, theatre clubs, etc.

As far as the Palestinian context is concerned, one has to admit from the outset that there is no formal peace education as part of the formal curriculum. However, the MoEHE encourages school participation in programs and projects sponsored and administered by local, national, regional, and international organizations in the public, private, and UNRWA school sectors, and at the university level. In addition, personnel from the MoEHE and from other Palestinian ministries and institutions have taken part in various workshops and training sessions aimed at providing them with knowledge and skills relating to peace, tolerance, reconciliation, human rights, justice, and communication.

Over the past decade or so, a good number of schools, colleges, teacher training institutes, civil society institutions, and NGOs in the West Bank and the Gaza Strip have sought out innovative strategies and adopted a proactive approach to counteract the increasing incidence of violence, stereotyping, intolerance, and prejudice.

Generally speaking, these social and educational initiatives have areas of overlap with peace education and with each other. These programs include children's/human rights education, civic literacy, conflict resolution and conflict transformation, peer mediation, violence prevention, cooperative discipline, education for development, gender training, global education, environmental awareness, life skills education, and psychosocial rehabilitation.

It is hoped that these programs will lead to a decrease in the levels of hostility and tension in schools and might promote peaceful, cooperative behavior among students. The combination of creative policies, training to enhance students' skills in understanding conflict, and efforts to create a more caring school environment is bringing the issue of youth violence out of the shadows and into the spotlight.

Children's/human rights and democracy education

Non-academic context

Children's/human rights and peace education are closely linked activities that complement and support each other. Rights education encourages the development of skills that will enable children to act in ways that uphold and promote rights, both their own and those of others. In such programs children are encouraged to understand the impact of rights violations, both at home and in school, and to develop empathy and solidarity with those whose rights have been denied.

On the ground, the Office of the High Commissioner for Human Rights (OHCHR) has been very active in the field of human rights education. Workshops and training target individuals from all walks of life, but mostly educators and personnel from the various ministries in the Palestinian Authority (Ministries of Women's Affairs, Labor, Local Government, Social Welfare, Health, Agriculture, Sports, and Youth). Training courses cover human rights principles and standards with the focus on children's/women's rights. Workshops and training sessions focus on building skills in documentation and reporting human rights violations. The OHCHR also co-organizes workshops and training sessions with the Commission of Human Rights and NGOs on relevant topics, such as the separation of powers and the rule of law. Some of these trainings target government personnel and officers from the Palestinian security apparatus.

Academic context

A number of local and international NGOs (e.g., the Teacher Creativity Center, the Educational Network, Al-Mawred, the Palestinian Center for Human Rights, among others) conduct training sessions and workshops for students, teachers, administrators, counselors, etc. These activities target educators out of a conviction that they are the most important people in society capable of effecting and implementing change and reform.

Projects and training courses aim to provide teachers from public, private, and UNRWA schools with the knowledge, skills, and competencies they need to integrate democracy and human rights in education. Training includes both theoretical and practical aspects relating to the topics addressed, such as the primacy of law and order, political pluralism in a democratic system, branches of government, accountability, citizens' responsibilities and rights, and independence of the judiciary. Other topics include: the Universal Declaration of Human Rights; the International Covenant on Economic, Social, and Cultural Rights; the International Covenant on Civil and Political Rights; the Convention on the Elimination of All Forms of Discrimination against Women; the Convention on the Rights of the Child; international humanitarian law; and the role of NGOs in the promotion and protection of human rights.

Pedagogical themes and skills in the workshops and training sessions include classroom and time management, active communication, cooperative learning, interactive learning, problem-solving, critical thinking training, etc. Other projects focus on designing and developing instructional materials and training manuals on the topic of integrating civic education concepts and counseling.

In practice, participants gain experiential as well as received knowledge by actively participating in role-plays, simulations, case studies, scenarios, dramatizations, and other active learning and interactive teaching strategies and methods.

Religious institutions are also involved in the informal teaching of peace, reconciliation, and social justice. For example, Sabeel, an organization that is part of a youth action plan for human rights, justice, and peace initiated by the Church of Sweden in Lund, facilitates the coordination of ecumenical youth groups (from the West Bank, Jerusalem, and Galilee) representing their own denominations. The program challenges and encourages local youth through various opportunities to develop leadership skills while exploring the meaning and roots of the Palestinian Christian identity. Participants discuss historical and contemporary issues that deal with peace, justice, human rights abuses, etc.

New challenges and controversy

Controversy erupted on the eve of the sixtieth anniversary of the Universal Declaration of Human Rights (UDHR), when UNRWA decided to build on its prior experience in the field of human rights education. Since 2002, UNRWA has integrated human rights into the teaching of Arabic, Islamic studies, and the social sciences as part of its nonviolent conflict resolution and human rights program. The Gaza Field Office announced that it was planning to introduce new instructional materials on the topics of human rights and several instruments of international law. This time, the plan had provision to teach: the individual responsibilities required to achieve human rights for all, including tolerance in thinking and behavior and the historical context that gave rise to the UDHR (the Second World War and the Holocaust); the history of the global struggle for human rights, using case studies including the civil rights movement in the US (Martin Luther King), colonialism in India and nonviolent resistance (Gandhi), apartheid in South Africa and the role of Nelson Mandela in the struggle to abolish it, genocide in Rwanda, and ethnic cleansing in the Balkans; and the global human rights context in terms of accountability and enforcement mechanisms.

The new UNRWA initiative is multifaceted and includes provisions for development of the curriculum, monitoring and evaluating progress and attainment of goals, and community outreach. The last dimension is of great interest since it entails ensuring community support through the use of committed and respected teachers, regular community outreach sessions, and fostering the recognition and support for the centrality of human rights in the human development of the next generation of Gazans.

When reports surfaced about UNRWA's intention to include the Holocaust in its school curriculum, Hamas initiated a campaign to denounce it. Officials in the Ministry of Education (in Gaza) said that they would consult with UNRWA officials and demand that the subject be eliminated from the new eighth-grade curriculum, which is supposed to include basic lessons about the Holocaust within the framework of overall human rights studies. A Hamas spokesman claimed that inclusion of the Holocaust in the new curriculum aimed to justify "the Israeli occupation" of the land of the Palestinian territories (Reuters, 2009). For his part, Abd al-Rahman al-Jamal, head of the Palestinian Legislative Council's Education Committee for Hamas, told a BBC correspondent that the Holocaust was "a big lie." He said that teaching it would serve Israel, which had been fighting Hamas for years. Instead, he said, the UN should teach the Nakba, the term used by the Palestinians to describe the establishment of the state of Israel and specifically the expulsion of hundreds of thousands of refugees (BBC, 2009). He said that Hamas would not allow UNRWA to include the Holocaust in the curriculum of its schools (Al-Bayan Center, 2009).

It is worth noting in this context that the Holocaust is not taught in Palestinian Authority schools. In PA textbooks, including those printed between 2005 and 2007, there is no mention of the Holocaust in connection with the Second World War. However, one textbook – an eleventh-grade "contemporary issues" textbook – makes a single reference to "what the Nazis did to the Jews."

At the grassroots and teaching community levels, the decision to include the topic in the curriculum, along with other activities carried out by UNRWA schools (e.g., sending students to participate in summer camps in the US and Western Europe), has met with opposition from parents, teachers, supervisors, and school principals. For example, the principal of one of the UNRWA schools, who asked to remain anonymous, attacked UNRWA's education policy of the last few years for sending fourteen–sixteen-year-olds to summer camps as a reward for excelling in human rights studies. The principal's criticism stems from his belief that these students are in the throes of adolescence and a trip abroad might negatively influence their behavior (Filastin al-'An, 2009). Another UNRWA employee, a school supervisor who also asked to remain anonymous, attacked the Agency for integrating material about human rights into the curriculum on the basis of a UN General Assembly resolution passed a year earlier. According to the supervisor, "the material is good but problematic," because it stressed the rights the Palestinians do not have but also stressed that every conflict "can be resolved by dialogue" while ignoring the role of the "resistance" in liberation (AP, 2009). A parent whose child attended an UNRWA school expressed his opposition, too: "I don't want them teaching my children Jewish lies. It will just be Zionist propaganda" (AP, 2009).

Until the plans to include the Holocaust in the curriculum of the human rights program, reactions had been mostly positive. For example, Farid El Haffar, from Gaza, reported in March 2007 that some teachers, both male and female, who attended a training course in human rights conducted by the Palestinian Center for Human Rights (PCHR) expressed their satisfaction with the workshop that was held as part of UNRWA's human rights program (El Haffar, 2007). The workshop is held annually as part of an agreement between UNRWA and PCHR to train teachers in the principles and methodologies of teaching human rights. Examples of comments and reactions from participants and trainers included:

- "We are learning about human rights conventions and bodies, and the role of human rights organizations."
- "The training course covers a variety of human rights topics, including the historical development of human rights, the Universal Declaration of Human Rights, the Convention on the Rights of the Child, and the right to education."
- "After finishing this course, teachers will develop a better understanding of human rights and will be able to integrate them in their teaching."
- "Among other things, the course aims to strengthen human rights understanding at school and at home. This will impact the way we interact and the way we look at society and others in general."
- "The Palestinian people live in a very complex reality and learning about human rights is a key to its understanding."

UNRWA's reaction

In response to Hamas's outcry, UNRWA initially denied it had any immediate plans to teach the Holocaust in the schools it runs in Gaza. Sources said that no decision had yet been made about the new curriculum. Adnan Abu Hasneh, UNRWA spokesman, said that there was no mention of the Holocaust in the current curriculum, but he refused to say whether that was about to change (Reuters, 2009). Karen Abu Ziyyad, UNRWA's commissioner general, said that the study unit for human rights was currently being developed and so far it was only in draft form. She added that, in any case, before it was taught, it would be examined by various groups that would be free to give their reactions. UNRWA spokesman Chris Gunness said that a final decision had not yet been made (AP, 2009).

The dispute with Hamas has serious implications for the education system in the Gaza Strip as both Hamas (as the *de facto* government) and UNRWA run their own schools. While Hamas controls the education system in the Gaza Strip, UNRWA still has considerable advantages, relatively speaking, in its far greater financial and logistical resources and its broad network of teachers and schools. At the time of writing the issue remained unresolved and was awaiting intervention from regional and international organizations and the good offices of the Palestinian Ministry of Education in the West Bank.

Conflict resolution/transformation and mediation programs

Peace requires more than an end to fighting. The underlying causes of violent conflict must be addressed to prevent its resurgence. Very often, the protracted processes that lead to a peace agreement represent the beginning of a much longer process of peace implementation and reconciliation.

Governments follow "track one" (or "conflict diplomacy"), while NGOs typically pursue "track two" – "unofficial diplomatic activities" that directly impact the people most affected by the conflict. While many peacemaking and peace-building efforts focus on governments, there is a widespread belief among educators and conflict resolution/transformation experts that the entire system will benefit from coordination between and among all the tracks. Projects dealing with political, racial, ethnic, or religious conflicts, such as the Israeli–Palestinian conflict, usually focus on "conflict transformation." This refers to the process of moving from conflict-habituated systems to peace systems. It is distinguished from the more common term "conflict resolution" because of its focus on "systemic change."

In the Israeli–Palestinian context, the conflict is deep-rooted. In addition, the social, educational, religious, and political systems have embodied the conflict, and the population has absorbed these conflict patterns at a very deep level. This means that the peace agreements and accords and the official negotiation venues comprise only one piece of the solution. To create lasting peace and transform the conflict, it will take a concerted effort that engages all stakeholders simultaneously, over a period of time.

On the ground, international and local NGOs and centers (Israel–Palestine Center for Research and Information (IPCRI), Palestinian Center for Conflict Resolution and Reconciliation (CCRR), PRIME, the Arab Educational Institute (AEI), and UNRWA, among others) are involved in the conflict transformation/resolution process because of their interest in changing the approach to conflict resolution within the Palestinian community and among the people of the region, and because they possess expertise in mediation, negotiation, and peace-building.

These organizations provide professional training programs and ongoing consultation that aim to enhance participants' knowledge and skills. In many cases the target groups are key "multipliers" in Palestinian society, with priority given to schools (students, teachers, administrators, counselors, and parents), youth security forces, leaders of NGOs working for peace and reconciliation, student leaders, women's groups, government officials, and others.

More specifically, uni- and bi-national programs implemented by the various organizations provide participants with the conflict resolution skills of mediation, communication, teamwork, active listening, trust, respect, anger management, and violence reduction. They also promote the creation of nonviolent communities by empowering marginalized groups to participate in the decision-making processes that affect their lives. Moreover, they work to strengthen democratic relations and understanding inside the Palestinian community by addressing the issues of conflict resolution, conflict reduction, and conflict transformation. Another aim of such programs is to promote the values of reconciliation and forgiveness inside the Palestinian communities and build peace between different races, religions, and groups.

Practically, and in addition to holding training sessions and workshops, these organizations promote the creation of nonviolent and peaceful environments in the region through national and bi-national projects and programs, hosting and/or supporting peace initiatives and conferences, printing and disseminating materials (booklets, etc.) on tolerance, conflict resolution, nonviolence, mediation, etc. Some (e.g., CCRR and PRIME) also have joint history dialogue projects that address the role of history in conflict creation and conflict resolution.

Other institutions address peace and reconciliation issues through learning about the monotheistic faith. For example, and in addition to its work in promoting non-violent alternatives to conflict, AEI has been coordinating a joint Palestinian–Israeli interfaith dialogue project. This has now been running for nearly a decade and is implemented in private, public, and UNRWA schools in the West Bank and public and private schools in Israel.

For its part, UNRWA has been very active in the field of conflict resolution and human rights education. It also receives external funds from international organizations such as the Friends of UNRWA. These organizations and groups supported the development of a unique curriculum created by UNRWA that has taught conflict resolution and human rights to a large number of refugee children in UNRWA schools in the West Bank and the Gaza Strip. The program is expected to remain in place in the coming years because such programs "would give Palestine refugee children the tools necessary to resolve conflicts peacefully through non-violent means."[10]

IPCRI has also been very active in the field of peace education. In addition to producing instructional materials, the Center, with financial help from Israel–Palestine Peace Partners, has provided joint training for Israeli and Palestinian public and private schoolteachers and students in conflict resolution and peer mediation.

Programs outside the region

Outside the region, Palestinian youth and educators have actively participated in the projects sponsored by the Seeds of Peace organization. Activities in the form of encounters, workshops, joint projects, lectures, summer camps, etc. offer participants (Israeli and Palestinian) opportunities to acquire, develop, and cultivate leadership skills and to engage in meaningful dialogue with their peers. In these programs, emphasis is placed on team-building, cross-cultural communication, and academic excellence in order to encourage participants to become leaders in both their schools and the global community.

Gender training

Gender conflicts are found in societies around the globe, and gender discrimination, stereotyping, and conflict are leading causes of violence.

In the Palestinian context, many initiatives and programs promote attitudes and values that emphasize the rights of girls and women to safety, respect, non-discrimination, and empowerment. More specifically, the CCRR, UNRWA, Palestine Red Crescent (PRCS), the Red Cross, the Gaza Community Mental Health Program (GCMHP), and other organizations and centers provide information for targeted sections of the population and conduct training programs for teachers and women on the topics of women's rights, assertiveness, self-esteem, personal statute law, marriage conditions and prerequisites, childbirth, kinds of divorce and their preconditions, and empowerment. For example, the GCMHP offers training sessions, on a regular basis, for women and girls interested in learning more about their rights and responsibilities.

Other workshops and training sessions address the concepts of gender culture and stereotyping. Gender culture refers to the existence of different social experiences for each sex. Gender stereotyping refers to preconceived and oversimplified ideas about the characteristics of the two sexes. In the process, the lectures and activities examine and challenge the tacit acceptance of sex-role stereotypes by examining the behaviors, attitudes, values, and beliefs that determine what is considered appropriate for males and females. In addition, participants gain knowledge of the value of gender equity and are encouraged to engage in critical thinking around issues of gender, including their own internal, and possibly unexamined, assumptions.

Psychosocial rehabilitation

Psychosocial rehabilitation programs are mostly therapeutic in focus, aiming to promote self-expression, coping skills, and psychological healing. However, peace education is not a form of individual or group therapy. Psychosocial rehabilitation programs complement and support peace education when, in promoting recovery from post-traumatic stress, they help participants learn new skills for dealing with conflict.

In the Palestinian context, several organizations and centers in the West Bank and the Gaza Strip offer psychological support through the PRCS's Psychosocial Support Program (PSP). They also offer training for health personnel, teachers, and parents. In addition, these centers and organizations offer counseling on individual and group bases. Many of these programs target ex-prisoners and injured individuals. Major contributors in this field include the Red Cross/Crescent, the YMCA/YWCA, and GCMHP.

More specifically, the PRCS provides psychosocial support services to selected communities through two psychosocial family centers. It has also integrated psycho-social activities into various health programs.

The GCMPH regularly conducts training courses on "mental health and human rights." These courses target personnel from the Ministry of Prisoners and Ex-detainees. Topics include Palestinian personality, mental health and mental illness, effects of detention on prisoners' mental health, treatment and rehabilitation of prisoners, violence and its effects on family and society, burn-out, and culture and mental health.

Other activities organized by the GCMPH include training courses for Palestinian law-enforcement personnel. Topics include the psychology of the victim, human rights, communication skills, and common psychological consequences of torture and human rights violations.

The CCRR is also active in the field of psychosocial rehabilitation and coun-seling. Over the past several years, they have conducted a psychological counseling program that provides participants with the skills to cope with crises in addition to conflict resolution skills. The Center has also been active in training security personnel in dealing with stress and violence, and has trained Palestinian and Israeli security personnel serving at border crossings.

As part of its emergency programming, UNRWA also provides educational psychosocial support for students. Over the past few years, the program has provided a large number of group and individual counseling sessions and parent meetings. In Gaza, workshops have been held on trauma, crisis management, human rights, tolerance, and conflict resolution. In the West Bank, workshops have included stress management and communication skills.

Education for development and global education

Education for development is an approach to teaching and learning which builds a commitment to global solidarity, peace, accepting differences, social justice, and environmental awareness. Its aim is to empower children and youth to participate in bringing about constructive change, both locally and globally. Some of the basic concepts in education for development are interdependence, images and perceptions, social justice, conflict and conflict resolution, and change and the future. Practical dimensions include interactive, participatory, cooperatively structured teaching methods. These allow learners to grasp complex concepts, build problem-solving abilities, and develop social communication and interaction skills.

Global education incorporates some of the themes covered in education for development programs, such as environment and ecology, peace, tolerance, conflict avoidance, personal health, cooperative skills, multiculturalism, comparative views on human values, and human rights. Pedagogically, global education gives priority to active, learner-based teaching methods, peer learning, problem-solving, community participation, and conflict resolution skills. It is value-based and future-oriented. Classroom activities address the overarching themes of "learning to live together," "images of ourselves and the others," and "futures."

In the Palestinian context, the MoEHE and the Palestinian Water Authority have been supportive of a joint Israeli–Palestinian–Jordanian project entitled "Watercare" that involves the design and development of supplementary materials (textbook, teacher's guide, website) on the topics of water conservation and environmental stewardship (water resources, water pollution, water uses, water management). The production of the textbook was a joint project that lasted almost three years and benefited from local, regional, and international expertise. The project is currently implemented in private, public, and UNRWA schools. It involves teacher and student encounters and joint environmental projects.

In addition, the MoEHE and UNICEF have collaborated in executing a "Global Education" program aimed at promoting the development of responsible Palestinian children. Through this project, children are helped to develop and acquire skills to interact with their own community and the outer world.

At the civil society level, for more than a decade IPCRI has been involved in building sustainable partnerships through organizing and administering joint Israeli–Palestinian projects and programs in the fields of negotiation, the environment/

water issues, final status issues, economic cooperation, legal affairs, leadership, good governance, grassroots mobilization, and other peace-building activities.

IPCRI and CCRR have also conducted conferences, workshops, and training sessions for peace activists from both sides and have co-facilitated a large number of programs in peace activism, conflict resolution, the environment, and creating a culture of peace.

Life skills education

Life skills education is an approach to education that enables children and young people to translate knowledge, attitudes, and values into action. Life skills can include cooperation, negotiation, communication, problem-solving, decision-making, coping with emotions, self-awareness, empathy, critical and creative thinking, dealing with peer pressure, risk awareness, assertiveness, and preparation for the world of work.

Many life skills are "generic" in that they can be applied to a number of specific contexts. The emphasis of life skills education on developing attitudes and values, and translating those changes into observable behaviors, is an important perspective to incorporate in peace education programs.

In the Palestinian context, the MoEHE and UNICEF have been collaborating for almost a decade in the development of formal and non-formal life skills-based education (LSBE). In that context, life skills are defined as "The abilities we need to solve our problems, cope with pressure, search for positive changes and promote available positives in order to improve our situation and reach security, peace, harmony with the society and the environment."[11]

LSBE in the Palestinian context rose as a need in two ongoing programs: the "Health Promoting School" project and the "Global Education" project. These two projects are supported by UNICEF and coordinated by the MoEHE, in partnership with the Ministry of Health, the Ministry of Social Affairs, UNRWA, and several NGOs. They started with the training of a core multisectoral group in LSBE who became the driving force for the initiatives by drafting materials for three age groups (six–nine, ten–twelve, and thirteen–sixteen years). A follow-up stage is to mainstream LSBE in the national curriculum in pilot primary, secondary, and vocational schools.

Other initiatives

According to an IPCRI document, creating a culture of peace "necessitates not only evaluating textbooks, joint projects, student and teacher encounters, as has been done until now, but the development of new learning materials in the form of curricula, textbooks, lesson plans, and teachers' guides."[12] To fulfill this vision, IPCRI will produce a set of new multidisciplinary textbooks for Palestinian and Israeli schools (grades one to twelve) on peace, mutual understanding, pluralism, diversity, and democracy.

Education and NGO work under the Hamas government

The victory of Hamas in the January 2006 Palestinian elections was met with concern in the international community because of the movement's covenant, its policies, and its ideology. For many observers in the region and throughout the international community, it was feared that the victory would result in a shift in the nature and dynamics of the peace process. In educational circles, there was a fear that Hamas's assumption of the leadership role in the Palestinian MoEHE would accentuate the already strained relationship with international donors over the Palestinian curriculum that was almost complete. It was also feared that the new cabinet would place some restrictions on the work of local and international NGOs, especially in joint projects in the economic, environmental, and educational fields.

However, under Hamas, work on the last set of textbooks (grades six and twelve) continued as planned with few changes at the top of the Center for Curriculum Development. In addition, the work of most of the local and international NGOs in the West Bank and the Gaza Strip (e.g., IPCRI, Seeds of Peace, CARE, PRIME, AEI, GCMHP, WI'AM, Panorama, Sabeel, the Holy Land Trust, Hope Flower School, Al Hadaf Association, among others) continued, although at a lower intensity and less frequently.

In addition, as recently as February 19, 2007, the Palestinian Minister of Education and Higher Education called for "reinforcement of the principles of acceptance and respect of the other in our sons and daughters so as to create a civil generation that respects the law, justice and discipline . . . Our people and its leadership have provided a lot and have shown willingness to respect international treaties and agreements."[13]

The formation of the Palestinian unity government gave us more hope that things would proceed in the desired direction. We were especially encouraged by the official pronouncements presented in the context of the government's program (March 17, 2007), originally published in the Palestinian daily *Al-Ayyam* in Arabic and translated by the Jerusalem Media Center. We note in particular statements relating to the political level and international relations:

- At the political level, "the government will work with the international community for the sake of ending the occupation and regaining the legitimate rights of the Palestinian people so that we can build a solid basis for peace, security and prosperity in the region." The government "shall respect the international legitimacy resolutions and the agreements that were signed by the PLO" and will work "to consolidate the relations with the Arab and Islamic countries and open up and cooperate with the regional and international surroundings on the basis of mutual respect."
- With respect to international relations, the government "shall work on establishing sound and solid relations with the various world countries and with the international institutions, including the UN and the Security Council and the international regional organizations, in a manner that assists reinforcing world peace and stability."

Challenges for creating a culture of peace in the Palestinian conflict

At the start of the twenty-first century, many people are looking to peace education to create a new, more tolerant, less bloody world order based on mutual respect, nonviolence, justice, and environmental sustainability. However, this nascent academic field faces key challenges in the future. Some of these challenges are generic in nature while others are more context-oriented.

Some of the major generic challenges relate to the difficulty of replacing a belief in peacekeeping with a commitment to peacemaking and peace-building strategies to address the multifaceted forms of aggression and violence that exist on this planet. Other challenges include: convincing policy-makers and educators to put resources into supporting peace education, producing research that demonstrates the value of teaching young people how to behave peacefully, and developing peace-building strategies in schools.

Context-oriented challenges include the existence of strong, contradictory, and deeply rooted Palestinian and Israeli collective narratives and historical memories, inherent economic, political, and military inequalities between the two parties, different conceptions of peace and the peace agenda, the outbreak of the second Intifada and the ensuing violence, and the excessive emotionality surrounding final status issues.

Enhancing the chances of success

What can be done to enhance the chances of successfully creating a culture of peace in the region? Some final remarks and recommendations, categorized into four domains, follow. These can also serve as preconditions for peace education programs to succeed.

Theoretical and general remarks and recommendations

* Palestinian education reform is important not only for Palestinians and for Israeli–Palestinian peace, but for broader regional and global interests. In this context, a diverse, balanced curriculum may serve as a foundation for greater peace, democratization, and the development of a vibrant civil society in the Palestinian territories.
* More attention should be given to "positive peace" as opposed to "negative peace." The former involves the development of a society where social justice and active civil society prevail. The former simply implies the absence of violence on a large scale.
* Along the same lines, and for peace education to be effective and beneficial, there is a need for a radical reconstruction of relations at the interpersonal as well as the international level. At the heart of these relations are the principles of social justice and law.

- In the same context, it is of great importance that political action accompanies other steps and actions in the educational arena. Stakeholders need to take an active role in peace movement activities in support of the causes of peace, tolerance, and reconciliation.
- Peace education needs to be proactive in its approaches. This means that its goals and aims need to be those of educating individuals and society at large in the principles and behaviors of nonviolence, tolerance, equality, social justice, and respect of differences, all of which contribute to eventual peaceful coexistence.
- To enhance the chances of success of peace education, programs need to bring in all relevant actors that, in addition to teachers and administrators, include appropriate government departments, local community-based, and international organizations, among others. Moreover, the strategies adopted in peace education need to be realistic and within the capabilities of the different agents and actors involved in the conflict. Most importantly, different responses to conflict need to be presented in the form of peacekeeping, peacemaking, and peace-building strategies.
- Building "peace" requires that we teach *for* peace, not just *about* peace. The latter implies learning facts and theories that may or may not result in a change in attitudes or a desire to work for peace. It also deals with creating awareness about peace and the complexities of peacemaking. The former deals with teaching skills and creating new attitudes and perceptions (in the areas of ideology, morality, and philosophy) and modifying existing structures in the educational system toward peace-building.
- In the same context, the national curriculum needs to be "regionalized" in the sense that it should include themes from the culture, heritage, religion, politics, and so on of the "other." This coverage involves including within the curriculum the contributions of Jews and Israelis to literature, history, art, and the general cultural heritage. Educating students about cultural, political, social, and religious similarities and differences is an important element in reducing prejudice and promoting tolerance. In addition, the lessons, strategies, and skills taught need to be age appropriate.

Pedagogic remarks and recommendations

- To be effective, the principles of peace education should be embedded in the regular school subjects rather than introduced as a separate program.
- There is a need to improve both the pedagogy and practice as they relate to peace education. In that context, a robust theoretical framework needs to be established.
- Along the same lines, there is a need for more empirical and qualitative research and evaluation projects to discern the effectiveness of peace education programs. This practice is likely to enhance the long-term success of such programs.
- Moreover, peace education should strive to be comprehensive and holistic rather than piecemeal in nature. This means that knowledge, skills and

strategies, attitudes, values, and behavior go hand in hand. It also means that the skills and concepts need to be taught in a systematic approach through formal education and in such informal settings as workshops, seminars, conferences, encounters, and joint projects.

- From a pedagogical standpoint, "cooperative learning," as a general teaching and learning method, is recommended in this context. This method requires participants to work in small groups and study in face-to-face interaction, cooperating to complete a common task.

- In addition, and since students encounter different types of violence, they should be informed about and trained in different forms of peace-building. These include teaching tolerance, conflict resolution, discussion and peer mediation skills, human rights, knowledge of national, regional, and international organizations, awareness of environmental issues, strategies for sustainability, different types of violence and conflicts and their roots and origins.

Teacher education

- Teacher effectiveness is very important in the educational process. Unfortunately, most teachers, having spent much of their lives in academic environments that do not foster the acquisition and development of critical and life skills (critical thinking, critical reflection, historical thinking, problem-solving and the like), may find it difficult to show students how to develop and employ these skills in real-life situations. Schools of education and teacher training colleges should provide significant exposure to these skills and competencies, thereby preparing young people to become active citizens of their country and the world.

Technology

- Peace education should benefit from the computer age. Local and regional programs could take on global dimensions as the possibilities for linking up with educators and stakeholders in distant areas become realities.

Final thoughts

Education for peace is the best vehicle to ensure that the next generation of Israelis and Palestinians have the skills, the knowledge, and the motivation to create a truly peaceful Middle East. However, peace education does not always lead to conflict resolution, but rather to greater mutual understanding, tolerance, and some reduction of violence. Regardless of that, Palestinian children must be provided with the skills and knowledge to live in peace and to create mutual respect and understanding that will enable them to transform their lives and this region into one of cooperation, prosperity, and freedom.

Educators' success will be measured by our ability to help children and youth to transform the conflict and embrace the principles and values of peace, tolerance, and reconciliation. Our success will also be a function of investing in human resource capacity through outreach and learning at the community level and of engaging local, regional, and international organizations in the process.

Success will also be measured by the degree to which we create a learning environment characterized by sharing and cooperation, shared decision-making and problem-solving, and critical reflection; and it will be contingent on promoting learners' skills and faculties of active listening, self-esteem, creative self-expression, their ability to act on ideas, and their understanding of the links between the personal, local, regional, and global.

Notes

1 Although specialists and professionals distinguish between "peace education" and "education for peace," in the context of the present chapter the two terms are used interchangeably.
2 *Peace Education.* Working paper. UNICEF: Education Section, June 1999.
3 Ibid.
4 MoEHE's Five-Year Plan: 2001–2005.
5 Clarification from the MoEHE-Palestine, May 12, 2001.
6 "Palestinian Curriculum Plan." MoEHE-Palestine: Palestinian Center for the Development of Curriculum, 1998.
7 Update on the Palestinian Curricula Project. MoEHE-Palestine, n.d.
8 Ibid.
9 "The Myth of Incitement in Palestinian Textbooks: Response to Allegations against Palestinian Textbooks." Position paper. MoEHE-Palestine, June 8, 2005.
10 Working Group 1, "Promoting the Well-being of the Palestine Refugee Child." Discussion paper. Geneva Conference: Meeting the Humanitarian Needs of the Palestine Refugees in the Near East: Building Partnership in Support of UNRWA, June 7–8, 2004.
11 "Occupied Palestinian Territory: Formal and Non-Formal Life Skills-Based Education (LSBE)." Available at <http://www.uncif.org/lifeskills/index_8797.html>.
12 IPCRI, "Peace Education Text Books for Israeli and Palestinian Schools: Project 'Educational Reform in Palestinian and Israeli Schools' – The Development of Curricula and Text Books in Democracy and Peace."
13 MoEHE-Palestine press release.

BIBLIOGRAPHY

Abdel Hadi, M. (1999) *Waqe'a Al-Mar'ah Fi- Felastine, Wujhat Nadhar Islamiyyah*. Nablus: Center for Palestinian Research and Studies.

Abu Alouf, R. and Ellington, K. (2007) "Hamas Targets Fatah Prayer Rallies in Gaza Strip." *LA Times*, September 7. Available at <http://www.latimes.com/news/nationworld/world/la-fg-gaza9sep08,0,200376.story>.

Abu Amre, Ziad (1993) *"Al-Eslamiyyoon Wa Mas'alah Al-Democratiyyah" Fi: Al-Mou'tamar Al-Felasteney Al-Auwal Hawl Al-Democratiyyah*. Jerusalem: Panorama Center.

Abu-Lughod, I. (ed.) (1971) *The Transformation of Palestine*. Evanston, Ill.: Northwestern University Press.

—— (1989) "Book Review: The War of 1948: Disputed Perspectives and Outcomes, Reviewed Work(s): *The Birth of Israel: Myths and Realities*, by Simha Flapan; *The Birth of the Palestinian Refugee Problem, 1947–1949*, by Benny Morris; *Palestine 1948: L'expulsion*, by Elias Sanbar." *Journal of Palestine Studies* 18 (2):119–127.

Abu Lughod, I. *et al.* (1993) *Al-Entikhabat Al-Felastiniyyah*. Nablus: Center for Palestinian Research and Studies.

Abunimah, A. (2006) "Hamas Election Victory: A Vote for Clarity." *Electronic Intifada*, January 6. Available at <http://electronicintifada.net/v2/article4425.shtml>.

Abu-Nimer, M. (2000) "Peace Building in Postsettlement Challenges for Israeli and Palestinian Peace Educators." *Peace and Conflict: Journal of Peace Psychology* 6 (1):1–21.

Abu Sitta, S. (1999) *Palestinian Right of Return – Sacred, Legal and Possible*. London: Palestinian Return Center.

—— (2001) *From Refugees to Citizens at Home*. London: Palestine Land Society and Palestinian Return Center.

Adalah (2003) *Special Report: Ban on Family Unification*. Available at <http://www.adalah.org/eng/famunif.php>.

Adelman, M. (2003) "The Military Militarism and the Militarization of Domestic Violence." *Violence Against Women* 9:1118–1152.

Adva Center (2004) "The 20005 State Budget Proposal: A Gender Perspective." Report, December. Herzliya: Adva Center.

Agi, M. and Cassin, R. (1998) *Père de la Déclaration universelle des droits de l'homme*. Paris: Perrin.

Aharoni, S. (2005) "Facing Denial: The Challenge of Feminist Conscious Rasing in Times of Conflict – an Israeli Perspective." Paper. Haifa.

—— (2006) "The Influence of the State of War on the Lives of Israeli Women: A Gender Analysis." Haifa: Isha l'Isha.

Al-Bayan Center (2009) "The Battle for Hearts and Minds in the Gaza Strip." August 31. Available at <http://www.terrorism_info.org.il/malman-multimedia/English/eng_n/>.

Albeck, J.H., Adwan, S., and Bar-On, D. (2002) "Dialogue Groups: TRT's Guidelines for Working through Intractable Conflicts by Personal Storytelling in Encounter Groups." *Peace and Conflict: Journal of Peace Psychology* 8:301–322.

Aliewi, A. and Assaf, K. (2003) "Assessment of Water Demand Management in Palestine: Identifying the Gaps and the Constraints, Envisioning Challenges and Opportunities." Paper presented to the Second Regional Conference on Water Demand Management and Pollution Control, Sharm Al-Sheikh, Egypt, December 14–17.

Aliewi, A.S. (2005) "Sustainable Development of the Palestinian Water Sector under Arid/Semi-Arid Conditions." Paper presented to the Workshop on Arid/Semi-Arid Groundwater Governance and Management, Cairo, April 3–7.

Allon, Y. (1976) "Israel: The Case for Defensible Boundaries." *Foreign Affairs* 55:38–53.

Alpher, Y. (1994) *Borders and Settlements*. Tel Aviv: Jaffee Center for Strategic Studies, Tel Aviv University.

Alpher, Joseph and Shikaki, Khalil (1998) *The Palestinian Refugees Problem and the Right of Return*. Cambridge, MA: Harvard University Press.

Al-Shu'aibi Azmi (2005) "A presentation." Fi: Mou'tamar Ramallah Al-Awal-Ashr Sanawat Ala Wojod Al-Sultah Al-Watanneyyah Al-Felastineyyah. Ramallah: Panorama Center.

Al-Sultah Al-Wataniyyah Al-Felasteniyyah (1996) *Al-Democratiyyah Fi-Felastine, Al-Entekhabat Al-Felastiniyyah*. Ramallah.

Amnesty International (2007a) *Report on Israel and the Occupied Territories*. Available at <http://report2007.amnesty.org/eng/Regions/Middle-East-and-North-Africa/Israel-and-the-Occupied-Territories>.

—— (2007b) *Palestinian Authority: Fatah and Hamas Violations Leave Gaza's Civilians Trapped in their Homes – Growing Concerns about Violence Spreading to the West Bank*. Available at <http://domino.un.org/UNISPAL.NSF/eed216406b50bf6485256ce10072f637/2f234 68462bd3e65852572fe006cb854!OpenDocument>.

Amre, Nabil (2005) *Taqiem Al-Ada'a Khelal Al-Sanawat Al-Ashr Al-Madeyah'*. Fi: Mou'tamar Ramallah Al-Awal- Ashr Sanawat Ala Wojod Al-Sultah Al-Watanneyyah Al-Felastineyyah. Ramallah: Panorama Center.

Anderson, P.O. (1957) *They Are Human Too: A Photographic Essay on the Palestine Arab Refugees*. Chicago: H. Regnery Co.

AP (2009) "Hamas Opposes Teaching about the Holocaust in UN Schools." August 31. Available at <http://www.blogrunner.com/snapshot/D/7/3/hamas_condemns_holocaust_lessons/>.

Arab Association for Human Rights (n.d.) *Land and Planning Policy in Israel*. Available at <http://www.arabhra.org/factsheets/factsheet2.htm>.

Arab Thought Forum (1999–2005) *Democratic Formation in Palestine*. Jerusalem: Arab Thought Forum.

Arasoughly, A. *et al.* (eds.) (2000) *Witness to History: The Plight and Promise of the Palestinian Refugees*. Jerusalem: MIFTAH.

ARC (Austrian Research Centers) (2001) *The ARIJ Report in Developing Sustainable Water Management in the Jordan Valley: Joint Synthesis and Assessment Report*. Seibersdorf: Austrian Research Centers.

Arendt, H. (1998) *The Human Condition*. Chicago: University of Chicago Press.

Aruri, N. (ed.) (2001) *Palestinian Refugees: The Right of Return.* London: Pluto Press.

Arzt, D.E. (1997) *Refugees into Citizens: Palestinians and the End of the Arab–Israeli Conflict.* New York: Council on Foreign Relations.

Ashkenasi, A. (1990) "The International Institutionalization of a Refugee Problem: The Palestinians and UNRWA." *Jerusalem Journal of International Relations* 12 (1):45–75.

Asia News (2007) "Gaza Priest Slams Barbaric Attack against Sisters of the Rosary." June 19. Available at <http://www.asianews.it/index.php?l=en&art=9601>.

Assaf, K. (2004) *Water as a Human Right: The Understanding of Water in Palestine.* Global Issues Papers No. 11, Heinrich Boll Foundation.

Assaf, K., Al Khatib, N., Kally, E., and Shuval, H. (1993) *A Proposal for the Development of a Regional Water Master Plan.* Jerusalem: Israel/Palestine Center for Research and Information.

Asser, M. (2007) "Obstacles to Peace: Water." *BBC News,* May 23. Available at <http://newsvote.bbc.co.uk>.

Associated Press (2005) "Israel Ends Demolition of Palestinian Homes." February 17.

—— (2007) "Hamas Forcibly Breaks up Rally in Gaza, Confiscates Cameras." August 13. Available at <http://www.haaretz.com/hasen/spages/892872.html>.

—— (2009) "Palestinians Believe Armed Struggle Led to Pullout." January 8.

Barak, E. (1999) "Inaugural Address to the Israeli Knesset." Available at <http://www.mfa.gov.il/mfa>.

—— (2002) "Interview: Camp David and after: An Exchange." *New York Review of Books,* June 13.

Bard, M. (1989) "Homeless in Gaza: Arab Mistreatment of Palestinian Refugees." *Policy Review* Winter: 36–42.

Bard, M. and Himelfarb, J. (1992) *Myths and Facts: A Concise Record of the Arab–Israeli Conflict.* Washington, D.C.: Near East Report.

Barghouthi, M. (1997) *"Al-Nedham Al-Ssiyasi Al-Felastini Wa Al-democratiyyah" Fi: Eshkaliyyat Ta'athour Al-Tahawwol Al-Democratey Fi Al-Watan Al-Arabi.* Ramallah: Muwatin.

Barnea, T. and Abdeen, Z. (2002) "The Function of Health Professionals in Advancing Israeli–Palestinian Co-existence." In T. Barnea and R. Husseini (eds.), *The Virus Does Not Stop at the Checkpoint.* Tel Aviv: Am Oved, pp. 355–372 (Hebrew).

Bar-Siman-Tov, Y. (ed.) (2004) *From Conflict Resolution to Reconciliation.* Oxford: Oxford University Press.

Bar-Tal, D. (1998) "Societal Beliefs in Times of Intractable Conflict: The Israeli Case." *The International Journal of Conflict Management* 9:22–50.

—— (2000a) *Shared Beliefs in a Society: Social Psychological Analysis.* Thousand Oaks, Calif.: Sage.

—— (2000b) "From Intractable Conflict through Conflict Resolution to Reconciliation: Psychological Analysis." *Political Psychology* 21:351–365.

—— (2001) "Why Does Fear Override Hope in Societies Engulfed by Intractable Conflict, as it Does in the Israeli Society?" *Political Psychology* 22:601–627.

—— (2002) "The Elusive Nature of Peace Education." In G. Salomon and B. Nevo (eds.), *Peace Education: The Concepts, Principles, and Practices around the World.* Mahwah, NJ: Erlbaum, pp. 27–36.

—— (2007a) "Sociopsychological Foundations of Intractable Conflicts." *American Behavioral Scientist* 50:1430–1453.

—— (2007b) *Living with the Conflict: Socio-psychological Analysis of the Israeli–Jewish Society.* Jerusalem: Carmel (Hebrew).

Bar-Tal, D. and Bennink, G. (2004) "The Nature of Reconciliation as an Outcome and as a Process." In Y. Bar-Siman-Tov (ed.), *From Conflict Resolution to Reconciliation.* Oxford: Oxford University Press, pp. 11–38.

Bar-Tal, D., and Sharvit, K. (2008) "The Influence of the Threatening Transitional Context on Israeli Jews' Reactions to Al Aqsa Intifada." In V.M. Esses and R.A. Vernon (eds.), *Explaining the Breakdown of Ethnic Relations: Why Neighbors Kill*. Oxford: Blackwell, pp. 147–170.

Bar-Tal, D. and Rosen, Y. (2009) "Conditions for the Development of Peace Education in Societies Involved in Intractable Conflict." In D. Berliner and H. Kupermintz (eds.), *Fostering Change in Institutions, Environments, and People*. Mahwah, NJ: Lawrence Erlbaum, pp. 231–249.

Bar-Tal, D., Halperin, E., and de Rivera, J. (2007) "Collective Emotions in Conflict Situations: Societal Implications." *Journal of Social Issues* 63:441–460.

Bar-Tal, D., Halperin, E., and Oren, N. (2009) "Socio-psychological Barriers to Peace Making: The Case of the Israeli Jewish Society." Manuscript submitted for publication.

Bar-Tal, D., Rosen, Y., and Nets, Z.R. (2009) "Peace Education in Societies Involved in Intractable Conflicts: Goals, Conditions, and Directions." In G. Salomon and E. Cairns, (eds.), *Handbook of Peace Education*. New York: Psychology Press, pp. 21–43.

Baskin, G., Dajani, M., Schwartz, R., and Perlman, L. (2002) *Yes, PM. Years of Experience in Strategies for Peace Making: Looking at Israeli–Palestinian People to People Activities, 1993–2000*. Jerusalem: Israel–Palestine Center for Research and Information.

BBC (2006) "Hamas Sweeps to Election Victory." January 26.

—— (2009) "Hamas Condemns Holocaust Lessons." August 31. Available at <http://www.news.bbc.co.uk/2/hi/middle_east/8230483.stm>.

BBC News International (2007) "Dozens Hurt in Mid-East Protest." November 28. Available at <http://news.bbc.co.uk/2/hi/middle_east/7117110.stm>.

Beilin, Y. (2004) *The Path to Geneva: The Quest for A Permanent Agreement, 1996–2004*. New York: RDV Books.

Bekerman, Z. and McGlynn, C. (eds.) (2007) *Addressing Conflict through Peace Education: International Perspective*. New York: Palgrave Macmillan.

Belenky, M., Clinchy, B., Goldberger, N., and Tarule, J. (1986) *Women's Way of Knowing*. New York: Basic Books.

Ben Ami, S. (2001) *A Front without a Rearguard*. Tel Aviv: Yediot Ahronot Books (Hebrew).

Ben-Porat, Y. and Marx, E. (1971) *Some Sociological and Economic Aspects of Refugee Camps on the West Bank*. Santa Monica, Calif.: Rand.

Benvenisti, E. (1994) "International Law and the Mountain Aquifer." In J. Isaac and H. Shuval (eds.), *Water and Peace in the Middle East*. Amsterdam: Elsevier Press, pp. 229–238.

—— (2002) "The Right of Return in International Law: An Israeli Perspective." Mimeo. Available at <http://www.arts.mcgill.ca/mepp/new_prrn/research/research_papers.htm>.

Benvenisti, M. (1995) *Intimate Enemies: Jews and Arabs in a Shared Land*. Berkeley: University of California Press.

—— (2000) *Sacred Landscape: The Buried History of the Holy Land since 1948*. Berkeley: University of California Press.

Berlowitz, M. (1994) "Urban Educational Reform: Focusing on Peace Education." *Education and Urban Society* 27 (1):82–85.

Bin Talal, H. (1981) *Palestinian Self-Determination: A Study of the West Bank and Gaza Strip*. London: Quartet Books.

Birzeit University Development Studies Center (2000) *Taqreer Al-Tanmeyah Al-Bashariyyah 1998–1999*. Ramallah: Birzeit University Development Studies Program with UNDP Program.

—— (2002) *Taqreer Al-Tanmeyah Al-Bashariyyah 2000–2001*. Ramallah: Birzeit University Development Studies Program with UNDP Program.

Bjerstedt, A. (ed.) (1993) *Peace Education: Global Perspective*. Malmo: Almqvist and Wiksell.

Blass, S. (1960) *Mai-Miriva v'Maas*. Tel Aviv: Massada (Hebrew).

Bowker, R. (2003) *Palestinian Refugees: Mythology, Identity, and the Search for Peace*. Boulder, Colo.: Lynne Rienner.

Bradley, K.R. (1978) "The Palestinian Refugees: The Right to Return in International Law." *American Journal of International Law* 72(3):586–614.

Bramwell, A.C. (ed.) (1988) *Refugees in the Age of Total War*. London: Unwin Hyman.

Braverman, A. (1994) *Israel Water Study for the World Bank*. Beersheba: Ben Gurion University of the Negev and Tahal Consulting Engineers.

Brawer, M. (1990) "The Green Line: Functions and Impacts of an Israeli–Arab Superimposed Boundary." In Carl Grundy-Warr (ed.), *International Boundaries and Boundary Conflict Resolution*. Durham: International Boundaries Research Unit, pp. 63–74.

—— (2002) "The Making of an Israeli–Palestinian Boundary." In Clive Schofield *et al.* (eds.), *The Razor's Edge: International Boundaries and Political Geography*. London: Kluwer Academic, pp. 473–492.

Brown, N. (2001) "Democracy, History, and the Contest over the Palestinian Curriculum." Paper prepared for the Adam Institute, November. Available at <http://www.geocites.com/nathanbrown1/Adam_Institute_Palestinians_textbooks.htm>.

—— (2003) *Palestinian Politics after the Oslo Accords: Resuming Arab Palestine*. Berkeley: University of California Press.

—— (2005) *Evaluating Palestinian Reform*. Washington, D.C.: Carnegie Endowment for International Peace.

Brynen, R. (2003) "The 'Geneva Accord' and the Palestinian Refugee Issue." Mimeo. Available at: http://www.arts.mcgill.ca/mepp/new_prrn/research/papers/geneva_refugees_2.pdf.

Budieri, M. (1995) "Al-Felastinniyyoun Bayn Al-Hawiyyah Al-Qawmiyyah wa hawiyyah Addinnyyah." *Majallat Addirast Al-Felastineyyah* 21:3–28.

Buehrig, E.H. (1971) *The UN and the Palestinian Refugees: A Study in Non Territorial Administration*. Bloomington: Indiana University Press.

Burghardt, A. (1973) "The Basis for Territorial Claims." *Geographical Review* 63 (2):225–245.

Bush, G.W. (2002) "President Bush Calls for New Palestinian Leadership." Press release, June. Available at <http://www.whitehouse.gov/news/releases/2002/06/print/200206 24-3.html>.

—— (2004) "Letter from US President George W. Bush to Prime Minister Ariel Sharon." April 14. Available at <http://www.mfa.gov.il/MFA/Peace+Process/Reference+Documents/Exchange+of+letters+Sharon-Bush+14-Apr-2004.htm>.

Cairns, E. and Roe, M.D. (eds.) (2003) *The Role of Memory in Ethnic Conflict*. New York: Palgrave Macmillan.

Callaway, R.L. and Matthews, E.G. (2008) *Strategic US Foreign Assistance: The Battle between Human Rights and National Security*. Aldershot, Hampshire: Ashgate Press.

Cambell, C. (1992) "Learning to Kill: Masculinity, the Family and Violence in the Natal." *Journal of Southern African Studies* 18 (3):614–628.

Cassese, A. (1993) "Some Legal Observations on the Palestinians' Right to Self-Determination." *Oxford International Review* 4 (1):10–13.

Castellino, J. and Allen, S. (2003) *Title to Territory in International Law*. Aldershot: Ashgate.

Cattan, H. (1982) *Solution of the Palestinian Refugee Problem*. Vienna: International Progress Organization.

CDM/Morgant (1997) *Study of the Sustainable Yield of the Eastern Aquifer*. Report for the Palestinian Water Authority.

CH2MHILL (2002) *Aquifer Modeling Groundwater Model for the Eastern Basin*. Report for the Palestinian Water Authority.

Chaklai, S. (2004) "Report on Water Use in 2004." *Agamit: Journal of the Israel Water Commission* 170:12–14 (Hebrew).

Cheal, B. (1988) "Refugees in the Gaza Strip, December 1948–May 1950." *Journal of Palestine Studies* 18/69 (1):138–156.

Childers, E. (1961) "The Other Exodus." *Spectator*, May 12.

Chodorow, N. (1978) *The Reproduction of Mothering: Psychoanalysis and the Sociology of Gender.* Berkeley: University of California Press.

Christison, K. (1999) *Perceptions of Palestine.* Berkeley: University of California Press.

Clarke-Habibi, S. (2005) "Transforming World Views: The Case of Education for Peace in Bosnia and Herzegovina." *Journal of Transformative Education* 3:33–56.

Clinton, W.J. (2000) "The Clinton Parameters – Clinton Proposal on Israeli–Palestinian Peace." December 23. Available at <http://www.peacelobby.org/clinton_parameters.htm>.

CNN (2008) "Abbas: Israel Settlements 'Greatest Obstacle' to Peace." November 6.

Coakley, J. (ed.) (1993) *The Territorial Management of Ethnic Conflict.* London: Frank Cass.

Cohen, A. (1985) *An Ugly Face in the Mirror: Reflection of the Jewish–Arab Conflict in Hebrew Children's Literature.* Tel Aviv: Reshafim (Hebrew).

Cohen, H. (1984) *Human Rights in Jewish Law.* New York: Ktav.

—— (1992) *Human Rights in the Talmud and the Mikrah.* Tel Aviv: Ministry of Defense (Hebrew).

Cohen, S.B. (1986) *The Geopolitics of Israel's Border Question.* Boulder Colo.: Westview Press.

Cohen, S.B. and Kliot, N. (1981) "Israel's Place Names as Reflection of Continuity and Change in Nation Building." *Names* 29:227–246.

—— (1992) "Place Names in Israel's Ideological Struggle over the Administered Territories." *Annals of the Association of American Geographers* 82:653–680.

Cole, C.F., Arafat, C., Tidhar, C., Zidan Tafesh, Z., Fox, N.A., Killen, M., Ardila-Rey, A., Leavitt, L.A., Lesser, G., Richman, B.A., and Yung, F. (2003) "The Educational Impact of *Rechov Sumsum/Shara'a Simsim*: A *Sesame Street* Television Series to Promote Respect and Understanding among Children Living in Israel, the West Bank and Gaza." *International Journal of Behavioral Development* 27:409–422.

Cole, E. (2007) "Attack on 80-Year-Old Christian Escalates Fears in Gaza." *Christian Post*, September 30. Available at <http://www.christianpost.com/article/20070930/29512_Attack_on_80-Year-Old_Christian_Escalates_Fears_in_Gaza.htm>.

Coleman, P.T. (2003) "Characteristics of Protracted, Intractable Conflict: Towards the Development of a Metaframework." *Peace and Conflict: Journal of Peace Psychology* 9 (1):1–37.

Council on Foreign Relations (2006) "Peace versus Democracy in Palestine: A Conversation with Jimmy Carter." March 2. Available at <http://www.cfr.org/publication/10024/peace_versus_democracy_in_palestine.html>.

CPAP (1994) *Palestinian Refugees: Their Problem and Future: A Special Report.* Washington, D.C.: CPAP.

Daibes-Murad, F. (2005) *A New Legal Framework for Managing the World's Shared Ground Waters: A Case-Study from the Middle East.* London and Seattle, Wash.: IWA.

Dajani Daoudi, Mohammed S. (2009) "The Arab Peace Initiative: Lost in the Translation." *CrossCurrents* 59 (4):532–539.

Diehl, P.F. (ed.) (1999) *A Road Map to War: Territorial Dimensions of International Conflict.* Nashville, Tenn.: Vanderbilt University Press.

Dodd, P. and Barakat, H. (1969) *River without Bridges: A Study of the Exodus of the 1967 Palestinian Arab Refugees.* Beirut: IPS.

Donnelly, J. (2002) *Universal Human Rights in Theory and Practice.* Ithaca, NY: Cornell University Press.

Doyle, M. (1986) "Liberalism and World Politics." *American Political Science Review* 80 (4):1151–1169.

Dreeben, R. (1968) *On What is Learned in School*. Reading, MA: Addison-Wesley.

Drucker, Yoav (2001) *Harakiri: Ehud Barak: The Failure*. Tel Aviv: Yediot Ahronot Books (Hebrew).

Dwyer, K. (1991) *Arab Voices: The Human Rights Debate in the Middle East*. Berkeley: University of California Press.

Elazar, D. (ed.) (1979) *Self Rule – Shared Rule: Federal Solutions to the Middle East Conflict*. Ramat Gan: Turtledove Press.

Eldar, A. (2002) "Moratinos Document – The Peace that Nearly Was at Taba." *Ha'aretz*, February 14.

Electronic Intifada (2006) "Palestinian Parliamentary Elections." Available at <http://electronic intifada.net/bytopic/416.shtml>.

El Haffar, F. (2007) "Future Generations Depend on Our Efforts." Report for UNRWA, March 9. Available at <http://electronicintifada.net/v2/article6648.shml>.

El-Hindi, J.L. (1990) "The West Bank Aquifer and Conventions Regarding Laws of Belligerent Occupation." *Michigan Journal of International Law* 11:1400–1423.

Enderlin, C. (2003) *The Shattered Dreams: The Failure of the Peace Process in the Middle East 1995–2002*. New York: Other Press.

Enloe, C. (1983) *Does Khaki Become You*. Boston: South End Press.

Falah, G. (1996) "The 1948 Israeli–Palestinian War and its Aftermath: The Transformation and Designification of Palestine's Cultural Landscape." *Annals of the Association of American Geographers* 86:256–285.

—— (1997) "Reenvisioning Current Discourse: Alternative Territorial Configurations of Palestinian Statehood." *Canadian Geographer* 41 (3):307–330.

Falah, G. and Newman, D. (1995) "Small State Behaviour: On the Formation of a Palestinian State in the West Bank and Gaza Strip." *Canadian Geographer* 39 (3):219–234.

Filastin al-'An (2009) "The Battle for Hearts and Minds in the Gaza Strip: Hamas Attacks UNRWA." August 30. Available at >http://www.terrorism-info.org.il/malam_multimedia/English/eng_n/>.

Finkelstein, N. (1991) "Myths, Old and New." *Journal of Palestine Studies* 21(1):66–89.

Firer, R. (1985) *The Agents of Zionist Education*. Tel Aviv: Hakibutz Hameuhad (Hebrew).

Firer, R. and Adwan, S. (2004). *The Israeli–Palestinian Conflict in History and Civics Textbooks of Both Nations*. Hanover: Verlag Hahnsche.

Fischbach, M. (2008) "Palestinian Refugee Compensation and Israeli Counterclaims for Jewish Property." *Journal of Palestine Studies* 38 (1):6–24.

Fischhendler, I. (2004) "Legal and Institutional Adaptation to Climate Uncertainty: A Study of International Rivers." *Water Policy* 6: 281–302.

Fisher, F. *et al*. (2005) *Liquid Assets: An Economic Approach for Water Management and Conflict Resolution the Middle East and beyond*. Washington, D.C.: Resources for the Future.

Flapan, S. (1987) *The Birth of Israel: Myths and Realities*. New York: Pantheon Books.

Gabbay, R.E. (1959) *A Political Study of the Arab–Jewish Conflict: The Arab Refugee Problem*. Geneva: Droz, Minard.

Gallagher, A.M. (1998) "Education Policy Approaches in Multiethnic Societies." Paper prepared for the UNICEF International Child Development Center, Italy.

Galnoor, I. (1991) "Territorial Partition of Palestine: The 1937 Decision." *Political Geography Quarterly* 10 (4):382–404.

Gazit, S. (1995) *The Palestinian Refugee Problem*. Tel Aviv: Jaffee Center for Strategic Studies.

Geertz, C. (1993) *The Interpretation of Cultures: Selected Essays*. London: Fontana Press.

Geneva Initiative (2003) *The Geneva Initiative: Yes to an Agreement*. Available at <http://www.geneva-accord.org/>.

Giacaman, G. (2005) *Mostaqbal Al-Nedham Al-Siyassi Al-Felasteni wa Afaquhu Assiyassiyyah Al-Mustaqbaliyyah" Fi: Mostaqbal Al-Nedham Alssiyasi Al-Felasteni Wa Afaquhu Al-Ssiyasiyyah Al-Momkennah*. Ramallah: Ibrahim Abu Lughod Center, Birzeit University, and Muwatin.

Gild, I. (2008) Interview with the author. Ramat Gan: Women's Counseling Center.

Gilligan, C. (1982) *In a Different Voice*. Cambridge, MA: Harvard University Press.

Gilmour, D. (1982) *Dispossessed: The Ordeal of the Palestinians*. London: Sphere Books.

Gleick, P.H. (ed.) (1993) *Water in a Crisis: A Guide to the World's Fresh Water Resources*. New York: Oxford University Press.

Goemans, H. (2006) "Territoriality, Territorial Attachment, and Conflict." In M. Kahler and B. Walter (eds.), *Globalization, Territoriality and Conflict*. Cambridge: Cambridge University Press, pp. 25–61.

Goertz, G. and Diehl, P.F. (1992) *Territorial Changes and International Conflict*. London: Routledge.

Golan, G. (1997) "Militarization and Gender: The Israeli Experience." *Women's Studies International Forum* 20 (5–6):581–586.

Goldberger, S. (1992) "The Potential of Natural Water Sources in Israel: Quantities, Quality and Reliability." In *Proceedings of the Continuing Workshop on Israel's Water Resources*. Rehovot: Center for Research in Agricultural Economics, pp. 4–7 (Hebrew).

Goldenberg, D. (1998) "The Influence of Democratic School on its Sudents' Knowledge and Attitudes." Master's thesis, Tel Aviv University.

Goodwin-Gill, G.S. (1996) *The Refugee in International Law*. Oxford: Clarendon Press.

Government of Israel (1996) "Guidelines." June. Available at <http://www.fmep.org/reports/archive/vol.-6/no.-4/guidelines-of-the-government-of-israel-june-1996>.

—— (2003) "Israel's Response to the Road Map." May 25. Available at <http://www.knesset.gov.il/process/docs/roadmap_response_eng.htm>.

Grahl-Madsen, A. (1972) *The Status of Refugees in International Law: Refugee Character*. Leyden: Sijhoff.

Grondahl, M. (2003) *In Hope and Despair: Life in the Palestinian Refugee Camps*. New York: American University in Cairo Press.

Gulf News (2007) "Hamas to Form Coast Guard Unit in Gaza." August 11. Available at <http://archive.gulfnews.com/indepth/palestiniancrisis/more_stories/10145873.html>.

Gurr, T.R. (1967) *Why Men Rebel*. Princeton, NJ: Princeton University Press.

Hadawi, S. (1988) *Palestinian Rights & Losses in 1948: A Comprehensive Study*. London: Saqi Books.

Haddad, M. (2007) "Politics and Water Management: A Palestinian Perspective." In H. Shuval and H. Dweik (eds.), *Water Resources in the Middle East: Israel–Palestinian Water Issues – from Conflict to Cooperation*. Hexagon Series on Human and Environmental Security and Peace. Berlin etc.: Springer-Verlag, vol. 2, pp. 41–52.

Haddad, S. (2003) *The Palestinian Impasse in Lebanon: The Politics of Refugee Integration*. Brighton: Sussex Academic Press.

Halbwachs, M. (1992) *On Collective Memory*. Chicago: University of Chicago Press.

Halperin, E. (2008) "Group-Based Hatred in Intractable Conflict in Israel." *Journal of Conflict Resolution* 52:713–736.

Halperin, E., Sharvit, K., and Gross, J.J. (2010) "Emotions and Emotion Regulation in Conflicts." In D. Bar-Tal (ed.), *Intergroup Conflicts and Their Resolution: Social Psychological Perspective*. New York: Psychology Press.

Harstock, N. (1983) *Money, Sex and Power*. London: Longman.

Herzog Hospital (2001) "Trauma Center Survey Reveals 70% of Israeli Children Impacted by Intifada." Available at <http://www.herzoghospital.org/index.asp?id=134&newsid=73>.

Hilal, J. (1995) *"Modakhaluh Hawl Eshkaliyyat Ma'assasat Al-Democratiyyah Fi Al-Hiyaat Al-Felasteniyyah" Fi: Al-democrateyyah Al-Felastiniyyah'*. Ramallah: Muwatin.

—— (2006) *Al-Tandhimat wa- Al-Ahzab Assiyasiyyah Al-Felastiniyyah Bayn Mahham Al-Democratiyyeh Al-Dakheliyyah, Wa Al-Democratiyyah Assiyasiyyah Wa-Al-Taharor Al-Watani*. Ramallah: Muwatin.

Horowitz, D. (1975) *Israel's Concept of Defensible Borders*. Jerusalem Papers on Peace Problems, No. 16. Jerusalem: Leonard Davis Institute for International Relations, Hebrew University.

Hourani, F. (1980) *Al-Fikr Assiyasi Al-Felastini 1964–1974*. Jerusalem: Abu-Arafeh Agency for Press.

Human Rights Watch (2004) "Israel: West Bank Barrier Violates Human Rights." February 22. Available at <http://www.hrw.org>.

—— (2007) "Gaza: Armed Palestinian Groups Commit Grave Crimes." June 13. Available at <http://hrw.org/english/docs/2007/06/13/isrlpa16156.htm>.

International Crisis Group (2002) "The Clinton Parameters in Endgame II: How a Comprehensive Israeli–Palestinian Peace Settlement Would Look." Report.

—— (2004) "Palestinian Refugees and the Politics of Peacemaking." Report.

International Law Association (2004) "Report of the Seventy-First Conference of the International Law Association: Water Resources Law, 'The Berlin Rules' (Berlin 2004)." London: International Law Association.

Iram, Y. (ed.) (2006) *Educating towards a Culture of Peace*. Greenwich, CT: Information Age Publishing.

IPCRI (Israel/Palestine Center for Research and Information) (2003) *Analysis and Evaluation of the New Palestinian Curriculum: Reviewing Palestinian Textbooks and Tolerance Education Program*. Report.

—— (2004) *Analysis and Evaluation of the New Palestinian Curriculum*. Report.

—— (2006) *Analysis and Evaluation of the New Palestinian Curriculum: Reviewing Palestinian Textbooks and Tolerance Education Program Grades 5 & 10*. Report.

Isaac, J. (2003) "Towards a Sustainable Peace between Israelis and Palestinians." In Majid Al-Haj and Uri Ben–Eliezer (eds.), *In the Name of Security: Sociology of Peace and War in Israel in A Changing Era*. Haifa: Haifa University Press, pp. 575–595.

Isaac, J. and Saad, S. (2004) *A Geopolitical Atlas of Palestine: the West Bank and Gaza*. Bethlehem: Applied Research Institute-Jerusalem.

Isaac, J. and Salman, N. (2003) *Undermining Peace: Israel's Unilateral Segregation Plans in the Palestinian Territories*. Available at <http://www.arij.org/paleye/Segregation-Wall/index.htm>.

Isaac, J. et al. (2000) *An Atlas of Palestine: The West Bank and Gaza*. Bethlehem: Applied Research Institute-Jerusalem.

Isacoff, J. (2006) *Writing the Arab–Israeli Conflict: Pragmatism and Historical Inquiry*. Oxford: Lexington Books.

Isha l'Isha (2005) "On Violence: Women in the Israeli–Palestinian Conflict." Report. Haifa: Isha l'Isha (Hebrew).

—— (2007) "Women in the Economy of the War: Personal Witnesses." Report. Haifa: Isha l'Isha (Hebrew).

Israeli Ministry of Foreign Affairs (1993) "Declaration of Principles on Interim Self-Government Arrangements." September 13. Available at <http://www.mfa.gov.il/MFA/Peace%20Process/Guide%20to%20the%20Peace%20Process/Declaration%20of%20Principles>.

—— (2005) "Israel's Disengagement Plan: Renewing the Peace Process." April. Available at <http://www.mfa.gov.il>.

Israel Women's Network (2007) *Women in Israel 2006: Between Theory and Reality.* Ramat Gan: Israel Women's Network.

Issacharoff, A. (2006) "Textbook Controversy in Gaza." *Ha'aretz*, September 9.

—— (2007) "At Least 10 Killed as Hamas Forces Seize Fatah HQ in Northern Gaza Strip." *Ha'aretz*, June 13. Available at <http://www.haaretz.com/hasen/spages/870095.html>.

Jacobs S., Jacobson, R., and Marchbank, J. (eds.) (2000) *States of Conflict: Gender, Violence and Resistance.* London: Zed Books.

Jarymowicz, M. and Bar-Tal, D. (2006) "The Dominance of Fear over Hope in the Life of Individuals and Collectives." *European Journal of Social Psychology* 36:367–392.

Jerusalem Post (2007) "Interview with Ehud Olmert." March 29.

Jihad Harb (2004) "Al-Eslah Al-Mali Fi Al-Sultah Al-Wataniyyah Al-Felasteniyyah." July.

Ju'beh, N. (2002) "The Palestinian Refugee Problem and the Final Status Negotiations." *Palestine–Israel Journal* 9 (2):5–11.

Kahler, M. and Walter, B. (eds.) (2006) *Globalization, Territoriality and Conflict.* Cambridge: Cambridge University Press.

Kally, E. (1990) *Water in Peace.* Tel Aviv: Sifriat Poalim Publishing House and Tel Aviv University (Hebrew).

Kam, E. (2003) "Conceptualising Security in Israel." In H. Brauch, P. Liotta, A. Marquina, P. Rogers, and M. Selim (eds.), *Security and Environment in the Mediterranean: Conceptualising Security and Environmental Conflicts.* Berlin: Springer, pp. 357–366.

Kansteiner, W. (2002) "Finding Meaning in Memory: Methodological Critique of Collective Memory Studies." *History and Theory* 41:179-197.

Kaplan, D. (1959) *The Arab Refugees, an Abnormal Problem.* Jerusalem: R. Mass.

Karmi, G. and Cotran, E. (eds.) (1999) *The Palestinian Exodus, 1948–1998.* Reading: Ithaca Press.

Kaufman, E. (1999) *Human Rights in World Politics.* Tel Aviv: Ministry of Defense Publishing House (Hebrew).

Kaufman, E. and Abu-Nimer, M. (2007) "Bridging Conflict Resolution and Human Rights: Lessons from the Israeli/Palestinian Peace Process." In J. Helsing and J. Mattus (eds.), *Human Rights and Conflict.* Washington, D.C.: United States Institute of Peace Press.

Kaufman, E. and Bisharat, I. (1998) "Human Rights and Conflict Resolution: Searching for Common Ground between Justice and Peace in the Israeli/Palestinian Conflict." *NIDR Forum* December: 16–22.

—— (1999) "Humanizing the Israeli/Palestinian Peace Process." *Israel–Palestine Journal* 6 (1):8–13.

—— (2002) "Introducing Human Rights into Conflict Resolution: The Relevance for the Israeli–Palestinian Peace Process." *Journal of Human Rights* 1 (1):71–92.

—— (2003) "Are Human Rights Good for the Top Dog as Well?" *Palestine–Israel Journal* 10 (3):89–95.

Kaufman, E. and Hassassian, M. (2006) "A Way out for Prisoners? New Parole System Could End One Part of Mideast Deadlock." *Baltimore Sun*, August 27.

Kellerman, A. (1993) *Society and Settlement: Jewish Land of Israel in the Twentieth Century.* Albany: SUNY Press.

Kelman, H.C. (1999) "Transforming the Relationship between Former Enemies: A Social-psychological Analysis." In R.L. Rothstein (ed.), *After the Peace: Resistance and Reconciliation.* Boulder, Colo.: Lynne Rienner, pp. 193–205.

Kerr, M. (1980) *America's Middle East Policy: Kissinger, Carter and the Future*. Washington, D.C.: The Institute for Palestine Studies.

Khalidi, R. and Cotran, E. (eds.) (1999) *The Palestinian Exodus, 1948–1998*. Reading: Ithaca Press.

Khalidi, R. and Rabinovich, I. (1990) *The Palestinian Right of Return: Two Views*. Cambridge, MA: American Academy of Arts and Science.

Khalidi, W. (1987) *From Haven to Conquest: Readings in Zionism and the Palestine Problem until 1948*. Washington, D.C.: The Institute for Palestine Studies.

—— (1991) *Before Their Diaspora: A Photographic History of the Palestinians, 1876–1948*. Washington, D.C.: The Institute for Palestine Studies.

Khan, M. and Giacaman, G. (2004) *State Formation in Palestine, Viability and Governance during a Social Transformation*. London: Routledge.

Kimmerling, B. (1983) *Zionism and Territory: The Socio-Territorial Dimension of Zionist Politics*. Berkeley: University of California Press.

Klaus, D. (2003) *Palestinian Refugees in Lebanon: Where to Belong?* Berlin: Klaus Schwarz Verlag.

Klein, A. (2007) "Hamas Accused of Intimidating Christians." *World Net Daily*, November 6. Available at <http://www.wnd.com/news/article.asp?ARTICLE_ID=58531>.

Klieman, A. (1980) "The Resolution of Conflicts through Territorial Partition: The Palestine Experience." *Comparative Studies in Society and History* 42:281–300.

Klinov, R. (2002) "Reparations and Rehabilitations of Palestinian Refugees." *Palestine–Israel Journal* 9 (2):102–110.

Kriegel, D. and Waintrater, R. (1986) *Cette nuit Golda ne dormira pas: Les femmes et la guerre en Israel*. Paris: J.C. Attes.

Kriesberg, L. (1998a) "Intractable Conflicts." In E. Weiner (ed.), *The Handbook of Interethnic Coexistence*. New York: Continuum, pp. 332–342.

—— (1998b) "Coexistence and the Reconciliation of Communal Conflicts." In E. Weiner (ed.), *The Handbook of Interethnic Coexistence*. New York: Continuum, pp. 182–198.

Kurzman, D. (1970) *Genesis 1948: The First Arab–Israeli War*. New York: New American Library.

Lapidoth, Ruth (2002) "Do Palestinian Refugees Have a Right to Return to Israel?" Report, September 1. Jerusalem Center for Public Affairs.

Lavie, E. (2003) "The Road Map: Political Resolution Instead of National Narrative Confrontation." *Palestine–Israel Journal* 10 (4):83–91.

Lederach, J.P. (1997) *Building Peace: Sustainable Reconciliation in Divided Societies*. Washington, D.C.: United States Institute of Peace Press.

Lesch, A.M. (1988) "Review: *Creating Facts: Israel, Palestinians and the West Bank*, by Geoffrey Aronson." *Journal of Palestine Studies* 18 (1):214–216.

Lustick, I. (1993) *Unsettled States – Disputed Lands*. Ithaca, NY: Cornell University Press.

Ma'an News Agency (2007) "Huge Palestinian Demonstrations against Fake Annapolis Peace Conference Suppressed by Palestinian Authority Police, Journalists Covering Protests Also Attacked." November 27.

McGowan, D. and Ellis, M. (1986) "The Causes and Character of the Arab Exodus from Palestine." *Middle Eastern Studies* 22 (1):5–19.

—— (eds.) (1998) *Remembering Deir Yassin: The Future of Israel and Palestine*. New York: Olive Branch Press.

Majdalani, Ahmad (2002) *Al-Majless Al-Tashre'ei Al-Felastini: Al-Waqe'a Wa Al-Tomoh*. Ramallah: MAS.

Makovsky, D. (2004) *A Defensible Fence: Fighting Terror and Enabling a Two State Solution*. Washington, D.C.: Washington Institute for Near East Policy.

Mansour, Jamal (1999) *Al-Democratiyah Wal Islam*. Nablus: Palestinian Research and Studies Center.

Maoh, Hanna and Isaac, Jad (2003) "The Status of Transportation in the West Bank." In John Whitelegg and Gary Haq (eds.), *World Transport Policy and Practice*. London: Earthscan, pp. 259–274.

Maoz, I. (2000) "An Experiment in Peace: Reconciliation-Aimed Workshops of Jewish-Israeli and Palestinian Youth." *Journal of Peace Research* 37:721–736.

—— (2004) "Peace Building in Violent Conflict: Israeli–Palestinian Post Oslo People-to-People Activities." *International Journal of Politics, Culture and Society* 17 (3):563–574.

Maoz, M. (1999) "The Oslo Agreements: Towards Arab–Jewish Reconciliation." In R. Rothstein (ed.), *After the Peace: Resistance and Reconciliation*. London: Lynne Rienner, pp. 67–83.

Martine, A. (2007) "Prominent Palestinian Christian Kidnapped, Murdered." *One News Now*, October 10. Available at <http://www.onenewsnow.com/2007/10/prominent_palestinian_christia.php>.

Masalha, N. (1988) "On Recent Hebrew and Israeli Sources for the Palestinian Exodus, 1947–1949." *Journal of Palestine Studies* Autumn: 121–137.

—— (1990) "Israeli Revisionist Historiography of the Birth of Israel and its Palestinian Exodus." *Scandinavian Journal of Development Alternatives* March: 71–97.

—— (1991) "Debate on the 1948 Exodus: A Critique of Benny Morris." *Journal of Palestine Studies* 21 (1):90–97.

—— (1992) *Expulsion of the Palestinians: The Concept of "Transfer" in Zionist Political Thought, 1882–1984*. Washington, D.C.: Institute for Palestine Studies.

—— (1997) *A Land without a People: Israel, Transfer, and the Palestinians*. London: Faber and Faber.

—— (1999) "The 1967 Palestinian Exodus." In Ghada Karmi and Eugene Cotran (eds.), *The Palestinian Exodus, 1948–1998*. Reading: Ithaca Press, pp. 63–109.

—— (2000) *Imperial Israel and the Palestinians: The Politics of Expansion*. London: Pluto Press.

—— (2001) "The Historical Roots of the Palestinian Refugee Question." In Naseer Aruri (ed.), *The Palestinian Refugees: The Right of Return*. London: Pluto Press, pp. 36–67.

—— (2003) *The Politics of Denial: Israel and the Palestinian Refugee Problem*. London: Pluto Press.

Massad, J. (1999) "Return or Permanent Exile? Palestinian Refugees and the End of Oslo." *Critique* Spring: 5–23.

Matz, D. (2003) "Why Did Taba End?" *Palestine–Israel Journal* 10 (3):96–105 and (4):92–104.

Maxwell, B. (1999) "Israel's Schools Mirror a Culture of Violence." *St. Petersburg Times*, June 6. Available at <http://www.sptimes.com/News/60699/Perspective/Israel_s_schools_mirr.shtml>.

Mazawi, M. (1968) *The Arab Refugees: A Tragic Human and Political Problem*. London: Council for the Advancement of Arab British Understanding.

Mezerik, A.G. (ed.) (1980) *Arab Refugees in the Middle East*. New York: International Review Service.

Michael, K. and Ramon, A. (2004) *The Wall Surrounding Jerusalem*. Jerusalem: Jerusalem Institute for Israel Studies (Hebrew).

Ministry of Foreign Affairs (1995) *Israeli–Palestinian Interim Agreement on the West Bank and Gaza Strip*. Jerusalem: State of Israel.

Moratinos, M. (2001) *Taba Negotiations: The Moratinos Non-Paper*. Available at <http://www.mideastweb.org/moratinos.htm>.

Morris, Benny (1987) *The Birth of the Palestinian Refugee Problem, 1947–1949*. Cambridge: Cambridge University Press.

—— (1990) *1948 and after*. New York: Oxford University Press.

—— (1991) "Response to Finkelstein and Masalha." *Journal of Palestine Studies* 21 (1):98–114.

Murphy, A.B. (1990) "Historical Justifications for Territorial Claims." *Annals of the Association of American Geographers* 80:531–548.

—— (2002) "National Claims to Territory in the Modern State System: Geographical Considerations." *Geopolitics* 7 (2):193–214.

Muslih, M. (1993) "Palestinian Civil Society." *Middle East Journal* 77:258–274.

Nabulsi, Karma (2003) "The State Building Project: What Went Wrong?" In Michael Keating *et al.* (eds.), *Aid, Diplomacy and Facts on the Ground: The Case of Palestine*. Bristol: Chatham House, pp. 117–128.

Nashif, Y. (1990) "The Return of Palestinian Refugees." *New Outlook* 33 (4):38–39.

Nazzal, N. (1978) *The Palestinian Exodus from Galilee, 1948*. Beirut: The Institute for Palestine Studies.

Neff, D. (1988) "US Policy and the Palestinian Refugees." *Journal of Palestine Studies* 18/69 (1):96–111.

Negotiations Affairs Department–PLO (2001) "The Clinton Parameters." Available at <http://www.nad-plo.org/listing.php?view=nego_nego_clinton>.

Newman, D. (1989) "The Role of Civilian and Military Presence as Strategies of Territorial Control: The Arab–Israel Conflict." *Political Geography Quarterly* 8 (3):215–227.

—— (1993) "The Functional Presence of an 'Erased' Boundary: The Re-emergence of the 'Green Line.'" In C.H. Schofield and R.N. Schofield (eds.), *World Boundaries: The Middle East and North Africa*. London: Routledge, pp. 71–98.

—— (1995) *Boundaries in Flux: The Green Line Boundary between Israel and the West Bank – Past, Present and Future*. Monograph Series, Boundary and Territory Briefings No. 7. Durham: International Boundaries Research Unit, University of Durham.

—— (1998a) "Metaphysical and Concrete Landscapes: The Geopiety of Homeland Socialisation in the 'Land of Israel.'" In H. Brodsky (ed.), *Land and Community: Geography in Jewish Studies*. College Park: University Press of Maryland, pp. 153–184.

—— (1998b) "Creating the Fences of Territorial Separation: The Discourse of Israeli–Palestinian Conflict Resolution." *Geopolitics and International Boundaries* 2 (2):1–35.

—— (1999a) "Territorial and Geographical Dimensions of the Security Discourse." In D. Bar-Tal, D. Jacobson, and A. Klieman (eds.), *Concerned with Security: Learning from the Experience of Israeli Society*. Stamford, Conn.: JAI Press, pp. 73–94.

—— (1999b) "Real Spaces – Symbolic Spaces: Interrelated Notions of Territory in the Arab–Israel Conflict." In P. Diehl (ed.), *A Road Map to War: Territorial Dimensions of International Conflict*. Nashville, Tenn.: Vanderbilt University Press, pp. 3–34.

—— (2002a) "Territorial Identities in a Deterritorialized World: From National to Post-national Territorial Identities in Israel/Palestine." *Geojournal* 53 (235–246):1–12.

—— (2002b) "The Geopolitics of Peacemaking in Israel–Palestine." *Political Geography* 21 (5):629–646.

Newman, D. and Falah, G. (1995) "The Spatial Manifestation of Threat: Israelis and Palestinians Seek a 'Good' Border." *Political Geography* 14 (8):689–706.

—— (1997) "Bridging the Gap: Palestinian and Israeli Discourse on Autonomy and Statehood." *Transactions of the Institute of British Geographers* 22 (1):111–129.

Newman, D. *et al.* (2006) "A Framework for Demarcating a Border between Israel and a Palestinian State: Parameters and Principles." Working paper, Herzliya Conference, United States Institute for Peace Research Project on Borders as Bridges or Barriers.

Newsweek (2009) "Interview with Ehud Olmert." June 13.

Norval, A.J. (1998) "Memory, Identity and the (Im)possibility of Reconciliation: The Work of the Truth and Reconciliation Commission in South Africa." *Constellations* 5:250–265.

Nussiebeh, S. (1993) *"Al-Mustaqbal Al-Siyyasi Al-Felastini wa Al-democratiyyah" Fi: Al-Mou'tamar Al-Felasteni Al-Awal Hawl Al-Democrateyyah*. Jerusalem: Panorama Center.

Olmert, E. (2007) "Annapolis Speech." November. Available at <http://www.haaretz.com/hasen/spages/928669.html>.

Oren, N. (2005) "The Impact of Major Events in the Arab–Israel Conflict on the Ethos of Conflict of the Israeli Jewish Society (1967–2000)." Dissertation, Tel Aviv University.

Oren, N., Bar-Tal, D, and David, O. (2004) "Conflict, Identity and Ethos: The Israeli–Palestinian Case." In Y.-T. Lee, C.R. McCauley, F.M. Moghaddam, and S. Worchel (eds.), *Psychology of Ethnic and Cultural Conflict*. Westport: Praeger, pp. 133–154.

Oz, A. (2002) "Doves Should Re-examine their Perch." *Guardian*, January 5.

Paasi, A. (1996) *Territories, Boundaries and Consciousness*. New York: John Wiley.

—— (2002) "Territory." In John Agnew, Katharyne Mitchell, and Gerard Toal (eds.), *A Companion to Political Geography*. Oxford: Blackwell, pp. 109–122.

Palestinian Center for Human Rights (1998) *Al-Majless Al-Tashre'ei Al-Felastini, Taqieem Al-Ada'a Khelal Al-Dowrateen Al-Ola wa Al-Thaneyah (1996–1998)*. Gaza: Palestinian Center for Human Rights.

—— (1999) *Al-Majless Al-Tashre'ei Al-Felastinie, Taqieem Al-Ada'a Khelal Al-Dowrateen Al-Ola wa Al-Thaneyah (1998–1999)*. Gaza: Palestinian Center for Human Rights.

—— (2000) *Al-Majless Al-Tashre'ei Al-Felastinie, Taqieem Al-Ada'a Khelal Al-Dowrateen Al- wa Al-Thaneyah (1999–2000)*. Gaza: Palestinian Center for Human Rights.

—— (2001) *Al-Majless Al-Tashre'ei Al-Felastinie, Taqieem Al-Ada'a Khelal Al-Dowrateen Al- wa Al-Thaneyah (2000–2001)*. Gaza: Palestinian Center for Human Rights.

—— (2001–2002) *Al-Majless Al-Tashre'ei Al-Felastini: Taqieem Al-Ada'a Khelal Dawrat Al- Al-Sadesah*. Gaza: Palestinian Center for Human Rights.

—— (2007a) "Black Pages in the Absence of Justice: Report on Bloody Fighting in the Gaza Strip from 7 to 14 June 2007." Press release, October 9.

—— (2007b) "PCHR Condemns Excessive and Lethal Use of Force against Civilians in Gaza." Press release, November 13. Available at <http://www.pchrgaza.org/files/PressR/English/2007/160-2007.html>.

—— (2007c) "PCHR Calls for an Immediate End to Attacks against Offices of Fatah Movement and Affiliated Institutions in Gaza." Press release, December 30. Available at <http://www.pchrgaza.org/files/PressR/English/2007/178-2007.html>.

—— (2007d) "CHR Calls for Investigation into the Use of Force against a Peaceful Demonstration and the Detention of a Number of Demonstrators in al-Shati Refugee Camp." Press release, November 26. Available at <http://www.pchrgaza.org/files/PressR/English/2007/168-2007.html>.

—— (2007e) "PCHR Condemns Continued Torture by Security Forces in the West Bank." Press release, October 1. Available at <http://www.pchrgaza.org/files/PressR/English/2007/130-2007.html>.

—— (2007f). "PCHR Calls for Investigating Torture and Abuse by Palestinian Security Forces in the West Bank." Press release, September 19. Available at <http://www.pchrgaza.org/files/PressR/English/2007/122-2007.html>.

—— (2007g) "PCHR Condemns Torture Practiced by Security Services in the West Bank and Calls for Investigation." Press release, October 23. Available at <http://www.pchrgaza.org/files/PressR/English/2007/145-2007.html>.

—— (2007h) "Families of Detainees Assaulted and Detainees Tortured and Mistreated." Press release, September 3. Available at <http://www.pchrgaza.org/files/PressR/English/2007/113-2007.html>.

—— (2007i) "PCHR Condemns Arresting and Torturing Iqra TV Media Crew in Ramallah by the Preventive Security." Press release, October 8. Available at <http://www.pchrgaza.org/files/PressR/English/2007/135-2007.html>.

—— (2007j) "PCHR Condemns the Detention of 2 Journalists by Preventive Security Service in Hebron." Press release, November 8. Available at <http://www.pchrgaza. org/files/PressR/English/2007/157-2007.html>.

—— (2007k) "PCHR Calls for Rescinding the Decision of the Nablus Police Chief for Licensing Peaceful Demonstrations." Press release, August 26. Available at <http:// www.pchrgaza.org/files/PressR/English/2007/108-2007.html>.

—— (2007l) "PCHR Condemns Use of Force to Disperse Student Conference and Attacks on Journalists in Hebron." Press release, September 10. Available at <http://www. pchrgaza.org/files/PressR/English/2007/119-2007.html>.

—— (2007m) "Palestinian Security Uses Force to Disperse Peaceful Women's Rally." Press release, September 23. Available at <http://www.pchrgaza.org/files/PressR/English/ 2007/125-2007.html>.

—— (2007n) "PCHR Condemns Excessive Use of Force to Disperse Peaceful Demonstrations in the West Bank." Press release, November 28. Available at <http:// www.pchrgaza.org/files/PressR/English/2007/170-2007.html>.

Palestinian Independent Commission for Citizens' Rights (2007) "Arrests in the West Bank Following the Declaration of the State of Emergency of June 14, 2007." Report.

Palestinian National Authority (2002) "100 Days Plan of the Palestinian Government, with Reference to the Presidential Decree of 12 June 2002." June 23. Available at <http:// www.pna.gov.ps>.

Palumbo, M. (1987) *The Palestinian Catastrophe: The 1948 Expulsion of a People from Their Homeland.* London: Faber and Faber.

Panorama Center (1994) *Men Al-Hokm Al-Thaty Ela Al-Hokomah Al-Thateyah.* Jerusalem: Panorama Center.

Pappe, I. (1994) *The Making of the Arab–Israeli Conflict, 1947–1951.* London: I.B. Tauris.

PASSIA (2004) *Palestinian Refugees.* Jersusalem: PASSIA.

Peretz, D. (1954) "The Arab Refugee Dilemma." *Foreign Affairs* 33 (1):134–148.

—— (1969) *The Palestine Arab Refugee Problem.* Santa Monica, Calif.: Rand Corporation.

—— (1993) *Palestinian Refugees and the Middle East Peace Process.* Washington, D.C.: US Institute of Peace.

Perry, G.E. (ed.) (1986) *Palestinians: Continuing Dispossession.* Belmont: AAUG.

Peters, J. (1996) *Pathways to Peace: The Multilateral Arab–Israeli Talks.* London: Royal Institute of International Affairs.

—— (1997) "The Multilateral Arab–Israel Peace Talks and the Refugee Working Group." *Journal of Refugee Studies* 10 (3):320–334.

—— (1998) "The Arab–Israeli Multilateral Talks and the Barcelona Process: Competition or Convergence?' *International Spectator* 33 (4):63–76.

Pettigrew, T. (1998) "Intergroup Contact Effects on Prejudice." *Personality and Social Psychology Bulletin* 23:173–185.

Pinner, W. (1959) *How Many Arab Refugees?: A Critical Study of UNRWA's Statistics and Reports.* London: McGibbon and Key.

—— (1967) *The Legend of the Arab Refugees: A Critical Study of UNRWA's Reports and Statistics.* Tel Aviv: Economic and Social Research Institute.

Plascov, A. (1981) *The Palestinian Refugees in Jordan, 1948–1957.* London: Frank Cass.

Podeh, E. (2001) *From Fahd to Abdallah: The Origins of the Saudi Peace Initiative.* Gitelson Peace Papers. Jerusalem: The Harry S Truman Research Institute Advancement of Peace, Hebrew University.

—— (2002) *The Arab–Israeli Conflict in Israeli History Textbooks, 1948–2000.* Westport, Conn.: Bergin and Garvey.

Pressman, J. (2003) "Visions in Collision: What Happened at Camp David and Taba?" *International Security* 28:5–43.

PRIME (2003) *To Teach the Historical Narrative of the Other.* Beit Jallah: Peace Research Institute in the Middle East.

Pryce-Jones, D. (1979) *The Face of Defeat: Palestinian Refugees and Guerillas.* New York: Holt, Rinehart and Winston.

Pulfer, G. and Al-Mashni, A. (1999) *West Bank and Gaza Strip: Palestinian Refugees Five Years after Oslo.* Bethlehem: Badil.

Qasis, M. *et al.* (1999) *Al-Mouasher Al-Democratey Al-Felastinie (1996–1997).* Nablus: Center for Palestinian Research and Studies.

Quandt, W.Q. (2001) *Peace Process: American Diplomacy and the Arab–Israeli Conflict since 1967.* Berkeley: University of California Press.

Quigley, J. (1992) "Family Reunion and the Right of Return to Occupied Territory." *Georgetown Immigration Law Journal* 6 (2):223–251.

—— (1998) "Displaced Palestinians and a Right to Return." *Harvard International Law Journal* 39 (1):171–229.

Rabah, R. (1996) *Palestinian Refugees, Displacement and Final Status Negotiations.* Beirut: Arab Press House.

Ram, U. (2004) "The State of the Nation: Contemporary Challenges to Zionism in Israel." In A. Kemp *et al.* (eds.), *Israelis in Conflict: Hegemonies, Identities and Challenges.* Brighton: Sussex Academic Press, pp. 305–320.

Ramras-Rauch, G. (1989) *The Arab in Israeli Literature.* Bloomington: Indiana University Press.

Regular, A. (2006) "Hamas' Platform Pushes for Armed Fight." *Ha'aretz*, January 11.

Reich, B. (ed.) (1996) *An Historical Encyclopedia of the Arab Israeli Conflict.* Westport, Conn.: Greenwood Press.

Reiss, W. (2004) "Evaluation of Palestinian Civic Education." Paper presented to the Teaching for Tolerance, Respect and Recognition Conference, Oslo, September.

Reuters (2007) "Fatah Men Rally for Gaza Prayers, Defying Hamas." *Alert News*, August 31. Available at <http://www.alertnet.org/thenews/newsdesk/L31919714.htm>.

—— (2009) "Hamas Slams UN over Holocaust Classes in Gaza." August 30. Available at <http://www.reuters.com/article/idUSTRE57T1JW20090830>.

Richburg, K.B. (2004) "US Court Rejects West Bank Barrier." *Washington Post*, July 10. Available at <http://www.washingtonpost.com/wp-dny/articles/A38285-2004Jul9.html>.

Rokard, M. *et al.* (n.d.) *Taqweyat Moassassat Al-Sulta Al-Wataniyyah Al-Felastiniyyah, Taqreer Fareeq Al-Mall.* n.p.

Ross, Dennis (2004) *The Missing Peace.* New York: Farrar, Straus and Giroux.

Ross, M.H. (1998) "The Cultural Dynamics of Ethnic Conflict." In D. Jacquin, A. Oros, and M. Verweij (eds.), *Culture in World Politics.* Houndmills: Macmillan, pp. 156–186.

Rouhana, N. and Bar-Tal, D. (1998) "Psychological Dynamics of Intractable Conflicts: The Israeli–Palestinian Case." *American Psychologist* 53:761–770.

Sack, R. (1986) *Human Territoriality: Its Theory and History.* Cambridge: Cambridge University Press.

Safran, Nadav (1969) *From War to War: The Arab–Israeli Confrontation, 1948–1967.* New York: Pegasus.

Said, E. (1978) *Orientalism.* London: Penguin Books.

—— (1979) *Orientalism.* New York: Vintage Books.

—— (1994) *The Politics of Dispossession.* London: Chatto and Windus.

Sakhnini, Issam (1986) *Felastine Addawlah.* Acre: Al-Aswar.

Salam, N. (1994) "Between Repatriation and Resettlement: Palestinian Refugees in Lebanon." *Journal of Palestine Studies* 24/93 (1):18–27.

Salem, W. (1999) *Al-Moundhamat Al-Mogtamaeyyah Wa Al-Sulta Al-Wataniyyah Al-Felastiniyyah*. Ramallah: MAS.

—— (2000) *Al-Masalah Al-Wataniyyah Al-Democratiyyah Fi- Felastine*. Ramallah: Muwatin.

Salomon, G. (2002) "The Nature of Peace Education: Not All Programs Are Created Equal." In G. Salomon and B. Nevo (eds.), *Peace Education: The Concept, Principles, and Practices around the World*. Mahwah, NJ: Lawrence Erlbaum Associates, pp. 2–14.

Salomon, G. and Nevo, B. (eds.) (2002) *Peace Education: The Concept, Principles, and Practices around the World*. Mahwah, NJ: Lawrence Erlbaum Associates.

Sanbar, E. (1984) *Palestine 1948: The Expulsion*. Paris: Institute for Palestine Studies.

Sandler, N. (2007) "Women Fight for Equality in Israel." *Business Week*, April 30. Available at <http://www.businessweek.com/print/globalbiz/content/apr2007/gb20070430_20 4117.htm>.

Sasson-Levy, O. (2003) "Feminism and Military Gender Practices: Israeli Women Soldiers in 'Masculine' Roles." *Sociological Inquiry* 73 (3):440–465.

Sayigh, F. (1952) *The Palestine Refugees*. Washington, D.C.: Amara Press.

Sayigh, R. (2001) "Palestinian Refugees in Lebanon: Implementation, Transfer or Return?" *Middle East Policy* 8 (1):94–105.

Schechtman, J.B. (1952) *The Arab Refugee Problem*. New York: Philosophical Library.

Schiff, Ze'ev (2000) [No title.] *Ha'aretz*. October 10.

Segev, T. (1986) *1949: The First Israelis*. New York: The Free Press.

—— (2000) *One Palestine, Complete: Jews and Arabs under the British Mandate*. New York: Henry Holt.

Shalhoub-Kevorkian, N. (2004) "Racism, Militarisation, and Policing: Police Reactions to Violence against Palestinian Women in Israel." *Social Identities* 10 (2):171–194.

Sharansky, N. (2002) *Democracy for Peace*. Washington, D.C.: American Enterprise Institute.

—— (2004) *The Case for Democracy: The Power of Freedom to Overcome Tyranny and Terror*. New York: Public Affairs.

Sharvit, K. and Bar-Tal, D. (2007) "Ethos of Conflict in the Israeli Media during the Period of the Violent Confrontation." In Y. Bar-Siman-Tov (ed.), *The Israeli–Palestinian Conflict: From Conflict Resolution to Conflict Management*. Houndmills: Palgrave Macmillan, pp. 203–232.

Shehadeh, R. (1997) "Land and Occupation: A Legal Review." *Palestine–Israel Journal* 4 (2):25–30.

Sher, G. (2001) *Just beyond Reach*. Tel Aviv: Yediot Ahronot Books (Hebrew).

Shiblak, A. and Davis, U. (1996) *Civil and Citizenship Rights of Palestinian Refugees*. Ramallah: Shaml.

Shikaki, Khalil (1996) *Attahawul Nahwa Addimocratiyyah Fi-Felastine*. Nablus: Center for Palestinian Research and Studies.

—— (2005) "The Current Internal Political Setting." In *Impact of the Legislative Elections on the Palestinian Political Map, Proceedings of the Conference Held in September 2005*. Jerusalem: Arab Thought Forum.

Shikaki, Khalil et al. (1997) *Al-Entakhabat Al-Felastiniyyah Al-Ola: Al-Bi'ah Al-Siyasiyyah, Al-Solok Al-Entekhabi Wa Al-Nataej*. Nablus: Center for Palestinian Research and Studies.

—— (2005) *Meqias Al-Democrateyyah Fi-Felastine (Taqreer 2003–2004)*. Ramallah: Palestinian Center for Policy and Survey Research.

Shlaim, A. (1988) *Collusion across the Jordan: King Abdullah, the Zionist Movement, and the Partition of Palestine*. New York: Columbia University Press.

—— (2000) *The Iron Wall*. New York: Norton.

Shohat, E. (1989) *Israeli Cinema: East/West and the Politics of Representation.* Austin: University of Texas Press.

Shuval, H. (1992a) "Approaches to Resolving the Water Conflicts between Israel and Her Neighbors: A Regional Water for Peace Plan." *Water International* 17:133–143.

—— (1992b) "Approaches for Finding an Equitable Solution to the Water Resources Problems Shared by the Israelis and Palestinians over the Use of the Mountain Aquifer." In G. Baskin (ed.), *Water Conflict or Cooperation: Israel/Palestine Issues in Conflict – Issues for Cooperation.* Jerusalem: IPCRI, vol. 1, no. 2, pp. 26–53.

—— (1994) "Proposed Principles and Methodology for the Equitable Allocation of the Water Resources Shared by the Israelis, Palestinians, Jordanian and Syrians." In J. Isaac and H. Shuval (eds.), *Water and Peace in the Middle East.* Amsterdam: Elsevier Press, pp. 481–486.

—— (1996) "A Water for Peace Plan: Reaching an Accommodation on the Israeli–Palestinian Shared Use of the Mountain Aquifer." *Palestine–Israel Journal* 3 (3/4):75–84.

—— (2000) "Are the Conflicts between Israel and Her Neighbors over the Waters of the Jordan Basin an Obstacle to Peace? Israel–Syria as a Case Study." *Water, Air, Soil Pollution* 123:605–630.

—— (2003) "An Equitable Approach to Resolving the Water Conflicts on the Jordan River Basin under Condition of Scarcity." *Proceedings of the XIth World Congress on Water Resources of IWRA, Madrid, October 5–9, 2003,* pp. 310–315.

Shuval, H. and Dweik, H. (eds.) (2007) *Water Resources in the Middle East: Israel–Palestinian Water Issues – from Conflict to Cooperation.* Hexagon Series on Human and Environmental Security and Peace. Berlin etc.: Springer-Verlag.

Soffer, A. (1994) "The Relevance of the Johnston Plan to the Reality of 1993 and beyond." In J. Isaac and H. Shuval (eds.), *Water and Peace in the Middle East.* Amsterdam: Elsevier Press, pp. 107–122.

Sparrow, A. (2008) "Israeli Settlements Are Blockage to Middle East Peace, Says Gordon Brown." *Guardian,* December 15. Available at <http://www.guardian.co.uk/politics/ 2008/dec/15/gordonbrown-middleeast/print>.

Spero News (2007) "Christians Fear Threats by Islamist Hamas." August 18. Available at <http://www.speroforum.com/site/article.asp?idarticle=10736&t=Christians+fear+thr eats+by+Islamist+Hamas>.

State of Israel (1994) *The Refugee Issue: A Background Paper.* Jerusalem: Government Press Office.

St. Aubin, W. de (1949) "Peace and Refugees in the Middle East." *Middle East Journal* 3 (3):249–259.

Sullivan, Dennis (1995) *Non-governmental Organizations and Freedom of Association.* Jerusalem: Passia.

SUSMAQ (2001) *Technical Background on Water Issues for the Final Status Negotiations.* Newcastle: University of Newcastle upon Tyne and the Palestinian Water Authority.

—— (2005a) *Developing and Implementing Water Policy under Changing Social and Economic Conditions in Palestine.* Newcastle: University of Newcastle upon Tyne and the Palestinian Water Authority.

—— (2005b) *Sustainability Assessments of Water Sector Management Options for the Palestinian Territories.* Newcastle: University of Newcastle upon Tyne and the Palestinian Water Authority.

Sussman, G. (2005) "Ariel Sharon and the Jordan Option." *Middle East Report.* Available at <http://www.merip.org/interventions/sussman_interv.html>.

Swisher, C. (2004) *The Truth about Camp David.* New York: Avalon.

Takkenberg, L. (1998) *The Status of Palestinian Refugees in International Law*. Oxford: Clarendon Press; New York: Oxford University Press.

Tamari, S. (1996a) *Return, Resettlement and Repatriation: The Future of Palestinian Refugees in Peace Negotiations*. Washington, D.C.: Institute of Palestine Studies.

—— (1996b) *Palestinian Refugees Negotiations: From Madrid to Oslo II*. Washington, D.C.: Institute of Palestine Studies.

Thicknesse, S.G. (1949) *Arab Refugees: A Survey of Resettlement Possibilities*. London: Royal Institute of International Affairs.

Toameh, A. (2007) "Gaza: Christian–Muslim Tensions Heat up." *Jerusalem Post*, September 25. Available at <http://www.jpost.com/servlet/Satellite?pagename=JPost%2FJPArticle%2FShowFull&cid=1189411486459>.

Tovy, J. (2003) "Negotiating the Palestinian Refugees." *Middle East Quarterly*. Available at <http://www.meforum.org/article/543>.

UNICEF (n.d.) *Basic Education and Gender Equality*. Available at <http://www.unicef.org/girlseducation/index_focus_peace_education.html>.

United Nations (1978) *The Right of Return of the Palestinian People*. New York: UN.

—— (1999) *Declaration and Program Action of a Culture of Peace*, A/RES/53/243. New York: UN.

UN Office for the Coordination of Humanitarian Affairs (2008) "Israel–OPT: Palestinian Water Boss Reduced to Crisis Management." August 28. Available at <http://www.irinnews.org/PrintReport.aspx?ReportId=80044>.

UN Peace Education (n.d.) *Origins of Peace Education*. Available at <http://www.un.org/cyberschoolbus/peace/index.asp>.

UN Relief and Works Agency for Palestine Refugees (UNRWA) (n.d.). Report. Available at <http://www.un.org/unrwa/refugees/p1.htm>.

UN Security Council Resolution 1325 (2000) October 31. Available at <http://www.un.org>.

Urian, D. (1997) *The Arab in the Israeli Drama and Theatre*. Amsterdam: Harwood.

US Department of State (2003) "A Performance Based Roadmap to a Permanent Two State Solution to the Israeli–Palestinian Conflict." Press statement, April 30.

US Government (1950) *A Decade of American Foreign Policy: Basic Documents, 1941–49*. Prepared at the request of the Senate Committee on Foreign Relations by the staff of the Committee and the Department of State. Washington, D.C.: Government Printing Office.

Wakim, W. (2002) "The Exiled: Refugees in Their Homeland." *Palestine–Israel Journal* 9 (2):52–57.

Wartenberg, T. (1988) "The Concept of Power in Feminist Theory." *Praxis International* 3:301–316.

Washington Post (2009) "Abbas' Waiting Game." May 29.

Waterman, S. (1987) "Partitioned States." *Political Geography Quarterly* 6 (2):151–170.

—— (2002) "States of Segregation." In Clive Schofield *et al.* (eds.), *The Razor's Edge: International Boundaries and Political Geography*. London: Kluwer Academic, pp. 57–76.

Wishart, D.M. (1990) "The Breakdown of the Johnston Negotiations over the Jordan Waters." *Middle Eastern Studies* 26:536–546.

Wolf, A. (1997) "International Water Conflict Resolution – Lessons Learned from Cooperative Analysis." *International Journal of Water Resource Development* 13 (3):333–365.

Wolfsfeld, G. (1997) *Media and Political Conflict: News from the Middle East*. Cambridge: Cambridge University Press.

Working Group on the Status of Palestinian Women Citizens of Israel (2005) "NGO Alternative Pre-Sessional Report on Israel's Implementation of the UN Convention on the Elimination of All Forms of Discrimination against Women (CEDAW)." Working paper, January.

Xinhua (2007) "RPG Fired at Haneya House as Hamas–Fatah Clashes Going on." *People's Daily Online*, June 12. Available at <http://english.peopledaily.com.cn/200706/12/eng20070612_383380.html>.

Yahoo News (2008) "West Bank Barrier is a Model for War on Terror: Olmert." December 23.

Yahya, A. (1998) *The Future of the Palestinian Refugee Issue in Final Status Negotiations.* Jerusalem: Israel/Palestine Center for Research and Information.

Yang, B. and Lester, D. (1997) "War and Rates of Personal Violence." *Journal of Social Psychology* 137 (1):131–132.

Yiftachel, O. (1997) "Israeli Society and Jewish–Palestinian Reconciliation: Ethnocracy and Its Territorial Contradictions." *Middle East Journal* 51 (4):505–519.

—— (2000) "The Homeland and Nationalism." In Athena Leoussi (ed.), *Encyclopaedia of Nationalism.* New Brunswick: Academic Press, vol. 1, pp. 359 –383.

—— (2001) "Right-Sizing or Right-Shaping? Politics, Ethnicity and Territory in Plural States." In I. Lustick, B. O'Leary, and T. Callaghy (eds.), *Right-Sizing the State: The Politics of Moving Borders.* Cambridge: Cambridge University Press, pp. 358–387.

—— (2006) *Ethnocracy: Land and Identity Politics in Israel/Palestine.* Philadelphia: University of Pennsylvania.

Yoav, Yuval (2005) "Justice Minister: West Bank Fence is Israel's Future Border." *Ha'aretz*, December 1.

Zedalis, R. (1992) "Right to Return: A Closer Look." *Georgetown Immigration Law Journal* 6 (3):499–517.

Zureik, E. (1994) "Palestinian Refugees and Peace." *Journal of Palestine Studies* 24/93 (1):5–17.

—— (1996) *Palestinian Refugees and the Peace Process.* Washington, D.C.: Institute for Palestine Studies.

INDEX